THE
WISDEN
— BOOK OF —
CRICKET MEMORABILIA

THE
WISDEN
— BOOK OF —
CRICKET MEMORABILIA
MARCUS WILLIAMS & GORDON PHILLIPS

**Foreword by
JOHN ARLOTT**

*Lennard Publishing
1990*

To Wendy and Maggie

Lennard Publishing
a division of Lennard Books Ltd
Musterlin House, Jordan Hill Road, Oxford OX2 8DP

British Library Cataloguing in Publication Data
Williams, Marcus
The Wisden book of cricket memorabilia.
1. Cricket. Memorabilia
I. Title   II. Phillips, Gordon
796.35'8

ISBN 1 85291 054 2

First published 1990
© Marcus Williams and Gordon Phillips, 1990

Editor Michael Leitch
Designed by Forest Publication Services
Jacket design by Pocknell & Co
Jacket photograph by Tony Pickhaver
Printed in Great Britain by
Butler & Tanner Ltd, Frome and London

CONTENTS

FOREWORD   7

PREFACE   10

COLLECTING   15
Auctions

PAINTINGS   30
Watercolours; Portraits; Naïf School; Cricketers as artists

PRINTS   58
Engravings; Aquatints and mezzotints; Woodcuts and a miscellany;
Lithographs; Chromolithographs; John Corbet Anderson (1827-1907);
Vanity Fair; Albert Chevallier Tayler (1862-1925); Oleographs;
Photogravures; Modern prints

OTHER PICTORIAL MATTER   95
Sheet music covers; Cartoons and caricatures; Photographs; 'Flickers';
Lantern slides; Stevengraphs; Handkerchiefs

BOOKS AND PERIODICALS   119
Wisden Cricketers' Almanack; Other books; Early rarities;
Lillywhite publications; Early tour books and 19th-century limited
editions; 20th-century books; Overseas publications;
County annuals; Periodicals

CERAMICS AND SCULPTURE   149
Ceramics; Plates, plaques and tiles; Miscellaneous; Sculpture, statues
and statuettes

ORNAMENTAL OBJECTS   179
Silverware and silverware trophies; Medals and medallions; Jewellery;
Clocks and watches; Vesta cases; Enamels; Glassware

PRINTED EPHEMERA   197
Autographs; Letters; Scrapbooks; Assorted ephemera; Club records
and archives; Handbills and posters; Admission tickets and tokens;
Advertising ephemera; Legal documents; Menu cards; Scorecards
and scoresheets; Scorebooks

EQUIPMENT AND CLOTHING   227
Bats; Miniature bats; Batting and wicketkeeping gloves; Pads;
Balls; Bowling machines; Stumps and bails; Miscellaneous
equipment; Belts and sashes; Buckles; Blazers and sweaters;
Boots, shoes and slippers; Boxes (protective); Buttons;
Caps and hats; Costume; Shirts and trousers; Ties

POSTCARDS, CIGARETTE CARDS AND STAMPS   255
Postcards; Cigarette cards; Trade cards; Cigarette packs;
Matchbox labels and book matches; Philately

MISCELLANEOUS   280
Badges; Calendars and diaries; Games; Computer games;
Gramophone and other recordings; Greetings cards;
Playing cards; Pub signs; Pub tables and other breweriana;
Souvenirs; Video recordings; Films; A miscellany

APPENDIX   307
The collectors – ancient and modern; Museums and collections;
Bibliography

INDEX   320

PICTURE ACKNOWLEDGEMENTS   328

FOREWORD

John Arlott began collecting cricketana at the age of 12 and rose to become the best-known figure in the field. At its peak his collection consisted of some 3,000 items and was based on annuals from all the major cricketing countries and on extensive groupings of selected authors. Aquatints and modern first-editions later became a dominant interest. The collection was compiled largely during visits to secondhand bookshops all over England, especially when he was broadcasting Any Questions *or cricket commentaries. He established a formidable reputation, for other seekers after cricketana would be met with: "I'm sorry, Mr Arlott has been." When John moved to Alderney after retirement in 1980, many of the scarcer items passed to Tony Winder, but he retained complete sets of* Wisden *(all original editions),* Scores and Biographies *(the first four volumes signed by the compiler, Arthur Haygarth); and a collection of Neville Cardus, with all the items published in the author's lifetime signed by him.*

The collection of cricketana is one of the major symptoms of cricketomania and it may honestly be described as incurable. It is not, though, as must be added, often fatal – even if it has been known for bookshelves to collapse on the sufferer who has overloaded them. It can be caused by playing or watching the game; it may be argued that watching – even through the means of television – is the most frequent cause of the complaint. In this connection it may be said that the complainants are often wives.

All the sufferers tend to be egomaniacal and to discuss their own collections almost endlessly and, to those who have never known it themselves, almost nauseatingly. The real problem is – as this book demonstrates all too clearly – that the subject and the material to fuel it, are virtually inexhaustible. It includes every kind of pictorial art from the work of great painters down to song sheets; and, probably the reason for an early phase of collecting – the postcards of teams or individual players which, roughly speaking, originated at the beginning of this century and created a whole special branch of collecting within easy financial reach.

The main body of most collections is probably books, and the earliest of them are the scorebooks dating from the end of the 18th century. Soon, though, the literature – and, indeed, some work which would stretch the imagination to call literature – covered every aspect of the game: and even spawned a dice-on-board game which some sufferers took hideously seriously.

The writer of this Foreword is inescapably afflicted. There was a time when collections of esteemed authors, aquatints, topography, wine and gastronomic books, some art books and histories so filled his house that he felt compelled to sell his cricket books. Then came the genuine trauma: some books simply *had* to be retained – for instance, the set of *Scores & Biographies* – the first four volumes inscribed by Arthur Haygarth to an Etonian cricketer; the set of first editions of *Wisden*; the signed first printings of Neville Cardus simply could not be spared. Then it became difficult to allow it to be discovered that he had disposed of signed copies of books by his friends. Finally, writing a review of each year's cricket books for *Wisden* made it increasingly difficult – and finally impossible – not to collect them. Then, of course there were the Staffordshire cricket figures, the genuinely decorative folk art, which even wives are happy to permit. Then, also, no man could part with those cricket paintings – not, at least, one who was crucially infected with the mania.

It had all begun in childhood, the keeping of cheap cricket annuals in boot boxes with one side cut off to make shelves. Like so many boys, he collected cigarette cards and autographs – pestering smoking elders and, sometimes, fuming players, for the material of the collections. When the time came to put away childish things, surely those two remnants of childhood could go – after all, he was now grown up, in years if not in hobby. Then it suddenly occurred that the cigarette cards could be pasted on a board, framed and hung like a picture, while at least three publishers put out birthday books which would take the signatures of the cricketers, in dignified fashion in lieu of the "childish" autograph album. Gradually the books extended to more and fresh shelves. It was lunatic, of course, but eventually he had to buy a fresh and larger house to contain the evidence of all his collector ailments. His only justification now is that he has never collected membership cards – or at least only a few of them – match boxes, place mats, tea towels, legal documents, match balls or caps. That could be said with a horribly righteous air – no watches either – only one, that is – and only one toast rack.

It is impossible to escape the conclusion that this book has been written out of genuine enthusiasm and with a high degree and width of knowledge and, most obviously, by two incurable sufferers. Equally it may be stated that it could lead on the maniacs who, at the time of first reading, suffer from only a few branches of the ailment, to others which would not have occurred to them if these fresh germs had not been thus inculcated. Seriously - and this is serious indeed - it would be a rare cricket book collector who, having read this, did not move into fresh fields. Already, even while attempting to limit new facets of the complaint, the writer had been trapped into videos and sound recordings. Once, too, he could not make up his mind whether a wine label which hinted at cricket should be put in the cricket or the wine section.

What the authors call "adverts (non-cricket but using cricket motif/scene)" plus "smaller collectables/miscellaneous" also cover a multitude of items which may be levered in.

The fact is, of course, that the scope is wide – wider perhaps than most people know – because the game is older than almost any other and more widely spread about the globe – hence the postage stamps from distant parts that demand their place because of the cricket picture they bear; there are even some postmarks which qualify. The blood sports, of course, have probably inspired a greater number of finer paintings: but they cannot match, for instance, the *Vanity Fair* cartoons in popularity in the extent of the demand for them, which over the last forty or so years has elevated them from the junk heap to a state where they can be torn out of the bound volumes and sold separately at prices the annuals themselves never commanded.

This is by far the finest, most extensive and authoritative work ever produced on a subject which, in its turn, seems to claim more enthusiasts as the years go by. Let no one imagine, however, that it will stand alone. Soon many of its sections and subjects will demand books to themselves – such as badges, pub signs – very costly, these latter, if they are the real thing. Already, too, books are being issued of the handiwork of scorers – and Bill Frindall has stepped clear of the men who used to write books about the matches of which he reproduces the scores.

Neither are some collectors discouraged by space-consuming items. Once bats were rarely collected, but no sooner were the antiques in that kind bought up to a state of relative unobtainability than the autographed blades given as sweepstake prizes to help benefit funds became even – if not more – desirable "collectables".

Meanwhile, photography did not merely make the postcard widely available but no one can dream of the extent to which amateur photographers have taken and collected pictures of players, grounds, and strokes. Cricket, indeed, virtually created the "team photograph" which, printed off, often at great size, also commanded – and no doubt still does – solid prices and earnest collectors. Indeed, Beldam's action photographs, quite apart from C.B. Fry's accompanying text, are costly, cherished and handsome in their kind. Let no one, either, think that the day could not possibly come when cricketers' finger prints are collected.

Our authors here are to be admired and congratulated: behind all their air of scholarly authority, however, they must be cricketomaniacs to the same extent as all of us who read this mighty work; our thanks are due to them.

John Arlott,
Alderney, Channel Islands, 1989.

PREFACE

This book is the first attempt at a detailed description of the many-faceted field of cricket memorabilia; after seemingly hundreds of hours of research and toil we now have a shrewd idea why others have restricted their efforts to a specific aspect! At least our passage in trying to chronicle the leading items (to cover everything would have required an encyclopaedia) has been eased by the fact that so many collectors and other involved parties have given generously of their time and energy in the face of our often persistent enquiries.

Cricket memorabilia may be broadly defined as any object connected with this most English of games, be it 18th-century book or woodwormed bat, cigarette card or postcard, panoramic painting or polychrome print, 78rpm gramophone record or jam maker's golly badge, cherished autograph album or yellowing scrapbook, new-fangled video cassette or computer game, an abdominal protective box – yes, one of these did appear at auction – or a chunk of masonry from the perimeter wall at The Oval. In fact, as readers will discover in the pages which follow, the subject is almost boundless. Every one of the items is collectable, and collected by devotees, and, though the appeal of some items may be too personal or esoteric for others, there exists a ready and established market for just about anything associated with cricket.

Material can turn up in the most unlikely places, although some leads can prove to be, almost literally, red herrings: more than one cricket collector has been seduced by a book entitled *A Summer on the Test, 1930* – only to discover that it is about fishing. However, examples of two unlikely but genuine sources, which came to light even as this book was in its final stages of production, can well illustrate the point: the first involves militant women, the second rubbish, and both stories also prove that the thrill of making a new discovery is far from lost.

It was a casual remark by John Kennedy Melling, an historian and critic (though not of cricket), which revealed that he did in fact own one item connected with the game.

It was a ball – could it be one with which Botham or Trueman performed great deeds, perhaps?

No, older than that – used by Bedser, maybe, or Laker?

No, earlier – Tate, Verity, Freeman?

No, before the First World War – Barnes, Rhodes, Richardson?

No, delivered by a female arm – female arm? Perhaps one of the Original

English Lady Cricketers, who were chaperoned around the country playing games of a strictly sporting nature in the 1890s? One of those special blue cricket balls once developed for the women's game and on display at Lord's? Still no.

And so he unfolded the tale. The ball had found its way into Melling's possession nearly 20 years earlier. He was given it by a former Alderman of Essex County Council, Miriam Eileen Edwards, who had inherited it from her father. He was Superintendent Wilcox of the Metropolitan Police, whose face, beneath his flat cap, became familiar as the officer who regularly arrested Emmeline Pankhurst during the struggles of the Suffragettes. (Wilcox carried out his duty, apparently, in a most gentlemanly way, telephoning Mrs Pankhurst first to say that he was on his way.) On 21st May 1914 the campaigners' order of the day was a window-smashing protest in Whitehall. While Mrs Higginson used as ammunition stones collected in Southend – such things were said to have been not easily found at that time in London – her companion on the raid, Mrs Marshall, hurled a more expensive missile, namely this cricket ball, through a Cabinet Minister's window, whence it was retrieved and came into Wilcox's hands. The ball carries in gold lettering the retailer's name, Army & Navy, and in black ink the protesters's message, "A PROUD & COWARDLY KING" and, beneath the stitching, "1914". The leather surface of the ball is intact apart from a few black stains and half a dozen tiny punctures, which may have been caused by the glass as the ball shattered the window. A piece of British, if not exactly cricketing, history, but a prize piece of cricketana[1] rescued and preserved.

Rescue, too, as well as a feminine connection, was the keynote of our other late entry, involving a blazer from the 1929-30 MCC tour of the West Indies. This navy blue garment, adorned with the familiar George and Dragon badge and red and yellow piping, was found in a rubbish skip in Cheltenham by a husband whose wife had been diligently clearing out piles of unwanted stuff found in the loft. Seeing the name tag, he telephoned a friend to ask whether anybody named R.E.S. Wyatt had played for England. By happy chance the friend was also the chairman of Derbyshire County Cricket Club, and the rest is another bit of history. The blazer turned out to be the only one missing from Wyatt's collection, and Warwickshire, his former county, arranged for it to be returned to him during the Edgbaston Test match of 1989. Sixty years on, England's then oldest living Test player, and captain, was thus reunited with a treasured item presumed lost forever. What was it doing in Cheltenham? The house outside which it was rescued was believed to have belonged to Wyatt's brother.

Until quite recently the collecting of cricketana was an apparently arcane pursuit, dominated by a handful of collectors and part-time dealers, but the advent of regular sales by leading London auction houses in 1978 has

Footnote:
[1]   According to *The Oxford English Dictionary* (Second edition, 1989) the word cricketana was first used as a heading in *London Society*, August 1862, with the meaning of "Literature, sayings, or items of gossip about cricket". The earliest entry for the secondary, but now more accepted, meaning of "Collectable objects associated with cricket; cricket memorabilia" is 1950, but it was certainly current before then. An article entitled 'Cricket as a Hobby' by F.S. Ashley-Cooper in *The Cricketer* Winter Annual 1921-2 (p.48) included: "...the collection of "cricketana" has again come in vogue"; in October 1929 The Cricketana Society was founded with, among other aims, a register of collectors and a census of rare publications and cricketana. It folded, incidentally, in 1935 and there was no similar body until the formation of the Cricket Memorabilia Society in 1987.
 Surprisingly there was no entry for cricketana in *The Language of Cricket* by W.J. Lewis (1938) or *The Dictionary of Cricket* by Michael Rundell (1985).

brought it to a far wider audience and attracted a far wider range of material on to the market. This has, inevitably, led to an escalation of prices, much to the chagrin of some collectors who feel themselves squeezed out by the greater buying power of the full-time dealers and who question the morality that lies behind the commercial ethos, feeling that cricketana belongs to the world of cricket, not to the world of business. It has to be accepted, however, that the market-place is now dominated by the auctions, although in global terms the levels are still those of a hobby when compared to the vast sums expended on works of art. Whereas these may be calculated in millions of pounds, cricketana still rates in hundreds and sometimes in thousands. Among competitive sports, however, cricket is rivalled for range and demand only by golf, horse racing, and possibly boxing; the presence of American and Japanese money, particularly in golf, makes for increased competition and thus higher prices than in cricket, although Australasian bidders, first prominent at the MCC Bicentenary auction in 1987, are making their dollars felt.

It has been a criticism of previous works on cricket memorabilia that they have given little or no indication of values and, while aware that our approach may not meet with universal approval, we have set out to fill this void. We are neither dealers nor valuers, so we have used the most reliable yardstick: the prices achieved on the open market, i.e. at auction, where collector and dealer can contend on equal terms (for obvious reasons we do not take account of charity or benefit auctions). Where auction prices cannot be applied, we have quoted those asked by dealers. Clearly the levels will be different, as dealers have overheads to meet and profit levels to maintain – though they must not frighten away their customers!

Auction prices must, of course, be viewed in the light of the market forces pertaining at the time, and experience here, as in most things, is an invaluable aid to understanding. Thus, rarer and more desirable items, in good condition, will usually achieve a high price, with dealers, private collectors and perhaps museums in competition. At other times a seemingly ordinary piece may fetch a price well above expectation, because a collector needs it to complete a set or an institution needs it for a display or merely because of sale-room fever, which can grip the gathering, as on the occasion of the MCC sale. Conversely, pieces may sell well below estimate, because of poor condition (perhaps not noted in the catalogue) or perhaps because of doubts about authenticity.

Where freakishly high prices have occurred, we have endeavoured to point them out. The test comes when the items are re-offered, and the market was awaiting with interest the sale of the Pilkington collection by Phillips at the end of September 1989, when many lots bought at the Bicentenary sale were due to reappear.

A few points to note about guidelines we have followed in assembling the book:

In selecting illustrations we have chosen, wherever possible, objects which have been rarely or never reproduced and have largely avoided those which have become clichéd through frequent appearances in print.

While ideally we would have inspected every item about which we have written, a lifetime was not available for the preparation of the book, so we have had in many cases to depend on entries in auction and other catalogues, finding our way, we trust, past occasional misprints, variant spellings and tantalisingly incomplete descriptions.

For the sake of a modern audience we have in many instances converted £.s.d. into decimal currency, with figures calculated to the nearest full penny following the demise of the ¹/₂p.

The figures given for auction realisations are hammer prices, i.e. the winning bid announced by the auctioneer, unless otherwise stated. Since the mid-1970s the major London auction houses have charged buyers a premium of 10 per cent on top of the hammer price, which means that, with the addition of VAT, the purchaser actually pays, for example, £111.50 for every £100 bid, which produces a further level of value.

References to Christie's refer, in most instances, to their South Kensington sale rooms.

As already indicated, the preparation of this book would not have been possible without the assistance, so gratefully received, from many individuals and organisations. We duly acknowledge them, with the *caveat* that any faults in the text are our responsibility and that we apologise to any who may have been inadvertently overlooked. The authors' thanks are due to:

David Rayvern Allen, John Arlott for his most felicitous foreword, Association of Cricket Umpires, John Atkins, Tony Baer, Mark Baring, A.R. Barker, Brian Bassano, Austin Bennett, Enid Bloom, Bonhams (Duncan Chilcott), William Bowyer, Geoffrey Boycott, Sir Donald Bradman A.C., Mike Brown (Plumstead Library), Michael Brownlow, Burlington Gallery (Nicholas Potter and Helen Gazeley), James Butler, Harold Cantle, Chris Beetles Ltd., Christie's South Kensington (Rupert Neelands), David Coates, Peter and Mark Coombs, Julia Coote, S.C. Cowman, Geoffrey Crambie, Cricketana (John Dixon), Don Crossley, Andrew Cunningham, Curry Rivel Gallery, David Dalby, Nigel Dalley, David Messum Gallery, Richard Davis, Deighton & Mullen Ltd. (Tony Muranka), Bonar Dunlop, Dyson Perrins Museum (Wendy Cook), E & J Software (Alan Clayton), I. Edwards (Secretary, Derbyshire CCC), Lt.-Col. I.G. Elliott, D.Ettlinger, L.A. Ettlinger, Felix Rosenstiel's Widow & Son Ltd. (David Roe), Mark Ferrow, Jacqui Figgis, First Impressions (John Gill), Franklin Mint Ltd., Friends of Grace Road (Leicester), David Frith, Richard Furness, Jocelyn Galsworthy,

Garrard & Co. (Nicholas Winton), Simon Garrow, Geering & Colyer (Mervyn F.P. Carey), Robin Gibson (National Portrait Gallery), Gordon Banks Sales & Promotions Ltd., David Gourley, Graves Son & Pilcher (Hove), Donald Green, Stephen Green, Terry Grose, Halcyon Days, Ron Harries, Chris Harte, John Hawkins, Keith Hayhurst, Roger Heavens, Murray Hedgcock, Clare Hemstock, Mike Heslop, Peter Hicks, Hove Museum and Art Gallery, Carl Howard, Hilary Humphries, John Hurst, David Inshaw, Ironbridge Gorge Museum (Yvette Miller), John Rylands University Library of Manchester (John Tuck), Andrew Johnson, Hayward Kidson, Lalonde Fine Art (Bristol), Lambourne Games (T.R. Goodchild), Peter Lawrence, J.B. Leather, Jonathan Lee, Rev. Malcolm Lorimer, Margaret Loxton, Jocelyn Lukins, J.W. McKenzie, Peter MacKinnon, Keith McMahon, Maidstone Museum, Roger Mann, Roger Marsh, Mike Marshall, John Kennedy Melling, Michael Messenger, Mitcham Library, Moët et Chandon (London) Ltd. (Nancy Jarratt), Morphot (A.E.J. Morris), Murray Cards (International) Ltd., Nubern Products (Eric Bernardes), H.A. Osborne, Oxford University Press, Panini Publishing Company (Peter Dunk), W. Prosser, Joan Redman, R.H. Reed (Archivist, National Westminster Bank), Colin Richards, Michael Roffey, RONA Gallery, Royal Crown Derby Museum, Joe Scarborough, Rosalind Scott, Mary Setchfield, Geoffrey Seymour, Hermon Shapiro, Tony Sheldon, Jackie Shipster, Martin Smith, Mike Smith, Sotheby's (Lucy Hodson), Sporting Heritage (June Stather), Sporting Moments (D.E. North), D.A. Stephenson, Jean Stockdale, Richard Streeton, Mike Tarr, John Townsend, Derrick Townshend, Toye, Kenning & Spencer, Treadwell's Art Mill, Graham Turner, Dr. J.B. Turner, David van der Plank, Martin Venning, Walton Fine Art Ltd., Charlie Watts, Terry Watts, Wedgwood Museum (Gaye Blake Roberts), Willow Enterprises Company, Willow Stamps, Keith Wilson, Tony Woodhouse, Laura Wortley, Gerry Wright, Peter Wynne-Thomas, and last, but by no means least, our thanks to Adrian Stephenson, of Lennard Publishing, for his enthusiasm and patience, and to his staff.

We append for guidance to actual values an extract from a consumer goods and services index compiled by the Central Statistical Office; the figures are given at intervals for the earlier years and annually since the start of the cricketana boom in 1978 (January 1974=100):

1914	11.1	1970	73.1	1983	335.1
1920	27.7	1975	134.8	1984	351.8
1930	17.6	1978	197.1	1985	373.2
1938	17.4	1979	223.5	1986	385.9
1946	29.4	1980	263.7	1987	401.9
1950	35.6	1981	295.0	1988	421.6
1960	49.6	1982	320.4		

COLLECTING

The fun of cricketana collecting is not the simple acquisition by passing a cheque over a counter; it is the fun of search, discovery and attainment. All three are the fruits of accrued knowledge gained the hard way, for to be a real collector one needs a fatalistic outlook, a deep purse, boundless optimism and a good-natured woman about the house. David Frith has described many a time, in the columns of *Wisden Cricket Monthly* and elsewhere, how possession of some treasured object can "paralyse an addict with ecstasy". Collecting becomes a serious affliction that cannot be operated upon. No bookshop or gallery worth its salt is safe from attack. Triffid-like, what starts as a hobby mutates into a fascination that can become a compulsion.

Maybe Duleepsinhji's cap is something that should never be worn out of doors, but collecting is a happy, joyous thing, and, in an effervescent letter typical of him, collector Mike Smith outlined for our benefit his fantasy scenario utilising cricketana to the full. It went something like this:

The wicket [his back garden] *did not look as if it had been cut, so was likely to take spin. Best therefore to wear Clarrie Grimmett's trousers. Who could play on a turning wicket – Len Hutton certainly, so out came his cap. J.R. Mason was good enough to go in high in the order, followed by A.P.F. Chapman and Norman O'Neill. Their caps would do. Mike was unsure of Randall's ability to cope with the Grimmett googly, but his fielding alone earns him a place, even wearing his night blue trousers and cricket shirt.*

His bowling was adequate. The ball used by Bob Willis to ruin the Australian batting and Kim Hughes's career could be used to open with, and, sharing the other end, Jack Mercer (10 wickets v. Worcestershire in 1936) and a Scottish gent, Arthur Broadbent, who disposed of the mighty Trumper for 8.

The batting side guarding the stump Sid Barnes missed as a souvenir at Nottingham in 1948, found the bowling a bit wayward, or had the bowler noticed that Mike had come armed with Sutcliffe's bat of the 1934 season, and with those used by Bobby Abel, David Denton, Barnes again, and Tom Barling's 1946-47 bat, with which he scored over 2,000 runs and which has hardly a mark on the edge.

Just as the pace hotted up, the opposition growing ever more confused by frequent changes of MCC and Cambridge blazers and sweaters, the great scorer in the sky decided enough was enough, so out came an I Zingari umbrella, and then indoors to contemplate the rose bowl presented for the last-

Mike Smith, in an MCC touring blazer and Grimmett's trousers, shelters under an I Zingari umbrella.

wicket stand by Fielder and Woolley at Stourbridge in 1909, play the amusement arcade cricket game, or glance through A.P.F. Chapman's bits and pieces, noting telegrams from Stanley Baldwin and one from Buckingham Palace congratulating him on beating Australia in 1928-29. His school reports, and those of Percy Fender, made interesting reading.

The greatest collectors have always been, with exceptions such as R.G. Barlow, E. Rockley Wilson and Bob Appleyard, players of only mediocre ability, their pleasure derived from the ownership of things connected with the heritage of the game, not in itself a bad substitute. Writing in *The Cricketer* (2nd May 1936), the great collector J.W. (Joe) Goldman placed himself squarely in that category – and never collected bats and balls, which he claimed not to understand. It is hard to argue with Irving Rosenwater's perceptive comment that only those who speak from experience know of the warmth derived from obtaining a coveted item, such as a curved bat, an epergne, a prized volume, or giving in to the temptation of buying a smoker's pipe carved with an image of W.G. Grace.

For the collector, Heaven can wait, and bliss takes many forms and shapes. It could well be a sketch-plan done by Hedley Verity, showing each shot by H.B. Cameron at Sheffield in June 1935, when he was punished for 4, 4, 4, 6, 6, 6 in one over and the normally immaculate Verity was told by Arthur Wood, Yorkshire's wicketkeeper, "You've got him in two minds. He doesn't know whether to hit you for six or four." The actual bat used still exists in private hands. For someone like Tony Baer, bliss could be plaque-shaped, preferably one with the features of Bill Woodfull, which long eluded him. And for Don Crossley, Chairman of the Cricket Memorabilia Society (founded 1987) – who used to caress, clean and polish his *Wisdens* until his cricketing hero, Barry Richards, said the publication was nothing more than a telephone directory – there would be the delight of adding fresh signatures to the bat he carries around the country in his car boot.

But collecting has always been a mixture of honey and gall. The chase is often more exciting than the capture and with success can come anti-climax. The hunt for a set of *Wisdens* can dominate the hobby of a lifetime, summed up by collector Ron Harries in a not-to-be-forgotten phrase on television: "When I completed my set, something went out of my life."

No conclusions dare to be made as to why so few active first-class cricketers show so little interest in memorabilia, other than their own trophies and personal gear. Even their achievements or records of their representative sides are sometimes shrugged off. Perhaps life indeed is too short to be both a full-time player and collector, or do players become immune to inanimate historical objects dimly perceived while moving from one pavilion to another? The attitude was typified by Bob Willis, once captain of Warwickshire and England and taker of 325 Test wickets, who said he had no desire "to turn my home into a shrine to myself" - he had always kept his trophies in a suitcase. Willis put his memorabilia up for auction (at Christie's in October 1988) with the laudable wish that devotees, who truly appreciate the array of blazers, shirts, jerseys, balls and medals, might have a chance to own them.

By contrast, one of the first major collectors was that most amiable of men, Richard Gorton Barlow of Lancashire and England (1851-1919), who lived in a house surrounded by memories of bat and ball, cricket trophies and "presents innumerable". With Bob Appleyard, the only other significant collector to have played Test cricket was Evelyn Rockley Wilson (1879-1957). Possessed of a proud Yorkshire snobbery – "One doesn't necessarily know cricket just because one has played for Leicestershire" – Rockley Wilson was a scholarly, erudite man, "a firm believer in the straight bat", and, with a considerable knowledge of furniture, philately and silver, was as close to Renaissance man as cricket could claim since Felix. His home was crammed with cricket pictures, china figures, handkerchiefs and the dining room dominated by a picture of Fuller Pilch at the wicket. A library of over 3,000 items avoided ephemeral trash and ghosted autobiographies, and under the terms of his will MCC were blessed with first choice of the rich pickings.

Another considerable collector was said to be G. Leonard Garnsey (1881-1951), a Sheffield Shield player for New South Wales, of whom it has been written that he owned all the early Australian annuals. If that is so, "considerable" is an understatement.

How easy it must have been for the pioneer collectors. There were Padwick, Ford and Gaston advertising in *The Field* and *Exchange and Mart*, traversing the home counties, often in concert, purchasing eagerly everything offered for a song, while all around them the motherlode of memorabilia awaited collection with singularly little competition. Cricketana as a hobby was a genteel pursuit for a narrow, almost incestuous brotherhood of collectors. Among major collectors there was a close alliance: Thomas Padwick was at school with A.L. Ford, and his daughter married Charles Pratt Green; Padwick also happened to be a close friend of A.J. Gaston, who was in turn a close friend of W.L. Murdoch, the former Australian captain, then settled in Sussex.

Other than books, the cricketing cult came into being in the heyday of W.G., when it was fashionable for houses, both great and small, to be graced with a cricketing piece or two. Supply always rises to meet demand, so that a touch of cricket was applied to a plethora of household and personal articles – clocks, pottery figures, mugs, jugs, ashtrays and jewellery. Around the turn of the century, Gaston's articles in *Wisden* and *The Cricket Field* stimulated a keen demand for cricket books, but this was short-lived, so that by 1905 F.S. Ashley-Cooper noted that although interest in collecting was as great as ever, albeit within a tight-knit circle, prices were lower than at any period since 1890. With certain notable exceptions, prices actually remained stable and in favour of the collector virtually from Edwardian days to after the Second World War.

Such cricket items as did appear at auction were tiny portions of more cosmopolitan sales, but generally the collecting scene was moribund. There was a time between the wars when it was possible to enter an antique dealer's shop, ask for a cricketing piece, and either be met with blank astonishment, or a gruff remark that nothing of that kind had been seen for years, or be offered, from some dusty corner, an autographed bat.

Before they were usurped by auction fever, a line of booksellers and firms who specialised in cricket bats reigned supreme and some of their names are imperishable. The departure of Leslie Gutteridge of Epworth Books in 1967 left a yawning gap. Few matched his knowledge of cricket literature, and even fewer had a comparable knowledge of valuation in the years when collectors both over- and under-valued their possessions. His stock of second-hand books, all reasonably priced, was purchased by E.K. (Ted) Brown, a much-liked and respected man and a crucial link in the chain which stretches back to Gaston and forward to their modern equivalent, J.W. (John) McKenzie. Cotterell's and E.F. Hudson, both of Birmingham, were big in their day, but after the Second World War sold out to Epworth's in the City Road, London. Overlapping both firms was Henry Ling, a collector-dealer who advertised his books on sale from 1929 at least until the mid-1940s.

Cricket theme added to J.W. McKenzie's shop front in summer 1989.

Southern Booksellers & Publishing Company, of St Leonards-on-Sea, have since 1962 operated a largely mail-order service of some quality. The antiquarian content has decreased, but they are still widely appreciated by customers. Roland and Betty Cole, formerly of Colchester in Essex, whose various individual catalogues from the 1960s awaken happy memories for many collectors operating on a low budget, form an important role, too, in that their stock was bought by John McKenzie in February 1973. Catalogues by McKenzie have highlighted an incredibly rich selection of cricketana, although collector John Hawkins remembers the "innocent" days before McKenzie had a bookshop proper and operated from home, and how, when the dealer offered a choice between Sydney Smith's *With the 15th Australian XI* (Sydney, 1922) for £5 and one of the post-war tour books for £1, he chose the latter because it was a jolly good read. To this day Hawkins regrets giving in to a whim.

Collectors have seen it as a matter of regret that the major dealers, like McKenzie, Martin Wood, Almeida Books and others, have developed the hobby into such a lucrative business that bargains are but a memory. To be fair, however, for many people John McKenzie has been cricketana personified for some years and their sole source of supply, and even he has been seen at auctions shaking his head in disbelief at prices being paid cheerfully for items identical to those in his lists which sell for less.

David Frith's overview of cricketana in *Wisden* (1981), and then again with John Arlott, Stephen Green, David Rayvern Allen and others in the *Barclays World of Cricket* (1986 – and the closest thing there is to an encyclopaedia of the game), confirmed, for the thousands saturated in the knowledge that cricket is more than a game, that the quest for cricketana is absorbing for its remarkable ramifications and for the range of entry points to the quest.

Every household where there is a lively mind within collects something, and generally the first and most enduring pastime is books. If one starts with a basic interest in cricket, one wants to know its history, but books exclusive to the subject take one only so far. The enthusiast gets wrapped up in the social setting of the game, in attitudes to it that were then current and are now recollected, so the more that is collected from a particular age, the more the game can be understood as it was at the time. The jumps in prices reported in the press have of recent years brought an apparently inexhaustible stream of material into the market, not only the property of former great cricketers, but also the specially conceived issues of stamps and prints, and the flood of souvenir, memorial, anniversary and birthday plates, tankards, ties and pottery figures regarded by many as too blatantly commercial to care about. Purists may turn up their noses at modern mugs, clocks and book-ends, suggesting these are gifts rather than collectibles, but while even those who trade in them acknowledge their present lack of rarity or intrinsic value, they will, inevitably, become a potent force. The mass of material to be had means we are now deeply into the age of the specialist, with interests confined to a narrow field, for which collectors are prepared to make large outlays of time, money and mileage.

Of the more traditional items, books and prints – both old and new – remain the most popular category, running ahead of the other hardy perennials: autographs, scorecards, scrapbooks, photographs, postcards, cigarette cards, and Doulton and Staffordshire pottery. The majority of those who set out to build a collection restrict their energies to securing books, pamphlets and magazines only, and the first stirrings often seem to occur at the ripe old age of ten or thereabouts. A starting point might be an incomplete set of cigarette cards, or a not particularly fresh *Vanity Fair* cartoon, but primarily it seems to be the hard-earned acquisition of a second-hand *Wisden*. Anything obtained through an act of self-denial never loses its sentimental appeal, as many collectors will testify.

Printed books and pictorial material are always the nucleus, but there is room for peripheral and neglected areas, and the purpose of this book is to try to show that it can be equally rewarding to search for unusual items not immediately thought of in connection with cricket. These range from contemporary art and prints, through biscuit tins, matchbox labels, greetings cards, even cigarette packs. Cricketana collectors can and do ignore that which is most obvious, and concentrate on the past to the exclusion of today's unsung memorabilia.

Few are inclined, however, to give over their whole life to the hobby, but it is easy to become obsessive. In his review of Irving Rosenwater's highly desirable (from every point of view) privately printed *Cricket Books: Great Collectors of the Past* (1976), David Frith queried justifications for the blinkered determination to satisfy a craving, either along specialist lines or universal. The usual reasons were listed: a hedge against inflation, books for reference, entertainment and the possessive instinct. All are viable and somewhere in there lies the complete answer, for collecting, after all, is not more important than life, or the financial stability of one's family.

The criteria for valuation are straightforward and easily summed up. Any cricketing artefact surges past the humdrum by reason of its antiquity, previous ownership or use, and any special factor such as a significant innings, event or, obviously, scarcity. Australian collector Denis Tobin has applied to the collection of caps an apt rule of thumb which relates to many other forms of collectibles. In the case of modern players, he assessed a cap owned by a "basic" Test player (Greg Ritchie or Bill Athey) at £12-£15; an established Test star such as David Gower or Kim Hughes, £35-£50; superstars such as Ian Botham, Viv Richards (and Graeme Hick to come?), £120-£200; and, in a different dimension, Bradman and Grace, from £300 upwards. At all events, common sense dictates that you pay the price that pleases, evaluate top likely price thresholds you can afford, and do not go above them.

There is always the option to collect only material closely associated with cricket as a game, such as bats, balls, costume, autographs and menu cards of functions actually attended by both players and officials, confirmed by their signatures. This bears also on items associated with tours and matches, the players involved, and their ownership of things. For collectors of this genre, books, prints and ceramics are the creations of people at a remove, often undertaken solely for self-aggrandizement or with thought of financial reward. Whatever the option, collections are never static, and one has to think of duplicates and the replacement of inferior quality space-fillers. Newcomers to cricketana are urged to consult reference books and periodicals, libraries, clubs, auction and sale catalogues, trade lists, packaging material, museums and archivists. Furthermore, be microscopic in observation: shape, colour, splendour of decoration, all of these offer a wealth of information. The importance of authenticity cannot be over-stressed, especially when, with much modern material, the main value lies not in its antiquity but in its relation to a particular player or event. In cases of doubt some definite proof of origin should be obtained. There is no limit to cricketana, but the collector will secure things that interest him according to taste, the display facilities needed and available, and what can be afforded. County and regional archives can seem forbidding places, but too little use is made of them for learning the latest techniques in conservation and display.

In the end, it is a little bit of what you fancy, really, and faced with this embarrassment of riches some collectors have opted for limited periods or even particular players. No cricketer has been represented in more different ways than the most famous of them all, W.G. Grace, and there can be no better introduction to the financial adulation accorded to Graceiana by collectors than the little-known lithograph by I. Hamilton of W.G., seen in simulated wicketkeeping gear, poised to catch a bag of swag, the proceeds of a nation's gratitude. In a sense cash is still being pumped into the Grace legend, far in excess of the £4,281.9s.1d. raised by readers (and management?) of the *Daily Telegraph*, which launched a National Shilling Testimonial in 1895. Little wonder that, as a substitute for pads, the shins of the great man were protected by copies of the newspaper.

As it is, W.G.'s influence permeates every section of this book, but it may serve to gather together a few threads from the scattered mass, and for this we are indebted to Irving Rosenwater's study of G. Neville Weston, the most fervent of all Grace's admirers, in the *Journal of the Cricket Society* (Spring 1975). Rosenwater

W.G. Grace about to catch a bag of swag.

A GRACE-FULL CATCH.
STUDY BY A STUMPED R.A. 1895

With Seasons Greetings
and Best Wishes from *I Hamilton*

1898 cast-iron cigar cutter, featuring Ranjitsinhji. Might Grace have used one?

it was, writing with tongue firmly in cheek, who rated as far more rare than any Georgian snuffer-stand, one of W.G.'s cigars, duly preserved in its original case. This was a minuscule item in Weston's unbelievable collection of figures, large and small, mugs, pipes with bowls showing his head, a matchbox and glass paperweights, christening robe, silver-plated inkstands "with W.G. towering above", even a door-stop showing W.G. seated with a cricket ball.

The impressive oil portrait of him (49½in.x39½in.), seen in three-quarter length, painted in 1895 by J. Ernest Brewn and artist-signed, was a feature of Weston's study. The portrait shows England's premier batsman with his bat under the right arm, MCC scarf around his waist, and was reproduced as a frontispiece to his 1899 book, *Cricketing Reminiscences and Personal Recollections*. An artist's proof of the Wortley portrait of Grace was also there, together with two unpublished pencil drawings done by H.S. Tuke as his prelude to his watercolour of W.G. as an Ottoman potentate. This latter, of course, Weston owned, as well as two original engravings by George Hicks, one an action study of W.G. bat in hand and running, the other E.M. Grace in a batting stance.

All W.G.'s books stood on his shelves, three outstanding items being two extra-illustrated editions of his book *Cricket*, and Charles Pratt Green's special presentation copy, seemingly the "only one not presented to a relative of W.G". Of the specially commissioned works, Weston prized most a bronze head by Colin Miller, which was included in the Post Office's special exhibition to mark the centenary of county cricket held in the Memorial Gallery at Lord's in May 1973. Ruth Andrews executed for Weston a wooden action figure of Grace batting, and two further wooden figurines by Anton Wagner show him as batsman and bowler. The first of his commissioned pieces was a coloured wooden figure of W.G. as a batsman, carved and painted by F.H. Whittington in 1950, based on a watercolour by Sirra that appeared in the *Illustrated Sporting and Dramatic News* of 17th March 1934.

Another who made a fetish of Graceiana was Ron Yeomans, and on his sideboard 20 years ago were two statuettes, both 6in. high, one a bronze showing him walking out to bat and the other a mascot, chrome-like in appearance, showing him at the wicket, bat slightly raised off the ground.

This was reputed to have stood on the bonnet of the great man's car, and was a gift to Yeomans from Ken Barrington. In the hallway of his home was a 12in. high silver-plated figure of W.G., holding a ball reminiscent of an orb tucked into his midriff, while a smaller epergne figure showed him, bat in hand, under a tree. Artistry turns some strange corners, and Yeomans had a picture of Grace walking out to bat made entirely from matchsticks, as well as a statuette of him in the same medium. Both were the creations of a former Leeds bus driver, Victor Wilson, and nearly 600 matches were used in each. His masterpiece, however, was a bust, containing no fewer than 12,454 matches glued together, sandpapered and then varnished over. The cricket cap he is wearing is in MCC colours, five matchsticks deep to give it extra height off the head.

It was partially to satiate a thirst for cricket's history that John Hawkins overcame the Swinging Sixties and started a love affair with the memory of Victor Trumper. In common with many other beginners he was shown many kindnessses by E.K. Brown, but it was at his first auction at Graves Son & Pilcher at Hove in the early Seventies that he stood, dry-mouthed and with legs like rubber, until the hammer came down and £26 seemed of little consequence beside a Trumper-Beldam signed photograph. A sadly dilapidated limited edition copy of Warner's *England v. Australia* (1911-12) has been rebound by his wife in kangaroo vellum, with 22ct. gold tooling depicting cricket motifs and the Ashes urn, and silk headbands and

end-papers in MCC touring colours. The same skill is being applied to Trumper's Queensland contract, bought for £150 and bound in with the rare tour brochure.

Hawkins secretly covets the original Chevallier Tayler of Trumper owned by the editor of *Wisden Cricket Monthly*, David Frith, but finds consolation in a complete set of four lithographs by George Elgar Hicks, still in their original wrappers, part of a series showing how to draw the human figure. At the MCC auction a pair

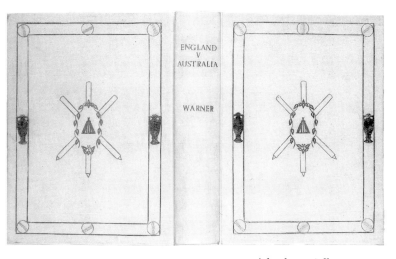

A book specially rebound by his wife for collector John Hawkins.

of these, dated c.1850s, fetched £600, and only one other has been seen at auction since 1978. Hanging proudly in an alcove is a specially commissioned Roger Marsh painting of Trumper in front of the Sydney "showboat" stand (see colour page i), but Trumper's passport document which scaled Grace-

Geoff Crambie's tribute to Frank Worrell.

like heights to reach £320 in October 1987, eluded him.

The sheer elegance and style of a superb century for Radcliffe by Frank Worrell late in 1948 was the talk of north Lancashire, and the very first item in what is now a memorable collection devoted to that lovely man by Geoff Crambie is a scorecard of 1950 with the rare "Frankie" Worrell signature. Among a host of tour brochures, scorecards, books, newspaper cuttings, photographs and the like are the only trade cards ever issued of Worrell, one of which is extremely rare, and, "my pride and joy", a photograph which once belonged to Frank of his only daughter. Clearest of all, however, Crambie remembers a summer's day at Old Trafford in 1959 when he spotted Worrell watching India batting. Having approached him for his autograph, he was told: "Sitting over there is a man whose autograph you must have for your book." The man was not young, and was supposed to be crotchety, but he did sign the book, and yes ... it was S.F. Barnes.

Today collecting is charged with energy, no longer a gentlemanly exercise conducted between friends, although a certain camaraderie still lingers on where talking about value is alleged to be distasteful; but anyone who collects seriously must keep abreast of current values, to comprehend why similar items make divergent prices. To the customary yardsticks of taste and knowledge is now added naked profit motive, with unpredictable realisations foisted upon the hobby by non-cricketing investors. This has given to overseas collectors an impression of "countless serious collectors putting up big sums of money", but if true, a good number of them have vanished into the woodwork.

During the last ten years the market has become the preserve of the auction houses Phillips, Christie's and Bonhams, and their competitive involvement is reflected in sharply rising prices with ordinary collectors compelled to circulate at a high-pressure level. Early in the 1980s it was felt that prices were settling down after a frenzy of activity which provoked the well-known absurdity of a pair of 1977 Centenary prints selling for £16, when they were to be had from the publisher for £5. During the mid and late 1980s one sensed a slight relief from the gloomy sight of a market growing ever more inflated, but fits of crazed buying do occur, when money seems little prized. The MCC Bicentenary auction brought prices to an unnatural head, and even seasoned, cynical collectors were genuinely taken aback. The inevitable mark-up of estimates ever since has left people floundering, wondering whether the Bicentenary auction was a freak, or are there simply more collectors around?

The escalation in prices since collecting became big business is a fact of life, but the market for cricketana is genuine enough. It reflects the state of the City. Prices at the auction in October 1987, held two days after "Black Monday", were significantly lower than would have been expected. Much has been made of the investment potential superimposed upon the indelible pull of nostalgia, so that collectors now see themselves in a bigger league, and when items are deemed to be valuable, they are better appreciated, better preserved and more worked upon in every sense of the word. Furthermore, since collecting became, almost inadvertently, a sort of financial cushion for the family, new problems have arisen that never dawned in earlier days. More than ever, one has to worry about insurance and the risk of theft. Is it still safe to have one's *Wisdens* on display where they might be spotted?

Auctions

Since the Phillips auction of September 1978, which caused a frisson to run up and down the backs of collectors, there have been over 40 auctions either wholly or partly devoted to cricketana. The regular pilgrimages to the London salerooms of Phillips, Christie's South Kensington and Bonhams have become mandatory for collectors, dealers and even just interested spectators, and they have also been drawn by the fund-raising auctions of county clubs and smaller sales at provincial houses. At a rough estimate, in ten years over £1 million has changed hands for approximately 11,000 lots, at an average of around £90 a lot.

All things are relative, of course, but this is, candidly, not a lot of money. The entire proceeds even of the momentous MCC Bicentenary sale in 1987, around £320,000, might have allowed the club's Arts and Library Sub-Committee a momentary fingerhold on a single Utrillo or Monet, but that is all. This serves to place cricketana in perspective, though certainly not to deny its enormous popularity; but while the auction houses now rule and dealers have to move sharply to outflank the new wave of private and institutional buyers, we are still talking, in global terms, of small sums in a quiet collecting backwater. There is none of the American or Japanese money that forces up prices in another area of fierce sporting collection, golf, or the competition from other parts of the world which fishes in the biggest oceans occupied by £20 million Van Goghs.

Auction catalogues, now items of cricketana in their own right.

The 1894 bazaar in aid of Sussex CCC resulted in a handsome balance of £700. No town in the world held so many cricket curios as Brighton and it was thought no comparable collection of pictures, balls, bats, early scorecards and relics in earthenware was ever got together. £50 was refused for the gem of the collection, on loan from the widow of a former county secretary, G.W. King, and described as follows: "Two valuable Quarto Books, containing 50 coloured illustrations by 'Felix', and copious notes of the doings of the All England Eleven of 1851 and 1852".

No high bids were recorded at the W.A. Bettesworth sale of cricket books in April 1929. Twenty-eight lots realised £43.16s. [£43.80]. A few private circulation items such as *Cricket 1742 to 1751* caused some competition, but prices ruled low and seven different editions of Pycroft's *Cricket Field* realised exactly 10s.6d. [53p]. Five guineas [£5.25] bought someone 15 volumes of *Scores and Biographies* with J.B. Payne's index to first-class matches. Henry Ling picked up several rarities at Sotheby's in May 1932, formerly the property of Philip Norman, including Love's *Heroic Poem*, Boxall's *Rules and Instructions* (1800), Lambert's *Instructions and Rules* (1816) and Bentley's *Correct Account of all the Cricket Matches played at the Marylebone Club from 1786 to 1882*. Ling paid just £26.

There was little to interest the cricketer at the sale of Jamnagar House, near Staines, the English home of Ranjitsinhji, in July 1933, "save the knowledge that once all these beautiful things had belonged to one of the greatest cricketers". The 96 sporting books fetched small prices, and the *Jubilee Book*, No.247, author-signed, was withdrawn before the sale commenced. Prices realised at the Sotheby's sale in 1936 of J.A.H. Catton's library were above average and there was brisk bidding making it obvious "that there is a good demand for second-hand cricket books of any merit". The chief items were purchased by J.W. Goldman and Sir Julien Cahn at what seem ludicrous prices: Love's poem for £2.15s. [£2.75]; a first edition of Nyren and Warner's limited edition *Imperial Cricket* for £1.15s. each [£1.75] and Denison's *Cricket* for a guinea [£1.05]. Mind you, Sir Julien lavished £43 on Boxall's rare first technical manual and £11.10s [£11.50] for 13 volumes of Catton's manuscript 'Dictionary of Cricketers'.

Just six months before the outbreak of war in 1939, Sotheby's sold about 50 books on cricket, the property of E.V. Lucas. The lots included a first edition of *Felix on the Bat*, Goldman's *Bibliography* and long runs of now rare annuals; *Scores and Biographies* fetched just over £11. After Cahn died in 1944 MCC were given first choice of any item from his collection not already in stock, but not items they already possessed, save in certain cases such as the richly annotated sets of *Scores and Biographies* which had been Haygarth's and Ashley-Cooper's. No one from Lord's made the trip to undertake the selection (admittedly it was wartime), and the result was that Lord's received volumes mistakenly taken up from both sets. Much of the remainder of the collection given away by Lady Cahn went to a collector and family relation, E.G. Wolfe. Primarily pictures and prints but also the Staffordshire figures of Caesar and Parr, they came, somewhat incongruously, to furnish eventually, The Yorker public house in Piccadilly, itself now no longer. The balance of the Cahn library was put up for sale, under Lady Cahn's property, at Sotheby's in October 1951 and it was a fiasco. An unexpectedly early start and misunderstandings between dealers meant over 350 cricket books going for next to nothing, and out of the other items, such as early Philadelphia brochures, a full run of Derbyshire annuals for the 1880s and 1890s, and a set of Natal and South African annuals, only some have come to light. Incidentally, Sir Henry Leveson Gower's cricketana collection also went to Wolfe, and parts of this great aggregation ultimately found their way to John Arlott, Geoffrey Copinger and Desmond Eagar.

A special feature of the Goldman collection, sold by Hodgson's on 24th November 1966, and one that made it especially valuable, was the large amount of 18th century material. The 301 lots realised £3,747.10s. and this was a record figure for a single day's sale of cricket books. The highest prices paid are worth repeating: Britcher's *Scores*, 1794-1805 (£350); Lillywhite's *Guides*, 1850-1866 (£195), a copy of Boxall (1804; £58); and Epps's *Scores*

(1799; £50). J.M. Barrie's Allahakbarrie book, published in 1899, ascended an arc as high as the author's slow bowling to reach £70, interesting to compare with the sale at Sotheby's in 1922, when four pages of Barrie's autograph manuscript of this work, with three proofs (one copiously corrected) and the book itself were sold for £41. Barrie himself did not possess a copy, and it was believed that no single cricket item had realised so large a sum at public auction since July 1914, when the Fletcher of Shelton pottery mug, commemorating the match between the Earls of Darnley and Winchelsea was sold for 43 guineas [£45.15].

The 'Tony Baer' auction at Phillips on 18th September 1978 was a wonderful occasion. It was rated by David Rayvern Allen as "surely second only to Goldman's since the War" and it served to open collectors' eyes to the investment potential of memorabilia. Most of Baer's collection had already gone to Melbourne, including an impressive library, but about 70 items from his peerless collection were offered in a sale which featured also non-cricketing oil paintings. The 40-page catalogue of oils, prints, pottery, silver and ephemera, the books of H.M. Cohen and property of others, is itself now awkward to find. Lest we forget, prices in the book section set standards which have now become the norm. Robin Marlar paid £280 for a first edition of Felix and £110 for Lillywhite's *English Cricketers trip to Canada and the United States*, while a second edition of Love's poem fetched £250, a Nyren £210, Denison's *Sketches of the Players* (1846) £200, Colman's *Noble Game* £460 and *Curiosities of Cricket* (1897) a fantastic £580.

Landmarks along the way since 1978 have included the sale of items from Sir Pelham Warner's estate in May 1980, when a total of 324 lots realised about £34,000, while also in 1980 Sussex CCC pulled in £10,000 and Worcestershire CCC just over £1,300 for a smaller number of lots. With *Wisdens* the staple of most sales and rarely failing to excite keen competition, the rest ticked over steadily until 20th and 21st November 1985, when modern collectors at last had a set-piece to match the legendary sales of yore. It was the most comprehensive private collection ever to go on public sale, 921 lots of pictures and prints, ceramics and metalware, ephemera, letters, and just about every significant book on cricket there had been. Although the collection was officially offered anonymously, it was discovered to have been that of A.E. (Tony) Winder, a Yorkshireman, who had acquired much of the material from John Arlott in 1980. The provenance of the collection – Gaston, Pratt Green, Ashley-Cooper, Weston, Goldman and Arlott – was a roll-call of the great figures in the field and the opportunity offered by "the sale of the century" was not missed by the massed ranks of dealers and collectors. Many of the individual realisations, notably among the books, are spread through this book and the overall total on the auctioneers' computer at the end of two days was £105,302, which grossed up to a total spent of £117,411 with the addition of buyer's premium and VAT.

A new record for a set of *Wisdens*, £15,565, followed at the G.B. Buckley sale in Bristol the following year, broken the next month, but even all this was as nothing compared to the hurricane, whirlwind, madness, call it what you will, which swept across Lord's on 13th April 1987. The occasion was the MCC Bicentenary auction – "the sale of the double century", even though all the material was from what MCC termed its reserve collection – and with an invasion of high-spending buyers from Australia (Melbourne CC and the embryo Bradman Museum) joining home-based bidders also seduced by the name of the world's most famous cricket club, all previous records were cast out of the window: the 829 lots actually sold grossed £323,878, as pre-sale estimates were beaten tenfold or more in the longest one-day fixture ever seen at Lord's, lasting nearly 11½ hours and superbly stage-managed by Christie's South Kensington. It was not, incidentally, the first auction there, as many had believed: George Robey, the entertainer, had conducted one in 1917, when 34 lots, primarily bats, raised £100 for war charities.

Of course it was widely acknowledged that prices went way over the top at the Bicentenary auction, and previously its very staging had been questioned by the Museums Association, who argued that the objects should have been offered first to other museums and accused MCC of "a sad insensitivity to the preservation of the country's cricketing heritage" by selling off items that had been donated to the club. MCC's response was that, as far as possible, they had given donors the chance to decide whether or not to support the sale and that some lots were indeed withdrawn. The items offered were duplicates of pictures or objects in the main collection, paintings whose repair would be uneconomic, or material not directly related to MCC. On the day ethical considerations seemed lost under the arc lights in the frenzy of the chase, and by the time the final sums were worked out, and all expenses and taxes had been paid, MCC were left with £225,000 to open a special fund to pay for restoration of the main collection and to make new acquisitions.

Prices at auction since the Bicentenary auction have not yet, and probably will not for a while to come, approach the same levels, apart from some exceptional pieces. However, the sale changed perceptions of collecting, both among those who have been involved in it for a long time and those who had not previously been interested. It was a factor, too, behind the formation of the Cricket Memorabilia Society, which aims to cater for the average, genuine, and probably lifelong, collector-enthusiast. There must always be a place for him in the world of cricketana.

The quarterly magazine of the Cricket Memorabilia Society.

PAINTINGS

Fortunately for cricketana addicts, cricket's pictorial art is anything but cosmically interesting. Few of the world's truly great artists have been drawn to the game, but those that have are now in the millionaire class. Out of reach and a world away are the stupendous paintings by J.M.W. Turner, 'The Lake, Petworth: Sunset, Bucks Fighting' (c.1830) and 'Wells Cathedral with a Game of Cricket' (c.1795), the former in Petworth House itself and the latter in the Lady Lever collection at Port Sunlight, Cheshire. Both of these typify a whole genre of paintings where cricket is but a passing reference within a wider artistic statement, scant appreciation being shown for the niceties of detail.

In this top bracket of rich, complex and satisfying art are two paintings by Camille Pissarro. 'Cricket on Hampton Court Green' (1890), seen by some as impressionistic to a startling degree, is, alas, lost to us in Washington, while 'Cricket at Bedford Park', painted in 1897, found its way to Paris. At this level, of course, the cricket enthusiast has to compete with institutional and private buyers wholly indifferent to any cricket content. This tends to make it a case of *non possumus*!

Of course there were the Gainsboroughs, Zoffanys and Hudsons who enjoyed a measure of patronage and a secure livelihood, but, generally speaking, it is a potpourri of works by unknown artists – often anonymous, itinerant and artisan, whose enthusiasm or need to paint outshone their skill – that has been left to collectors.

Johan Zoffany's conversation piece oil of the Sondes children, painted c.1764, is justifiably well-known, but there is an intriguing reference in cricket's periodical literature to another painting, an oil portrait of a boy cricketer, painted toward the end of the 18th century and attributed to Zoffany; in 1928 it was in the possession of Cyril Andrade. The boy is seated, holding a bat, gaitered and wearing silken cuffs, his cap lying on the right hand side of the picture.

Into the gilded salons of the patrons Henry Edridge fitted neatly. He was much in demand as a portraitist and by 1806 was able to confide, in a letter, that for a single full-length drawing he had raised his asking price from 15 to 20 guineas. A delightful watercolour of a boy holding a bat was exhibited at Agnew's in 1978. Possibly the same painting, but described as executed in pencil, with some delicate touches of colour, 'A Young Cricketer', $14^3/_4$in.x$10^1/_4$in., sold in May 1980 for £420; at the MCC Bicentenary auction another $8^1/_4$in.x$5^1/_2$in. pencil and watercolour of a boy holding a bat and standing beneath a tree, attributed to Edridge, was bid up to £800. Meticulous in attention to detail, 'A Young Cricketer' adhered to the aristocratic conventions of the age, the sitter perfectly dressed, totally devoid of expression, and posed against a studied background of country house or formal garden. Elegance, refinement and restraint mattered most, and a horse or a fowling piece could have served as well as a bat.

'A Young Cricketer' by Henry Edridge.

A step or two down the scale of international desirability, we come to the British Impressionist School, but these, too, are ardently collected. Spencer Gore's pointillist 'The Cricket Match' (1909), in the Wakefield Art Gallery, has something in common with the Pissarro painting of Bedford Park, but shows a greater appreciation of the game *per se*. Gore's father held the first Wimbledon Championship in 1877, and he himself was a useful all-rounder at Harrow, both boxing for the school and keeping wicket for the second XI.

What one critic called the "embrasured serenity" of county grounds between the wars, rich in commentary on English class and society, is made vivid in a piece by another British Impressionist. Arthur Spooner's 'Cricket, Tea Interval, Trent Bridge', signed and dated 1938 (the ground's centenary year), has shafts of sunshine which transform a quiet corner of the ground, the old tea gardens behind the pavilion, into a warm, southern European townscape. The date, plus the Nottingham background of the artist, makes one wonder whether Sir Julien Cahn, the great patron of Nottinghamshire cricket, can be identified in the scene (see colour page iii). Recently acquired for something like £60,000 through the David Messum Gallery, London, this must be one of the most costly pictures in private hands with any reference to cricket, and it stayed in Britain despite intense pressure from American buyers.

In 1959 a retrospective exhibition of Spooner's work included another cricketing subject, 'At the Test Match'. Nothing seems to be known, however, even by the artist's daughter, about what must surely constitute a major work.

That such high-calibre material can simply disappear is extraordinary. Some sort of art equivalent of Padwick's *Bibliography* seems essential, and with desk-top publishing making life a lot easier, would it be a disservice to collectors for the MCC Arts and Library Sub-Committee to earmark some of the proceeds from the Bicentenary sale to underwrite a project of this nature?

For anyone new to the collecting scene, the Bicentenary sale catalogue – itself assuredly a collector's and student's piece – is a valuable introductory guide to the pictorial arts. The illustrated catalogues (1986, 1987 and 1989), issued by the Burlington Gallery since the arrival there of Nicholas Potter, conform also to high standards of taste and scholarship. They concentrate on the peak period of fine print production from 1790 onwards, but give lavish attention to oils, watercolours, ceramics, silverware and ephemera.

Almost all the best-known and most coveted works date from the 1840s and 1850s when few people had much in the way of disposable income. The getting of money was harder and its spending stingier. With so little consumer demand, it is impossible to disagree with John Arlott's contention that cricketing pictorial art is "neither particularly distinguished nor extensive".

Wide-ranging contributions in the cricketing press by J.W. Goldman, Rockley Wilson, Rowland Bowen, Irving Rosenwater and, notably, Stephen Green, signposted the way for the outstanding 'Baedeker' work by Robin Simon and Alastair Smart, entitled *The Art of Cricket* (1983). Despite its claim not to be exhaustive, so extensive is its coverage of who owns what and where, that we need mention only a sample, purely as a taster. There is, for example, 'Three Young Cricketers' by George Elgar Hicks at the Southampton Art Gallery; a W.G. miniature at Bristol Art Gallery, and at the Greaves Art Gallery in Sheffield 'A Game of Cricket' by Purlee Parker. Hastings Town Hall has an attractive view of the local cricket ground, painted by Charles Cundall, whose painting of the Lord's Test of 1938 has been so frequently reproduced that copies promoted by Gillette virtually as giveaways adorn study walls all over the place.

Cricket has long been regarded as an ingredient in a rural scene, often purely a device by the artist to add a human dimension or make a point of social comment. The more illustrious landscapes begin with permutations of Hayman's 'Cricket on the Artillery Ground', such as the small oil on panel sold for £300 at Phillips in June 1988, and progress through such works as the russet and ochre lines of Thomas Barker's 'Cricket at Pontypool', T. Bristow's oil of 'The Australian XI of 1878 v. XI Gentlemen of Kent and Surrey', Charles Dean's 'Cricket Match at Wittersham, Kent, c.1845' and 'A Cricket Match at Canterbury c.1760' by Henry Hodgins. Paintings by anonymous artists are legion, but it may be enough to single out 'Cricket Match at Christchurch, Hampshire', c.1850, which has been exposed as an ingenious fake, created some time between 1920 and 1945.

Ashley-Cooper's notes in *Cricket*, 1891, refer to an enormous painting – some 5ft.x3ft.6in. – of cricket on Bembridge Common, Isle of Wight, as played in 1761. It was found in an old lumber room, where it had probably lain for the best part of a century. Including spectators, some 300 characters appear in this massive work, a treasure trove for students of period costume.

Overseas and Continental paintings also make their presence felt. A wrinkled oil of the Calcutta Cricket Club, painted in 1861, was sold in November 1985 for over £1,000, while a couple taken at random from 1988

Thomas Barker's 'Cricket at Pontypool'.

auctions reveal £480 paid at Christie's for an early 19th-century 'Cricket Match in Meadows beneath a European City', and £200 for an early 20th-century oil of a 'Cricket Match on a Colonial Ground, possibly a military post, said to be Tasmania'.

Self-evidently outside the scope of the Simon and Smart book, there must be scores of suburban homes dotted across the country with paintings near and dear to their owners. The reasons for private pleasure would be as diverse as the scenes depicted, but particularly interesting are those where there is an element of family link.

Mike Marshall in Essex, for instance, has an evocative rural cricket scene by James Stark (1794-1859), a representative of the Norfolk School (see colour page vi). It is a pleasant, if not exceptional work, made more meaningful by Stark having been a distant relative.

When all is said and done, all roads lead to Lord's. The walls of the pavilion are festooned with the world's greatest collection of cricketing art, but while it is rumoured that 'enterprise culture' has invaded the *sanctum sanctorum*, the sad fact remains that, at the time of writing, much of cricket's artistic heritage is inaccessible.

The collection makes no claim to be complete, indeed many years ago (*The Cricketer*, 27th June 1931) E.V. Lucas wrote, enigmatically, that "it could not be complete when the Pavilion at the Oval has the Morland" (alas, no longer there). Neither, to be perfectly honest, have the authorities at Lord's ever pretended that all the paintings are originals, despite the alarums off-stage created by the *Mail on Sunday* in 1983 about fakes and forgeries.

In 1864 MCC boasted just two pictures, both by or attributed to Francis

Hayman. The collection was begun in the 1850s by James Dark, for almost 30 years proprietor of the ground, and vastly expanded by Sir Spencer Ponsonby Fane. By the turn of the century, long before the arrival of the magnificent ensemble from Sir Jeremiah Colman, there were some 200 depictions of cricket scenes. Ponsonby Fane then co-compiled the 1902 and 1912 catalogues, and collectors await an up-date.

Meanwhile, thanks to postcard reproductions, many of the club's paintings are legendary. There is the masterly gouache ascribed to Paul Sandby, 'Landscape with a Cricket Match' (1774); Garland's 'The Winner of the Match'; 'Tossing for Innings'; 'Cricket at Kenfield Hall' (dated c.1780, and attributed to W. Pratt); and Thomas Henwood's portrait of the Pickwickian scorer for Lewes Priory, one William Davies, and known to the world simply as 'The Scorer' (1842). A now very rare lithograph of this was issued the same year with the Chesterfield tape-measure and stumps, included in the original work, omitted from the scene.

The happy discovery of a single sheet from George Shepheard's sketchbook, which lay hidden at Lord's for many years, enables us to visualise the postures adopted by the 'Hambledon Men'. "Lumpy" Stevens is one of those shown, the greatest bowler of his time, and a man actively concerned in the introduction of a third stump. Legend has it that, at least until 1860, there was a picture of Stevens, dancing with a jug of ale in hand, in the Waterloo Inn, Bath Green, near Hambledon, later the Heroes of Waterloo Inn at Waterlooville.

The other Test match grounds are more reticent. Trent Bridge has Frank Batson's epic 'Playing Out Time in an Awkward Light', presented by his daughter to the Nottinghamshire club in 1904 and impossible to walk past and not feel instant sympathy for the unseen batsman taking strike.

Among a host of others, Surrey at The Oval have an engraving dated 1846, showing a view of the ground as seen from what is today the Vauxhall end, and a painting of 1847 by C. Rosenburg jnr, on the back of which is inscribed 'Kennington Oval, with the Market Gardeners' Dwelling turned into a Club House'. More compelling, and rarely seen, is an intriguing oil on composition painting panel of the site of The Oval around 1810. It is from much the same angle as the later pictures, but three decades and more before the first recorded game. It may have been commissioned by Frederick Laudensark, owner of The Oval, and one of the three men seen in the picture. Then there is the George Morland alluded to by Lucas, but no longer known at The Oval. Are we to assume it is 'A Cricket Match at Laleham Green', painted in the 1790s, and found by Thomas Padwick at a pub, the Cricketer's Arms in Chertsey?

Outside the galleries, stately homes and great national collections, amply dealt with in *The Art of Cricket*, the supply of expensive objects for

The Oval around 1810 as seen in the painting probably commissioned by Frederick Laudensark.

veneration and worship is limited, whereas the amount of cash chasing any still in private hands is basically a lot less limited. So what will inevitably go up is not supply, but prices, and it could be that the export market will exert the strongest pull.

Australia's ethnic mix, and the wide assortment of financial counter-attractions such as dream townships, the America's Cup and a large chunk of the world's media, has so far distracted a nation with an unquestioning belief in its own capacities from true involvement in cricketana. The Melbourne Cricket Club and the fledgling Bradman Museum at Bowral may yet rival Lord's for artistic treasures, reflected already by aggressive bidding at auctions, prices paid locally for Bradman scraps, and the attractive format and presentation of Rick Bouwman's *Glorious Innings: Treasures from the Melbourne Cricket Club Collection* (1987).

Literally anything by Sir Russell Drysdale, that distinguished visual narrator of the Australian bush scene since the 1950s, is rampantly collected in his native country. The sporting angle to 'The Cricketers', the famous scene of two youngsters practising against a wall in some bush town, is probably secondary to the warmth of ownership. Recently, we understand, it was sold for a fantastic Aus$2 million to the "L.B.J." collection in Melbourne, a record for a Drysdale work and one of the highest prices for an Australian painting – and, by several pitch lengths, the top price for an item of cricketana.

Back in the UK, it is hard to conceive of a finer or sweeter selection than the 'duplicates' on offer at the MCC sale, when, as often happens, human nature ensured an excess of cash over sense. On the other hand, the indifferent attitude of most county committees to their own heritage may assist collectors as awareness grows that if it's cricket, then it's saleable.

In the interim, collectors can tuck into a reasonable trickle of largely second-rank material, decanted from houses decorated with a comfortable array of cricketing scenes or from pavilions faced with theft, vandalism, local government cutbacks or closure.

The year 1973 was a vintage one for sales. There was a tiny watercolour from Myles Birket Foster, just $1^3/8$in.x$5^1/2$in., seen briefly at Sotheby's before it disappeared into private hands. He is better known as one of the country's greatest wood-engravers, so this 1860 example of his later Surrey landscapes is most desirable. The ball is shown coming directly at the viewer from a square-cut, and its reappearance on the market would cause an agreeable stir.

The same could be said about an $11^3/4$in.x10in. kaleidoscope of Victorian schoolday memories compiled by Edward George Handel Lucas into 'When We Were Boys Together' (1881). Picked out in detail are marbles, bat and ball, and that other crisp reminder of those days, a cane. In similar vein is the oil on canvas by Rupert Dent. Priced by the Burlington Gallery at £2,750 in 1987, 'A Schoolboy's Treasure' represented an affectionate recollection of the childhood pleasures of 1890 (see colour page ii): a case of butterflies on the wall, a dog by the door, and a bat, ball, pair of pads and set of stumps.

Appreciably more watercolours and sketches descend upon the market than the number of oil canvases, but from the latter we have chosen an eleven, plus twelfth man and a reserve or two, which seem to reflect popular appeal. The blue riband might well go that choice example of bucolic rusticana, Alexander Hohenlohe Burr's 'A Game of Cricket: Youth and Age', which was painted at Arlington in Sussex in 1878. There are other versions of this composition, and one of them, 'The Veteran Bowler' (see colour page vi), was a hot property in September 1979 at £2,800, rising to £8,000 at Phillips in June 1989. Browns and greens are the predominating colours, and one version, size 15in.x$24^1/2$in., was bought by Ron Yeomans at Sotheby's in 1960, and regarded as one of his greatest treasures. 'Youth and Age', size 18in.x26in., was sold at auction in September 1978 for £7,500, and this may well be the one listed in the Simon and Smart book as property of Harvert Consultancy (Holdings) Ltd., based in Dundee.

In both, the setting is a farmyard, with a venerable rustic bowling lobs to a small boy defending a rudimentary wicket. It has become widely known both as a greetings card and as the frontispiece to a menu card for the Northern Cricket Society's dinner to the champion Yorkshire team of 1960.

Burr was a Scotsman and it is remarkable how often painters from north of the border have contributed to the canon of cricketing art. At the Tate Gallery is John Robertson Reid's 'Country Cricket Match' (1855), a painting which reaches beyond the extremes of Victorian sentiment to show how all the vigour and motion of nature can be conjured up in the momentum of the paint itself.

'Her First Lesson' by James Hayllar did well at £300 in September 1980, while an early copy of Richard Wilson's painting of Hampton Wick and Moulsey Hurst realised £600 in 1981, not surprising in view of the link with the famous actor, David Garrick, who sponsored local matches. Showpiece items at the Sussex CCC sale in 1980 were an oil, size 23in.x31in., with additions, of 'A Match between Kent and Sussex near Malling' (late 18th or early 19th century), and a tiny sketch of 'Sussex v. Cambridge at Hove 1895', which cheered up the county treasurer to the extent of £1,650.

The creations of E.P. Kinsella are discussed in the chapters on Ceramics and Postcards. In the field of painting, anything "after Kinsella" usually finds an appreciative audience, although one senses that latterly they have tended to drag somewhat. The pair of boy cricketers, modelled on his cheerful Cockney lad, 'Hope of His Side' and 'Out First Ball', signed by F. Vitale, were seen on offer recently at the Burlington Gallery around the £700 mark, while 'Waiting for a Delivery' and 'Clean Bowled', a pair of signed canvases on the same theme, sold at Bonhams in November 1987 for £400.

Watercolours

It is in the realm of the smaller watercolours, along with crayon sketches and pen-and-ink drawings, that the collector can really find bargains. There is a large amount of material available at budget prices, most of it uncomplicated, readily understandable and easy to live with.

There is, of course, a plethora of trivia, but some notion of the game's tangible tradition and the splendour that accompanies it, is easily gained by a glance at the Tony Baer collection as it was in 1965, pre-Melbourne. His earliest watercolour is dated c.1730 and shows two boys playing cricket in a rural setting, while another, dated 1831, has the Stonehenge CC playing in the majestic environs of the great stones. Earlier watercolours by named artists are relatively scarce, and Ron Yeomans, while he relished the dappling of colour and tone in a landscape thought to be Rudding Park, with a game of cricket in the middle foreground, could only dubiously ascribe it to J.W. Carmichael (1800-68).

A particularly delicious feat of water painting is 'The Boundary Bench' by James Mathews, the Sussex-based artist, signed and dated 1901, and sold by Burlington Gallery for £2,000 (see colour page iv). Rather earlier in date, there was some pleasant handling of paint in 'Cricketer at the Crease', by Henry Garland (1841), 12in.x17in., sold in 1980 for £220.

James Thorpe was well represented at the MCC sale, and subsequently six of his pen-and-ink studies of batsman, bowlers, wicketkeeper and a sleeping spectator came up at Christie's for auction the following year. Seemingly modestly estimated at between £80 and £120, they only managed £55.

In a different dimension altogether, we come to the singular, shining talent of N. Felix (a.k.a. Nicholas Wanostrocht). He will loom large in the chapter on Prints, but an album of his watercolours sold for over £1,000 in November 1985, and a lookalike 'Game of Cricket' for £7,500 in 1984. Two watercolours by him in a single frame, 'The Wood-wain' and 'Cows in the Pool', once a presentation gift to Jack Hobbs, seem in retrospect to have been a snip at £300, but then the Sussex CCC sale of 1980 seems to have been curiously overlooked.

It is in the 'English School', embracing numerous subjects, that collections can still be assembled at a reasonable cost. Typical of this genre are 'Four Boys Playing Cricket before a village church', a pen-and-ink brown wash dated 1783, signed with the monogram "F.R.", which realised £200 at Christie's in 1988, and 'Figures playing cricket before the village church', with figure studies of cricketers on the reverse, sold seven years previously at Phillips for £60. At the rampant hysteria of the MCC sale, 'The Jubilee Cricket Match' wildly exceeded its estimate of £100-£200 to zoom over £1,500, and 'Two Young Girls/Two Young Boys holding bats' did much the same, almost £3,000 against an estimate of £400-£600.

The anonymous watercolour 'Grand Cricket Match for One Thousand Guineas'.

As much a leitmotif for cricket art as the Hayman picture is the anonymous 'Grand Cricket Match for One Thousand Guineas' between the Earls of Winchelsea and Darnley, played at Thomas Lord's ground at Dorset Square, Marylebone on 20th June 1793. A watercolour of this frequently copied scene climbed to £550 at Phillips in June 1988, with one of scores of prints of the same scene touching down at £50.

Portraits

Artists are dreadful voyeurs, yet, perversely, so much of cricket portraiture strikes one as bland and anodyne. There can be finely focused attention to detail, but most are basically board-room paintings, the subjects dignified in mien, but the treatment arid and lifeless.

For a lack of any real human presence, take the James Archer portrait of A.G. Steel. Although it was spoilt by over-varnishing when offered by Christie's in June 1988, there is little evidence of integration between the artist and his sitter in this rather pedestrian study of the great Lancashire and England Test player. It was commissioned by R.G. Thoms and MCC in 1901, and little of the subject's inner self emerges; but in Lancashire they look after their own and keen bidding pushed the price up to £600. Mind you, he will be in excellent company at Old Trafford. A striking portrait of the inimitable Cardus by Holesch, commissioned in 1951, arrived there in 1975, and it is interesting to note that in a May 1982 auction at Phillips there was an unframed sketch by Cardus himself of his press-box position at The Oval, which made £55.

If one's idea of a portrait is a contour map of features, every wrinkle highlighted, then a photograph is sufficient. If, however, portraiture is meant to probe the spirit of the sitter, then the fresh eye can be more courageous, evocative and disturbing.

John Bellany's work deals with urgent psychological perceptions, often autobiographical, a factor overlooked when his highly expressionistic portrait of Ian Botham was unveiled at the National Portrait Gallery to a largely incredulous public. Some reactions are worth recalling: "a perfect specimen of a malformed wimp", "a thin, weedy aesthete", "an attenuated Byzantine saint" and "Paul Allott after an incident with the heavy roller". Yet for Bellany, Botham was a hero, a cult figure, as much a colossus as Grace, whose portrait is also to be found at the Gallery. Both of them are shown half-length and full-face, powerful and immense. The massive Botham torso contrasts with a small, almost epicene head, but this was deliberate artistic licence, the artist trying to capture not the physical likeness but a deeper perception of "aura", a figure of Bellany's imaginative world, typical of his symbolic work, religious and mythical.

Images of W.G. transcend time, and to this day he is probably the only cricketer recognised by non-cricketing women when buying for the men in their lives. The best-known image of Grace is Archibald Stuart Wortley's much-reproduced study of him at the wicket at Lord's (1890), commissioned by MCC through £1 subscriptions and for which the artist was paid £300. The oil (48in.x34in.) emphasises Grace's bulk and strength, as well as his masterly technique. The brown shoes and cocked left toe cause wry amusement now and the eagle-eyed will note that the clock in the background, on the wall

Wortley's famous portrait of 'W.G.', and a letter from the great man referring to a sitting.

W.A.J. West, possibly a model for the Grace portrait.

of the old real tennis court, shows 2.30 – which would have been during the lunch interval in W.G.'s day at Lord's. We have also found an intriguing reference (*The Cricketer*, 13th June 1953, p.218) to the possibility that W.A.J. West, a first-class (later Test match) umpire based at Lord's, was used as a model by the artist. West, who was a noted heavyweight boxer and played cricket for Northamptonshire and Warwickshire in their second-class days, was also a large man and would certainly have fitted the bill.

Among watercolours of the "Grand Old Man" is a cool and disciplined work by Cecil Cutler, signed and dated 1895, the year Grace completed 1,000 runs in May at the age of 47. Shown in three-quarter length, he is wearing an I Zingari blazer and MCC cap, and the supposition of the Burlington Gallery, which sold this fine painting for some thousands of pounds, is that it may have been executed for the IZ. Another unforgettable study is the portrayal by Henry Scott Tuke, RA, of Grace as an Eastern potentate. The occasion was a dinner following a match at Shillinglee Park, Sussex, seat of the Earl of Winterton, in May 1908, when Grace donned one of Ranjitsinhji's turbans and sat for the artist in it again the following afternoon before going out to bat. This choice item, once owned by the leading figure on Graceiana,

G. Neville Weston, reached £3,000 at Christie's in October 1987. Tuke was also responsible for a charcoal portrait of W.G., inscribed "Crystal Palace. June 24, 1905" (20cm.x26cm.), which achieved £2,200 at Phillips in June 1987, but was unsold when they reoffered it a year later.

The turbanned Grace by Henry Scott Tuke, and the charcoal portrait by the same artist.

Two other rather nondescript oils have appeared; one, on board (18cm.x25cm.), by Dr Geo. Dale came as part of a "W.G." lot and realised £48 at Phillips in October 1985, and another, an anonymous study inscribed "W.G. Grace, '79", but painted this century, £180 at Christie's in October 1988. A modern oil, by Harold Cantle, has a charm of its own. No.1 of a print run of a thousand, it hangs in the Grace Suite at the County Ground in Bristol.

Mostly, though, W.G. appears in caricature. A "handsome drawing", attributed to Harry Furniss, was acquired for over £1,000 at the MCC sale, and nine action sketches, also by Furniss, estimated at between £600-£900, reached over £3,000 on that epic occasion and what has been criticised as an "ugly" caricature, by J.W.T. Manuel, exceeded estimate tenfold to clamber over £1,000.

Presumably they were not West Country buyers, for it has been

Portrait of an
anonymous bearded
cricketer by A.
Ludovici.

'Lewis Cage as a
Batsman' by Eleanor
Hughes D'eath.

suggested to us that in the cider counties he is still not totally forgiven for quitting Gloucestershire in favour of his mercenary London County XI, and prints of W.G. sell well everywhere, save in his heartland. Nevertheless, the name of Grace casts an eternal spell. Witness a compelling oil by A. Ludovici of a bearded cricketer in a garden setting, dated 1879, and sold for £400 in June 1986. It has quite definite style and presence and shows the influence of Ludovici's mentor, J.M. Whistler, in the rendering of the floral background. It is now reckoned to be a member of the clan Grace and the asking price has escalated to £4,000.

If the full-length, opulent picture of a supremely arrogant-looking W.E. Roller going out to bat, painted by his brother c.1880, bulks large in the pavilion at The Oval, the same can be said of the influential portraits of Jardine and Bradman in the Long Room at Lord's. As may be imagined, the pavilion and Memorial Gallery are replete with pictures of the mighty. Thomas Lord, and another acquisition from a grand-daughter, the unsigned, undated picture of John Nyren in mid-life hold one's fancy, as does yet another figure from the dim past, Lord Frederick Beauclerk.

Beldham is there, and Disraeli, too, along with a surprisingly amiable looking Spofforth, also by H.S. Tuke. Probably the best-known, if only because it cost so much, is Jacques Sablet's full-length portrait of Thomas Hope of Amsterdam (1792), purchased by the MCC in 1968, through grants and subscriptions, for 9,500 guineas – the equivalent today of some £65,000. Fit for a lord (or Lord's?) was a portrait of a boy, 60cm.x44cm., resplendent in royal blue coat and holding a cricket ball, which was offered as part of the Pilkington Collection by Phillips in September 1989. Estimate for this choice item, by John Russell c.1800, was £7,000 - £10,000.

William Bromley's illustrations of Wisden, Parr and Mynn add lustre to Lord's, but one at least – that of James Dean, painted c.1850 – escaped to Melbourne via Tony Baer, the last link in a chain extending back to Goldman and the Jeremiah Colman sale of 18th September 1942.

Barring another aberration on the scale of the MCC sale, rarely do household-name portraits appear on the market, and then, as in the case of Eleanor Hughes D'eath's full-length oil of 'Lewis Cage as a Batsman' (1768), only as a later copy. The original by Francis Cotes is the property of Lord Brocket, John Nutting has the replica illustrated in *The Art of Cricket*, while a modern copy hangs in the Long Room. Typical of the formalised style of heroic pose, current at the time and suggestive of manly character, this universally known canvas, estimated at £1,800-2,500, sold at the Bicentenary for £10,000.

The same sale dispersed to happy ownership a pair of earlier works: Henry St Clair's large oil portrait of John H. Chandler for close on £6,000 (estimate £1,000-1,500) and a picture of William and Thomas Earle by C. Wellings for £6,500 (estimate £300-500).

Portraits are strung across a number of county pavilions, but research suggests three legendary names worth seeking out. There is a charming portrait by "Felix" of G. Lionel King, which hangs in the Hove pavilion. King bowled the lob ball struck with tremendous power by Thornton in a practice match at Brighton in 1871, a prodigious hit variously measured between 148 and 168 yards.

C. Wellings' painting of William and Thomas Earle.

Two drawings, 'Lillywhite of Home' (*sic*), 5in.x7½in. and 4½in.x7in., together with a photograph of the same subject, appeared at the Sussex sale in 1980, when a watercolour portrait of Lillywhite was also sold.

Digging around in a dingy shop, Ashley-Cooper was told that all there was for sale, kicking around in a lumber room, was a "picture of a man in cricketing dress". Playing it close to his chest, he proffered the necessary shilling or so, and quietly stole away with a hitherto unpublished painting of Alfred Mynn, which, prior to its disappearance, had once been on a wall in the pavilion at Southgate.

A mini-rash of English School primitives and pseudo-primitives depicting "boy cricketers" erupts at regular intervals. An oil on canvas, 71cm.x91cm., 'The Young Cricketers', was sold at the seminal Phillips sale in 1978 for £2,600; then came 'Boy with a Bat', inscribed "G.R. 1862", 18in.x23in., £250 in August 1980; 'Boy with a Bat' another oil on canvas, at Bonhams, £700 in 1987; yet another of the same, late 18th century, £450 also in 1987; 'Boy with a Bat' at Christie's in October 1988, £220, and 'The Young Cricketer and his Sister', £240 at Bonhams in June 1988, this time a pencil and watercolour of the pair seated beside a cricket bat and ball, underneath the shade of trees in a woodland vista. 'Portrait of a Young Boy' (1834), identifiable to the artist, Thomas Kirby, realised £750 in 1979.

Studies from life, as opposed to photographic retrieval, occur infrequently. There was a quite brilliant pastel of Herbert Strudwick, painted by Frank Eastman in 1949, while a chalk drawing by W.H. Gill of

Wilfred Rhodes, an
action portrait by
Ernest R. Moore.

Warwick Armstrong at the wicket, signed and dated 1902, attracted £60 at Phillips in July 1981. But for most people, and not necessarily just Yorkshiremen, a realisation of £380 in May 1982 for an immaculate study by Ernest R. Moore of Wilfred Rhodes in action would seem a rich dividend.

In the pecking order, material relating to England v. Australia fetches the highest prices, followed by England v. India and scarce Caribbean items. There is little demand for South African interest, hence the lack of takers for a portrait of the first captain of a South African cricket team, Owen Robert Dunnell, painted by Charles Victor. The situation is worsened by currency restrictions and general apathy in that country, so it is with great pleasure that we include here a hitherto unpublished portrait of N.B.F. (Tufty) Mann (see colour page ix) by the widely-honoured medical scientist, Dr. William Hofmeyr (Don) Craib. Mann's married daughter carries it around the world with her, and at the time of writing it resided in New Delhi. India is the natural home for spin bowlers, whatever their nationality, so where better for anyone who bowled ten consecutive maiden overs to an England top order of Hutton, Washbrook, Compton and Edrich in the golden summer of 1947.

It may be, as was suggested to us by a staff member of the National Portrait Gallery, that since cricketers used not to congregate in the same circles as artists, there are no nationally displayed portraits of Compton and Edrich as they were in their heyday. The situation is not quite the same now.

The spread of affluence to the county cricket circuit has meant that not only top-flight collectors like Mike Smith of Tunbridge Wells are in a position to have Roger Marsh originals of Sobers and Bradman, but also Test and county players are able to commission some exceedingly good likenesses. For every Keith Fletcher and Neil Smith of Essex that we have heard of, there must be dozens more.

Tony Baer, of course, is and was a law unto himself. In his former London flat there were 19 oils in the lounge and over 50 watercolours around other rooms, including studies of Bradman, Sobers and Hobbs by Leslie Wilcox. To these have been added Graeme Pollock. Notwithstanding all this, the overall pattern of indifference to and ignorance of modern art has not excluded portraiture, and, frankly, collectors are the poorer for not being aware of its existence.

Best known as the artist commissioned by MCC to paint Lord's during the 1987 Bicentenary Match, William Bowyer has for the last few years sent a cricket portrait to the Royal Academy. Gower and Gooch preceded his chosen subject for 1988, the one and only Richard Hadlee, and for 1989 the record breaking Indian opener, Sunil Gavaskar (see colour page ix). The rich swirls of colour in his painting of Botham's impassioned plea to the umpire show the influence of Ruskin Spear, one of his teachers, and the first artist to convey the raw menace of F.S. Trueman.

Bowyer is a former league cricketer in Staffordshire, self-described as "finely honed to kill as a slow off-break bowler", and his figurative work literally cries out for reproduction on a wider scale. In 1988 the National Portrait Gallery, largely due to the influence of Robin Gibson, added to its meagre stock of sporting subjects Bowyer's enthralling vision of I.V.A. Richards in full flow. Another of his portraits, a dramatic 1984 head of Arthur Scargill, was accepted at the same time, a dual event of some note, largely unreported except by the well-informed Sports Diary column in *The Times*.

Another prolific and dedicated artist, twice profiled in the cricketing press, Juliet Pannett first started making sketches of visiting players to Hove around the edges of her scorecard for the day. Sadly, none of these have survived, but "Cushy", a regular cushion salesman at Hove, was so taken by her sketch of him that he had it reproduced as a postcard and sold it on the

William Bowyer's portrait of Viv Richards.

ground. She includes, among innumerable pictures of cricketers dating back to 1929, a small charcoal drawing of John Arlott, and a pastel of Colin Cowdrey at his Limpsfield home, wearing a sweater, immediately prior to leading the 1968-69 MCC tour of Pakistan. Notable oils have been done of A.E.R. Gilligan (1972), John Snow (1974), George Cox (1977) and Bob Wyatt (1978). Earlier, in 1961, she visited Edgbaston and did lightning sketches of a number of veterans present at the match: Barnes, Woolley, Rhodes and Canon J.H. Parsons.

John Ward has to his credit a masterly study of G.O. Allen at Lord's, but his watercolours for *The Cricketer* – Cowdrey at Canterbury, Greig and Bedi at Lord's, Knott and Illingworth in Sydney and Clive Lloyd in a fantasy Caribbean locale – have not captured popular imagination and reproductions at auction in June 1988 made little impression, averaging £60 for the set.

Ninety per cent perspiration and a lot of photographic research, plus expert outside comment and protracted scrutiny of typical Viv

Richards movements, went into Michael Heslop's gouache, painted in 1982. All this needs to be weighed against the fee involved, and it is reckoned that it is a stiff task for an artist to make a decent living solely out of sporting themes. Of 850 offset colour litho signed prints reproduced on high-quality board, around 350 were sold, including a number to Australia, Richie Benaud taking a couple.

Mike Tarr is another who embodies an aspect of contemporary cricket art. He works on both a private commission and commercial sale basis. Viv Richards owns the original of a sparkling print of himself, a medley of centre portrait, action shots and vignettes of grounds associated with his career. A similar work was done for Richard Hadlee, as well as collages of pencil sketches of over 100 Somerset and Hampshire players. Duncan Fearnley has a large collection of cricket bats illustrated with Mike Tarr's caricatures, and these are also produced for beneficiaries.

Rosemary Taylor had two of her canvases, ranging in price from £500 to £1,200, on show at the Qantas Gallery in Piccadilly in July 1976. One spotlights Tony Greig at the wicket, Rod Marsh crouching behind the stumps, both of them in a characteristic pose, while the other has Jeff Thomson blurred into an image of sheer speed recorded in a series of horizontal lines.

Bill Frindall, scorer and statistician, immortalised as a batsman by Mark Coombs.

Mark Ferrow's first cricket painting, a life-size, almost photographic portrait in oils of David Gower (see colour page viii), was discussed on BBC Radio 4 in connection with fund-raising for the Leicester-based Centre for Stress in Education and Research, and Gower himself sounded well satisfied with the delineation by an artist who otherwise concentrates on marine and animal studies. After problems finding a purchaser the canvas was destined in summer 1989 for Gower's home ground, Grace Road, Leicester.

Mark Coombs enjoys painting players from the vintage days because, for a young man, painting is a time machine. Jessop and Trumper can be summoned back to life at a brushstroke, as easily as Greenidge and Botham laying bat to ball, Bill Frindall carving into the covers and an anonymous England batsman reacting to a particularly vicious piece of pace like fire. Over 30 of his paintings have been sold, either directly or through the Burlington Gallery, the smaller pieces, 6in.x5in., at around £150. Twinned with Coombs for an exhibition at the gallery in July 1989 was the work of of Colin Richards, who seeks out club and village grounds with the aim of capturing their special flavour. His list of works includes 'Run Out, Lyndhurst, Hants'; 'Threat of Rain, Chiddingly C.C., Sussex', and 'Lancashire League Cricket at Lowerhouse'.

Original commercial artwork is rare: indeed it is unique. All the more gratifying, therefore, to chance upon a sensitive, tender appreciation of C.Aubrey Smith (see colour page ix), and a burlesque on Michelangelo's 'The Creation of Adam' from the Sistine Chapel in the Vatican (see colour page xxviii), both incorporated in a cricketing calendar issued by the London advertising agents, Deighton and Mullen, for the year 1988. John Dixon, proprietor of Cricketana in Bath, mentioned to us that he had come across some paintings used as covers for *C.B.Fry's Magazine* and now moved with their owner to Scotland, while cigarette card original artwork is still safely under lock and key in Bristol.

Modern cricketing art, other than portraiture, has been eloquently described as ranging from the near-representational – although not necessarily depicting a specific setting or match – to surrealist chunks of action, unfettered by disciplines of proportion, composition and perspective, and thence onwards into the realms of the "Super-Humanist" school.

Clearly identifiable matches and grounds have been afforded lavish treatment by artists of the calibre of Sherree Valentine-Daines, Roy Perry, Jocelyn Galsworthy and John Ward. Their work is difficult to dislike, for it is so obviously painted with pleasure, a love of the game, of life itself, plus a passion for naturalism. These plein air pictures enjoy a widespread response, for much in the manner of their better known forebears, they act as a mirror of the way the game appears now.

The fierce irony, however, is that artists like these work either to direct commissions, or tend to be bought by the casual buyer, people who respond positively to cricket, but who would not normally consider themselves part of the cricketana fraternity. By their very nature, many of these paintings elude the normal cricketana channels, and conversations with numerous collectors reveal a retreat from modernism at any price. The argument seems to be that they are minor distractions from the big business of acquiring the cherished, popular and traditional images, but we suggest that collectors are short-changing themselves and may yet regret it.

Cricket, after all, is part of an everlasting England, replete with landscapes so hauntingly caught in David Inshaw's much reproduced 'The Cricket Game'. The original is with a member of the Showerings family, makers of Babycham, but it was diverting to note a postcard copy of this scene standing at first-slip position to Harold Pinter, when he was interviewed recently on television, seated in his study. For personal reasons, this picture of the ground at Bride Head in Dorset is Inshaw's only cricketing picture, but even when deserted the ground is important to him, for it is where he finds peace and tranquillity of mind.

New-wave tastes will inevitably win out and salerooms will sift market-weary material in favour of fresh arrivals, the net result being that the hitherto quiet backwater of modern art will come alive and be priced ever more extravagantly. Prices for rural nostalgia are not dropping, and the extraordinary revival of taste elsewhere for a fond, rural mystique must permeate through to cricket. No matter how fanciful its portrayal, cricket outside the Test arena is part of that mystique, and while this yearning appears to sit oddly in our hard, fast age, there are sufficient people of substance to ensure modernity will sell – and sell well.

Gerry Wright is a case in point. His instantly recognisable creations are ablaze with colour, striking and original in conception. They are widely admired, widely disliked, the balance being about even. What is really interesting is that a veritable pantheon of top personalities and cricket devotees have purchased his work: Tim Rice, Charlie Watts, Michael Parkinson, Mick Jagger, Robert Powell and J. Paul Getty, jnr. He has been called the first "Ruralist" and the two great loves of his life are cricket and gardens. His paintings act as a device to combine the two. While he was playing for a works side on a June day in the grounds of a large country house near Maidstone, the heady scent of musk roses drifting across the ground struck a chord deep in his soul. It counted among "the happiest days of one's life, sixteen, and trying to bowl as fast as you can".

'The Cricket Match' by Gerry Wright.

Outstanding individuals – portraits of two of cricket's most talented modern exponents, Imran Khan and Viv Richards – blend with village and school sides, teas and cucumber sandwiches, in his ever-widening choice of subjects. His book, *Cricket's Golden Summer. Paintings in a Garden* (1985), with commentary by David Frith, looks back to the halcyon days of truly Corinthian characters, "heroes who stare back at us from their garden in Arcady".

His earlier paintings are by no means cheap, and the price range for his October 1988 exhibition at the Hurlingham Gallery, London, was from £500 to £3,750. 'The Cricket Circle' (1977) sold for £2,500 some time ago, as did the 'Village Cricket Match' and 'Cricket and Elderberries' for £850 each.

He did not like his sombre portrait of W.G. going out to bat for the last time, and refused to sign it. Yet 'His Last Innings', owned by Roger Mann, throws a shadow of poetic melancholy across the canvas to create a truly memorable picture, enduring enough to dominate Roger's cricket room.

Jocelyn Galsworthy's paintings of cricket venues such as Burton Court, Vincent Square and Hurlingham, have also gone directly into a wide circle of private collections. A great niece of the poet and playwright, who happens also to have founded his own village team, she knows the game intimately. Her first cricketing theme, back in 1965, shows a match between the Royal Green Jackets and Free Foresters, played on the lovely St Cross ground, near Winchester, and reproduced in *The History of I Zingari*. Twenty years later the Green Jackets were proud to hang in their new officers' mess at the Sir John Moore Barracks a pastel of their centenary match against IZ, and a few of the signed, limited-edition prints are still available. Among many others privately owned, Lord Annaly has 'Eton v. Winchester' on Agar's Plough ground and the 'Duchess of Norfolk's XI v. IZ at Arundel', while Jeremy Cowdrey has 'Tonbridge School v. MCC at Tonbridge'. Typical, too, of her work is 'Gemini v. IZ (Australia)' at Sunningdale in June 1988 (see colour page v).

'Hook' by Lawrence Toynbee.

Television and the sweep of modern photographic technology have forced artists to dig deep into new dimensions of abstract art, so as to find expression for their personal vision of cricket in a series of strongly imaginary and expressionistic canvases.

Foremost to mind comes Lawrence Toynbee, son of the renowned historian and a one-time bustling outswing bowler of good club standard, whose sense of fleeting movement and sudden activity comes closest to the split-second nature of personal involvement at any level of the game. His 'Catch at First Slip' – offered for sale recently at the Burlington Gallery for £550 – spotlights the blur of real speed reactions (see colour page vii), yet, mystifyingly, but so typical of the stereotyped reaction among collectors, three of his works were left unsold at auction not long ago at between £240 and £300.

Two of his paintings are in the MCC collection and a further eleven in the Toynbee Rooms of the Lord's Banqueting Suite, but most of his other works, such as 'Arundel', 'Canterbury Festival', 'Hook', 'Stumping', 'Driving Off-spin' and 'Sweep' have found private billets. Other than Ruskin Spear's almost disturbing portrait of F.S.Trueman, to be seen in the Lord's Memorial Gallery, few artists have better probed the ferocity of really quick bowling than Toynbee in his pictures of Trueman, Wes Hall and Jeff Thomson.

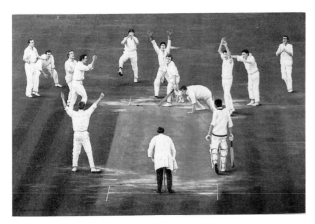

More of the dynamism of modern cricket is seen in Terry Macklin's dramatic canvas, based on a photographic original and done in 1986. Described in the Burlington Gallery's catalogue as one of the "most exciting and animated of cricketing oils", it recalls the moment when Derek Underwood had Graham McKenzie caught close in by David Brown as Australia's fate was all but sealed at The Oval in 1968.

Terry Macklin's re-creation of the famous photograph which showed all eleven England players in the frame.

Much less frantic in pace, more preoccupied with shades of light, skyscapes and atmosphere, are the group of artists who have painted various grounds usually deep in the countryside, but often metropolitan in setting.

Sherree Valentine-Daines is one who will long be remembered for the media attention focused on the blonde who was such a part of the 1985 Ashes scene, when she set up her easel at the six Test match grounds. Since then two of these have come up at auction, one at £2,600, and 'Old Trafford' sold at Bonhams in 1988 for £1,600. She is a long-time admirer of "the lovely old-fashioned English scene" of village cricket greens in Surrey, and her paintings of the cricket grounds at Ashtead (1983) and Cobham did much to prompt a Surrey member to commission a view of The Oval. Her latest work, 'Ashes

'Old Trafford' by Sherree Valentine-Daines.

'89. The Lord's Test', 30in.x15in., was made available as a limited edition print at £85, numbered and signed by the artist and the opposing captains, Gower and Border.

Roy Perry is another who has done appealing canvases of the grounds at Canterbury, Trent Bridge (see colour page iii) and Worcester. All have appeared as prints, either published by the counties or on their behalf, and are possibly as well known as his 'Opening Match', the pictures of Chelmsford, Taunton and Donhead CC, or a view of the Chobham ground, sent many a time as a greetings card.

Perry has been a Lord's Taverner since 1986, with painful memories of trying to draw accurately details of Worcester Cathedral with a sore hand, injured when fielding a Kim Hughes off-drive during a knock-up session. His more recent pictures include coverage of Harrow, Arundel and Bath, the Bath print (1988) being claimed as a double first in the histories of art and marketing. The sponsor's banner is deliberately left blank, so that individual corporate prints can be produced to order. The first was sold, appropriately enough, to Just Leather of Salisbury, Wiltshire, the very modest fee being handed directly to charity.

The original of John Ward's painting of the St Lawrence Ground at Canterbury was donated by the artist to Kent CCC, and roughly half of the subsequent print run of 500 have been sold at £35; but as a commercial venture it was viable and the county has no regrets.

The lovingly compiled watercolour by E.R. "Dick" Sturgeon, entitled `The Cricket Match', epitomises the artist's absorption in an olde worlde village idyll and is based on a scene recalled from early life in Curry Rivel, Somerset. Issued as a four-colour lithograph by the Curry Rivel Gallery in 1981, it was very nearly sold out in early 1988, a time-span regarded by the gallery as very reasonable for a non-limited edition print.

A stride away from Gerry Wright in concept, if not in style, paintings by Roger Marsh are almost conversation pieces, and he confesses a preference for the narrative content of the game to straightforward portraiture or action shots. The past, preferably an imagined past, appeals most, nowhere seen to better effect than on the jacket of David Frith's majestic *Pageant of Cricket* (1987), whereon an army of "les immortels" advances towards the spectator. Most of his work is uncommissioned, and besides portraits of Pollock, Procter, Warner and a miniature of Constantine, his mellow inspiration is seen to good effect in 'The Illustrious Game of Cricket', 'Spofforth bowling to Hornby, Oval Test, 1882', and the pavilion architecture which frames other heroes of the Golden Age.

More provocative, yet comprehensible to the public at large, are the vivid, story-telling images, full of human content, which are the hallmark of "Super-Humanist" art, exhibited and handled by the Treadwell Art Mill in

Facing Page
Top 'The Cricket
Match' by E.R.
Sturgeon.
Bottom Roy Perry's
highly adaptable
painting of the ground
at Bath.

Roger Marsh's
'Spofforth bowling to
Hornby, Oval Test,
1882'.

'Score Bored' by Guy
Gladwell.

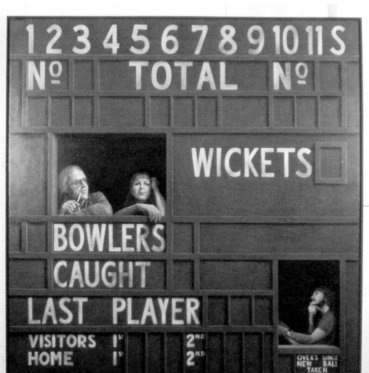

Bradford. Examples of cricket scenes by exponents of this figurative, ultra-realist school are Guy Gladwell's 'Score Bored', in which the artist himself can be seen, and priced at £1,650, and 'Summer Days No.2: Maiden Over' by Robert Knight. This blend of fibreglass and other mixed media was exhibited in "Sporting Pictures 1976", priced at £1,850, and, like so much else, has found its way to Australia.

"Cricketscapes" mark the work of Simon Garrow, for whom cricket and art are an obsession. These strongly imaginative pieces cover in a single work panoramas and close-ups. He tries to capture the opposites in the game: long days in the field when the concentration wanders, opposed by moments of exhilaration in action, even a sense of fear.

A pair of paintings by Gary Keane were sold at the Phillips sale in 1978: 'World Team', acrylic on canvas board, signed and dated 1975 (£90), and 'Portrait of Ted Dexter', signed and dated 1968 (£75), the latter a pencil and colour wash sketch, heightened with body colour and white. The asking price in 1976 for 'West Indian Daydream' by Paul Roberts (152cm. square) was £850. It is a fantasy idyll – a beach scene, waves breaking gently on a shoreline seemingly created by Saatchi and Saatchi. Maurice Foster takes strike in the middle ground, the Jamaican batsman seemingly oblivious to the rather tasty lady to whom the eye inevitably strays.

The American artist LeRoy Neiman, better known for his paintings of horse-racing, night-clubs, and jazz musicians, made a brief excursion into cricket; prices of £1,600 for 'Caught and Bowled' (see colour page vii) and £1,200 for 'Running In' (both inscribed "Lord's, June 1961"), achieved way back in April 1979 at Phillips, were probably appreciably more than anything Keith McMahon derived for the set of four Rotring sketches of Golden Era cricketers. Still, as he wryly remarked, "I can take some small comfort from the fact that I sold fourteen more than Van Gogh did in his lifetime."

Naïf School

It is easy to be very sophisticated and cynical about the Naïf School "fringe of surprise" art. To many it looks amateurish and crudely coloured, but it has the blessings of being inborn, spontaneous, natural and outrageous. It is frankly unworldly and ingenuous, and tries to resuscitate the innocent childhood eye as a deliberate revolt against materialism. Granted they are an acquired taste, but for mainstream cricketana collectors they represent almost virgin territory.

Generally only a tiny proportion of their work alludes to cricket, but when it does, the intensity of colour and humour is eye-catching. 'The Cricket Match' (1982) by Mark Baring, now owned by a director of BP, shows Vincent Square, and, in common with 'Westminster School Cricket Club', it has all the architectural elements characteristic of his sparse, decorous landscapes.

Larry Smart's 'Cricket Match at St Mary's Grange, Wiltshire' (see colour page x) has a stately ornamental pavilion centre stage, and the rural landscapes of patterned grass and trees are typical of this school, as are the Beryl Cook-like figures in 'Cricket Match' by Michael Lewis (1986).

The girlhood heroes of Margaret Loxton were Edrich and Compton, and though she has drifted away from cricket, among a group of pictures are two oils, showing the same village and its green one hundred years apart, 1884-1984.

Former colliery worker Joe Scarborough's paintings reflect the family nature of Yorkshire cricket: "back to back living and back to back fighting". His work is earthy, in the music hall tradition, big, bold and brassy. His latest painting, 'Yorkshire v. Essex at Scarborough' was exhibited at the RONA Gallery, London, in June 1988, and is but one in a long line, including 'The Opening Pair', 'I Met Him at Cricket', 'The Boundary' and 'Douglas Jardine playing Yorkshire CC 1934' (see colour page x).

Gloria Stacey is best known for her witty, crowded and highly original collage of Burton Court, Chelsea, the scene of the final of The Cricketer Cup and Möet et Chandon award, 1982. The original hangs in the company offices in Grosvenor Crescent, but prints were available, hand-touched in gold, at £63.50, and Felix Rosenstiel's have been responsible for smaller-scale reproductions.

Jean Stockdale's grandfather kept a pub called The Cricketers next

The Cricketer Cup final at Burton Court created by Gloria Stacey.

Premium Bond
illustration by Jean
Stockdale.

door to the Crabble Cricket Ground, Dover, deep in darkest Kent. Elaborate luncheons and teas were all part of the service for visiting players, immaculate in their whites and colourful blazers. Her mother could just recall being given a threepenny bit by W.G., who invariably stayed at a local boarding house when bringing down his London County side.

A cricket illustration advertising Premium Bonds brought her work before a wider audience, an imaginary scene at Bearsted and Barming Heaths as they were in the 1950s. Since then she has done 'Going in for Tea at Manorfield', acrylic on board and priced at £500, and, completed in the summer of 1988, 'A Summer at Riverfield', a time-warp picture with W.G. Grace, David Gower and Ian Botham in a fantasy Edwardian setting (see colour page x), hot-air balloons overhead.

Cricketers as artists

Works by cricketers with distinct artistic skills of their own are always worth noting. In the train of the prime Renaissance man, "Felix", still the only man to have played cricket for England (albeit in pre-Test match days) and to have his work hung in the Long Room, come a couple of Australians: Arthur Mailey, one of whose paintings, the cricket ground at Sandringham, was presented to Queen Mary, and E.L. McCormick, fast bowler and designer of

'Watching the Cricket'
by Australian artist
Narelle Wildman.

the Frank Worrell Trophy. English representation would include Charles Shaw Baker, a member of the 1911 Warwickshire side; Bernard Hollowood of *Punch*, a Shropshire player before the war; George Hillyard Swinstead, a member of the Middlesex second XI and famous for his ornate menu cards; Ken Taylor of Yorkshire, noted for some attractive portraits of his fellow county players; Roy Abell, a former leg-spinner for Warwickshire, commissioned to paint Edgbaston for a presentation to Leslie Deakins in 1976. A reproduction print was donated to Neal Abberley for his benefit and 200 black and white signed copies were given to £20 donors.

The latest recruit to this group is Jack Russell, the trim Gloucestershire and England wicketkeeper, who took up sketching in the summer of 1987 and put his new hobby to good use during the traumatic tour of Pakistan the following winter. An atmospheric drawing of the National Stadium, Karachi, sold for £225 in December 1988, when more than three dozen of Russell's cricket and rugby sketches were exhibited at the Richmond Hill Gallery and raised more than £1,300 in the first two hours. Reproductions of the sketches appeared in *A Cricketer's Art*, published to coincide with the exhibition.

PRINTS

Print collecting, like book collecting, is a private satisfaction, and there is no accounting for the vagaries, variables and vicissitudes of taste. Prints are for many people the bare bones of works of art, cool and disciplined, untrammelled by the sensual distractions of paint.

Whereas the market for all prints in Britain slumped in the 1930s, so that book illustration became almost the only way to achieve publication, there is no disguising the present stimulus of interest. Despite this, Nicholas Potter, of Burlington Gallery, contends that prints in general in Britain are still undervalued, and cricket is but one small area. Such an assertion confirms Stephen Green's point that print collecting is the best way to enjoy cricket art "at only a modest cost". People who acquired material for small sums do not know how lucky they are. Despite the boom of recent years cricket prints are still inexpensive, many tucked away in portfolios or accorded only secondary notice as illustrations, but this is a short-lived situation.

Buyers want a good provenance because they are always at risk, and dubious *Vanity Fair* items have been seen at important auctions, to the dismay of specialists who are only too aware how difficult it is to detect originals from the accumulations of reproductions. Collector emeritus, Irving Rosenwater, has observed incomplete copies of his large-format book, *A Portfolio of Prints* (published in 1962 and itself hard to find now), turning up at auction. Having ourselves seen people scrabble through dealers' print cabinets, jettisoning almost everything in the frenetic search among artistic paraphernalia for something even remotely familiar, a sub-trade in Rosenwater prints has already developed. With the hype in price levels and public morality not quite what it used to be, the turn-around time for a good print, already as brief as a telephone conversation or two, may cause us to give further thanks for reputable dealers.

Besides provenance, what matter most to collectors are condition and subject. The ugly chariot of time brings in its train foxing, fading, rust and damp stains, cuts, tears, abrasions, rubbings, margin trimmings and uncouth framing processes, all of which diminish prices. The *Vanity Fair* market, however, remains bullish and Chevallier Tayler is becoming ever more popular. Corbet Anderson never fails to engage an audience, and of his great lithographs the Burlington Gallery reckons to handle 10-12 annually.

Almost sixty years ago, F.S. Ashley-Cooper casually remarked that while the collection of cricket art was akin to embarking upon a shoreless sea, some of the more famous lithographs by Corbet Anderson and the 1849 engravings of the W.H. Mason 'Sussex and Kent' match had been so heavily reprinted that acquiring them was no difficult matter. The portraits published by Mason were less easy to find, but a selection of these, leavened with *Vanity Fair* cartoons, plus a few from *Baily's Magazine* would be a good starter, while a set of Watts's batting strokes, with their zestful life and movement, would enhance the novice collection. By way of contradiction, an essay written in *The Cricketer* (February 1965) by John Arlott, the unassailable authority on cricket art, inquired why cricket prints which had lain unheeded in dusty piles wherever "antiques" collect, had suddenly become scarce. Victorian lithographs and aquatints, which Stephen Green felt could be found "without too great a difficulty", had in Arlott's view suddenly appeared in smarter frames and at alarming prices. Steel-engraved plates such as 'The Bowler' (William Clarke) and 'The Batsman' (Fuller Pilch), extracted from Pycroft's *Cricket Field*, and enhanced by water colouring –

A highly unusual representation - a two-pane glass silhouette picture - of the familiar Mason engraving of Sussex v. Kent.

which was never done at the time – were available at £5 each when the book itself could be had for 12s.6d. [63p.].

Victorian print publishers, like the rest of tradesmen of that period shrewd operators of the enterprise culture, and uninhibited by copyright control, freely adapted new printing developments so as to keep operating costs low. The same picture was thus reproduced wholesale by a variety of print-copying techniques, some with above-average competence and greater sympathy with the subject than others, although this was probably a secondary consideration in a cut-throat, low-budget business.

Engravings

One area where prices have little room to manoeuvre is among the founding father prints, in the quest for which most collectors are reduced to the role of spectators. Anything pre-1830 can be said to lie in a realm beyond rarity, and although repeats of the handy phrase "after Hayman" are not that uncommon, the earliest representations lie beyond the pockets of many. First among these is little more than a decorative border design by Hubert Gravelot, engraved and sold by J. Cole and dated 7th May 1739. It was used as a decoration transfer-printed on ceramics such as the notable sugar bowl in the Tony Baer collection, dealt with elsewhere in this book. Gravelot happened to teach at the same art academy in St Martin's Lane as Francis

Hayman (1708-76), and it was the latter who has handed down to posterity the most frequently reproduced early visual records of cricket.

Hayman's two immortal oils, 'Cricket in the Artillery Ground' – itself a painting after an engraving by Bénoist, based on a now-lost Hayman picture called 'The Play of Cricket' – and 'Cricket in Marylebone Fields', are both at Lord's. The earlier of the two was the ninth of a series of 12 paintings done in 1743 for Jonathan Tyers, proprietor of the Vauxhall Gardens. Said to have shown off popular amusements, they hung in yesteryear's equivalent of hospitality boxes at the Rotunda in the Gardens. The 12 subsequent engravings were then stitched together as an undated pamphlet, probably printed soon afterwards. The best known of the set, published by Thomas and Jno. Bowles, is No.9: 'The Game of Cricket as played in the Artillery Ground London', which was engraved by Antoine Bénoist (1721-70) and issued on 4th April 1743 (13$\frac{3}{4}$in.x11$\frac{1}{4}$in.). In the centre is the title 'Cricket' and on either side a quatrain of verse extolling manly 'Swains', all robust for war.

William Hogarth, a contemporary and friend of Hayman, worked along with Bénoist as a joint commission, and some have theorised that Hogarth himself is the wicketkeeper playing on the most famous ground of the day in the picture. On it was played the celebrated match between Kent and England, made famous by Love's poem of 1744 and the first 11-a-side fixture for which individual scores are known. A second and smaller form of this engraving appeared in *The New Universal Magazine* (1752) above a printing of the 1744 Laws.

A number of differences have been identified in the backgrounds, but in one variant copper line engraving of 1743, 'Playing at Cricket - Engraved after the Original Painting in Vaux Hall Gardens' (9$\frac{1}{4}$in.x14in.), at the Burlington Gallery, there was little apparent change in the foreground scene.

Any early impressions of this engraving are rare and we doubt whether more than three or four have been handled since the last War. A fleeting reference was found that plate No.9, hand-coloured, was sold for £18 many years ago after Lord Rosebery's sale. Prices therefore must be conjectural and tempered by condition and caution. Perhaps £1,500 for a first-edition engraving, but anything "after Hayman" can fall as low as the £110 paid for a 19th-century copy in May 1988.

The other picture by Hayman is his only surviving autograph painting, generally known as 'Cricket in Marylebone Fields', often preceded by the words 'Royal Academy Students playing...' On 16th July 1748 it was engraved by Charles Grignion (1716-1810), and sold by George Smith, the keeper of the Artillery Ground and also landlord of Pyed House in Chiswell Street, at the main entrance to the ground. Only 300 copies (26in.x29in.) were made at 5s. [25p.] each, and Rockley Wilson, writing in 1941, believed that only seven of

'Cricket in Marylebone Fields' engraved by Charles Grignion.

the originals survived. The words "The Royal Academy Club in Marylebone Fields " were written in ink by William Ward on the back of one of Grignion's engravings, and while the whole of cricket's heritage owes a debt to Ward for taking over the lease of the Lord's Ground from Thomas Lord in a deal which included Hayman's pictures, he was probably incorrect in diverting attention from the fact that this painting might be the Artillery Ground in more detail.

A "rarer, smaller version" (9$^{1}/_{2}$in.x13$^{1}/_{2}$in.) of the copperplate engraving "after Hayman", probably published by Bowles c.1750, was for sale from Burlington Gallery a year or two back for £750. A copy, placed as mid-19th century, overmounted, framed and glazed (61.5cm.x49.5cm.), went for £600 at Phillips in October 1988, while a coloured mezzotint, signed by the engraver, Lawrence Josset, "after Hayman", was sold at Bonhams in April 1987 for £100.

The year 1744 was significant in the history of cricket for it saw the codification of the Laws at a meeting of the London Club at the Star and Garter in Pall Mall, London. A folded engraving of these Laws, attributed to Henry Roberts, appeared in the first cricket pamphlet, *The Game of Cricket*: 6d. with folding engraving, published by W. Reeve, Cheapside, London: 1755. Among the most widely circulated permutations on the Hayman engraving were those reproduced on handkerchiefs and as headpieces in colour to broadsheet editions published by J. Wallis in 1785, 1800, 1809 and so on. Any of these would be high fliers indeed, and a hand coloured copper line engraved oval view, dated 1809, (15in.x9$\frac{1}{4}$in.), above the 1785 'Laws of the Noble Game of Cricket', introduces more contemporary attire, a scorer's tent, an entourage of lady spectators and a price of £325.

The rather primitive oil painting by W.R. Coates, 'Cricket Match', was based on a Henry Roberts copper engraving of a 'Curious drawing of Cricket from the Life', published by Jno. Bowles, itself derived from Louis-Pierre Boitard's original oil entitled 'Exact Representation of the Game of Cricket' (1743). Contemporary with the first engraving after Hayman's last picture, the Boitard print has a mellow colouring and enormous cricketing interest in that it shows the proper double-wicket game. Boitard, too, served as the model for a match entrance ticket of 18th June 1744, fee 2s.6d., a miraculous survivor in the MCC collection.

All the old engravings now run into hundreds, if not thousands of pounds. Thomas Rowlandson's 'Cricket in White Conduit Fields' (c.1790) has eluded potential buyers for many years, but his coloured, satirical sketch, 'Rural Sports, or a Cricket Match Extraordinary', (1811; 8$\frac{1}{4}$in.x13$\frac{1}{4}$in.), sardonically observing Rubensesque maidens at play and based on a watercolour in the MCC collection, appeared as an etching at the Sussex CCC sale in May 1980. "Once barely considered, but lately become rare" said *The Noblest Game* (1969), of the 'Grand Cricket Match played in Lord's Ground, Mary-le-bone...between the Earls of Winchelsea and Darnley...' - and it has become even rarer. The print first appeared as the frontispiece to *The Sporting Magazine* of June 1793, and this 3$\frac{1}{2}$in.x5$\frac{1}{4}$in. copper engraving by Cook was accompanied in the one we saw for sale by a printing of the Laws.

Two noteworthy prints in private hands which would double any predicted estimate are the engraving by Grignion of the painting 'Richmond Park' by August Hekel (1752) and that other early favourite, 'Cricket Match at Copenhagen House, Islington', by the sporting artist James Pollard (1797-1867). Possibly engraved by the artist himself from his original oil on panel (9$\frac{1}{4}$in.x11$\frac{3}{4}$in.), it has been seen by us for sale as a coloured aquatint published by Dean and Munday in 1824, price undisclosed.

A selection of other engravings which have changed hands include: Thomas Lord's first cricket ground shown in a colour copperplate engraving by Spear (22$\frac{1}{2}$in.x19$\frac{3}{4}$in.), which was issued as sheet No.1 of Horwood's detailed survey of London, 1794 (£230); 'View of the Mary-le-bone Club's Cricket Ground' (3$\frac{1}{4}$in.x5$\frac{1}{4}$in.), an original engraving published by Effingham Wilson in 1833, which appeared as the frontispiece to the first edition of John Nyren's *Young Cricketer's Tutor*; a wood engraving (7$\frac{3}{4}$in.x9$\frac{3}{4}$in.) by Gustave Doré, typical of his work in that more attention is paid to the spectators than the game, but nevertheless alleged to be a true representation of Oxford v. Cambridge at Lord's, 1872; 'The Cricket Bat Maker', engraved by W. Washington, signed and titled in pencil by the artist, which at Phillips in June 1986 realised £170. *The Cricketer* in 1979 carried an intriguing advertisement for an oak-framed and glazed engraving (14½in.x11¼in.) of a 'Grand Cricket Match between the England XI and 33 of Norfolk 1797'. The match was played at Swaffham for a 500 guineas wager, and together with the scorecard the engraving had been in the family of a participant ever since.

Surpassing all these for fame is 'Ireland's Royal Gardens, Brighton', published about 1827 (6½in.x11¼in.). Originally issued both plain and coloured, it was engraved by George Hunt after a drawing by H.Jones, and published by C.&R. Sickelmore of Brighton as plate No.4 of his 'Select Views of Brighton' (c.1827). Joseph Ireland opened his gardens for recreational facilities in 1822, prior to their closure as a commercial undertaking 14 years later. This print gave rise to an unpublished brochure by A.D. Taylor, of which only 50 copies were issued, and as an aquatint it was for sale for £375 in 1986, whereas, rather surprisingly, the asking price in 1988 was £350. Was this an inferior specimen, or does the commercial failure attached to the ground also attach to the print?

While on the subject of classic prints, perhaps the best known of them all is the composite panorama of a fictitious 'Cricket Match between the counties of Sussex and Kent, at Brighton', set in Ireland's Gardens. It was judged by Goldman to be one of the truly seminal prints in that the basic layout – a portrait group in front, a match in progress behind, and the location denoted by background landmarks – was to be repeated in scores of images throughout the Victorian era. The 72 portraits of the most influential cricketing persons of the time were taken by W. Drummond and C.J. Basébé, and engraved over several years by G.H. Phillips. First published by W.H. Mason's Repository of Arts, Brighton (with E. Gambart & Co.) on 1st May 1849, it was reprinted from the original copper plate in 1879.

For prints the original price was 3 guineas, for proofs 6 guineas, and for artists' proofs 8 guineas. Each of the 8 guinea subscribers received a 24-page prospectus and a large descriptive key, the latter now one of *the* rarities. A.D. Taylor published a booklet on the print in 1923; copies were available in 1936 from the Eagle Press in Hove at 3s.6d., and in the same year copies of both coloured and hand-coloured prints were freely available from the Yardley Art Gallery.

Mason's print has been much pirated, notably by S. Lipschitz, and is found wherever cricket is loved. The original was never issued in colour, but of the pirated versions the most attractive are those agreeably tinted. In an original Victorian frame, £10 would not have been considered exorbitant in the mid-1960s. At the Sussex CCC sale in 1980 a copy was sold for £1,650, which makes one of the earliest impressions, a proof before lettering, seen in the original frame as issued to subscribers, worth at least £3,000. Various forms have appeared at auction: monochrome, framed and glazed, at Geering & Colyer in 1979 (£70); a defective copy at Bonham's in 1987 (£400) and, size 23in.x35¼in., at Christie's in October 1988 (£800). An aquatint price was noted at £180 in 1979 and for a "pirated" version in 1985, £220.

Dickinson and Foster's engraving 'Charterhouse, 1889'.

In the late 1880s Dickinson and Foster of New Bond Street published an extensive series of fine engravings of schools from drawings by Barraud. Every school was published in two editions, either signed by the artist and/or engraver, or titled, but unsigned. They were obtainable at prices from 15s. [75p.] to £2, but it proved not to be a financially rewarding enterprise. The majority of the schools have three or four different views, and their appeal depends as much on the cricket action and old-boy nostalgia as on the chosen medium for reproduction.

Signed artist's proofs of etchings of an assortment from the public schools are often available from the Burlington Gallery around £385. Prices, though, seem to have stabilised around £200, and, to illustrate the point, from the large number at auction since 1980 a random selection shows: 'Eton v. Harrow' (1980, £170); a signed photogravure of 'Eton v. Harrow' after Dickinson, published as a limited edition of 200 in 1908 (24½in.x36in.) by Messrs Dickinson, Publishers to the Queen (£450); 'Harrow' (May 1985, £220); 'Rossall School', after Francis Philip Barraud, signed by artist and engraver in pencil (£240). Barraud has his coterie of admirers, and at the Phillips auction of May 1982 'Canterbury Cricket Week, 1877', a permanent carbon print, realised £85 and 'MCC and Ground, 1881', £45.

There are also a great many pictures executed in a number of media of small grammar schools and playgrounds, some to be had for as little as £40, but bargains are more likely to be found in the £250 range. Cricket is often incidental to the scene, but Goldman pointed out the curious feature that often the batsman is left-handed, probably so that the frontal aspect of the batsman is shown, particularly when he is on the right-hand side of the picture - the direction to which the eye naturally strays.

Cricket is in the foreground of the scarce aquatint/litho/ engraving of 'Bark-Hart House Academy, Orpington, Kent', seen at Phillips in June 1986, and knocked down for £280 with 'Hackney School'. 'Salvadore House Academy,

Tooting', an aquatint by F. Jukes after a drawing and engraving by J. Walker, was published in 1787. A very vibrant playground picture, full of incident, it proves, as the Burlington Catalogue stated, that "colour is by no means essential to the decorative qualities of an engraving" (£300). Other aquatints occasionally seen are 'Leytonstone Academy, Essex' by J. Merigot, after T. Atkins, 'Hackney School' and 'Rugby School', both by R. Reeve. 'Eton College', an original colour aquatint engraved by J. Bluck, after G.H. Angelo, highlights the average figure of £220 for this genre. 'Goodenough House, Ealing' by Robert Carrick, RA (fl.1853-80) is a little-known print but with special appeal in that one of the headmasters, Dr Dodd, was the last man hanged for forgery in England, and E.M. Grace was at the school from 1850 and played his first innings there. Since the date of the picture coincides roughly with his time at Goodenough, "The Coroner" might well be one of the boys depicted.

A highly decorative sheet, 'Lord's Cricket Ground Centenary', celebrates a match between MCC and Hertfordshire in 1814, and with vignette views of the ground in 1814, 1885 and 1914, this coloured engraving, printed for Tom Browne & Co. of Nottingham, was on sale recently for about £110.

We round off this section with the steel line-engraving by Edward Finden of 'A Game of Cricket by Ships' Companies of HMS *Fury* and *Hecla*. Latitude 69.22°N, March 1823'. Published in 1824 by John Murray and reproduced as a card by Cricketana, of Bath, the two ships set anchor at Igloolik, and mad dogs and Englishmen took to the ice for sport, cricket being one of the more sensible pastimes.

'Salvadore House Academy, Tooting', aquatint by F. Jukes.

Aquatints and Mezzotints

The colour aquatints by one of the leading print publishers of the period, Carrington Bowles, captioned either as 'Representation of the Noble Game of Cricket, as played in the celebrated Cricket Field near White Conduit House' (7in.x8in.) or 'Cricket Played at the Gentlemen's Club, White Conduit House', which appeared in the 1780s, show the site of the ground on which gambolled the founders of the MCC. Prominent among the gentlemen who gathered at the White Conduit Fields in Islington to play cricket was a servant of the club, one Thomas Lord. Although it is often reproduced, early impressions are very rare and £400 would not be far-fetched.

The aquatint of the 'North East View of the Cricket Grounds at Darnall near Sheffield, Yorkshire', after a sketch by R. Thompson and superbly engraved by Robert Cruikshank in 1827, needs no introduction. Under the managership of W.H. Woolhouse, Darnall was one of the leading venues for cricket in the north of the country. Gatherings in excess of 10,000 were not unheard of, and the rich, complex and crowded nature of the scene, squeezed into an image 8in.x12in., endorses the need felt at the time for personalised entrance passes. After 1829, however, its glory departed, supplanted by the Hyde Park Ground, much nearer to the centre of Sheffield town. Every serious collector knows the scene, but few have been able to find one to buy. When a print turned up at auction, in May 1982 at Phillips, it was worth every bit of the £80 paid.

One of the very small number of mezzotint engravings with cricket as a theme, 'The Juvenile Cricketer' (6¼in.x7¼in.), possibly from a steel plate, c.1830, was on sale at Burlington Gallery at £195. Another, 'The Soldier's Widow', by W.R. Bigg, 1800, has children with long-handled bats with a hint of a curve to them, clustered around the lady who is very much down on her luck. Described by Burlington as a "fine impression... of a mezzotint that rarely appears in any state", it contrasts neatly with a lady who does appear

'The Soldier's Widow'.

very much in state. 'Miss Wicket' leans on her curved bat, foot firmly placed on the crease, a fine early example of female militant tendency. The image of 'Miss Wicket and Miss Trigger', after John Collet (1725-80), printed for Carrington Bowles in London, 1778, shows to best advantage as a hand-coloured mezzotint engraving. Collet was a popular artist in his day and produced a number of works engraved mainly on standard 18th-century themes – sport, fashion and genre scenes. The print is now rare, either in the larger (13½in.x10in.) or smaller (6in.x4¼in.) format. At Phillips in June 1988 bidding started at £500, ultimately tailing off at £1,000.

'Miss Wicket and Miss Trigger'.

MISS WICKET and MISS TRIGGER.

Mifs TRIGGER you fee is an excellent SHOT, And forty five Notches Mifs WICKET's juft got.

From the Original Picture by John Collet, in the poffeffion of Carington Bowles.

370 Printed for & Sold by CARINGTON BOWLES, at his Map & Print Warehoufe, N°69 in S.Pauls Church Yard, LONDON. Published as the Act directs 1778.

Woodcuts and a miscellany

Among an amorphous mass of other prints accessible to the average collect
or are illustrations from *Baily's Magazine* and *The Sporting Magazine*.
Engravings showing the game as the principal feature in the oldest medium
of all, wood, are not often encountered, but a handful merit notice. A very
rare woodblock engraving in original colour of a 'Grand Female Cricket
Match', published in October 1811, highlighting the then popular ladies'
matches, is valued around £250, and equally rare is a pair of neatly executed
woodblock engravings of 'The Batter' and 'The Bowler' by J.T. Woods, dated
c.1835 and sold by Burlington at £150. From Australia there is a woodcut
after Calvert of a 'Grand International Cricket Match', from the Melbourne
offices of *The Herald*, c.1880 (5in.x10in.) and thought to be England v. XXII
of Victoria.

Talking of periodicals, there is that good old stand-by, the *Illustrated
London News*. It became in 1842 the first magazine to introduce pictures
and, along with other magazines of that nature, has provided ample scope
for imaginative embroidery ever since. It has been gutted to its core, and
among the multitudinous colourations seen are 'Australian Cricketers at
Kennington Oval' (September 1880) and 'The English Lady Cricketers: Miss
Stanley Batting' (May 1890). Priced around £70, they invariably find a home.
Punch can also prove fruitful. Letterpress verses with a colour border, of
May 1893, commemorate the first match of the Australians against Lord
Sheffield's XI and have been on sale for £85, and, among picture books
broken down and ravished, drawings by Ernest H. Shepard (of 'Pooh' fame)
in *Mr Punch's Book of County Songs*, by E.V. Lucas, published in 1928, are
delicately dappled in colour. Framed colour front pages of *John Bull*,
Britain's counterpart to the American *Saturday Evening Post*, remind us of
the innocence of pre-helmet days and are worth every penny of a tenner
spent.

By way of conclusion, hands up those ignorant of 'Captain of the
Eleven' by the splendidly named Philip Hermogenes Calderon. Perhaps the
best known to cricketing illiterates and yet among the least illustrious of
cricket prints, it was first engraved in mezzotint in 1883, but became a
national figure after it was purchased for £180 by A.&F. Pears from the
Fine Arts Society in July 1897, and after publication as a supplement with
the 'Pears Annual' for 1898, transformed into advertising medium for their
well-known brand of soap. A recollection (*The Cricketer*, July 1973) of the
same boy shown with his stumps spreadeagled cannot be confirmed in the
House of Pears archives, but hands up, too, those who have handled a proof
print of a 'Grand Match' on the Magdalen Cricket Ground, Oxford, dated
c.1835. It is alleged that only two copies were made, and there is a query
whether one of the figures depicted is the immortal Reverend Pycroft.

Lithographs

The earliest lithographs were issued plain, in a sepia or yellowish hue, with a likeable period quality and feel, but the majority of the plain prints have been coloured to meet demand. Although better known as a coloured engraving, a fine specimen of the first is described in a Burlington Gallery catalogue as a rare and outstanding Clark and Company lithograph of the well-known sketch by C. Atkinson of the Lord's ground. The view shows the ground as it was before 1837 when the Church of Our Lady was built, but showing the post-1826 pavilion. Even with a dealer's mark-up it is hard to imagine a print in prime condition for under £500.

A handsome lady, handsomely portrayed, appears in the hand-coloured lithograph 'Keeping the Wicket against All-England'. Originally published c.1848 for a shilling, the lady now expects £200 at auction. Another hand-coloured litho, simply called 'Cricket', and signed only with a monogram (6in.x10$\frac{1}{2}$in., c.1835), offers a finely detailed social and historical perspective of a village match (see colour page xii). It could be anywhere, but the scorers are ostentatiously placed at their desk in front of a marquee, there is a goodly throng in attendance and the artist has found room for two wicket-keepers. A charming piece, very rare, and priced at £240.

At the outset, coloured or tinted lithographs were only sparingly issued. One original finely coloured lithograph of the residence of HRH the Princess Sophia in Blackheath by W. Bligh Baker, (6$\frac{1}{2}$in.x8$\frac{1}{4}$in., c.1830), shows boys playing next to a pavilion tent in the grounds of the Princess's residence. Priced by Burlington at £130, this print has been described elsewhere as set in the grounds of the estate of Princess Charlotte, daughter of George IV. A pair of tinted lithos from J. Ryman's scenes of Oxford and Eton, c.1850, entitled 'Bullingdon on a Summer's Afternoon' and 'Cricket Match at Eton',

Tinted litho from J. Ryman's 'Cricket Match at Eton'.

are especially vivacious, with more hand-colouring than was usual. In superb condition, £550 for the pair seems generous, though 'Bullingdon' on its own has now advanced to almost £400.

Since the total output of vintage cricket lithographs, teams and single-figure portraits, has often been calculated as less than a hundred it is still possible (just) to accumulate a reasonable cross-section. Most of the portraits of known cricketers, in what Goldman called the "top hat" era and later, were issued between 1849 and 1860 by the publishing trio of W.H. Mason, Corbet Anderson, and

Baily Brothers of Cornhill. These images represent the pinnacle of artistic and lithographic representations of art in England, and the work of Watts, Felix, Basébé and Drummond reinforces their claims to be the most potent draw cards for print collectors.

George Frederick Watts (1817-1904) may well have been one of the best British 19th-century artists, widely esteemed by the Pre-Raphaelite brethren, but, for many commentators, at the summit of cricket art are the six high-quality lithographs of batsmanship he drew directly on to the stone. Modelled in the main on Felix (Nicholas Wanostrocht), a leading amateur of the game in its formative years, they were both commissioned and published in 1837 by this man of infinite variety. The pencil sketches for these lithos show the translation of Felix from left-hand to right-hand, and 20 years ago Arlott pointed out that 'Play', 'Forward', 'The Draw', 'The Cut', 'Leg Half Volley' and 'Leg Volley' were all never common and certainly hard to find. Watts's other two lithographs are portraits of Alfred Mynn ('The Bowler') and Fuller Pilch ('The Batsman'). To suggest that they

'The Bowler' by Felix.

are rare would be typical British understatement. 'The Bowler' round-armed his way to an average price of £550 in the halcyon days of 1987, and 'The Batsman' clipped a tidy little innings of £380 at Christie's in October that year. Still in 1987, examples of the art of batsmanship drew in and then cut buyers to the tune of between £320 and £600, depending on print condition.

'Play', from the Burlington Gallery in 1986, showing a batsman preparing to take strike, suggested either the hand or the influence of Watts. It may well have been conceived as a trial run for a book which never appeared, and was an interesting number at £200.

Felix was called the "king of men" by the cricket writer, Frederick Gale, managing in one lifetime to be an author, inventor, dancer, linguist, ventriloquist and cricketer, becoming in his later years a prolific painter both in oils and watercolours. Some 300 of his paintings are known, some with their provenance, but not all collectors are aware of the circumference of his talent.

Some of his drawings were published as lithographs, but these are very rare, only 25 copies having been struck off. Inclined to self-flattery with the brush, he was nevertheless an artist of real ability, although expert opinion has it that his portraits vary in quality and likeness, that of Daniel Day being an accurate portrayal. The first three editions of *Felix on the Bat*, the first colour-plate book devoted to cricket, each used different sets of lithographs from 1845 onwards to illuminate the pioneer coaching manual. So many of the colour prints, based on drawings usually attributed to Watts, printed by C. Graf and published by Baily Brothers, have been abstracted that complete volumes are inordinately rare.

Felix's best-known original drawing is 'The Eleven of England Selected to contend in the Great Cricket Matches of the North for the Year 1847', a lithograph of which by N. Ploszczynski was struck off by Baily Brothers the same year. A time-stained specimen, 19in.x24in., with surface abrasions, found favour at Bonhams in April 1987 at £580, just below top estimate. At the November 1985 sale, a colour tint copy reached £1,450, while another, 70cm.x60cm., framed and glazed, with some damage, was sold to dealer John McKenzie for over £500. That a fine copy would climb into four figures is confirmed by the asking price of £1,350 for a hand-coloured lithograph from the Burlington Gallery at their 1988 Christmas Exhibition. Of the three major team groups executed in the heyday of lithography, easily the most rare is 'Two Elevens of the Town and University of Cambridge in 1847', drawn and published by Felix and lithographed by Ploszczynski. Compared

'Two Elevens of the Town and University of Cambridge in 1847'.

with his other group, it lacks true artistic stature. Commentary on this picture in *The Noblest Game* has it exactly right in that it is cluttered, effete, and of limited sales appeal when published. Modern appeal, however, produced a realisation of £1,100 at the MCC Bicentenary auction.

Of the non-Anderson portrait lithos, possibly the most popular is the one of Felix and Alfred Mynn, drawn on stone by C. Cousens and published by Baily Brothers in 1846. At auction in October 1987 this found a strong price at £1,000.

Basébé and Drummond are best known for their work on the massively copied Sussex and Kent match at Brighton, published by Mason and almost his ruination; but a set of about 20 of their original lithograph portraits of leading cricketers, based on their own drawings and published by Mason in 1841, are rather more rare than the Corbet Andersons which appeared four or five years later. Charles J.Basébé was responsible, moreover, for the series of sensitive aquatint portraits used to illustrate Lillywhite's *Hand-book of Cricket*.

Recent prices noted for these colour lithographs include a portrait of William Ward by William Drummond (May 1849), which hovers around the £100 mark, while some which reveal Basébé's clever use of white wash colouring include John Wisden (1849), now climbing over £200, and Edward Gower Wenman, a scarce item at £380 in October 1987.

Published either as single figures, plain or hand-coloured, or four to a sheet hand-coloured, all by Charles Hunt, one of the leading exponents of aquatint engraving, they are, despite an increase in numbers after the

Portraits of William Ward (left) and John Wisden (far left).

Bicentenary effusion, still awkward to find. Prints of Langdon (£220), Mynn (£220) and Taylor (£130) by Hunt emerged from that auction riding high, whereas a hand-coloured aquatint engraving of Fuller Pilch dipped to £80 later in 1987. At Christie's sales of 1987, 'The Gentlemen' – Mynn, Taylor, Langdon and Kynaston – grouped in four, averaged £400, with 'The Players' (Pilch, Lillywhite, Box and Cobbett) slightly down the pecking order between £190 and £420. All eight in a single frame combined well at £550 in October 1987.

A slightly foxed copy of 'The Cricket Match, played at Toronto, Canada on 2 and 3 Sept., 1872...', (23³/₄in.x35¹/₂in.) was on display at the Burlington

Canadian lithograph of R.A. Fitzgerald's side.

Gallery in 1986. Few prints of comparable size exist today, especially any depicting English touring sides to North America, and it is believed to be one of the three recorded copies from an edition of 22. It shows W.G. at the crease with R.A. Fitzgerald's side against XXII of Toronto, but at auction at Phillips in June 1986 it failed to find a market. Interestingly, a photographic reproduction, 48cm.x28cm., framed and with a key, realised £55 at Phillips in October that year. Another lithograph with a transatlantic flavour, and not often seen, is 'The Eleven of New England, Cricket Match at Boston', drawn and lithographed by J.H. Bufford in 1851.

W.G. always takes centre-stage, and much in demand is a large, autographed lithograph, a few copies of which were produced by him for presentation to friends. A popular print is one of him running between the wickets, beard streaming in the wind, but, as with anything to do with Grace, these are located only with some difficulty. In August 1895 *Cricket* reported that the latest reproduction of W.G. came in the shape of a collotype picture, the work of Fairburn and Co., of Bride Lane, EC. We have not recently come across copies of this, but an uncommon litho, probably of German origin and dated c.1885 (10³/₄in.x15¹/₄in.) was on sale at the Burlington Gallery for £165. A "stunning Victorian print" surrounds W.G. with vignettes of 15 prominent contemporary cricketers. Published c.1895, size 27¹/₂in.x21¹/₂in., it is highlighted in gold, and, described as "incredibly rare" in fine condition, it was another Burlington offer at £575.

A selection of lithographs typifying the quality still to be had for a modest outlay would include 'Cricket', 11 vignette scenes of "match stick men" in cricketing postures, $7^{1}/_{2}$in.x$9^{3}/_{4}$in., published by J.H. Dark at Lord's around 1846, and an undated, coloured lithograph of the pavilion at Lord's ($7^{3}/_{4}$in.x$10^{1}/_{2}$in.) sold for £110 at Bonhams in April 1987. The Sussex CCC sale had a tiny ($4^{1}/_{2}$in.x$7^{1}/_{2}$in.) print of 'Sussex v. All England, Broadwater Green', dated c.1837, while the pair of coloured lithos which appeared in an edition of H.D. Miles's book *British Field Sports*, 'International Cricket Match at Kennington Oval' and 'Lord's Cricket Ground', 1870-80, have a West End dealer's price of £395 for the pair.

The stream of topographical lithographs from the last century, priced between £80 and £400, burbles merrily on, seemingly endless, and from the many seen we have chosen a few: the colour litho by W. Burgess of a 'Match Played at Canterbury on Monday, August 4th 1845, between Kent and All England', published in Canterbury by H. Ward ($11^{1}/_{4}$in.x19in.); Cheltenham's 'Proprietory College', an original colour litho by L.T. Picken, c.1835 (£110); 'View of the City of Chichester', a coloured litho drawn on stone by Henry Burn in September 1852; an Eton sketch, lithographed by William Bambridge, 1852 (£175); 'The Cricket Ground, Harrow', another colour litho on stone, by N. Whittock (5in.x7in.); and 'Cricket Match at Tonbridge School', by W.L. Walton after the painting by C. Tattershall Dodd, c.1851 ($19^{1}/_{4}$in.x$31^{1}/_{2}$in.), highly rated by Arlott as "sensitively balanced and pleasingly coloured".

Chromolithographs

The perfection of the art of lithography coincided with the pinnacle of cricket print art, and assuredly one of the loveliest of all pictures, and once thought to be Hambledon, is 'Village Cricket' drawn by John Ritchie in 1855 (see colour page xii). Reproduced from his oil painting, it is a fine example of chromolithography, a technique wherein areas are carved into a special limestone block to produce colour images, still new in the 1850s, and as an artistic medium destined only for a brief lifespan.

Published to celebrate the Lord's Test of 1886, 'England v. Australia', drawn by I.F. Weedon and published by John Harrap the following year, forms the frontispiece to E.L. Roberts's *Test Cricket*

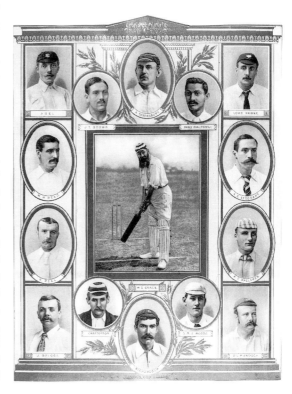

Victorian print, c1895.

Cavalcade (1947). A large chromo (25½in.x35¾in.), highlighted in gold, the imaginary composite of the match is surrounded by portraits of the players involved. In December 1979 a framed copy was sold for £150, scaling upwards to £600 in November 1985. A chromo of Cecil Aldin's only known cricket subject, one of the 12 scenes from his 'Old English Sporting Pictures', (10in.x13½in.), dated 1901, was seen at the Burlington Gallery for £200, and two others, 'An English Team' and 'An Australian Team', after Harry Bright, c.1890, (7½in.x19¾in.), fetched £180 at Bonhams in April 1987 and £475 for the pair at Burlington late in 1988.

Dearly beloved by some and hated by many, Charles Exeter Devereux Crombie cannot be omitted, if only because of an anniversary exhibition by Perrier proposing to accord him more wall space than he would have dreamt of in his lifetime. Most copies of the book of 12 coloured comic chromos by Crombie, sponsored somewhat improbably by the mineral water firm in 1907, and sold for 5s. [25p.], have been broken up for framing, and are ideally suited to pubs, hotels and billiard-rooms, where their sparkling colour, cheerfulness and frenzied nature are best suited.

Poster artist and cartoonist Crombie's anecdotal interpretations of *The Laws of Cricket* generally get the elbow from serious collectors, but this did not dissuade reproduction of the whole set in 1978 by Crombie Illustrations Ltd. at £25 or £2.50 per individual print. In the Phillips auction of 1978, eight of the original prints lotted as 'The Rules of Cricket' (15cm.x21cm.) managed £110, but for a good copy of the oblong, quarto book, with title-page and back advertisements, an asking price of £150 upwards would be in order. A non-cricketing gallery was expecting £40 each for an incomplete run, board-mounted, and this was well over five years ago.

One of Crombie's 'Laws of Cricket'.

The classical scenes have been reproduced as lithographs with almost monotonous regularity, so that in 1975 buyers were yet again offered the same old song and dance – 'Lord's in 1837'; 'The Oval in 1847'; 'Melbourne, 1864'; 'Sydney 1857'; 'Eton College in 1844'; 'Chichester in 1852'; Rowlandson's female bucolics and the quartet of Pilch, Box, Lillywhite and Cobbett on one sheet.

John Corbet Anderson (1827-1907)

Like many of that breed of adaptable Scots flung across the face of the Empire in its heyday, John Corbet Anderson had a multi-faceted talent, and his contribution to cricket's artistic heritage remains forever green.

Working often from The Three Tuns, a Southwark pub much frequented by visiting players to London, Anderson was the most prolific of the early lithographic cricket artists, as well as a keen historian and antiquarian, responsible for a series of views of churches in the south-west London area, and a technical innovator. In 1861 he took out a provisional patent for a bowling machine, consisting of a cup, two double bows and a winch handle to draw the ball back, very much on the "catapulta" principle. When the bow was released, the ball literally exploded forth. He also enjoyed a fine memory and a marked sense of humour, and delighted in recalling in old age how Alfred Mynn put away five pounds of beef and a quart of beer during the course of a two-hour conversation.

In the 1850s Anderson himself sketched 42 cricketers, excluding those in group pictures. Regrettably not all his portraits were published, for it is believed that his representations were truly lifelike, and many of them are the only known likenesses of old-time players. They have a delicate colouring, simplicity and so much period charm that we tend to forget that he lived into this century.

His 'United All-England XI' is one of the rarest prints, especially in prime condition. Drawn and lithographed by Anderson, and printed by Stannard and Dixon c.1852, this 18$\frac{1}{4}$in.x23$\frac{1}{2}$in. print is undoubtedly his most important cricket subject. This was a breakaway group from William Clarke's touring side of mercenaries, and among the players depicted are Wisden, Caffyn, Martingell and John Lillywhite. When auctioned in November 1985, a final figure in excess of £950 surprised no one, bearing in mind that this lithograph is rarer still than Felix's 'All-England XI', produced in 1847.

Anderson is best known for his 'Sketches at Lord's', but his set of eight batting strokes is very much rarer. Similar to the lithographs by G.F. Watts, they look stiffer in style, lacking the fluidity of movement to be seen in Watts's figures. Size 10in.x8in. and published in 1860, the pair entitled 'Standing in Attitude' and 'Leg Hit' would command something in the region of £350 in good condition.

'Sketches at Lord's' are among the best known, most cherished and celebrated of all cricket's images. Issued in two sizes, the main series of his portraits are probably the larger original colour lithographs, published in 1850, size 11in.x8in., the engraved surface 13 in.x9in. The smaller series, published in 1852 with the engraved surface of each measuring 7in.x5in., was, like the earlier set, issued in three sheets, four persons on each.

In 1965 the less scarce prints might be obtained for a fiver, and at the Phillips auction in 1978, prices ranged from £50 to £60. Although it is sadly lacking in catalogue details, what is extraordinary about the Sussex CCC sale in May 1980 was the number of Andersons for disposal, many of which are probably doing the rounds now, increasing in value each time.

As with any series issue, some plates are harder to find than others, and when Anderson lithos were relatively easy to obtain, it was reckoned that perhaps Hankey and Nixon were the most difficult. This remains true only of the latter, but prices for even those most regularly encountered are indicative of a strong following and a surge of renewed interest.

As mentioned above, many of the catalogues from the infant days of the cricketana boom are poorly lotted, so that statistics of Andersons for sale are hesitant and what you care to make of them. Of the players from those far-off days, itemised since 1978, different sizes of Mynn and Hillyer appear the most common, followed by Box, Joseph Guy and John Wisden. Then come, grouped in sequence, Dean and Martingell; Dark, 'The Umpire' (Caldecourt), Diver, Hankey, Miller and Pilch; Beagley, Bickley, Caesar, Cobbett, Lockyer, Parr, Taylor, Ward and Willsher; with copies of Brown, Clarke, Griffith, Tom Hearne, Kynaston, Langdon, Wm. Lillywhite, Royston, Sampson and Stephenson the most elusive.

The unframed colour lithograph of H. Royston of Harrow, printed by Stannard and Dixon ($11\frac{1}{2}$in.x$7\frac{1}{4}$in.) exceeds all others thus far with £750 at Christie's in June 1988, surpassing the £1,100 paid at the Lord's sale in 1987 for Stephenson and Tom Hearne. George Griffith "broke records" at the same sale at £460. The March 1858 coloured litho of Stephenson (12in.x$8\frac{1}{2}$in.) ran to £320 at Christie's in 1988, and very much in the same price bracket now of £320-£350 are: Bickley (£55 "in fair condition" in 1984); Dean (up from £160); Diver; Hankey (£380 at Christie's, 1988); Hillyer, Lockyer and Miller. Slightly down market, below £300, come Edgar Willsher (published by F. Lillywhite, April 1857, £260), John Wisden (printed by Richard Black, published by Anderson and Lillywhite, £280) and Joseph Guy of Nottingham (£85 in 1979 and £140 in 1988).

A selection of the smaller coloured lithographs of this famous series, drawn, lithographed and published by Anderson in 1852, were on sale at the Burlington Gallery for £175 each. Hand-coloured aquatints of Thomas Box and Alfred Mynn ($4\frac{3}{4}$in.x7in.) realised £80 each at Bonhams in June 1988.

A coloured Anderson lithograph of 'Lillywhite at Home', printed by Stannard and Dixon, was sketched from the cottage in which the Lillywhite family was born. Described as a very rare item at the Gaston exhibition in the last century, the auction price at Bonhams in April 1987 was £150.

'Sketches of the Surrey Cricketers', a hand-coloured tinted lithograph

LILLYWHITE AT HOME.
A REMINISCENCE OF THE PAST.
Sketched From the Cottage in which the Family were born

H. ROYSTON.
OF BRIGHTON.

STEPHENSON.

published on 16th July 1852 (38cm.x35cm.) is a very rare bird indeed. Sherman, Caesar, Caffyn and Lockyer are posed on a pitch, and possibly because of its localised, smaller appeal originally, after years without a sign of any, two surfaced at the Bicentenary auction in 1987, realising £1,200. At Phillips in June 1988, bidding for this mouth-watering item started at £500 and only ended at £1,700, the property of Michael Down, an authority on the Anderson prints. A copy, torn in several places, realised £700 later the same year.

Vanity Fair

The best known of all prints are the *Vanity Fair* caricatures and that doyen of collectors, J.W. Goldman, urged all novices to start with them. One young Australian collector indeed did start off with a bulk purchase at 7s.6d. [38p.] each from a young bookseller's assistant who had thoughts of going into business on his own. Now cricketana's leading dealer, John McKenzie no longer sells them quite so cheaply, but *Vanity Fair* prints themselves are stabilised as a national institution. As a reminder of the old Corinthian days, of chivalry and MCC social dominance, the 1,325 drawings by "Spy" alone form the staple diet for most men's clubs, pubs or wherever people gather in the name of cricket.

Original watercolour by Leslie Ward ("Spy") of R.A.H. Mitchell, executed at the same time as a similar portrait for *Vanity Fair* in 1896. Mitchell, an outstanding cricketer at Oxford, spent his career as a much-respected master at Eton.

Full lists have been published of the leading or keen cricketers portrayed *qua* cricketers, plus the other 40 or so past-presidents of MCC and men not shown in cricketing attire but who became famous in other walks of life and at some time in their lives achieved a measure of cricketing prominence. To this list is usually added a "Spy" drawing of J.R. Mason, which appeared as a supplement to *The World*.

All the pictures are chromolithographs in full colour and show single persons with an image surface of about 12in.x17in. The various artists' appreciation of their subjects range from the savage to carefully controlled near-portraiture of the later years. With the coming of the camera – which helped kill off the magazine itself – the differences between image and reality become more clearly defined, but while the camera is a more accurate recorder of actuality, it is a less effective indicator of how people perceive themselves. To that extent, we have lost the record of how the *Vanity Fair* generation saw itself through the eyes of "Spy", "Ape", "Stuff" Gownsman, Liberio Prosperi ("Lib"), "Owl" and other artists known only by their initials.

The first caricaturist recruited, Carlo Pellegrini (1839-89), originally drew under the name "Singe", anglicised to

"Ape". Responsible for only two sketches which are relevant to this book, 'English Cricket' (Alfred Lyttelton) and 'Australian Cricket' (George Bonnor), both dated 1884, he was witty, volatile and a bit of a gadabout. "Spy", otherwise Sir Leslie Ward (1851-1922) was droll, reserved, and an Establishment snob. Neither thought much of the other. Ward was born into a family of artists, educated at Eton, and lived most of his life in London's *haut monde*. Of the two he was by far the more methodical, studying his 21 cricket victims for hours and making numerous preliminary drawings.

Issue No.1 appeared on 6th November 1868, launched on a modest capital of £200 by a guiding genius, Thomas Gibson Bowles (1844-1922). Until its absorption into *Hearth and Home* in 1914, *Vanity Fair* was the most successful society magazine in the history of English journalism. Written by and for the Victorian and Edwardian establishment, it was aimed at "those in the know", the Smart Set. A barometer of changing taste, the way of life it chronicled perished like the magazine itself in the blood and mud of Flanders.

As the magazine evolved, its emphasis gradually degraded from formal political and literary comment, with intelligent word games devised by Lewis Carroll (C.L. Dodgson), into society chit-chat. The caricatures, however, never lost their interest. Beginning with Disraeli in January 1869, some 2,359 'Men of the Day' caricatures, with biographical notes usually by Bowles, were the lifeblood of the journal and kept society buzzing. Few eminent men refused the honour (the editor of *The Times* was one), for to be caricatured was to be admired by one's peers.

Given the range of social, political and picturesque personages from which to choose, and the relative obscurity of cricket's place in society, it is hardly surprising so few were accorded the nod of public acclaim. The first to appear in actual cricket gear was 'Cricket', personified by W.G. Grace, on 9th June 1877, and by August 1913 over 30 had been illustrated as cricketers, the last, 'The Champion County', Edward Wentworth Dillon of Kent (see colour page xiii).

The fascinating tale of the dispersal of *Vanity Fair*'s immense stock of 2-3 million unsold caricatures, proofs and original watercolours after its sale in 1914, until their final resting place with Clive Burden, reads like a detective thriller. For this we are indebted to Professors Roy Matthews and Peter Mellini, authors of *In Vanity Fair* (1982), who also unravel the evolution of each version, from the painted originals to the familiar weekly lithograph (or colour offset) or album print. The format, layout and dating of the caricatures are also spelled out.

For the purchaser of any *Vanity Fair* print it is still a case of *caveat emptor*. From the mid-1920s, David Weir, the London book and antiquarian dealer, desperate to dispose of this gigantic collection, assembled sets of cricketers in Cambridge blue folders, bound up with a ribbon, and then sold them, together with a sales list of available sets. Such sets have obviously not always remained intact, but a bound set of 70 did reach an astonishing £1,895 in 1985.

To complicate matters, each print was published in three forms. First they appeared as the loose-leaf centre feature of the weekly issue and were then reproduced as part of the bound yearly or sometimes half-yearly *Vanity Fair Album*. Thirdly, the cartoons were sold individually or in sets, framed or unframed. Sets of these personalised albums do exist, mostly in the hands of private individuals or organisations. One album, volume XVI, 1884, with 52 assorted plates but including Bonnor and Lyttelton by "Ape", in its original cloth, made a mighty £650 at Christie's in 1988.

To give a graphic example of the potential problem presented to collectors, let us take the well known "Spy" vision of W.G. As collectors know, VANITY FAIR, in capital letters, appears on the top left-hand corner, and the date on the top right-hand corner. Under the illustration, on the bottom left-hand corner, it was the house practice after 1873 to stamp in small type the name of the lithographer – Vincent Brooks, Day and Son, Lith. Below, centred under the caricature was contemporary editorial comment, written either by Bowles or another staff member.

It is important to note that the originals were on high-quality weight and grade of paper. In the 1890s and the first decade of this century, the sale of cartoons was a crucial source of income for the proprietors, and over the years they were reprinted in vast quantities. W.G., for one, was deliberately reprinted full-size on 14th April 1898, after a fire that destroyed the Vincent Brooks printing works. More recent copies, origins unknown, turn up for sale as originals. Care should be taken to determine whether it is the 1877 version, the 1898 reprint or a subsequent copy, or an authorised reprint when stocks ran low, and the magazine needed funds. It should also be noted that lithographs published in the 1890s show striking differences of colours and tones, a good example being "Spy's" portrait of C.B. Fry (1894).

Irving Rosenwater was not joking when he mentioned to us that the more ornate the framing, the less the likelihood of a first-edition print. Often the frame obscures the presence or absence of appropriate captions for dating, and many reproductions may be taken on board by hapless vendors at needlessly inflated prices. Russell March's *Cricketers of Vanity Fair* was published in 1982 and the first edition is now itself something of a collector's item. We have seen prices of £70 in the windows of print shops. Tasteful and authoritative, its valuable introduction sets cricket and the magazine firmly in the social context. At the same time as publication of the book, a limited number of reproductions of some of the prints were offered, and these, also, change hands at multiples of the original price. A selected eight of the most attractive and scarce prints – Dillon, Harris, Dalmeny, Bonnor, Hawke, Spofforth, Hobbs and Grace – appeared in 1987 at £12.50 each from March Publications. No reflection on Russell March, an ardent cricket lover, but we leave readers to ponder how many reproductions that makes of W.G. – five, six, or more?

It has been claimed that the later drawings, post-1900, are the hardest to find. True in the case of Dillon, for as the magazine's popularity declined so its circulation dropped, but a scarcity graph for the last century might show a hierarchy something of this order. Spofforth would vie with Grace, Hawke and Harris for top spot, with Bonnor and Lyttelton some way behind and "Sammy" (S.M.J. Woods by "Stuff") coming in with Philipson just before extras at £60-£70. In the present century, Hobbs (1912) and Dillon come out top, closely followed by Lords Dalmeny and Darnley (1904), Hayward (1906) and Hutchings (1907). The most commonly seen at auctions are Jephson (1902), Abel (1902), Warner (1903) and Gillingham (1906), firm favourites for last place, with rather surprisingly, Blythe (by AHS, 1910) not much above them.

Once treated like wallpaper, in the 1930s a hundred sets of 33 cartons were advertised by Weir at 2 guineas per set or 2s.6d. each. In 1939 the generality were reckoned a fair bet as low as a shilling, with some notable exceptions at 5s. Twenty years ago they had "not yet risen to high prices", and by 1965 single drawings could be had for 10s. By the mid-1970s, W.G., Spofforth, Harris and Hawke were still procurable at £8-£10, but prices were creeping up to peak at £40 for the rarest individuals. Then came cricket's equivalent of the "Big Bang" – the 'Tony Baer' and 'Tony Winder' sales – since when there has been no stopping escalating prices.

Hobbs (above) and Dalmeny (below) from the pages of *Vanity Fair*.

Jessop, signed by the mighty hitter, touched £75 in 1984; Spofforth and Lord Harris £110 in 1985; W.G. £110 in 1985 and £220 in 1987 (bought by a Mrs Grace). The two peers, Harris and Hawke, netted £500 and £400 respectively in 1987, while in 1988 W.G. varied between £110 and £180 and an overmounted, framed and glazed Spofforth reached £220 at Phillips. A signed 'Cricketing Christianity', otherwise the Rev. F.H. Gillingham, went to dealer John McKenzie for £75 also in 1988. It was once thought that W.W. Read by "Lib" was a tough one – indeed, in 1904 *Vanity Fair* advertised him at 10s.6d. as against other cricketers in a set of 22 priced at 1s.6d. and 2s.6d. each. Presumably the original stone had been lost. In 1988 a rather worn copy went for a mere £25. To quote *Private Eye*: "Shome mishtake, shurely?"

With original watercolour drawings, naturally, we are in a

different dimension. At Christie's during 1912, when *Vanity Fair*, in decline, was trying to raise some capital, 1,067 original drawings were sold for an average of £5.4s.6d. each. Among 15 cricketers offered, Grace, at 12 guineas, was for once beaten, by W.W. Read at 16 guineas; of the others Jessop made £9.10s., Jackson £9.5s., Spofforth £6.16s.6d., Lord Harris 6 guineas, and Bonnor and Lyttelton £5.15s.6d. each, down to Hirst at surprisingly only £1. When we next pick up the trail, at Phillips in May 1980, an original of Tom Hayward, plus print, went under the hammer for £300, then considered a record price. However, it was pushed into oblivion at the 'Winder' sale in November 1985, when Bonnor (by "Ape") steepled like the hits he used to make to £2,700 and the "Demon" Spofforth (by "Spy") was slightly in his wake at £2,200. With proceeds from the Bicentenary sale MCC purchased Hirst – but where are the rest?

Albert Chevallier Tayler (1862-1925)

If the *Vanity Fair* chromolithographs remain steadfast favourites, then coming up fast on the rails are the series of chalky-white drawings, folio size, and printed on grey paper, commonly known as 'The Empire's Cricketers; Season 1905', by Albert Chevallier Tayler.

He was a former pupil at the Paris *atelier* of the great Jean-Paul Laurens in the 1880s, and examples of his art are in the Birmingham and Liverpool Art Galleries, the Imperial War Museum and the Guildhall Art Gallery. His work appears also in a small impressionistic oil at Lord's entitled, 'Lord's Ground during an Eton and Harrow Match' (1886), showing spectators on the boundary near the old pavilion and a lone outfielder.

After decades of non-recognition, his robust series of tinted lithographs has at last attracted the attention they have long deserved. Long trivialised as "really cheap pictures" and condemned by John Arlott as lacking movement and colour, they catch the mood of the 1980s for action studies, and a selection enormously enhances the appearance of the Long Room bar in the Lord's pavilion.

Originally issued on a weekly basis in 1905 as a part-work by the Art Society, 12 parts with four portraits each, they were no great success story as a publishing venture. It is one of the minor perversities of cricketana history that while these refreshingly lively prints were "after" photographs by George W. Beldam, the pioneer sporting action photographer, who more than anyone else accelerated the turn-of-the-century preference for candid naturalism, it was Beldam who supplied the text when the full set of lithographs and appropriate career annotations appeared in the cloth-bound portfolio of 'The Empire's Cricketers'.

A complete folio of 48 in very good condition was offered by a Romford advertiser in *The Cricketer* (May 1978) for £150 – a remarkable bargain by comparison with 38 out of the set bought at auction the next year for £200. By May 1984 a complete set had advanced to £500; over £900 in November 1985, and by October 1987, a new high of £1,500. However, that was left far behind when a marginally imperfect set, but in original cloth portfolio, realised £2,200 at Christie's in October 1988.

Individual prints were popular at £9-£12 in early 1979, and W.G."made an amazing £50" (*Wisden Cricket Monthly*) in November 1984. The same journal noted in passing (May 1985 sale), "Even the Chevallier Tayler limited edition in *WCM* at £19.50 three years previously made double that framed."

Chevallier Tayler prints of Grace and Jackson.

In 1986 the top singles would have been Hesketh Prichard, Clem Hill, Monty Noble and Trumper at £85-£95, followed by a clutch of Australians such as Darling and Duff at around £80, with home players like H.K. Foster, Hirst and MacGregor very close behind. In tune with Chevallier Tayler's growing appeal some 120 prints have appeared at sales since then, with only J.J. Kelly missing from the dozen Australians with Haigh, Rhodes, Tyldesley and King making several appearances. In ascending order we find "Plum" Warner invariably bottom at £40; S.E. Gregory and Braund, £50; Rhodes and

George Thompson, £55; Denton and Iremonger at £70; H.K. Foster, £85; Hirst, £90, and F.S. Jackson supreme at £110. W.G., naturally, tops the century and goes on to £140.

There was some stirring in the nest when the June 1988 Christie's catalogue thumped on to doormats, announcing an original chalk drawing of Jackson for sale. The estimate of £600-£800 was soon left behind and bidding for the artist-signed and inscribed drawing (21in.x17$\frac{3}{4}$in.) finally ceased at £2,400.

Seemingly undeterred by the commercial failure of 'The Empire's Cricketers', Tayler went on in 1906 to draw one of cricket's most poignant images, 'Kent v. Lancashire, Canterbury 1906'. Blythe is bowling from the pavilion end to Lancashire's J.T. Tyldesley, with an attacking field of close catchers in the gully area, and the original canvas hangs in the pavilion at Canterbury. A vignette of Lord Harris, President of Kent in the championship-winning year, appeared below the picture, when it was issued as a limited edition photogravure (size 37$\frac{1}{2}$in.x21$\frac{1}{2}$in.), signed in pencil by the artist and Lord Harris. A copy, presumed to have been presented to J.R. Mason, one of the fielders depicted, made £280 at Phillips in October 1986 but another, offered by Christie's in June 1988, soared to £750.

'Kent v. Lancashire, Canterbury 1906' by Albert Chevallier Tayler.

Oleographs

Among prints not destined for glory are the "oleographs" of classic paintings, apparently issued as a limited edition in the early 1970s as the "MCC series". Realisations asserted themselves only gently after 10 years in circulation, when in May 1984 the series – 'Thomas Hope of Amsterdam', 'Cricket Match at Christchurch', 'W.G. Grace', 'Cricket at Eton', 'The Rustic Game of Cricket' and 'Cricket at Moulsey Hurst' – made or just exceeded estimates of £40-£60.

Again in November 1985 they yielded nothing sensational, and some critics allege they are not true oleographs, but prints touched up here and there with oil paint to give the illusion. 'Moulsey Hurst' is one of those prints so often seen that as early as 1927-28 the Medici Society were offering reprints at 30s. each or £3.15s. framed.

In 1979 the Courtenay Studio offered eight famous MCC paintings as oleographs in a limited edition of 150, with an agreed ten-year copyright embargo on reproduction. The prices were colossal for 1979, from £340 for 'Tossing for Innings', £275 for Boitard's 'Exact Representation' and 'Cricket Match at Brading', down to £175 for 'The Scorer' by Henwood. They were also sceptically received by some who alleged it was not easy to tell the difference between copy and original. Courtenay used a technique where the artist overpainted each individual picture, reproducing as faithfully as possible the brushstrokes of the original artist. Attempts to reach this studio have failed and a spokesman for MCC claims that contact has ceased. We are unable, therefore, to discover how many were actually sold to MCC members, who were given first offer.

A land of opportunity may, however, yet be signalled for genuine oleographs, which are similar to lithographs, except that the printed medium is oil paint rather than ink. A portrait of Ranji (36in.x23½in.), said to be an oleograph, realised £60 at the Sussex CCC sale in 1980, while Melbourne has a pleasant example by an anonymous artist of George Marshall, dated 1864.

Photogravures

For those with a predilection for all paper-engraved images, photogravure prints offer a finely focused attention to detail not always found elsewhere.

They are full of social comment and architectural interest, and one needs to plunder a lexicon to find anything new to say about one of the finest and most famous of all cricketing scenes, 'England v. Australia', after G.H. Barrable and R. Ponsonby Staples, published by Dickinson in 1887. Grace has stroked a delivery from Spofforth to what would become the Warner Stand, where T.W. Garrett fields the ball on the extra-cover boundary. Oblivious to the on-field activity, the Prince of Wales and his wife stroll towards the stand, forcing various "grandes horizontales" of the first rank to find pressing reasons to gaze elsewhere. Beneath the main image there are medallions of the two teams. A Boussod Valadon photogravure version of 1st October 1887 (20½in.x40in.), signed in pencil by both artists, showed the lasting interaction between collectors and this subject, sustained at £1,100 in October 1988 at Christie's; a limited edition of 325 – of which 200 were artist's proofs – signed by both artists and published by Goupil & Co., reached £1,500 at the MCC Bicentenary sale.

Then there are three large Dickinson and Foster views of Lord's, two of which show figures in and around the pavilion, and pose problems for the compilers in the inconsistencies of title and size and the omission of dates in catalogue entries. 'Awaiting the Start at Lord's' (49cm.x101cm.) or 'Before the Match - Gentlemen v. Players' was seen at Phillips in May 1982 (£45). The second of the crowd scenes, 'Lord's on a Gentlemen v. Players' Day. Stumps Drawn', in a proof copy before titles and signed by the publishers, although foxed and light stained, was offered by Bonhams in November 1987, with a rare framed key place, but failed to find a buyer. Differing sizes of the same scene realised £42 at Phillips in 1982. The third, 'Lord's on a Gentlemen v. Players' Day', c.1885, (19in.x38½in. with key), now valued around £600,

'Lord's on a Gentlemen v. Players' Day'.

features some 15 giants of the game on parade, among them Stoddart, Hearne, Shrewsbury, Peel, Lockwood and, coming in to bat, the awe-inspiring figure of Grace. A signed copy touched £50 at Phillips in May 1982.

'Portrait Group of Members of the Marylebone Cricket Club outside the Pavilion at Lord's', a gravure print by Dickinson after Henry Barraud, size 9½in.x20½in., realised £260 at Christie's in June 1988. A cryptic note in *Cricket* reported that 'MCC at Lord's' was on public view in June 1894, and close on its heels came the large work by Mayall & Co., showing some of the major Surrey personalities *in situ* at The Oval.

Copies exist signed by both artist and subject of Archibald Stuart Wortley's archetypal portrait, 'W.G. Grace at the Wicket', hymned to the sky as one of the ultimate images of the game. James Coldham, collector and

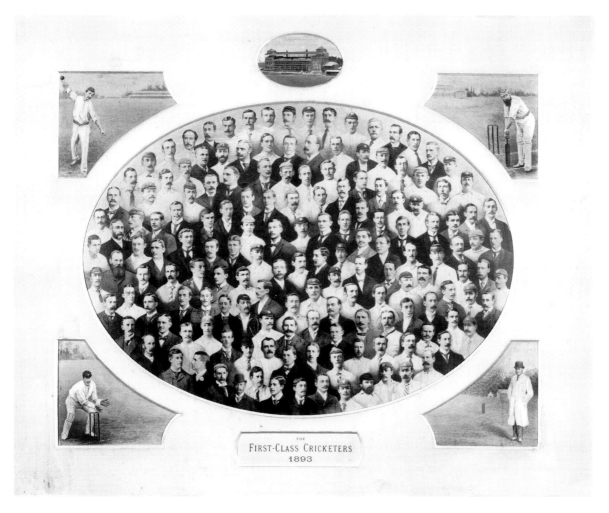

THE
FIRST-CLASS CRICKETERS
1893

leading researcher, described the example hanging above his study mantelpiece as "his icon". Dated 1st May 1891 and limited to an edition of 200 (22½in.x15¼in.), the photogravure version by Manson, Swan and Morgan is a hot property still despite fluctuating fortunes at auction. An example in the MCC Bicentenary sale reached, as with so much on that day, flabbergasting levels at £2,000, but a time-and-damp-stained edition, given as 23in.x18in., made only £150 at Bonhams in June 1988.

Cricket in May 1894 issued a composite oval collection of portraits of 150 or so of the leading players of the day, entitled 'The First-Class Cricketers of 1893' (23½in.x27in.). Surmounted by a view of the pavilion at Lord's, the corners have vignettes of Grace as a batsman, Trumble the bowler, a wicketkeeper and an umpire. For this impressive legacy, bid to £400 at the

'First-Class Cricketers of 1893'.

MCC Bicentenary sale, Burlington Gallery's asking price was £650, and, to quote from their catalogue, "Surprisingly perhaps, the group centres not on W.G. Grace but on Bobby Abel, while the great man and his brother are pushed out to the boundary". *Cricket* of 13th April 1899 contained a handsome coloured supplement, 30in.x20in., comprising a revised list of the principal fixtures, a picture of the Lord's pavilion, and portraits of the Yorkshire team as well as a number of distinguished individuals.

Of the few photographic studies by George Beldam issued as photogravure prints, quite the finest by general consent is the one of Victor Trumper leaping out to drive. It was issued in very limited numbers and is now extremely rare, especially when signed by that consummate batsman. For such a copy £450 would not be an exaggeration. Another Beldam classic, published by the Swan Electric Engraving Company of London in 1905, is the signed full-length study of F.S. Jackson in action (19in.x11in.). A realisation of £120 in 1983 has subsequently lifted to £280 by 1988. A sumptuously framed full-length gravure of Ranji at the wicket, taken from a painting by H. Jamyn Brooks, was a snip at the Sussex sale in 1980. Then £60, it ranged in 1987 between £320 and £380.

Modern prints

Diametrically opposed to the hubris of *Vanity Fair* and its fellows, and still neglected and deeply unfashionable, modern original cricket prints as an "industry" can be said to stem from the impetus given by the 1977 centenary of Anglo-Australian Tests. With other centenaries following on so closely, a largely unsolicited and feebly marketed mass was spawned. Commercial considerations apart, "limited editions" of 850 upwards are not only a misnomer but also a stumbling-block to sales. Some of these artist-signed and numbered prints were also priced outrageously. In retrospect, it all seems rather sad, for some enterprises were genuinely worthwhile, and we have to admit to an irrational affection for many of them, for their deep sincerity, their romanticism and a touching lack of cynicism, not always reflected on the playing fields themselves.

Consumer resistance was intensified by the ferocity of the tabloid urge towards the personality cults which became associated with the names of Ian Botham, Viv Richards and Geoffrey Boycott. Of course it cut both ways, and more than ever before it was a time when, as any celebrity could tell you, there was a price to pay for being famous. The proliferation of adulatory prints from the West Country, finding artistic hyperbole for Richards prior to his departure from Somerset, is a case in point. Disproportionate media coverage also caused a falling-off in sales of prints of Gower and Gooch. Nevertheless, prints continued to be produced, albeit, we suggest, in dwindling numbers, for specific events, an instance being the joint Ken Higgs-Chris Balderstone autographed Leicestershire benefit offering, lost in the general *mêlée*, and as a result enjoying only local consumption.

The July 1984 issue of *Wisden Cricket Monthly* neatly sized up the lacklustre attitude to contemporary offerings. Modern "originals of great post-war players by Ronald Wootton, Rodger Towers, Ivan Rose and Mike Francis, whose work was immortalised in *The Lord's Taverners Fifty Greatest*, barely exceeded estimate".

Reproductions of old sporting prints, individually hand-coloured and often with special complementary mounts, such as those from Sporting Heritage, find a place over many a hearthside, and W.G. still reigns supreme. The absolute bottom end of the market was reached, one felt, when to celebrate the first 11 years of the Gillette Cup, the sponsors gave away three reproduction prints. The Artillery Ground print of 1743, Lord's in 1839 and Charles Cundall's 'England v. Australia at Lord's 1938' were a very fair exchange for three tokens, yet, oddly enough, ornately framed, the last-named found a gullible buyer for £30 in 1988, and very good indeed it looks in his study.

Benefit year tribute to Viv Richards by artist Mike Heslop.

Many of the modern prints were limited-offer reproductions of new paintings mentioned in this book, and since they were often overlooked at the time or sales outlets have disappeared and artists' stocks have been discarded in despair, a brief A-Z of some of them may not be out of place. The question of who are the architects of change – the artists or their patrons – remains unanswered, and an outlay of £100 could reap the 21st-century counterparts to Chevallier Tayler. He, after all, took 80 years to leave the starting blocks.

The Adlard hand-coloured prints of 'The Batsman' (Pilch) and 'The Bowler' (Clarke), $11^3/_4$in.x$7^1/_2$in. (see colour pages xii and xiii), are, at the time of writing, still something of a mystery, though they could be by one Walter Leggit. Published by Felix Rosenstiel's Widow and Son in 1986 at £69 inclusive for the pair, they are regarded by the firm as a best-seller, but no one seems to know anything about them within the company. A collection of nine pen and wash and crayon sketches by Roland Baines, including Boycott, Mike Procter, and Dennis Lillee and others discussing "the matter of the aluminium bat", came up for auction at Phillips in October 1985, realising £25. Harold Cantle's 'W.G.' is based on his bold oil painting and, in a signed, limited edition of 1,000, was sold at £28 per print. Alan Fearnley's colour prints and pencil sketches of county and Australian grounds, based on the original paintings, are well known, as is the vivid action portrait of 'The Don', issued in 1980 as an edition limited to 850 at £45 each.

'Four Views of Lord's', an original lithograph in six colours, commissioned by MCC from David Gentleman for the Bicentenary, appeared in a limited edition of 195 copies, signed and numbered, for £100. A.L. Grace's 'A Century for England' and 'Visions of a Hat-trick' were offered as a pair, in a limited edition of 850, signed by Sir Len Hutton, with scorecards for the 1880 and 1980 Tests. Framed with a gold moulding, they were on sale at £35, and realised £85 at Phillips in June 1986. A delightful portrait plus action impression of 'Graham Gooch: Record-breaking year 1984', marked his

David Gentleman's lithograph for the MCC Bicentenary.

2,559 runs for Essex in 1984 and was issued in another limited edition of 500, signed by the artist, Terry Grose, and by the England opening batsman.

Behind the Ian Botham lithograph of John Hurst lies an interesting tale. The artist was for a time a neighbour of Ian and Kathy Botham, and having bought a couple of lithographs relating to agricultural subjects, Kathy originally commissioned an original watercolour, depicting Ian with pheasants and gun against a local landscape. For the lithograph, which was also reproduced on a souvenir stamp cover in 1984, Botham not only posed playing all manner of shots in the garden, but also loaned boots, pads and other equipment for technical study. He then signed the entire print run of 1,000 during the screening of the film 'Jason and the Argonauts', consuming at the same time two boxes of chocolates and a commensurate amount of liquid refreshment. On sale at £30, early copies were auctioned at benefit occasions, reaching up to £100 each, but media harassment eventually hit sales.

One revels in the sheer, mad time-warp of Roger Marsh's work. A small, hand-coloured lithograph of Grace, Jessop and Hammond at Cheltenham, entitled 'Three Gloucestershire Players' sold for £4 in 1977, and 'The Illustrious Game of Cricket' at £9 the same year. This representation of a fantasy match between two teams of some of the best players from 1877 to the present day, watched by 47 other players and personalities of the game, fetched £25 at Phillips in October 1986. The same auction featured at £30 a copy of the signed limited edition of 50 of 'Ramadhin and Valentine', originally published in 1978. Two other limited editions were 'Out for a Spin' (see colour page xi), with Ranji, Fry, F.S. Jackson and the parrot Popsey out for a run in a Lanchester car against the background of a canopied pavilion, based on childhood memories of Preston Park, Brighton (£39.50), and a 1986 publication, 'Tom Emmett and Grace' (£38).

Simon Painter's signed watercolour impressions of George Headley and Bradman appeared under the aegis of *Wisden Cricket Monthly*, while 1985 saw a signal effort by Bryn Parry to capture the elusive splendour of David Gower. Reproductions of Roy Perry's gracious paintings appeared both as prints and greetings cards, while Aylwin Sampson's set of eight black and white prints from his evocative (and now hard to obtain) book, *Grounds of Appeal* (1981), were published at £9.95 each. Malcolm Stead and Taunton artist Mike Tarr took as subjects Geoff Boycott and Viv Richards, while Royal Academician John Ward's set of portraits of six of the outstanding cricketers of our time, like the other two, reproduced in signed, limited editions, sold at £10 each, but rose only very slightly to £85 a set at Phillips in June 1988.

Polish-born Feliks Topolski was an unlikely entrant in the cricket art stakes, but his silk-screened, impressionistic sketch of the crowd in 'Eton v. Harrow '83' was a reasonable investment at £30. The original of Arthur

Weaver's signed print of the Centenary Test Match of 1980 hangs in the Long Room at Lord's. A limited edition print, individually signed both by the artist and 11 England Test captains, alphabetically from Allen to Yardley, was published by MCC at £100. Selected from his book, *Cricket's Golden Summer*, artist-signed sets of four of Gerry Wright's idiosyncratic portraits of Shrewsbury, Jessop, Lockwood and Stoddart were to be had for £20, while a special autographed print for the 1983 World Cup, signed by every participating player, was given as a prize in April 1984 to coincide with the launch of Wyvern Software's game Howzat.

From overseas, we enjoyed Kathleen Hawkins's modern depiction of the Garrison Savannah in Barbados as it was c.1865, and a lithograph marketed by the New South Wales Cricket Association of a painting by Wesley Walters, the original of which is in the possession of Sir Donald Bradman. The artist shows Bradman scoring the single that gave him a hundred first-class centuries, and included in the offer was a full-colour reproduction of the original scoresheet, dated 15th November 1947, for the match between an Australian XI and Amarnath's Indian touring side.

OTHER PICTORIAL MATTER

Sheet music covers

'When the day is done and the ball has spun from the umpire's pocket away' (Roy Harper, 1975), as a respite from our modern echo song, "Ere we go, 'ere we go, 'ere we go' (anonymous, forever) and before 'Death begins to bowl' (1839), those wishing to learn about cricket's abiding links with every form of musical entertainment should immerse themselves in David Rayvern Allen's book, *A Song for Cricket* (1981). It is among the most illuminating, original and imaginative books for years, and apart from the Bodleian Library and BBC Music Libraries, the names of those who helped read like a drumroll of major cricketana collectors. In the December 1983 issue of *Wisden Cricket Monthly*, he took us further down Tin Pan Alley, from the Vauxhall Gardens through club smokers to impromptu singalongs and the interminable verses of hallowed school songs.

Songs and recordings of all kinds have their own place in this book, but Rayvern Allen's allusion to a large silk handbill focuses attention here more on the visual appeal of music covers than the discords of bar room ballads and glee singers. The handbill referred to was printed for Hull Town Cricket Club's Grand Fete and Cricketers' Revel of August 1857, when a Throwing the Cricket Ball contest found suitable musical accompaniment from 'The Cricketers' Polka', "composed especially for the occasion".

The coloured print of 1839, featuring an outline engraving of the 'Baxter Cricket Song', finished in watercolours, with a figure at the wicket and the verses printed within a colourful border of flowers and butterflies, is, for many people, the most picturesque and lyrical of all song covers. Composed in honour of "Honest" Baxter of Surrey, the song is most probably the work of an unrelated namesake, John Baxter of Lewes, published in conjunction with his son, George, a noted colour print engraver in his own right. It appeared at the 'Tony Baer' sale of 1978, easily worth the £400 realised. A similar Baxter song, 'My Friends leave your work now to sport and play', possibly even earlier in date, with a reserve of a cricket bat, stumps and ball instead of the figure, and without the inset allegorical scene of Death as the Grim Reaper of all batsmen, was bought, not necessarily with a song, for £310 at the same sale.

Sheet music covers with a cricket theme are rare at auction. 'The Cricketer', written and composed by W.J. Bullock and priced at 3s., is typical of the ballads of the day, a wholesome and hearty variation of the perennial theme of "For cricket is a noble game". The chromolitho cover, printed by J.

& W. Pearman and published by Weippert and Co. of Regent Street, c.1870, has a singer, T. MacLagan, centre-stage in cricketing dress, flanked by vignettes of Clarke and Pilch, plus views of Lord's and The Oval. Surrounded by a decorative border, it has been priced by Burlington Gallery at £250. Its popularity is unimaginable to those of us who in 30 years of club cricket have never heard a cricket song bellowed out in the flesh. At least four editions were issued, and on the fourth the face of Howard Paul replaces MacLagan, the latter departed to wherever stentorian baritones find a haven.

'The Season's Gallop', c.1885, priced around £150, is a captivating period piece with a pleasant lithograph cover by I.H. Burnside, but it is with club dance music sheets that we learn that, while a gay time was undoubtedly had, they were not necessarily all-male occasions. The pastel-shaded colour lithograph cover of 'Cricket Polka' ('pour piano'), by Emile Ettling, published by Stannard and Dixon for 3s. around 1880, has a rear-view image of a round-arm bowler about to despatch calculated ferocity at a distant batsman, the umpire strategically placed to snap up a catch at fine leg-slip. In so far as anything can be called "common" in this rarefied field, then it has to be 'Cricket Polka', which has appeared more than once at auction but is still an attractive item around £150. Bearing the same cover price and roughly the same valuation now, is another music cover, $14\frac{1}{2}$in.x$10\frac{1}{4}$in., 'The Cricket Bat Polka', by Henry A. Sutch. The nationally recognised figure of W.G. appears as a monochrome portrait, probably to induce sales, and the sheet was published by Charles Sheard in London, c.1890. Both formed part of a lot of six music covers at Phillips in October 1985, and together with sheet music copy for 'Down Went the Wicket', realised £95.

I Zingari as a club was formed in 1845 and the theatricals, country house dances, soirées, dance ensembles and games put on by the club in connection with the Canterbury Cricket Week were spot-on occasions for music publishers to merchandise their products with the IZ image. The cover of Boosey and Company's 'Cricket' is plain by comparison with the 'I Zingari Galop', 'Zingari March' and 'Zingari Galop', but, having tried it out ourselves on the old joanna, the melody does not linger on, and one hopes the other tunes were less commonplace. Written by Alfred Scott-Gatty and received by the journal, *Cricket*, as "bright and pleasing", the chromolitho covers are in the famous red, black and yellow club colours. Prettiest by far is the faintly Ruritanian, chromolitho, castellated setting for 'Valse I Zingari', by A.D. Porter, dedicated to the wife of Sir Robert Peel, top man at Scotland Yard, which went for £80 at Phillips in June 1986. The chromolithographed sheet music cover for 'The Domum Galop' (c.1870), performed at the Domum Ball, Winchester, shows in sepia a sextet of cricketers taking a breather from practice against a backdrop of college buildings. This was another Phillips June 1986 lot at £30, sold with 'The Pelican Lancers'.

In 1976 Solarbest Limited (London) reproduced, as a limited edition of 1,000, a selection of 18 Victorian music covers, the one featuring cricket being J. Harcourt Smith's immortal 'Cricket. The Song of the Centuries'. Appropriate to the Grace fervour of 1895, it could be sung anywhere "provided the natives and the police don't object" and was originally published by Howard & Company at a price of 2s., a portion of the proceeds promised to the Grace Testimonial Fund. The reprint set, signed and introduced by the comedian Max Wall, was priced at £17. Harcourt Smith's earlier song, 'Cricket' (1882), dedicated to A.N. (Monkey) Hornby and sold from home in Wolverhampton for 18 stamps post free, is rarely, if ever, seen, and probably lies in a limbo land of unwanted ditties. With it is another desirable property, a "hidden and desirable relic", the Devon ballad entitled 'The Umpire', published in 1890 and dedicated to A.G. Steel, one of the leading amateur batsmen of the age.

Allan and Company's sheet music for 'Our Don Bradman' is quoted as selling over 40,000 copies in a matter of weeks in 1930. In his green years, Bradman then added music to the lyrics by Jack Lumsdaine for 'Every Day is a Rainbow Day for Me', published in Sydney in the 1930s, and saw it incorporated in a pantomime, 'Beauty and the Beast', at the city's Grand Opera House. Where in the world have all those copies gone, for the owners we have encountered of these two sheets would not part with them for £50 each, minimum?

For anyone with £200 to spend and an inglenook to fill, as seductive as any print is the blend of sienna walls, striped red marquee and flags, blue-green and ochre playing area on the cover of Frank Hall's 1870 song, 'Life is Like a Game of Cricket'. This time the artist, A.H. Concanen, has the umpire at mid-off, well placed for the shuffle outside the off-stump. Another heart-warming print, the 'Eton & Harrow Valse', dedicated to C.I. Thornton, vies with it for naivety, colour and likeability, and probably comes armed with the same sort of price tag.

Cartoons and caricatures

Humour is a transient thing; it dates quickly and is supremely a matter of taste. Until modern caricaturists such as Ralph Steadman seized upon a man's more prominent characteristics, to mould them, enlarge them and distort them, while all the time retaining the subject's essential personality, cricket cartoons were genial and affectionate.

But we live in a sharper, more acid society and tend to relish the flavour

Ralph Steadman's view
of Dennis Lillee.

"Rip" cartoon of
Albert Trott.

of 'Spitting Image' and the power generated in Steadman's fearsome interpretation of Dennis Lillee or the less than deified vision of C.B. Fry, one of the three originals used to promote *John Arlott talks Cricket*. Then there is the slightly sick, sad and tasteless illustration of Ian Botham on a "hashish" theme, worlds apart from the winsome and genteel manner of "Rip" (Roland Pretty Hill), the first of the popular cartoonists. Some modern collectors may indeed find his portrayals of the subtle nuances of class distinction mildly off-putting.

Although originals of "Rip" cartoons were available from the offices of *The Cricketer* early in 1922 at ludicrously low prices – the fledgling weekly in those days counted pennies carefully – the wide range and topicality of *Kricket Karikatures*, the *Evening News Cricket Annual* and other magazines has made the work of Hill foremost in the eyes of many collectors, and his sketches are strongly represented in all the major private collections. His style is gentle, civilized and thoroughly decent, and there is warmth engendered by his pen and ink sketches, such as those of Albert Trott and Sammy Woods in 'Second Innings', the Burlington Gallery's 1987 catalogue. Popular he may be, but it took a brave soul to pay over £2,000 at the Lord's sale for his framed drawing of W.G.

Another sketch of W.G. at the same auction by Frank Gillett found a buyer at £90 in May 1985, and the unforgettable sketches of the great man by the legendary Harry Furniss, originals too, "which ought to have stayed at Lord's" (*Wisden Cricket Monthly*) were acquired for £3,000 at the same historic sale in 1987. The Furniss sketches dated from c.1895 and were done on the spot when Grace was at his peak, and republished in *A Century of Grace* (1896).

He may not equal the eternal flame of W.G., but P.G.H. Fender was God's gift to cartoonists. A caricature by Francis Perachio, signed by the subject, was deemed "reasonable" at £55 in 1987, commonplace by comparison with £95 paid for an Arthur Mailey pencil and wash drawing of the long-sweatered Surrey captain done six years earlier. Mailey's cartoons and booklets of cricketers of his time are as whimsical as was his leg-spin, and with the blossoming of Australian institutional collecting recently, it is easy to imagine the £180 plus, paid in 1988 for an autograph album containing a signed caricature self-portrait in pen and ink by the immensely versatile artist, soon being overtaken many times over. Roger Mann has a brilliant Mailey cartoon, sent "with apologies" to A.P.F. Chapman, entitled 'After a hot day in the field' and showing the English skipper's growing pot belly. Anything to do with Clarrie Grimmett has would-be buyers leaping out of the crease to spot his googly, and already a Kerwin Maegraith black ink caricature of Grimmett, artist-signed and dated 1930, previously the property of Mailey's leg-spin successor, jump-bid upwards to £300, three times top estimate.

Harold Gittins, Harry Hargreaves and David Low were all newspaper cartoonists who frequently touched on the game, but few artists have captured cricketers with quite the brio of Tom Webster (1882-1962). His irresistible sense of fun and cheek, coupled with bold, brash strokes of the pen, captured both the cricketer and the inner man lurking behind the white flannels. On the *Daily Citizen* prior to the First World War, he invented the cartoon "running commentary" technique, later perfected on the *Daily Mail* immediately after his return from the trenches. Lord Northcliffe was then leading the mass circulation press battle in the 1920s tabloids via the *Mail*, so it is little surprise to learn that Webster was the highest-paid cartoonist in the world. Each issue of *Tom Webster's Annual* was a winner. Cartoons by him of Strudwick (autographed) and Maurice Tate turned up at the Sussex CCC sale in 1980, and Webster was in fine form at the Christie's October 1987 auction, both his individual and strip cartoons rising above normal newspaper instant disposability to average £52. From his first *Argus* drawing in May 1906 – 'Cricket Celebrities, No.1: WG Quaife', until his retirement from the *News Chronicle* in 1956, amid a wealth of colourful characters everywhere to be seen, his own particular favourites were Hendren, Duckworth, Tate, Hobbs and, of course, Fender.

Close behind Webster came Roy Ullyett of the *Daily Express*, singled out by John Arlott for his fire-eating impression of F.S. Trueman, and in the eyes of many critics the last of the great cartoonists. Whether he is collectable is debatable but some names simply cannot be ignored. Pairs of Frank Reynolds sketches were selling for £50 and £55 in 1980, with other originals just below those figures at the 1984 Hampshire CCC sale. At £30 plus, an original drawing of Macartney would have been a real bargain as well. A Phillips auction included his 'Butler falls victim to the Squire – standing close in' (pencil and black ink; £120), and a selection of his work in an album containing 16 hand-coloured *Punch* cricket cartoons realised £60 two years later. Originals of five eminent Royal Academicians caught by Reynolds in cricketing guise for *Punch* (Summer Number, July 1922) were hugely appreciated at the Bicentenary sale with realisations between £1,000 and £1,200.

David Langdon, a perennial *Punch* favourite, satirised Ted Dexter's 1964 electoral campaign against James Callaghan for the Cardiff South-East seat.

"There goes Dexter, vote-catching again...."

So long as good humour and the effervescence of the human spirit prevails there will always be cartoons, both ancient and modern. Max Beerbohm's caricatures, drawn in 1896 and again in 1905-09, are either witty and economical in style or grotesque, depending on the individual viewpoint; but, aesthetics apart, at any sale they are a drawcard. "Massie" cartoons of matches between Ivo Bligh's team and Australia (January-February 1883) were described by an advertiser as "scarce" in 1932. What price on these now, we wonder, for an original cartoon in ink and watercolour marking Middlesex's celebratory dinner to P.F. Warner from the Langford collection, sold at Phillips for £20 in May 1982?

We have to confess to a marked liking for the work of John Ireland. Although he is not self-confessedly a cricket fan, a long-standing admiration for "Spy" and other artists of that genre led him to wonder whether there might not be a place in the market for similar caricatures of today's sportsmen. The success of *Cricket Characters* – 7,000 books sold on the initial run and 5,000 as a second edition – argued that there was. A limited edition of prints of six illustrations has recently appeared, and the artist comments: " 'Cricket Characters 2' could appear in a few years' time if the England team continue to self-destruct." The originals are in the hands of our publisher, Adrian Stephenson.

Far left Richard
Hadlee, as portrayed
by John Ireland.

Left Alan Matthews of
Glamorgan,
caricatured by Victad.

An enigma wrapped in a mystery is Victor C. Tipping, self-styled 'The Cricket Artist'. Working from Londonderry just before the last war, he signed his work VICTAD, and we have been able to identify only half a dozen of his caricatures. They were mounted on stiff cardboard and sold at 2s.6d. each; one of them showing A.D.G. Matthews is actually signed, but most of the others drawn were of infinitely more illustrious players, of the Bradman, Hammond and Headley calibre. Graham Turner, our original informant, has come across two more - Duckworth and Brooks of Surrey – and there must have been at least 14 others, since 20 studies of "various [unnamed] cricketers" were offered by Graves and Pilcher in May 1984, realising £170.

Anyone familiar with the discard-at-any-cost ethos of national newspapers should laud the efforts of the University of Kent's Centre for Cartoon and Caricature, which tries to keep some sort of overview of a fugitive art form. It is to be hoped that they, at least, have preserved copies of the cartoon in *The Times* by Lurie (issued in an edition of 1,000, signed by artist and "victim"), which summed up the national image of Botham in 1981 wielding a spiked club. Another set from that year, a grouping of eight personally autographed caricature prints by artist David Waugh of prominent Kent players, appears to have sunk without trace, except maybe in Canterbury. *The Times* figures again with a 1986 original pen caricature by Gerald

Broadhead of Abdul Qadir, signed in pencil by the artist, which made over £70 at the June 1988 Phillips auction.

The Cricketer's own cartoonist, Neil Bennett, has extended his repertoire from paper to carving highly assured figures from wood. His first cartoon man shows a batsman in no-man's land, half forward and halfway back, a lethal delivery having turned him into a fielder's gift offering. Also working with wood is Joan Redman. With sales overseas as well as the UK, her caricatures are executed on cricket bats and mahogany plaques as well as on stone. She finished a set of ten caricatures of England captains (all 6in.x4in.) on full-size bats, and then went on to do Tom Richardson for David Frith. Another direct commission was a paperweight caricature for a fan of Geoff Boycott.

Cricket is a sacred business and, until Bodyline and Peter Hain, essentially apolitical. Perhaps the game comes too close to our innermost feelings for politicians, and the cartoonists who satirise them, to use it as a medium for their message. At all events, such cartoons are quite rare. 'Vacation Amusements. Cricket (A Long Innings)' and 'State Cricket Match' or 'A Game of Cricket', coloured lithographs after "H.B.", published from 1834 onwards and valued at over £100 each, are probably the best-known indigenous satires. John Doyle, an Irish artist, took refuge behind the monogram "H.B.", and of his long output of prints only these two variously titled and very "busy" sketches highlight a political imbroglio, all very passé now. Anyone interested enough to pursue the political content and details needs recourse to the British Library catalogue of caricatures. Another cartoon from those far-off political scandals is 'Bowl Fair Sir!', c.1820, and also costing perhaps £80-£100.

For all our national game is complicated and perplexing, and to many foreigners a form of buffoonery going nowhere very fast, not many satirical sketches of cricket have emanated from our natural enemies. A brightly coloured hand lithograph, by and after Draner, was published in Paris c.1870 as part of a large series of caricatures of military types. 'Angleterre – Oxford University Rifle Volunteers' has a member of the regiment visibly disconcerted by a sharply rising ball desperately close to his nose. The artist's knowledge of the game is of little consequence, being non-existent, and were it not for the date and proximity of the Franco-Prussian War, those depicted could for all the world have been Afghans, Zulus or South African Boers. The message may be obscure, but there is no denying the overt hostility and bristling near-flashpoint in a minor Anglo-Boer confrontation sweetly caught in a print which cost all of a fiver in a flea market.

Les Prisonniers des Boërs

Qu'on leur donne tout de même de la marmelade, dit Kruger

Photographs

We all share a deep-rooted, atavistic need to possess a pictorial record of the past and how often have collectors found, when showing visitors their books, pictures and engravings, that these receive only polite scrutiny, readily by-passed in favour of photographs of old-time cricketers. There is a greater affinity with former cricketers than with current players, the more so when photographs were once personal keepsakes, autographed and inscribed, so that any imperfections seldom inhibit value.

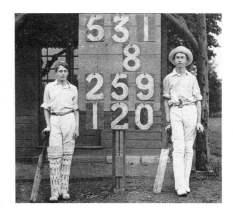

A 1912 photograph lovingly preserved by the sister of George Whitehead (right), who died in the First World War after an illustrious schoolboy career at Clifton, including this 259 not out against Liverpool College. His fellow centurion was J.R.F. Errington.

Below An informal moment from the '60s.

Whatever the motivation to collect cricket photographs, it is very much an individual imperative, as complex as any aspect of human nature. It could be a wish to superimpose a broader historical perspective on a cul-de-sac collection, or something as simple as a natural progression from printed books. J.W. Goldman wrote (*The Cricketer*, 1936) how the stimulus for cricketana in his case was an introduction to the photographs of every amateur who played in the Scarborough Festival, which he saw festooned on the walls of the Cricket Room at the Grand Hotel in Scarborough. Few could fail to be moved by photographs of, say, that mighty smiter of the ball, Albert Trott, long ago practising in the nets; the dapper, handsome Kenneth Hutchings with a small echelon of Kent admirers, or the two peers of the realm, the Lords Hawke and Dalmeny, tossing for innings at Walter Lees's benefit match at The Oval in 1905. These, admittedly, are not among the cheaper photographs, and would probably come in the £60 class, but from a personal recollection distinctly down-market photographs of Ted Dexter and his Sussex team-mates quaffing milk from the bottle, or a bespectacled Geoff Boycott with Ray Illingworth and Norman Yardley looking thoroughly relaxed with a mini-skirted 'milkmaid' of the early Cilla Black generation, are just as pleasurable.

Deeply felt personal affiliations aside, the real value of photographs is associative. A cabinet photograph of Ranji was sold for £18 in July 1983, but one signed "To Plum from an old comrade and friend" raises the ante to £40, as at Phillips in May 1982. An albumen print, 4in.x6in., of Ranji demonstrating a forward stoke, but enhanced by an autograph, was worth £420 at the Bicentenary sale. Then again, a large signed photograph of him at the wicket, framed and overmounted, a tantalising glimpse of the Golden Age, tempted bidding to £360 at Phillips in October 1985. On his own, Maurice Turnbull is a Glamorgan cult figure and therefore most collectable, but when associated with five other county captains of the 1930s, all resplendent in blazers and brilliantine, the combination of languid amateur grace and arrogance pushes its value into three figures.

Enmeshed in the past, we can also be haunted by reminders of previous ownership. An autographed photograph of 14 great cricketers of the past, including Woolley, Freeman, Jardine, Hendren, Strudwick and Hobbs, each one of them a hinge to former glories, takes on an even more gratifying hue when we know it came from Hobbs's own collection, and was worth £75 to a grateful recipient at Phillips in May 1982. A group photograph, titled in Clarrie Grimmett's hand 'Reception to Jardine's England team at Government House Adelaide', and inscribed with the names of most of the sitters, together with the autographs of 15 of the 19 players on the tour, left estimate far behind at over £300 in June 1988.

Memories of obscure tours, such as Macartney's Australian side taken to Malaya in 1927, normally relegated to footnotes in history, become rekindled when a signed team photograph becomes a setpiece at over £100. The same applies to tour matches, even the very earliest. It could never be called mundane, but an otherwise fairly orthodox photograph of play between Cambridge University and the Australians in 1882 becomes riveting, not just because the Studd brothers are at the crease, but because fielding in a sort of fly-slip position is Spofforth, the only known photograph of him on the field of play.

Unlikely settings, historic views of grounds while they were still being developed, or photographs of players taken out of normal context can cause ardent bidding. Don Bradman, playing tennis, from 'Souvenir of the Visit of the 1930 Australian team and Friends to Jodrell Hall', worth £220 in June 1988, or a candid camera view of W.G. chatting with a local vicar, can have an impact incredible to those who cannot understand the hold cricket exerts on those who love it. A most unusual early view of the far-flung presence of the game turned up at the Phillips auction in June 1988, when £460 was paid for a pair of photographs dated c.1865-75, which substantiated arguments that North American cricket had spread south of the border, down Mexico way. The inscription on the pavilion appears to read "City of Mexico Cricket Club".

As is generally known, cricket photography originates with Roger Fenton (1810-69), founder of the Royal Photographic Society and a member of the Calotype Club. He was an energetic publicist for photography as a medium of artistic expression, and was opposed to the general practice of creating artificial backgrounds or using backdrops in the style of, say, Lewis Carroll's nymphets. His preference was for natural settings, and his outdoor compositions have a serenity and calm, particularly evident in his view of the Hunsdonbury v. Royal Artillery match in 1857, now the property of the RPS and almost certainly the oldest surviving photograph of a cricket match.

A fine example of the newly emerging art of photography is 'England's Twelve Champion Cricketers', published by W.H. Mason of Brighton on 2nd October 1859. Taken on board ship, this is probably one of the most reproduced images of the first touring side to leave England, destination North America and a hellish trip ahead of them. This same group photograph reached £200 in July 1983, but is now valued nearer £550. A much less familiar group shot of the team, presented to MCC by the C.C. Morris Cricket Library of Haverford College, USA, is shown in Stephen Green's *Backward Glances;* if it ever came to auction, it must surely command four figures.

A case can be made that the first action photo of a cricketer, with the player frozen in real-life action, as opposed to simulated correct attitude, appears in *A Bawl for American Cricket*, by Jonas Wister, published in May 1893. The angle of the shadows on George Bromhead suggest that the action took place the previous summer, some three years ahead of the person generally regarded as the definitive pioneer of action photography, the legendary George William Beldam. His earliest surviving photograph (as yet unpublished) dates from 1895, and his name is synonymous with the Golden Age. He combined high shutter-speed expertise with the true artist's eye for a good picture, and over a thousand of his pictures appear in *Great Batsmen; their methods at a glance* (1905) and *Great Bowlers and Fielders* (1906). In a highly diverting article in the February 1988 issue of *The Cricketer*, Anthony Meredith discusses the salvage and research work done by George A. Beldam on newly discovered Beldam photographs, and hints at exciting publishing ventures yet to come.

Gilbert Jessop, photographed by George W. Beldam.

A unique set of three large action photographs taken by C. Nettleton in January 1862 at the Melbourne Cricket Ground, during the very first match played by an England team on Australian soil, XVIII of Victoria v. H.H. Stephenson's All England XI, were acquired by David Frith for a "trifling" £55 at Christie's in November 1981, and these are the earliest photographs of an international match, unless something survives from the English tour of North America in 1859.

As early as Grace's *annus mirabilis*, 1895, the journal *Cricket* bitterly lamented that "the photographing of cricketers, individual and collective, is never ending", mentioning that E. Hawkins and Company, of Brighton, regular suppliers to the trade for many years, had over a hundred negatives

Lord Sheffield's XI,
1890.

of W.G. and it was felt that Ranji was not far behind. Rated by Roger Mann as probably the most potent treasure trove awaiting rediscovery somewhere is the stock of original plates, glass negatives and prints of this firm, the race for which might occasion the first recorded case of manslaughter in cricketana history. Whereas a rare photograph of philanthropist Lord Sheffield's XI of 1890, specially published by Hawkins and including W.G., Stoddart and W.W. Read, was valued at £220 in October 1988 at Phillips, mounted photographs by Hawkins are not uncommon and a series of the Kent county sides of 1894,1897,1899,1900 and 1908 found buyers in the range of £38-£85 at Phillips in April that year. Tremendous competition in its centenary year took a mounted photograph of England v. Australia, 1888, with printed caption and team names, to £150 at Christie's. A signed and dated photo of F.S. Jackson from 1898 and one of the 1902 Middlesex team realised £130 and £80 respectively at the Lord's bonanza, while another, of the Cambridge XI of 1909, had with it a memorandum from Hawkins indicative of costs of 2s.6d. for the group scene and cabinet proofs of individual players at 1d. each. It was one of the few bargains in that sale at £25.

If the Hawkins holdings are irretrievably lost, what of the other accumulations of fragile, heavy and therefore woefully easily discarded glass

Contemporary with the Hawkins team groups were those that appeared in the periodical *Land and Water*, such as the Yorkshire team of 1888.

negatives which have perished? As any picture researcher will agree, the urge to preserve and protect scarcely touches the comprehension of such picture agencies and newspaper libraries which escaped major war damage. With the honourable exception of the Hulton Picture Library, memorably presented in *Starting with Grace* (1986), the equation of takeover equals chuck-out has, if anything, accelerated with the advent of the motorised camera. Chris Park's lucky find of several hundred plates by Leslie Overend, stacked in the offices of the *Dewsbury Reporter*, achieves near-miracle status. Patrick Eagar's suggestion, made as long ago as 1971, that a central body be set up to collect significant photographs, is a long way off fulfilment, and it has been left to a select gathering of highly gifted photographers like Eagar himself, Ken Kelly, Adrian Murrell, Graham Morris and others, to organise picture-retrieval methods for their own collections. Needless to mention, Stephen Green presides over a matchless MCC collection, and David Frith has spread his wings over the whole pageant of cricket with a collection calculated to embrace over 500,000 images. Dozens of other collectors have amassed pictures of the game at every level and arranged them in scrapbooks, collated either sequentially or by thematic interest. Modern restoration and conservation techniques are available to aware private collectors, portfolios with customised mounts and interleaving being turned into small masterpieces of preservation.

Few players since the resumption of cricket after the First World War have not been recorded on film, and the same applies to most of the outstanding events. That hundreds predating the modern camera have managed to survive was made abundantly clear by the scintillating variety of fine photos deemed to be surplus to requirements shown at the Bicentenary auction. From over 150 lots of gelatine silver prints, cabinet cards, *cartes de visite* mounted in sets, hand-tints, studio, albumen and copy prints, to pick a sample few is galling but necessary. Ignoring panoramic views of the first Test ever played on grass in South Africa as well as other views of overseas interest, there was the mid-19th century bowler Martingell in old age, the 1894 Eton-Harrow match in progress, a reunion grouping in a garden setting of former county captains in mufti (c.1900), and an unforgettable shot of two street urchins, one carrying a large cricket bat, reissued by the purchaser as a card.

Poor street urchins perhaps, but this 1930s photograph was bid up to £1,100 at the MCC Bicentenary auction.

Above right Boys enjoying a game of cricket in West Africa, 1905.

Roger Mann has probably the largest collection of W.G. photos, some 300 or so, dating back to his very first match at the age of 14, for Twenty-Two of Lansdown v. the All-England XI (he scored 0 in both innings). One turns also to a choice angle by G.M. Smith of the old man "in retirement", wearing cricket gear and a panama hat, taken in his conservatory at Mottingham around 1905 (before he retired), which realised £190 at Christie's in 1988. The Burlington Gallery can usually be relied upon for better-grade photographs and some have included W.G., one with the veteran

Gloucestershire bowler and Duleepsinhji's coach, W.A. Woof, dated c.1878, at £160 and another with Jupp, c.1885, for £165. A hand-coloured albumen print of W.G., taken in three-quarter length part-profile, made £360 at the Lord's sale, but other solo portraits of halcyon-day players also come down hard on the pocket. A photograph of S.F. Barnes on rare England duty cost around £20 as a part-lot at auction; Lord Harris, photographed c.1880, has been offered at £75, while a signed print from the Langford collection of Jack Hobbs, inscribed "To P.F. Warner", demanded £90 at Phillips back in May 1982. Over 180 studio photographs of cricketers from the 1870s and 1880s went to dealer John McKenzie for more than £800 at the November 1985 auction.

Group and team photographs are even more stringently priced. A dozen albumen portraits in matching oval frames on a red-plush mount, showing members of R.A. Fitzgerald's private English side to America in 1872, caught up in the Bicentenary sale, went for £700, while an even earlier and extraordinarily rare photograph of the team selected to visit Australia in

A chance to compare the golf and cricket swings of W.G. Grace.

1863-64, taken at Lord's on 1st October 1863, and published by McLean & Haes, is valued around £200. At a guess, £350-£400 would secure an equally rare 1862 photograph, issued in Melbourne by T. Hill, and over-painted by hand, of the first English touring side to visit Australia. A special affection has always attached to the "old enemy", and a very reasonable (by today's standards) price of £75 for an autographed group of Armstrong's great side of 1926 has subsequently been beaten by an awesome £320 paid in June 1987 for 15 signed photographs of that fairly useful side brought over in 1930. The pervasive *dementia praecox* of the Lord's sale saw a card-mounted team photograph of the 1902 side, with manuscript title, scramble up to £300.

A pair of photographs of Smokers v. Non-Smokers at East Melbourne Cricket Club, together with the scores, featured the then highest single innings score of 803 in March 1887 (Phillips, July 1981, £75), and a signed photograph of the three captains – Gregory, Fry and Mitchell – who participated in the ill-fated Triangular Tournament of 1912, sold for £50 in July 1983. The melancholy remembrance of the 1868 Aborigines never fails to draw collectors, and a composite of *cartes de visite* in an oval fetched £200 at Phillips in 1983, but failed to find a buyer at Christie's on the 120th anniversary of their visit to the United Kingdom. Also valued at over £200 in 1986-87, and once possibly part of the Goldman collection, is the mounted card with printed title reproducing photographs of 90 of the leading players of the day as an illustrious array of *carte-de-visite* type images. To record Bradman's last visit to this country in 1974, at the express invitation of the Lord's Taverners, a special photograph was taken at the Anglo-American Sporting Club of Sir Donald with most of the 1948 England team from the Oval Test, together with a number of other famous cricketers. An edition of 50 signed and mounted copies was made available by the Taverners at £50 each, and it will be intriguing to note what they fetch at auction one day.

Wisden Cricket Monthly (January 1987) carried a gripping account of the rescue by H.A. "Ossie" Osborne, from its dingy resting-place in a boiler room at the county ground in Hove, of the earliest known photograph of a Test match on Australian soil, Sydney 1891-92, with the home side in the field, and the trans-shipment of the massive panorama, thanks to David Frith, to

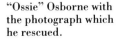

"Ossie" Osborne with the photograph which he rescued.

Photograph from the album presented to Victor Trumper.

its proper home at the Sydney Cricket Ground. The photo was originally presented to the Earl of Sheffield by the trustees of the SCG as a gesture of appreciation for his efforts in the revival of Australian cricket, and deposited with the county along with other mementos of the tour. This rescue by the curator of the Sussex CCC museum prompts the researcher to wonder how many copies exist still of the mammoth photo taken in five sections by the New South Wales "Government Department" of the final Test at Melbourne, the scene of Stoddart's victory in 1894-95. Its definitive measurements were given as 5ft. long and 3ft.4in. wide, and it was available in 1895 for £4. The idiocy of £38, paid at the MCC Bicentenary sale for a recent and fuzzy photo of a youngster bowling at the Nursery Ground, finds parallel in the grotesque picture, 28ft. long, of the Sydney Test 1894, which was sold at the same auction to the Bradman Museum for £1,200; some small panoramas, slightly later in date, went for just under £1,000.

Generous sums have been paid for four photo albums relating to A.P.F. Chapman, formerly the property of John Arlott, worth £180 in 1980, and £400 for another pair of Chapmanana in November 1985. An album of original photographs of the Ashes Tests of 1911-12 and 1920-21 realised £550 in June 1987 and an album of largely informal snapshots presented to Trumper by his 1899 tour colleague and keen photographer Frank Laver, was justifiably valued at £500 in October the same year. Laver made similar presentations on subsequent tours. "Ram" Ramamurthy, profiled in *Wisden Cricket Monthly* (March 1988), has another priceless album once owned by Trumper, all the photographs signed.

The 'flickers' of Bradman and Grimmett.

'Flickers'

G.D. Martineau, writing in 1936, regretted the disappearance from the market of the 6d. "flickers" from Flicker Productions Ltd. of Earls Court Road, showing Grimmett's bowling action and Bradman's batting style, "since when I have only seen one of Woolley batting and that one only gave two of his strokes". Unprepossessing in appearance, a signed Bradman and Grimmett were advertised in 1986, but not until the press previews of the sale of the effects of C.V. Grimmett did we discover their peculiar fascination. Obviously writing for the *arrivistes*, *The Times* felt it needed to describe them as "a kind of archaeological instant replay", allowing the viewer to flick the pages to create the illusion of movement, or freeze-frame for more detailed inspection. Provenance and rarity propelled some quite astounding prices once bidding started, between £65 and £220 showing what 1988 collectors at Christie's thought of googlies tossed their way half a century before.

Lantern slides

Not over-popular, being cumbersome and difficult to display to advantage, nevertheless a box of over 50 of these slides, some from informal photographs but the majority Beldam shots, secured £70 in December 1979. A very tasty 7in.x4in. hand-painted slide, set in wood, showing a comic batsman and wicketkeeper scene, with the action controlled by a hand-lever, moved to £320 at the Bicentenary auction. Collector Mike Smith now lays claim to over 300 magic-lantern slides, complete with original lecture notes, which show off Victorian cricketers and a history of the game as it was in those days. Mind you, Smith points out, "The lecturer appeared to have more time for E.M. Grace than W.G.!"

Lantern slide from the Bicentenary auction.

Stevengraphs

Stevengraphs are named after Thomas Stevens, born in 1828 at Foleshill, then a village on the outskirts of Coventry, where he learned the craft of ribbon-making as a boy. Well established in Coventry by 1854, then the centre of the silk-weaving industry, he capitalised on a ready market for silk ribbons, bookmarkers (often with a suitable moral, ideal for school prizes), Valentine and Christmas cards, sashes, silk calendars and hat bands. They were not then called by their better-known name, but as "Textlegraphs" could be bought as spaced-along ribbons by the foot or yard, or fitted into simple cardboard frames, at a shilling each, ready for framing and hanging in the home.

In 1879 he introduced Stevengraphs, some as small as 1½in.x4in., and with a shrewd appraisal of public taste began with sporting prints, before branching out into Royals, heroic figures of the time, or scenes from myth and legend. His work was something of a vogue in the latter part of the nineteenth century, but at its close the quality was deteriorating and the subject matter was imitative. Probably his company's last production was a portrait of King George VI and his Queen in 1938, and two years later the Luftwaffe destroyed the factory.

Eagerly sought after are those depicting a wide range of sporting subjects, but only two are known to feature cricket. A scarce and highly desirable item, 'The Last Innings', actually shows baseball. Stevens catered for the American market and there is a Stevengraphs Collectors Association dedicated to their acquisition in the United States. No one knows how many of the cricket scenes have migrated across the Atlantic, but the existence of this club has had an effect on prices and rarity.

When assessing value, ideally the card-mounts should be originals, uncreased, and bright in colour, unspoilt by direct sunlight.

One of the earliest Stevengraphs (May 1880) is 'The First Over'. Just 2in.x6in. image size, it portrays a stereotyped Victorian match, crudely designed, with underarm bowler, fieldsmen poised to pounce, and a scattering of spectators. Condition is paramount – the lush colours of the grass and players' outfits are often found faded – and prices for the four or so to have appeared in the last few years have swayed between £90 and £134. Elsewhere described as a "delicate little cricketing scene" and "a masterpiece of its kind", it was valued in an article on the Tony Baer collection in 1965 at a modest £25.

Despite being produced in large quantities in 1896, 'W.G.', 4in.x2½in., woven on the occasion of his hundredth century in 1895, is the rarer of the two (see colour page xiv). It shows him at the wicket, and is still scoring high: £145 in 1968, at a Phillips sale in October 1972 it was the highest bid of all at £200, and in more recent auctions has attracted bids of £300, £240, £320 and £480. A copy in excellent condition, but untitled, was on offer from the Burlington Gallery in 1989 at £495.

Handkerchiefs

Shelley's "slow stain of time" has eroded the quantity, physical state and colouring of cricket's handkerchiefs, but in a bullish market large sums are lavished on them. Granted the fragility and disposability of the product, and the fact that at least one of the handkerchiefs was a direct commission, by the early 1860s printed handkerchiefs or those woven on Jacquard looms became plentiful. Their use had been extended to commemorative events and personalities, and in this they were similar to the broadsheets of previous generations.

The anonymous nature of their manufacture suggests a wide retail outlet, yet remarkably few have survived. Fifty years ago J.W. Goldman doubted whether there were more than a dozen different cricket handkerchiefs in existence, a fact which renders condition slightly less crucial than in other areas of collecting and buyers are prepared to pay strong prices for even second-rank material.

In the 18th century the habit of using a pocket-sized piece of cloth for hygienic purposes was confined to western Europe, and then only to the more refined classes of society. Made of the finest silks and linens, they were still regarded as decorative rather than functional. *Oliver Twist* makes much of the eagerness shown by Fagin's youthful pickpockets looking for these expensive items, even when devoid of any sort of ornamentation.

To act as a deterrent, they were often stitched with the owner's name, and the handkerchief with the original Laws of Cricket in the MCC collection bears the initials "S.B.", indicating that it may have belonged once to the legendary scorer, Samuel Britcher.

The very early handkerchiefs printed on silk, apparently by Joseph Ware of Crayford in Kent, are now more than ever before in demand, since they bear the earliest printed laws of the game. There appear to be at least two closely allied versions of the illustrious commemorative which shows a reproduction of Grignion's engraving of cricket as played on Marylebone Fields, surmounted by the insignia "The Laws of the Game of Cricket", and variously quoted as puce, purple or blue. The original Laws (second edition) are inscribed along all four margins of what is assuredly one of the most coveted pieces known to collectors.

Goldman claimed a variant copy in perfect condition, printed it seems by J. Cray of Dartford (note the confusion with Crayford) and reckoned it to be earlier than the one in the possession of MCC. This dated around 1740; it was printed in blue, whereas Rockley Wilson's rather more battered specimen – formerly the property of the Baroness d'Erlanger – was more of a puce colour. The admirable museum at Melbourne Cricket Club claims their printed cotton, size 70cm.x79cm., ex-Goldman and in the Baer collection, is "one of the only three remaining versions of the second edition of these Laws, which were printed in 1744". A literature search also unearths a tantalisingly brief reference to an exact copy annotated "A.J.G.", possibly A.J. Gaston.

On the back of the framed cotton or linen handkerchief presented to Sussex CCC, which showed the same Marylebone Fields painting and was described as "light-brick red, hardly puce", was pasted a cutting from *The West Sussex Gazette and Courier* (17th May 1860), signed simply "W.J.H." It refers to a silk handkerchief handed to W. Humphrey by Daniel King on his death bed in 1836, carrying verbatim the Laws in the words of the first edition. Since this article appeared in 1860, it could be that Haygarth took his description from this cutting without having seen the handkerchief, and fell into the same error as Humphrey. Alternatively, they may have been referring to another handkerchief altogether.

A framed, glazed but faded cotton commemorative showing Hayman's other classic scene, cricket on the Artillery Ground, but with a different, longer title and letterpress border citing the 1744 Laws, dated mid-18th century and printed in red, was sold at the Lord's auction for £1,400.

Much more elaborate, indeed almost stately, is the linen handkerchief printed in purple, c.1785, the lengthy title at the base ennobling the game and showing a match in progress at the White Conduit Club. The Laws are printed on the remaining three sides, with the corner half-length portraits

Handkerchief now in the Bradman Museum.

of the Prince of Wales, Sir Horatio Mann, Colonel Tarleton and the Duke of Dorset. At the Lord's sale in April 1987 a copy was estimated at £3,000-£5,000 but went to the Bradman Museum for £7,000. Another, repaired, also exceeded estimate later in the year at Christie's at £5,500.

Ford's India Silk Handkerchief Warehouse, 185 Strand, were advertising at the turn of the century an 1847 "first rate view of Lord's Cricket Ground", printed, obviously, on silk. It reproduced within an octagonal border an early representation of a match in progress at Lord's, c.1833. The bowler has the standard Alfred Mynn action, with his typical field. Each corner has an image of Lillywhite, Box, Pilch and Cobbett respectively. A silk, edged in purple, 36in.x31½in., showing some wear, was auctioned at Christie's in October 1988 for £300, while Melbourne, again courtesy of Tony Baer, has a cotton version, dated by them c.1840.

Three versions (at least) exist of the silk commemorative to the MCC Jubilee Match of 1837, for all of which buyers are prepared to do anything other than sit on their hands. Properly entitled 'The Grand Jubilee Match Played Monday July 10th 1837 at Lord's ground between the North and South of England Box and Cobbett given to the former to commemorate the 50th year of the Marylebone Club', this printed silk has dark pink clover leaves against a cream background and is edged in red. Lillywhite, too, was prominent in this festival match, and handkerchiefs were presented to each of the men employed on the ground. One rumoured to have been the one actually given *en personne* to Box was sold at the Lord's auction for £450.

A similar handkerchief, but without the title or names of the players, with a different-coloured border and a plain cream field, formerly the property of Stephen Slatter, head groundsman at Lord's in the last century, reached £280 at the same sale. A third version, the central oval reserve showing the same match, has a stylised and foliate border, 105cm. square, and realised a remarkable £1,300 at the Phillips 'Tony Baer' sale in 1978.

The printed silk portraying 'The Eleven of England 1847', after a watercolour by Felix, within a broad yellow border, is another *rara avis*. A poor copy achieved just over £80 at the 1979 Phillips sale. Its purchaser, John Gill, carefully restored it and his company, First Impressions, had a black

'The Eleven of England 1847'.

THE ELEVEN OF ENGLAND.

and white replica on sale soon afterwards. Meanwhile, over £240 was paid for one in linen which appeared among the duplicates at the Sussex CCC sale in 1980, whereas a silk at the Lord's sale reached £1,600.

To our mind an outstandingly attractive handkerchief, with its richly embellished borders, is the cotton commemorative dedicated 'To the Admirers of the Noble Game of Cricket', printed in two colours (see colour page xiv). The centre has a group picture of the England XI of 1847, again after a Felix watercolour, and is flanked by vignettes of classic poses, Laws I,IV,VIII and IX in cartouches, and a village cricket game at the base. A visual pun on the word "bat" surmounts the whole. At least five have appeared for sale in the past few years. The Sussex sale realisation was £480, whereupon First Impressions offered a replica at £25, but of late prices have wavered between £100-£140, depending upon wear and tear, until a mounted copy soared to £2,500 at the Bicentenary sale, followed by £950 at Christie's in October 1987.

Another to catch the eye is 'Eleven of England in Australia with Mr Mallam', a commemorative silk marking the first English side to tour Australia. Captained by H.H. Stephenson and managed by Mallam, the team arrived on Christmas Day 1861, and after 60 days at sea almost immediately buckled to and took on a local XVIII at the Melbourne Cricket Ground. The company which sponsored the tour and commissioned the handkerchief, the catering firm of Spiers and Pond, had intended a lecture tour of Australia by Charles Dickens, so this was very much a second XI affair by comparison.

The centrepiece has the named cricketers with a wide blue border, size 75cm.x65cm. A copy was advertised for sale in 1979 for £350, and at the Phillips auction in April that year one went for £220. A white silk example climbed to £2,500 at Christie's in October 1987 and made £2,000 at Christie's in June 1988. Another First Impressions replica was on offer for £25.

A handkerchief was also struck for the expedition of the second English team to Australia in 1864. It is similar in style to the team group shown for 1861-62, but the corners show Lillywhite's scoring tent, pavilions, bats, wickets, balls, gloves and pads – images symbolic of cricket for that era, and widely used in prints and illustrations at the time. A framed and glazed example in silk was bid up to £1,650 at Christie's in October 1987.

The Australian cricketers visiting England in 1882 received the accolade of two commemorative printed cotton handkerchiefs. Both have a named team group as the traditional centrepiece, with one (59cm.x58cm.) printed in grey, carrying their 12 larger single portraits around the border, and the other has orthodox bat and stump emblems and batting and bowling figures. Both have an assured rarity. The former was bought by First Impressions in April 1979 for £340 and offered soon afterwards as a Habotai twill reproduction for £20. Two were on sale at Lord's, one with a corner inscription "William

Hall", reaching £500.

There was somewhat muted interest at Christie's in October 1988 for 'The Australian Cricket Team of 1878', the first to visit these shores. A commemorative cotton handkerchief, printed in grey, it shows the team at centre, with corner full-length portraits of Spofforth, Blackham, Murdoch and Bannerman, but made only £140.

The most popular of all cricket handkerchiefs formed lot No.224 at the 'Tony Baer' sale in 1978. Entitled 'Dr W.G. Grace, Champion Cricketer of the World', and printed in grey on cotton, it carries a central portrait and biography with a border surround enumerating his hundred hundreds. An outer border bears floral and cricketing motifs. Printed as it was in 1895, it does not include his further 26 centuries, but the bidding went several hundreds down the way to a staggering £850.

Of the dozen or more to have come on the market in the past decade, the 1980 Sussex sale had two to spare, both of which found buyers at around £100. Although more common than some of the other cricket-oriented handkerchiefs and scarves, it still commands prices between the "sentimental" £140 and £160 at the Gloucestershire CCC auction and the ridiculous sum paid in 1978. By 1980 prices had slipped to the £100 mark, while at the Lord's sale, of the three lots, two went for £160 and £320. First Impressions slipped in again with a £20 replica.

It would be idle to pretend that this survey exhausts the number of 19th-century handkerchiefs, but we must move forward. A commemorative silk marking the 1905 Australians exceeded £110 in 1984 but, strangely enough, prices for the Jack Hobbs 'England's Champion Batsman' have only just crept up from £80 in 1979 to £240 in late 1987, slipping back to £100 in June 1988. It is hard to reconcile this languor with the general enthusiasm for all Hobbsiana. It is a not unattractive item either, with an oval centre portrait of "The Master", vignettes of him in action, statistical data, and a surround of his centuries between 1905 and 1922.

In 1926 Messrs Merritt and Hatcher of Blackheath Road, London SE10, issued a silk commemorative "as a beautiful memento of a famous victory", but if any have emerged for sale they seem to have been tucked away among job lots. However, a photographic printed cotton handkerchief with a team group of the 1931 Lancashire team made £200 at the MCC Bicentenary auction.

Modern silk and cotton commemoratives appear not to have caught on. Two issued in 1982, with caricatures by Roy Ullyett and dedicated to the famous Headingley Test victory of 1981, and Laker's superlative bowling figures in 1956, both with complete scorecards, seem to be duds. Perhaps it is still too soon to comment, and collector regret will come later – or might they have been over-priced at £6 and £10 respectively?

BOOKS AND PERIODICALS

Wisden Cricketers' Almanack

The best-known and most collected cricket book is *Wisden Cricketers' Almanack*, known familiarly by its first name to its many devotees. It has been praised (mainly), criticised (occasionally), anthologised (quite often) and even televised (the subject of a documentary in 1987), and features regularly in the bestsellers' lists. Many rarer cricketing volumes exist, but the fervour with which *Wisdens* are pursued, and its wide recognition far beyond the boundaries of the game, are evidence, should any be required, of its pre-eminence in this area – perhaps all areas – of cricketana.

Older collectors, as they see three-figure and even four-figure prices become the norm for early editions, are left to look back nostalgically to the days when they might reasonably expect to enter a second-hand bookshop and acquire a second-hand *Wisden* of all but the earliest vintage for about half a crown [13p.] or at most ten bob [50p.]. Vendors, be they private or public, now seem only too aware of the demand, and thus the value, of old *Wisdens* and this makes redundant the dreams once cherished by collectors such as Richard Streeton of discovering a junk shop in an out-of-the-way village where a little old lady is happy to give away the compact volumes whose scoreboards and statistics she misinterprets as railway timetables. Indeed, such has been the escalation in prices that even J.W. McKenzie, the dealer in the forefront of the boom, admitted in 1988 that he was finding prices at auction too high.

The almanack was first published in 1864 by John Wisden, a leading professional cricketer in his day and latterly a dealer in sports goods. The first edition was a modest 112-page offering in paper covers, titled *The Cricketer's Almanack, for the year 1864* and containing much information unconnected with cricket. It opened with an almanack, cricketing information supplementing calendrical and historical, and a misprint for June giving the year as 1846 instead of 1864. The cricket section comprised primarily the laws of the game, detailed scores for the Gentlemen v. Players and All England XI v. United All England XI matches since their inception. The final 15 pages included the winners of the Derby, Oaks and St Leger; the rules of knur and spell (a game which involves hitting a ball released from a trap); a potted history of China and coinage; the rules of bowls and quoiting; the dates and results of the Oxford and Cambridge rowing matches; a list of principal British societies and canals; the battles of the Wars of the Roses; and a note on the trial of Charles I. All of this could "be had of all respectable

Booksellers in the United Kingdom" for one shilling [*5p.*] "or forwarded free by the Publisher to any part of Great Britain for 13 [*1 penny*] Stamps".

However, from little acorns grow mighty oaks and John Wisden's almanack has been published every year since its inception, seeing off several rivals along the way and enduring from its second edition as the only complete record of first-class matches played in the British Isles in the previous season. Coverage of overseas cricket has been less comprehensive (and plans for an Australian edition in the early 1980s never came to fruition) and though an extensive section of the game's records has been a feature of the book dubbed "the cricketer's bible" for many years, contrary to popular myth this does not – indeed cannot – contain every great or unusual feat on the cricket field; nor again does it list the name of every first-class cricketer, although the 'Births and Deaths' section, which began in 1867 and has since passed through several stages of excision and revision, misses few who have made a mark on the game. Notes by the Editor, instituted in 1901, are one of the strongest elements of *Wisden* and have featured trenchant comment from a distinguished line of editors, which has to date numbered only 13 throughout the book's existence. To correct another misconception, *Wisden* has never been infallible – what product of humankind has ever been? – but rigorous checking in modern times by the small and devoted team responsible for its production mean remarkably few errors for a book of 1,200-1,300 pages so packed with detail.

Wisden has had its quirks too, never being too good on cricketers' achievements outside the game. The classic example is the obituary of Rupert Brooke in 1916; it runs to six lines and after telling that he was in the Rugby School XI in 1906, heading the bowling averages with 19 wickets at 14.05 runs apiece, concludes baldly: "He had gained considerable reputation as a poet." For all that, *Wisden* remains the cornerstone of any cricket library and it is most collectors' ambition to possess a full set. One such, Ronald Harries, likened the pursuit to the quest for the Holy Grail or Jason's search for the Golden Fleece; when he acquired his final volume he might indeed have agreed with Robert Louis Stevenson's words, "Is there anything in life so disenchanting as attainment?" – but at least he could die fulfilled!

Wisden has been a desirable and collectable commodity ever since its earliest days. Thanks partly to an increasing amount of advertising from purveyors of sporting and other goods, such Dr J. Collis Browne's reliable medicine which was claimed to cure everything from gout to hysteria, and largely to the absence of the inflationary pressures that have since beset the national economy, the retail price of the softback edition (hardback was introduced in 1896 at 2 shillings) remained at a shilling right up to the First World War; by then it had grown to almost 800 pages. Lucky indeed, however, was the collector who by that ominous year of 1914 had assembled

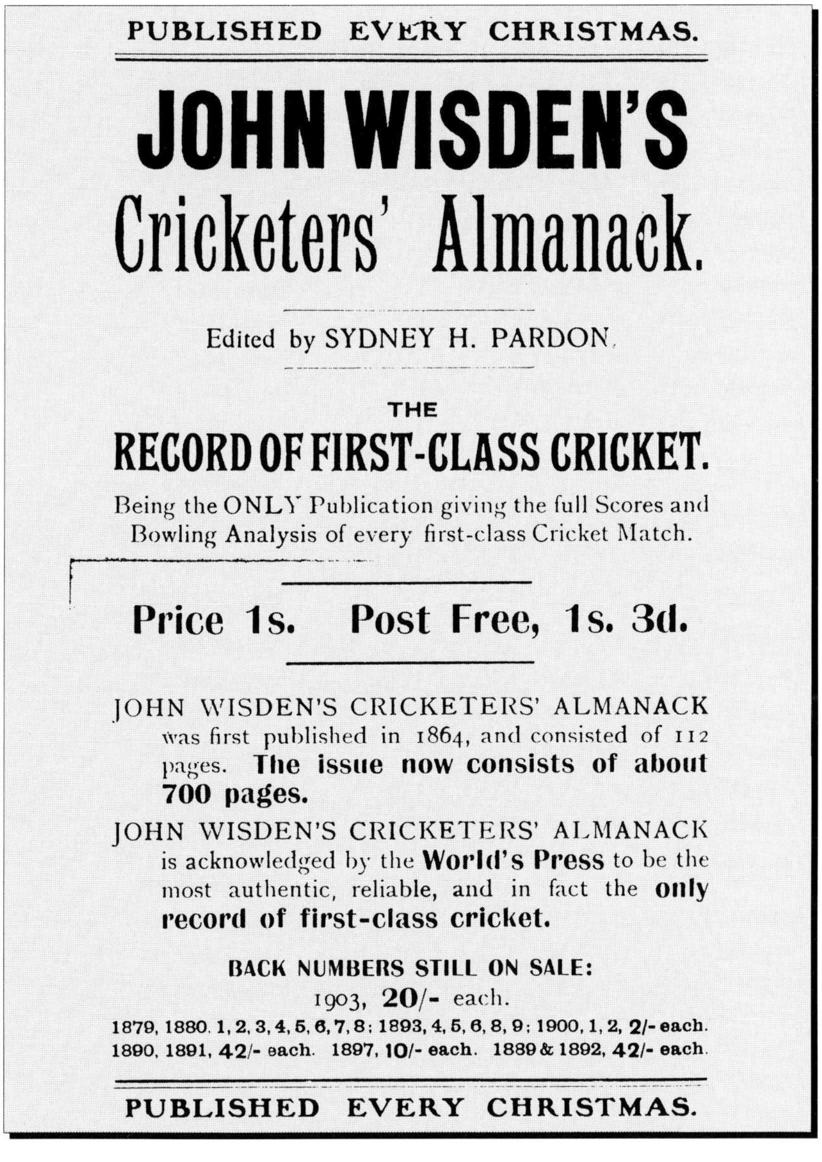

PUBLISHED EVERY CHRISTMAS.

JOHN WISDEN'S
Cricketers' Almanack.

Edited by SYDNEY H. PARDON,

THE

RECORD OF FIRST-CLASS CRICKET.

Being the ONLY Publication giving the full Scores and
Bowling Analysis of every first-class Cricket Match.

Price 1s.   Post Free, 1s. 3d.

JOHN WISDEN'S CRICKETERS' ALMANACK
was first published in 1864, and consisted of 112
pages. **The issue now consists of about 700 pages.**

JOHN WISDEN'S CRICKETERS' ALMANACK
is acknowledged by the **World's Press** to be the
most authentic, reliable, and in fact the **only
record of first-class cricket.**

BACK NUMBERS STILL ON SALE:
1903, **20/-** each.
1879, 1880. 1, 2, 3, 4, 5, 6, 7, 8; 1893, 4, 5, 6, 8, 9; 1900, 1, 2, **2/-** each.
1890, 1891, **42/-** each.   1897, **10/-** each.   1889 & 1892, **42/-** each.

PUBLISHED EVERY CHRISTMAS.

Flyer offering *Wisden*,
which was scheduled
for publication before
Christmas in those
days.

his run of the first 51 *Wisdens* at cost price, £2.11s. [£2.55], for even the
publishers themselves were seeking to acquire copies of the rare 1875 edition
at 10s. within half a dozen years of its publication; the reason for its rarity
is presumed to be a small, and possibly hurried, printing. Though Leslie
Gutteridge, than whom no one has known more on the subject of cricket
books, had in 1951 never heard of 1875 bought singly, several have been
offered in recent years (see further below). The noted cricket bibliographer,

Alfred D. Taylor, wrote in *The Catalogue of Cricket Literature* (1906) that the earlier issues were "exceedingly difficult to meet with, and even the more recent numbers are advertised at forty times the published price before they are twelvemonths [sic] old." He valued a "clean and perfect set, in original covers," at 18 guineas [£18.90], although *The Cricketer* (11th June 1927) said that Mr Harry Luff, proprietor of *Wisden*, sold a set to the Earl of Carnarvon for £25 at the beginning of the century.

Even allowing for the obvious fact that a full set of *Wisdens* grows by one each year, prices rose sharply in 1920s, when a set was reported changing hands for £150, but shopping around, as ever, would have been worthwhile, for a catalogue issued by A.J. Gaston, the Sussex collector-dealer, had a set bound in whole calf with original covers available in 1925 at 50 guineas [£52.50]. By then another rarity had risen in the shape of the 1916 volume. Wartime meant a cessation of first-class cricket and consequently a small volume of only 300 pages; austerity also meant a smaller than usual printing and the presence of W.G. Grace's obituary (not to mention those of Victor Trumper – and Rupert Brooke) meant that these were quickly snapped up. The publishers were offering copies a year later at 21s. (publication price had been 1s.6d. [8p.]) and by 1919 were indicating that the 1916 edition was out of print. Gutteridge, who wrote the definitive article on *Wisden* in the almanack's centenary edition in 1963, had stated a dozen years earlier in *The Cricketer* that the 1916 "is not so scarce as many would have you believe" and valued it at £2.10s.; but in the boom of the early 1980s collectors were paying more than £200 for it at auction. A marginally kinder light was cast on the astonishing £525 seen in one dealer's list in April 1989 for a copy in hard covers after bidding at Phillips in October 1988 soared to £320 for a soft-cover version of this elusive number and then to £400 for a near-mint example at Christie's in June 1989.

The Second World War, too, brought slimmer volumes and truncated printings, and this era has its particular rarity: 1941. The preface to 1942, referring to "the sustained efforts of the enemy [the publishers were bombed during the winter of 1940 and all the records lost] to prevent publication of its predecessor", provides apologies and an explanation: "In addition to war-time restrictions, there was an actual shortage in the making of the supply of paper for that issue which was too small to justify an additional supply being put in hand, but was sufficiently large to cause a serious shortage of copies. It is hoped that there will be enough copies of this new edition to go round." There scarcely seem to be nowadays, and the price of single copies, when they are offered by dealers, is well into three figures.

This is all a far cry from the bargain found by a bidder at Sotheby's auction in 1937 of the library of the sports journalist, J.A.H. Catton, when a set (1864-1936) plus 11 duplicate volumes went for only £33; it was, however, probably well thumbed, for *Wisden* is an essential point of reference for every serious writer on cricket. In 1954 a set complete to 1953 fetched £145 at a Hodgson's auction and by the following decade Gutteridge valued a set in good condition at £250. Since then prices have risen dramatically: a complete run was offered in 1972 for £750 by the then new Surrey dealer, J.W. McKenzie, and bought by the librettist and cricket fanatic, Tim Rice. The price caused many eyebrows to be raised in the hitherto fairly closeted world of cricket collecting, but Rice before long could answer them.

Signs of the new passion for *Wisdens* emerged at the Phillips sale of April 1979, when a Nottingham collector, Philip Jones, needing two to complete his set, bid £4,200 for a run from 1864 to 1969 lacking nine 19th-century volumes (including 1875). Two years later, in a special *Wisden* catalogue, £12,000 was being asked by McKenzie for a set and by 1986, at the culmination of what might be described as a period of Wisden-mania, a set brought a gross auction realisation of £16,669 (see below). Further signs of this were seen, for example, at Phillips in July 1981, when the *Index to Wisden 1864-1943* by Rex Pogson, an invaluable but not particularly rare book, soared to £50; the madness of it all was illustrated by a letter in *The Cricketer* of December 1981, which pointed out that copies of the index were still available from the publishers, Sporting Handbooks ... at £2.50! By May 1983 auction prices for the index had eased back to around £20 and by May 1985 to £15, by when was published an updated, though less tidily typeset, index updated to 1984 by Derek Barnard. It was the recognition by Rice – as by others such as Robin Marlar, the journalist, former Sussex captain and erstwhile active bidder for *Wisdens* – of the almanack's investment potential that prompted him to buy a second set at the great Phillips auction of November 1985, when it took a bid of £7,000 to secure a lot which Rice discovered only afterwards included photocopied pages among some of the early volumes. All potential bidders are well advised to take advantage of the pre-sale viewing of lots: otherwise, *caveat emptor*.

A number of other sets have been seen in the auction rooms, often with a famous provenance. In May 1980, along with other material from the late Sir Pelham Warner's collection, Phillips sold his set of *Wisdens*, complete to 1963, for £7,800; the successful bidder was Duncan Mutch, known in the cricket world as solicitor to Geoffrey Boycott. The books were uniformly and handsomely bound as 73 volumes in half green morocco and gilt, with Warner's initials on the spine; of these the editions up to 1904 had been given to him as a wedding present by the publishers. Rather less attractive in appearance (the binding was black hide), though not in the charisma of their owner, was P.G.H. Fender's set, which came up at Phillips in October 1985 and fetched a disappointing £4,500. There were several reasons: though the set was complete to 1985, the first 15 years were facsimiles; more importantly the big guns among the bidders were keeping their powder dry for the big 'Winder' sale the following month. Martin Wood, the Kent dealer who made the winning bid, cannot have been too unhappy with what he paid, but he had an extended search for a buyer.

Blue calf and the badge of Scarborough C.C. was the livery of the first 76 volumes of a set (complete to 1985) ascribed to Sir Henry Leveson Gower (pronounced Looson Goore) "by descent", which was offered by Phillips in June 1987 and went under the hammer for £10,000, a record bid for a set offered as a single lot. According to the sale catalogue, the earlier part of the set was believed to have been presented to Leveson Gower by Scarborough C.C. in 1948; that was the 50th year of his association with the Scarborough Festival and this may be one of the "handsome gifts" he records, in his autobiography *Off and On the Field* (1953), having received to mark the occasion.

As well as offering collections complete, auctioneers have taken to splitting up some properties into several lots, the early years singly and the later by decade or period. The effect of this is twofold: collectors seeking particular years do not, as Mr Jones in 1979, have to buy large numbers of duplicates; on the other hand the price for a set is raised ever higher. It has the additional effect that the work, perhaps of a lifetime, is undone at a few strokes of the auctioneer's hammer, the books are dispersed and the cycle begins all over again. As a result of splitting, in the space of a month in 1986 the record was twice broken. At Lalonde and Parham, Bristol, in May the *Wisdens* (complete to 1962) of Dr G.B. Buckley, a dedicated student of the game's early history, went under the hammer in 16 lots for a total of £13,960 (£15,565 when buyer's premium of 11.5 per cent, including VAT, was added), the first 15 years alone, bound into four volumes, contributing £9,420 to that total. At Phillips in June a set offered in 22 lots was bid up to £14,950 (£16,669 with premium), when the first 15 went for £10,860 and the last 100, as a single lot, for £3,000. The figure was all but matched at Phillips in June 1987, when the *Wisdens* (many *ex-libris* W.F. Curtis), in 18 lots, made £14,940. That sale also contained another near-complete run, split into lots, and, while the earliest years naturally commanded the highest prices, it may be helpful to illustrate the average realisations at these and later sales:

	Buckley sale May 1986 £	Phillips June 1987 £	Phillips June 1988 £	Christie's & Phillips June 1989 £
1880s	160	253	188	233
1890s	39	52	75*	82
1900s	24	28	30*	39
1910s	–	46	42	116†
First War (inc.1916)	88	88	–	135
1920s	38	55	30	46
1930s	32	36	35	35
1940s (inc.1941)	63	46	36	51
1950s onwards	21 (to 1962)	8 (to 1986)	8 (to 1987)	9 (to 1985)

* spines distressed	† original publisher's hardback cloth

These figures are intended as a statement of what was achieved at five particular sales; they do not take into account the varied bindings and lotting periods. It must also be remembered that condition is the overriding factor, as well as the mood of the saleroom and, on occasions, the determination of a particular bidder to secure a particular lot or lots. Copies in the publishers' original hard covers, particularly, or with original covers bound in will usually command a premium over those in soft covers, unless they are in prime condition, and dealers' prices will, naturally, be somewhat different, i.e. higher!

The highest price paid hitherto for individual volumes was also achieved at the Phillips June 1986 auction, when a previously unknown collector, Hugh Simmonds, presumably seeking to complete his set, bid an incredible £5,500 (which meant an actual payment of £6,132.50 including buyer's premium) for the first two, 1864 and 1865, and then a further £3,690 for six other early volumes, including £1,600 for the rare 1875, before hurriedly leaving the saleroom. A further twist was added to the story two years later by news of his suicide, amid allegations of financial scandal.

The previous record had been £950 (£1,059.25 inclusive of premium) for the 1868 issue in May 1985; the first "£1,000 *Wisden*" had been an 1864, for which John McKenzie paid an all-inclusive £1,003.50 in 1983. To drive home the point about condition, even a copy of 1875 – which, apart from the freak bid by Simmonds, fetched £800 even though disbound and lacking covers in the sale of the collector-dealer J.R. Batten's property by Graves and Pilcher, Hove, in July 1985 – slipped back to £200 at Phillips in June 1987 when it lacked a few front pages as well as its covers, and £350 at Christie's in June 1989 when the final leaf was lacking.

Because of the rarity of the early years and the difficulty in obtaining them, in 1960 and again in 1973 the then publishers, Sporting Handbooks, published facsimile reprints of the first 15 volumes (1864-78) in limited editions of 150. The first reprint sold at £40 boxed (or 3 guineas for individual years); the second at £50 for the set and £4 individually. These too have acquired their own value and they frequently realise in excess of £400 at auction, the peak so far being £800 for the first facsimile at Phillips in June 1989. With the amounts being paid for *Wisdens* from the 1880s also beginning to move out of range of all but the wealthiest collectors, an enterprising teacher from Stone, Staffordshire, David Jenkins, established the appropriately named Willows Publishing Company in 1984 and set out to reprint the years 1879-90. His excellent volumes, firmly and attractively bound as opposed to the flimsy Sporting Handbooks efforts and in an edition of 500, were widely welcomed by collectors. At an initial cost of £20-£24 each they were roughly one-tenth of the concurrent auction prices.

The presence of these reprints has brought the acquisition of a copy of every edition within the compass of many more collectors, although the purists will rightly argue that a truly complete set consists only of originals. It has often been asked just how many full sets of *Wisden* exist, but attempts at a census have, so far as we are aware, been unsuccessful. In view of the books' value the reluctance of some collectors to disclose their holdings is understandable. Leslie Gutteridge, in *The Cricketer* (26th May 1951), said that the owners of at least seven, perhaps eight, sets could be named by many readers, but he postulated that rather more sets actually existed, without suggesting a figure. We have established that MCC possess three sets at Lord's and other Test grounds have one; and we are aware by report or repute, of at least 20 collectors worldwide who have achieved this state of Nirvana, some with the help of reprints. We would guess that there may be nearly as many again – though surely none at present to match the legendary J.W. Goldman, who at one time could apologise to visitors for being able to show them only one of his *four* complete sets.

Other books

As all those even marginally acquainted with cricket books will know, there is an enormous output on the subject every year from publishers global and parochial. As early as July 1897 the periodical *Cricket* was stating: "Of cricket-books just now there is apparently no ending"; in the 1980s the annual total is regularly reported at upwards of 70. Two of the more striking features to the modern observer are that so many manage to cover, despite all that has gone before, fresh ground and that there is, apparently, even a ready market for reprints of books published only a few years previously. Because of the welter of titles, selectivity is obligatory for all but the giants of the collecting field.

Many books warrant a place in a cricket library for their content and large printings make most of the modern, i.e. 20th century, ones readily accessible in terms of both cost and availability; only a few will have a rarity value. For recent or older books the aspiring collector can turn to several specialist dealers and, of course, the secondhand bookshops, but he can do much worse than watch out for the multiple lots of books which emerge at the main cricketana auctions; prices for these often average little more – or sometimes even less – than £1 a volume, though inspection is essential to avoid too much dross.

Since this is such a vast field, we have chosen in what follows to concentrate on the rare, mostly – but not exclusively – early, books which are the quarry of bibliophiles (in view of the fervour displayed by some in the saleroom, should it be bibliomaniacs?) and dealers, all of whom now require capacious wallets. The books achieve their desirability by reason of their antiquity and/or limited production, though appeal of the author or previous

Arthur Mailey's original illustrations in David Frith's copy of *10 for 66 and all that.*

ownership (regrettably, for students, not always indicated by bookplate or signature) adds to the value. We can, in passing, exemplify this by pointing to items such as *10 for 66 and all that* (1958), reminiscences of the former Australian leg-spinner, Arthur Mailey, a book which might be acquired for well under £10 but in a different league when containing 31 of Mailey's original drawings from the book and eliciting a bid of £300 at Phillips in November 1985; also two devoted studies by G.B. Buckley, *Fresh Light on 18th Century Cricket* (1935) and *Fresh Light on Pre-Victorian Cricket* (1937), published at 15s.

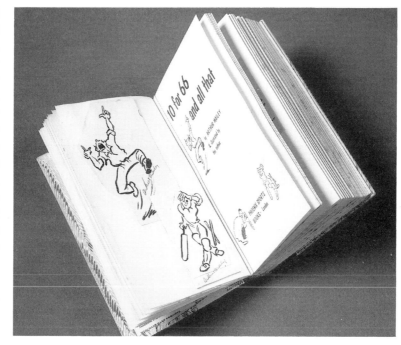

and 10s. respectively, soared to £200 when Dr Buckley's own annotated copies were offered by Lalonde and Parham, of Bristol, in May 1986.

Books have been written on every conceivable aspect of cricket from how to play and watch it to county and club histories, accounts of tours, players' biographies and reminiscences, and encyclopaedic works of records and statistics. For sheer curiosity value, however, there is nothing in all this range to beat a 500-page philological thesis – in German – which analyses cricketing terminology: *Studien zum Verbum in englischen Fachsprachen (Cricket)* by Ernst Burgschmidt, first published in 1970 and, remarkably, reprinted in 1977.

Another scholarly work, which is of inestimable value to cricketing bibliophiles and serious students of the game, is the prodigious *A Bibliography of Cricket*, compiled by E.W. Padwick and published by the Library Association on behalf of The Cricket Society. It was first published in 1977 at £32, listing all works known to the compilers up to the end of 1973; the edition ran to 750 copies and within a few months of publication it was almost impossible to buy a copy. A new edition appeared in 1984 at £50, amended and updated to the end of 1979, but because of publishing costs there is pessimism about the prospects of a third edition. Future revisions, if there are to be any, may sadly have to be confined to supplements.

The project aimed at comprehensiveness rather than the impossible goal of completeness – the description now occasionally seen, "not in Padwick", confirms the authority of the bibliography as much as kudos on the discoverer of the omission – and includes "separately published books, pamphlets, brochures, yearbooks and periodicals" together with "books known to include passages of cricket interest". The first edition contained 8,294 entries with a fully cross-referenced index. The figure is slightly misleading in that some publications warrant entries in more than one section and consequently have more than one number; however, "A" numbers, as well as single entries for multiple-edition or annual works, make it a pretty good working total. This was stated to have been increased by a third (i.e. to more than 12,000) in the second edition, which is illustrated and immensely stronger in detailing overseas publications.

Prior to the *Bibliography* there existed the early efforts of A.J. Gaston (published in *Wisden* 1892, 1894, 1900 and 1923; *The Cricket Field* 1893-95, and in pamphlet form in 1895) and A.D. Taylor (*The Catalogue of Cricket Literature*, serialised in the periodical *Cricket* in 1906 and then published in book form), and then J.W. Goldman's bibliography, published in a limited edition of 125 (of which 100 were for sale) and serialised in *The Cricketer*.

Part of the Goldman collection was offered in a famous sale at Hodgson's in November 1966 – the rest was dispersed privately – and the only other so far to match has been that at Phillips in November 1985, when they offered

"An Important Collection of Cricket Books, Pictures and Ephemera". It needed only minimal detective work to discover that it had belonged to the Yorkshire collector, A.E. "Tony" Winder, who had bought much of it from John Arlott in 1980 when the latter retired and moved to Alderney. As will be seen below from the many references to the 'Winder' sale, its catalogue is invaluable as a listing of rare and desirable material, and as a guide to the contemporary market, although such was the range of gems on offer that some realisations did not quite reach the peaks that might have been attained on lesser occasions.

As limited editions themselves the pre-Padwick bibliographies have acquired their own value. Gaston's 12-page offering – of which only 25 copies, on rich paper, were published for private circulation – holds the palm, for copy No. 8 (which belonged to Arthur Haygarth, of *Scores and Biographies* fame and was annotated by him) fetched a remarkable £400 at the MCC Bicentenary auction in April 1987; No.25 had made £190 at the 'Winder' sale in November 1985, and No.1, Gaston's own copy, resided for many years in the Goldman collection. Taylor's *Catalogue*, which for all its obvious outdatedness remains a highly valuable tool because of its notes, comments and valuations, was published in a numbered edition of 50 (although the appearance of apparently duplicated numbers has cast doubts on this figure), and its desirability was reflected at Hodgson's in 1954 in a bid of £41 for No.25. That was an enormous amount for an item of cricketana at that time – for comparison, in the same sale a complete set of *Scores and Biographies*, these days fetching up to four figures, made only £21 – but auction realisations since have slipped to £90 at the 'Winder' sale and £42 at Phillips in June 1986 for No.7 with distressed spine. The presence, since 1972, of a reprint probably accounts for the dramatic reduction.

The Goldman *Bibliography of Cricket*, which was founded on F.S. Ashley-Cooper's *Catalogue of the Cricket Collection of Sir J. Cahn* (1931, realised £140 at the 'Winder' sale), was in essence a catalogue of his collection and until the arrival of Padwick was the most comprehensive available. J.W. McKenzie in his sales list, *A Catalogue of Cricket Literature* (1972), offered a copy for £38, since when a top realisation of £160 has been achieved at the Phillips sale of May 1984. A typescript, updated to May 1956 and of which only two copies are known, reached £70 at the 'Winder' sale. Though not strictly a bibliography one should also mention here C.J. Britton's *Cricket Books: The 100 Best (old and new)* (1929); apart from the standard edition at 2s.6d. [13p.] there was a limited edition of three, with the text printed only on the rectos. A copy in the 'Winder' sale went under the hammer for £160.

Early rarities

Outside *Wisden*, the highest price paid for a single cricketing volume in the 'Winder' sale – and, indeed, in any open-market sale that we have been able to trace – was the £1,800 (£2,007 when buyer's premium and VAT are added) for a copy of the *New Articles of the Game of Cricket*, published by J. Williams in 1775 and containing the code of laws established at The Star and Garter, Pall Mall, the previous year, as well as the less often found laws they superseded. It runs to a mere 16 pages but has a folding frontispiece engraving captioned 'A Representation of the Game of Cricket, Inscribed to

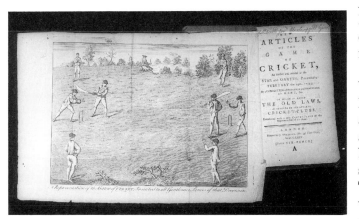

The 1775 edition of *New Articles of the Game of Cricket*.

All Gentlemen Lovers Of That Diversion'. Another version of the new code only, published by J. Ridley, went for £600.

There were other rare early items. We should treat with caution Florio's Italian-English dictionary of 1511, with an entry "Sgrillare, to make a noise as a cricket, to play Cricket-a-Wicket, and be merry", which turns out to have sexual rather than sporting overtones. There were some other early poetical works with but passing references to cricket: a copy of William Goldwin's *Musae Juveniles* (1706), which contains in Latin verse 'In Certamen Pilae', the first account of a cricket match, and fetched £260; also *Cricket, An Heroic Poem* by James Love (his real surname was Dance), the first account of a major match, the famous encounter at the Artillery Ground, London, between Kent and All-England, a second (1754) edition of which fetched £300; and *Surry* [sic] *Triumphant: or the Kentish-Mens Defeat*, a description in verse by the Rev. John Duncombe of Surrey's win over Kent in July 1773, which fetched £260. The last-named work had raised £21.10s. at a Hodgson's auction in 1954.

Many other books, particularly of instruction or scores from the late eighteenth or early nineteenth century, are as rare as hen's teeth and appear on the market perhaps once in a generation, if that often.

Books in this category are W. Epps's *Cricket, A Collection of all The Grand Matches of Cricket, Played in England, within Twenty Years, viz. from 1771, to 1791*, published in 1799 at Troy-Town, a district of Rochester, Kent, and *Rules & Instructions for Playing at the Game of Cricket* by Thomas Boxall, a leading bowler of the day. Neither book in its original form has been sighted on the market since Hodgson's offered the first part of the Goldman collection in 1966, when an Epps made £50 and John Small's copy of Boxall

£58. For once the 'Winder' sale was lacking, although it did offer a modern reprint of the Boxall (2nd edition, c.1802) in the MCC library at Lord's. The British Library has an incomplete first edition (c.1801), lacking four pages, of this work, which was the first practical treatise on the game. Taylor described it as "perhaps the most rare and coveted of the very few contributions to the literature of cricket in the early days" and "worth its weight in gold ... just as much as it will fetch". This was far in excess, at any rate, of the shilling for which Ashley-Cooper once secured two Boxalls and four Lambert *Guides*, "but the days of such bargains are over". Taylor was less effusive about the elusive Epps, criticising it for leaving out many important matches but acknowledging it as "a gem to collectors ... worth at least from 20s. to 30s.". Four or five copies are believed still extant, but a J.W. McKenzie reprint will make it more widely accessible.

The Lambert *Guides* – initially published by Baxter as *Instructions and Rules for Playing the Noble Game of Cricket* and latterly as *The Cricketers' Guide* – were successors to Boxall. Some have viewed them as strongly derivative, for which the publisher rather than the "author" is probably to blame. They appear under the name of William Lambert, the leading professional all-rounder of the period whose career in top-class cricket ended when he was accused of "selling" a match at Lord's, and they are a

A Lambert *Guide*.

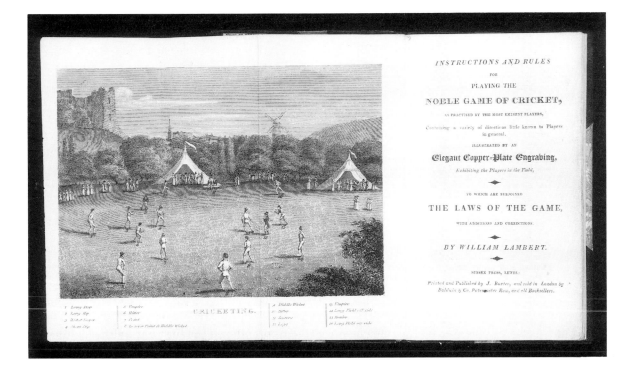

bibliographer's nightmare. Only the first two editions, of 1816 (price 2s.), were dated and it appears that there were 13 editions in all. To confuse the issue further, an edition marked twentieth was the penultimate, while the latest recorded edition, from the early 1830s, is marked the twelfth! Editions 13-19 have never been seen, and are unlikely to have been published, although the story of Thomas Padwick around 1890 finding Lambert's family using a pile of unsold *Guides* to light the fire provides fuel for speculation.

A publication of 1865 states that more than 300,000 of the Lambert *Guides* were sold, but such a tiny proportion has survived that they are highly prized by collectors. A perfect copy of the first issue was offered in 1927 for 9 guineas [£9.45] and the seventh made £8 at a Hodgson's auction in 1954, climbing to £32 in McKenzie's list of 1972. J.W. Goldman, who, remarkably, found one of his copies in a secondhand shop in a German village, claimed in his 1937 bibliography that the later editions were rarer than the earlier, but his view has not been supported by bidders in modern auctions. At the 'Winder' sale a first edition made £380, while a third edition went for £100 and an eighth for £120. Similarly, a first edition in the Batten sale of July 1985 reached £340 and a second edition £200 at Phillips in September 1978, but a fifth made only £150 at Phillips in November 1987.

Standing in rarity alongside the instructional works from this early period are the collections of scores. If Epps is all but unobtainable, the collector can at least aspire to the publications of Samuel Britcher and Henry Bentley, which preserve scores that might otherwise have been lost in the 1825 fire at Lord's. Britcher was official scorer to MCC and his *A List of all the Principal Matches* (later *A Complete List of all the Grand Matches*) of *Cricket That have been played in the Year* [1790-1805] ran to 15 editions. Taylor said it was "doubtful whether a complete run would ever be collected" but valued one at £50 (for comparison, he valued a set of *Wisden* at 18 guineas), and Ashley-Cooper lamented in *The Cricketer* in May 1930 that the books are so scarce "that a collector might well receive booksellers' catalogues for half-a-century without once finding even a single issue". Goldman managed to obtain 11 editions, which fetched £350 at the Hodgson's sale in 1966, but he was outdone by Dr William Brockbank, whose 12 copies are now in the John Rylands University Library of Manchester. David Rayvern Allen pulled together the strands of research, including a census of the 43 known copies, in *Samuel Britcher, the Hidden Scorer* (1982) and suggested that there were at least two sets completed with the photocopies as well as two sets made up entirely of photocopies. One of these photocopied sets came up at the 'Winder' sale, realising £100, but there was a greater gem in the shape of an original edition of 1795, which fell to McKenzie for £680. At Christie's in October 1988 the 1802 edition, ex-Goldman and K.J. Cole, was bid up to £800. As a footnote to encourage collectors overawed by the prices quoted for these and other rarities, we may mention that not long after Allen's monograph was published, he reported that 10 copies of Britcher were bought at a garage sale in Surrey for a few pounds!

By comparison with Britcher, copies of Bentley's *A Correct Account of all the Cricket Matches which have been Played by the Mary-le-bone Club, and all other Principal Matches, From the Year 1786 to 1822 inclusive* have been seen regularly on the market, though less so the supplements published for 1823 and 1824-25; the Goldman collection boasted a complete copy, which had been presented to the famous batsman, Fuller Pilch, in 1833. At the end of the last century copies of the main volume, containing 374 unnumbered pages, were reported at anything between 2s. and 3 guineas, and by 1972 McKenzie was offering one at £38. The price had leapt to £190 at the seminal Phillips auction of September 1978, since when a peak of £240 was achieved at the May 1982 sale. The scarcity of the supplements was indicated at the 'Winder' sale, when the 20-page 1823 supplement realised £120 against £180 for the main book.

John Nyren's *The Young Cricketer's Tutor* (later *Cricketer's Guide*) has long been held to be one of the game's classic works, not least for its account of the cricketers of Hambledon days. It ran to 11 editions between 1833 and 1858 and there have also been seven reprints, which make the text accessible to modern readers at more modest cost than the early editions now fetch.

John Nyren's classic.

While the first edition was valued in *The Cricketer* in 1927 at £2 and McKenzie had one in 1972 at £32, bidding soared to £210 and £170 for copies at Phillips in September 1978; prices have since levelled off to retail at £180 ten years later for the first edition and around £65 for later issues.

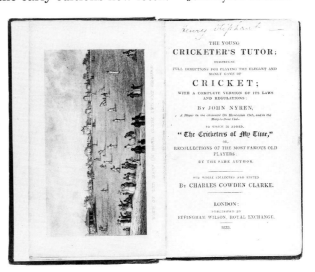

Also much sought-after from this period are the works of William Denison and Nicholas Wanostrocht, the latter a schoolmaster known to all but the parents of his pupils by his *nom de cricket* of Nicholas Felix. Denison, the father of daily newspaper cricket reporting and a parliamentary reporter as well, is remembered for two works: *The Cricketer's Companion*, a precursor of *Wisden* which covered four seasons, 1843-46, and *Cricket, Sketches of the Players* (1846). The *Companions* are rarely seen, only 32 copies in private hands being recorded in 1963, and a copy of the second issue of 1844 soared to £400 at Phillips in June 1988, more than three times the realisation at the 'Winder' sale in 1985. *Sketches*, which has three times been reprinted, is also scarce:

two copies surfaced in the Phillips 1978 sale, setting a high level at £200 and £180, which had advanced only to £220 a decade later in a sale at Christie's. *Felix on the Bat* (see colour page xv), which ran to three editions between 1845 and 1855, was the first cricket book to be illustrated with coloured lithographs and these, not least the frontispiece showing Felix himself flying on the wings of a large bat (the mammalian variety), have always ensured its appeal to collectors. Many copies have been gutted for the prints, thus reducing its availability, but J.W. Goldman insisted in 1936 that there was no need "to pay more than £1 for any edition". By 1972, however, McKenzie was listing a third edition at £28 and, as with so much else, prices really took off with the Phillips auction of September 1978: £280 for a first edition and £240 for a third, roaring to £500 for first editions at the same house in 1987 and 1988.

From this mid-19th century period we must also draw attention to the works of Charles Box – *The Cricketers' Manual* (1848-51), under the pseudonym "Bat", and *The English Game of Cricket* (1877) – and the Rev. James Pycroft's *The Cricket Field*, which ran to nine standard editions (1851-87), an American edition (1859) and a limited edition of 1922, edited by F.S. Ashley-Cooper; the last two of these are least frequently seen. So too Clark's *The Cricketer's Handbook*, of which the so-called tenth edition (of 1849 or 1850) made £260 at Phillips in September 1980, and a similarly titled work published by R. Tyas, of which an 1841 edition fetched £150 at the 'Winder' sale. A particularly lavish work from this period is *The Canterbury Cricket Week* (1865), which has a coloured half-title page and gilt edges and is the first cricket book to contain (sepia) photographs; though it is described as

The tenth edition as sold by Phillips.

"Volume First", no other appeared. Taylor, who says the announced second volume fell through because of lack of support, described it as very rare, valuing it at 35-40 shillings; McKenzie offered a copy for £18 in 1972, and its desirability was further reflected in a peak bid of £260 at Phillips in June 1987.

Lillywhite publications

Four-figure realisations have been achieved for runs of famous multi-edition works, such as : £1,600 for the rare Frederick Lillywhite's *Guide to Cricketers (1849-66)*, knocked down to the brother of the late, lamented comedian Tony Hancock, at the 'Winder' sale, and the £1,000 at the MCC Bicentenary auction of April 1987 for the first 14 volumes of the 15-volume *Scores and Biographies*. Vols. I-IV were published by Frederick Lillywhite and V-XV by MCC, and the fearsome work of compilation was almost entirely done by Arthur Haygarth, although Lillywhite was loath to acknowledge the fact.

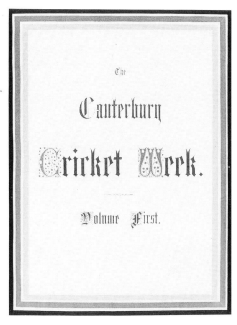

The first and only edition.

Taylor stated that a complete run of the Lillywhite *Guides*, which began life as the *Young Cricketer's Guide* was "perhaps the most cherished of works in connection with the literature of the game" and offered the view that there were "only three perfect sets in existence" – this despite Frederick Lillywhite's claim of a sale of 10,000 copies of the penultimate edition. According to Taylor the sixth edition of 1853 was "of especial value" and a set was worth 20 guineas [£21]; Leslie Gutteridge, writing in *The Cricketer* in 1951 opined that a set, if you could find one, "would be a good investment at fifty pounds". The reason for the paucity of surviving copies is that in those mid-Victorian days few people collected cricket books and most of them must have been thrown away. One of the recorded complete sets belonged to the famous collector, the Rev. R.S. Holmes, and it passed to G. Neville Weston; another was owned by the Rev. C.E.M. Wilson, whose brother and fellow Yorkshire cricketer, E. Rockley Wilson, had a set which included the 1853 edition containing more than 230 pages written out word for word in his own hand by Thomas Padwick. This extraordinary item was offered by McKenzie in May 1983 for £225.

Scores and Biographies, covering the period 1744-1898, is an unparalleled work of reference for those years and is prized by some, among them the leading collector and writer, David Frith, more highly than a set of *Wisden*. Despite their value to collectors now, they were by no means bestsellers: Lillywhite needed financial assistance from F.P. Miller, the

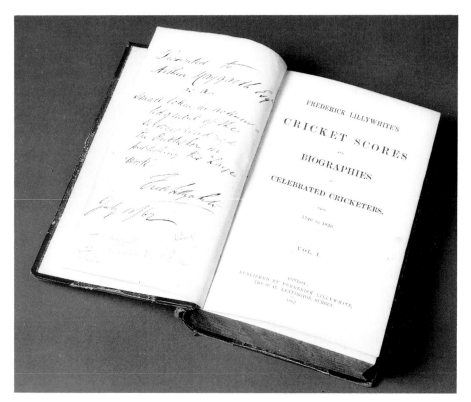

Lillywhite's *Scores and Biographies*: an edition inscribed to Haygarth by Lillywhite '... in acknowledgement of the services rendered...' and also by Haygarth himself reading 'Arthur Haygarth compiled himself the whole of the work vols. 1 to 14 inclusive'.

Surrey captain, to publish Volumes III and IV, but the response from the public was so tepid that Miller is said to have destroyed all unsold copies of the third volume, which, in consequence, is regarded as the rarest – so much so that another devotee, with even more staggering patience than Padwick and the Lillywhite *Guide*, wrote it out, all of nearly 700 pages, a curio that emerged in a lot at a Phillips auction in October 1986. Moreover, MCC were not exactly overwhelmed by purchasers for the volumes they published (Volumes V to XI originally offered at 10s. and later ones at 15s.) and it was as late as the 1960s that they finally disposed of their stocks, which until that date could be purchased at or near cost price at Lord's.

Scores & Biographies has shown a marked increase in value in recent years, progressing from a now-laughable £5 in an advertisement in *The Cricketer* in May 1940 through £21 at a Hodgson's auction in 1954, £120 in McKenzie's first sale catalogue of 1972, £380 at Phillips in May 1982, £650 at the 'Winder' sale and £900 at Phillips in June 1987 (a pencil marking, undated, in Volume I of this set stated, mockingly, to the new purchaser: "£15 complete"). The retail level was established by a McKenzie catalogue in 1988 offering a full set for £1,250, though a bid of £1,200 at Christie's in

June 1989 will have prompted revision. The scores in *S & B* cover the period up to 1878, since when, of course, the student of the game is able to find his English scores in *Wisden*; the biographies, updated by Ashley-Cooper, in Vol. XV, had no comparable source until the publication in 1984 of the *Who's Who of Cricketers*, compiled by Philip Bailey, Philip Thorn and Peter Wynne-Thomas, all members of the Association of Cricket Statisticians. This equally monumental work, which retailed at £30, had a print-run of 15,000 copies, so, though an essential reference tool, it is unlikely ever to acquire a great monetary value.

The name of Lillywhite, still familiar through the outfitters at Piccadilly Circus, London, is found on other sought-after publications. *Lillywhite's Illustrated Hand-book of Cricket* (1844), containing the laws and hints on playing of the game, is extremely rare. There were three versions, topped by the de-luxe, which has portraits of eight cricketers and was published originally at 3s.6d. [18p.]. Taylor rated a perfect copy "from thirty shillings to two pounds" in 1906 and of those we have been able to trace, one belonging to W.A. Bettesworth which with one portrait defective went for 52s. [£2.60] at a 1929 auction, while the price had soared to £290 when Graves and Pilcher, of Hove, offered J.R. Batten's collection in July 1985, and £320 at the 'Winder' sale soon afterwards – when also the middle edition (with portraits of four players at 2s.) reached £80. This book was edited by Frederick William Lillywhite; his son, Frederick, the *Scores and Biographies* man, wrote and published *The English Cricketers' Trip to Canada and the United States*, a thoroughly readable account, published at 4s. [20p.] of the first overseas tour by an English team in 1859 which he accompanied with the printing tent and press that were a familiar feature on English grounds. Taylor valued this at 6s. in 1906 and McKenzie offered a copy at £20 in 1972; however a choice copy, signed by the author and bound in green cloth and gilt, fetched £220 at the 'Winder' sale, while unsigned copies made £110 at Phillips in September 1978 and another – despite having one page replaced by a photocopy – climbed to £170 in May 1982.

Then there are the annual publications, brother John Lillywhite's *Cricketers' Companion*, which ran from 1865 to 1885 (incorporating the Lillywhite *Guide* from 1867) and is known familiarly as "Green Lilly" from its covers, and brother James's *Cricketers' Annual* (1872-1900), known likewise as "Red Lilly", although sometimes orange, yellow or brown would seem nearer the mark; it absorbed the *Companion* from 1886. The "Greens" have usually been regarded as rarer, Taylor valuing a set around five guineas as opposed to 50s. [£2.50] for the "Reds", though the first four issues of the red Lillywhite are rare and it is harder overall to find well-preserved copies of the red than the green in original (as opposed to rebound) state. Despite containing much useful information not to be found in *Wisden*, the Lillywhite annuals have always suffered by comparison with that almanack because, with a handful of exceptions, they do not carry the full scores of first-class matches, hence *Wisden*'s ability to outlast them and, indeed, all other rivals. Recent years have, however, seen renewed interest and the *Companions*, while realising £240 (bound in seven volumes) at Phillips in May 1984, achieved double that in the 'Winder' sale 18 months later and a complete run, some in original covers, made £440 in June 1988. For a set of the *Annuals* a price in the region of £240-£300 has been the norm at auction during the boom of the late 1970s and 1980s, but two bids stand out: a remarkable £500 at Phillips in September 1979 for a set in which 1872-89 were bound in nine volumes and a "lunatic" (according to one leading bidder) £600 in the 'Winder' sale, this set bound in 10 volumes.

Early tour books and 19th-century limited editions

Apart from Fred Lillywhite's account of the inaugural tour to North America, books on early tours have established a niche in the market, with modern reprints by J.W. McKenzie helping to satisfy a demand that cannot be met by original copies. A copy of Argus's (P.E. Reynolds) account of the Australians' tour of 1878 was offered by McKenzie for £150 in 1986, while R.D. Beeston's *St Ivo and the Ashes* (published in Australia, 1883), a light-hearted and illustrated description of the Hon. Ivo Bligh's tour to Australia, on which he was presented with the Ashes urn, fetched £130 at the 'Winder' sale in 1985 and then £240 at Christie's in October 1988. The 'Winder' sale, as ever, also set the benchmark for C.F. Pardon's *The Australians in England 1882* (£110) and *The Australians in England 1884* (£120), while the rarer *The Cricketing Record of Major Warton's Tour, 1888-9*, published by Charles Cox in South Africa, was bid up to £240 and A.B. Price's *English Cricketers at Barbados*, published there in 1897 but not hitherto reprinted, made £260.

While some books may eventually achieve their scarcity by dint of small print runs and low survival rates, others begin life as limited editions, sometimes numbered and circulated only among the author's close acquaintances. Notable among these, though more as a collector's item than for historical value (Taylor: "The compilation contains many defects"), is *Sussex County Cricket Scores from 1855-1878* by Major George Ewbank, who compiled the scores to help while away the hours during his posting in India. Four copies only, it is said, were printed on a small hand press by an army colleague; two are at Lord's, a third went under the hammer for £180 at the 'Winder' sale, but the location of the fourth is unknown.

Positively "popular" editions by comparison were two small works by Lord Charles Russell, *Some Recollections of Cricket* (1879) and *Cricket, 1757-1889* (1890); the latter was published in an edition of 12, the former is assumed to have been so. Taylor valued *Recollections* at 50s., Goldman at 5 guineas, and the only one on the market in recent times, at Phillips in September 1978, rocketed to £250. Again a McKenzie reprint has brought it to a wider public, as too has his production of *Curiosities of Cricket* (1897) by An Old Cricketer, whose identity has been established as that of the early collector and compiler, A.L. Ford. Only 25 copies were issued for private circulation and when No.5 emerged at Phillips in September 1978 pre-sale hype helped to push the price up to an astronomic £580, whence it descended to £300 when resold by the same auctioneers in September 1980. It is

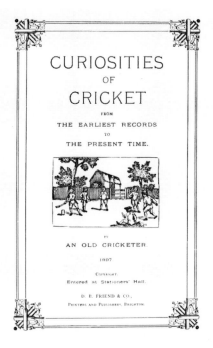 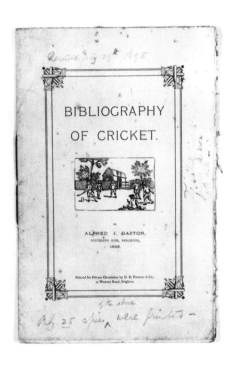

Two surprisingly similar covers.

incidental, but seemingly unremarked elsewhere, that the cover of this work bears a strong similarity to that of Gaston's *Bibliography of Cricket*, published two years earlier; they bear the same imprint, D.B. Friend, of Brighton, who were also Gaston's employers, and an illustration of a game with a two-stump wicket, which is described in Haygarth's hand on the cover of the *Bibliography* as "The earliest cricket picture known to date".

If not all strictly limited editions, though they were published privately in, of all cricketing places, Madrid, we may mention here three detailed statistical works compiled by, of all people, a Spanish nobleman, Anthony Benitez de Lugo, later the Marquis de Santa Susana. A devotee of Surrey, presumably from his schooldays in Croydon, he celebrated the county's first

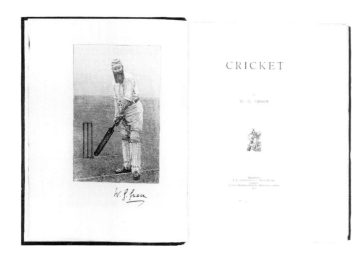

CRICKET

A signed edition of W.G. Grace's Cricket.

championship for two decades with *Surrey at the Wicket, 1844-1887,* followed with *The Surrey Champion* (1895), an exhaustive account of W.W. Read's career, and concluded with *A Summary of Surrey Cricket, 1844-99* to celebrate another championship title. The first made £11 at Hodgson's in 1954 and all three came up at the 'Winder' sale, where they fetched £90, £100 and £80 respectively. Since then *Surrey at the Wicket* has reached £140 at Phillips in June 1987.

Another class of limited edition are those de-luxe versions, published alongside the ordinary book and commanding a premium by way of fine binding, coloured plates, author's signature, etc. Thus, while *Cricket* by W.G. Grace (1891), might be had of a dealer for £3 in 1972 and even in 1988 for only £24, the de-luxe, large paper edition of 652 numbered copies, signed by Grace and valued over the years at 2 guineas (1898), 5 guineas (1956) and £28 (1972), now commands prices in the region of £200-£260 at auction and £300 retail. There were also 10 presentation copies, bound in white vellum, and No.1 went under the hammer for £350 at the 'Winder' sale. Similarly, Ranjitsinhji's wide-ranging *The Jubilee Book of Cricket* (1897) ran into several basic editions; it was published at 6s., could be had for £1 in 1972 and even now may be had for under £10. However, there was a de-luxe edition of 350, issued at 5 guineas with 22 additional plates, and this reached a new level of £140 at Christie's in October 1987.

From the very end of this period we must not forget a publication by a name etched on the minds of English-speaking children, J.M. Barrie, the creator of Peter Pan. Less widely known was Barrie's passion for cricket. He was not very good at the game – "I can bowl so slow that if I don't like the ball I can run after it and bring it back" – but he ran a social team called the Allahakbarries (an adaptation of the Arabic word *allahakbaris*, God help us, to accommodate Barrie's name as founder of the club). In 1893 he issued 12 copies of *Allahakbarries CC*, one of which fetched £58 at Sotheby's in 1938, and followed this with *The Allahakbarrie Book of Broadway Cricket* for 1899 to commemorate that summer's match in the Worcestershire village. Fifty copies of this were printed and were treated protectively by their author. In response to Taylor's application for a copy, Barrie wrote: "The pamphlet you refer to is of no value, and as it is strictly private I must ask you to forgive my not sending you a copy." To which Taylor added rather icily: "The fame of the author has, nevertheless, made this book valuable."

This was confirmed in a general books auction at Sotheby's in April 1928, when bidding, spurred by the worldwide repute of the author, soared to £108; this was to remain the largest amount paid for a single volume on cricket for many years. The Goldman sale at Hodgson's in 1966 saw £70 paid and at the 'Winder' sale in 1985 a copy was bid up to £450. The purchaser was Tim Rice, who, with his own club, the Heartaches (who have issued their own almanack since 1975), likens himself to Barrie as a cricketer "without talent who obtained a few bob from writing".

Twentieth-century books

Straddling the turn of the century and an active figure until his early death in 1932 was F.S. Ashley-Cooper, an authority on cricket whose output, according to the type of special obituary notice in *Wisden* usually awarded only to outstanding players, amounted to 103 books and pamphlets and 40,000 biographical and obituary notices. Ashley-Cooper assembled a superb collection of books and pictures, which was bought by Sir Julien Cahn shortly before Ashley-Cooper died. A typescript listing of the collection fetched £140 at the 'Winder' sale and a *Bibliography of the Cricket Works of the late F.S. Ashley-Cooper* (1933), compiled by another noted student of the game, G. Neville Weston, in an edition of 100, offered at £15 by McKenzie in 1972, was bid up to £100 at Phillips in June 1987. The works of Ashley-Cooper are keenly-sought by collectors; some of the pamphlets, apart from *Noteworthy Events of 1905* at £18, were offered for between £3 and £6 in 1972, since when we note a realisation of £80 at Phillips in September 1980 for *Cricket and the Church* (1904, an edition of 30); and, at the 'Winder' sale, £90 for *Eton v. Harrow At the Wicket* (1922, edition of 100), £85 for *Curiosities of First Class Cricket* (1901, edition of 100) and £80 each for *Feats, Facts and Figures of 1899* (20 copies) and for *Cricket 1742-1751* (1900, 15 copies). A particular Ashley-Cooper curiosity, too, was *Cricket and Cricketers* (1907), published in Philadelphia, which was then, albeit in its late stages, an outpost of first-class cricket. J.W. McKenzie listed a copy at £160 in 1986 and the same year had an even rarer *Indian Cricket Chronology and Memorabilia* (1911), A.J. Gaston's copy from an edition of 30, at £350.

To the true bibliophile it is the appeal of the book itself that counts rather than the monetary value of his library – although it would be an unusual collector indeed who did not draw some satisfaction from the rising worth of his volumes. While it remains the case that limited editions of particular interest in subject or author show the greatest rises, the investment success of all limited editions is not guaranteed. Take the case of Sir Pelham

Warner's *Imperial Cricket*, which in its de-luxe form is probably the most luxurious cricket book ever published (Gaston in his bibliographic supplement published in *Wisden* 1923 recorded that the book was "Now a Remainder" without specifying whether it was the de-luxe, subscribers' or ordinary edition). Goldman called it "the Magnum Opus of Cricket" and it offers a comprehensive review of the game throughout the Empire. It was published in an edition of 100 at 25 guineas, an enormous sum in 1912, when, in cricketing terms, it would have bought 21 of the highest-quality cricket bats; the equivalent outlay required for the bats in 1989 would be in the region of £2,000 and while it might not be a totally valid comparison to expect Warner's book to be worth that amount, the realisation of £150 at Christie's in June 1988 represents a paltry return – although few, if any, of those who made the initial outlay are likely to be around to lament the fact! As a footnote, we might add that copy No.1 was presented to King George V, who in turn gave it to the stationmaster at Sandringham, from where, in due course, it migrated to Australia.

Warner's book is perhaps the exception which proves the rule, for all other limited editions for which market trends can be established have shown dramatic rises. Distinction must, of course, be drawn between the de-luxe type of limited edition and the booklet/pamphlet type intended for limited or private circulation, although both command a premium. From the first half of the century we must also mention in the de-luxe class the edition of 230 of Roland Wild's biography of Ranjitsinhji (1934), a copy of which was bid up to £320 at Phillips in June 1987, and the lavish 434-page *The Noble Game of Cricket*, illustrated from pictures, drawings and prints in the "Mustard Millionaire" Sir Jeremiah Colman's collection, much of which passed to MCC after his death in 1942.

The Noble Game of Cricket: a lavish production during wartime austerity.

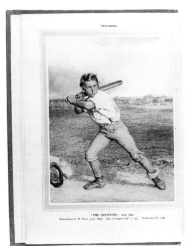

Notwithstanding the constraints of war-time it was published in 1941 by Batsford at 5 guineas in an edition of 150, of which 100 were for sale, and has from early on been a target of collectors. One made £52 at Sotheby's in 1947, another £42 at Hodgson's in 1954; at the start of the modern boom in the September 1978 sale at Phillips the new price level was set at £460, which, despite the protestations of one outstanding collector that the book was "undervalued", was not topped until a bid of £520 in June 1988; realisations in the interim ranged between £380 and

£460. We have also noted that in 1986 McKenzie offered for £350 a unique proof copy, annotated by the publisher. One of the notes records: "165 copies returned after sewing. Hold balance for instructions."

In modern times the names of John Arlott and Irving Rosenwater feature prominently among the pursued limited editions in both categories. To take the "luxury" class first, Rosenwater's *A Portfolio of Cricket Prints*, published in 1962 at 35s., was being offered in 1989 at £110, while his *Cricket Books: Great Collectors of the Past*, privately published in a sumptuous edition of 200 in 1976 at £10, realised up to £65 in sales at Phillips during the mid-1980s. Arlott, in collaboration with the best-known of all cricket writers, Sir Neville Cardus, was responsible for the handsome *The Noblest Game* (1969). The standard edition at 5 guineas was accompanied by a special edition of 100 in green morocco at 15 guineas, which by 1980 was being offered at £100 and at Phillips in June 1987 a copy soared to £280; in 1985 even the ordinary edition was being offered at £55, encouraging soon afterwards a disappointing reprint, which retailed at £25. There have been too since 1977 several limited editions of Cardus anthologies or reprints but despite the author's reputation the wide availability of his works has meant there has been no appreciation in value. Of far greater appeal to the collector, however, are original Cardus manuscripts, for which 28 pages on Victor Trumper and 34 on S.F. Barnes were bid up to £340 and £320 respectively at the 'Winder' sale.

In the limited-edition pamphlet class, highly prized are Arlott's works on players (mainly from his native and beloved Hampshire) and great events, published in numbers sometimes as low as 12; many of these are offprints from the county's annual handbook. The Sevenoaks cricket bookseller, Martin Wood, secured something of a bargain with a bid of £320 for a collection of 19 of these, including a memoir of the collector and Hampshire captain/secretary Desmond Eagar, in the 'Winder' sale; his success was apparent at Phillips in June 1987 when 14 Arlott limited editions, offered as separate lots, totalled £900. Best price was £120 for *The Master* (1979), a 20-copy offprint of the appreciation of Jack Hobbs in *John Arlott's Book of Cricketers*, while biographical cameos of Horton, Ingleby-Mackenzie, Marshall and Rogers, all of Hampshire, reached £75 each. Eagar himself produced a limited-edition *Readers' Guide to Hampshire Cricket* (1964), which made £60 at the 'Winder' sale and £55 at Phillips in June 1986. H.S. Altham, another man with strong Hampshire connections, was the subject of *The Compleat Cricketer* (1960) in an edition of 25 by the distinguished cricket correspondent, E.W. Swanton, which achieved £70 at Phillips in June 1987, though the same copy slipped to £50 in October 1988.

We are led, finally, to wonder whether those who have expended huge sums on some lavish modern tomes will have no satisfaction beyond the albeit great one of possessing a beautifully produced book. We have in mind publications such as a de-luxe edition of 100 of R.L. Arrowsmith and B.J.W. Hill's *The History of I Zingari* (1982), which was published at £100, remaindered at £45 and then £65, but went under the hammer at the 'Winder' sale for £85; an edition in quarter morocco of 500, signed by the artists and the selectors of the subjects (Bailey, Benaud, Cowdrey and Laker) of *The Lord's Taverners Fifty Greatest* (1983), which sold at £60, and a leatherbound edition of 452 (Bradman's highest score and signed by the Don) of *Australian Cricket* (1983) by Jack Pollard, for which £125 was the asking-price in Britain where only 50 copies were available. We shall watch too for the £100 MCC members' edition of 100, leather-bound and gilt-edged, of Tony Lewis's *Double Century* (1987), commemorating the club's bicentenary and a £225 leather-bound edition of 200, signed by Sir Donald Bradman, of David Frith's monumental *Pageant of Cricket* (1987), with its 2,000 illustrations and 120,000 words covering the game from its infancy. Success, however, seems assured for the largest cricket book hitherto published, the hand-bound *Men in White: The History of New Zealand International Cricket 1894-1985* in an edition of 1,200 which measures $21\frac{1}{2}$in.x16in.x2 $\frac{3}{4}$in. and cost £420 (see colour page xv). It was sold out before publication, almost exclusively in New Zealand, and its appearance on the market will be watched with great interest.

Overseas publications

Unlike England no other country has a full-time professional cricket circuit; unlike England no other country has managed to sustain a cricket annual such as *Wisden* for even half a century of continuous publication, let alone the century and a quarter that it has been published. The two facts cannot be unconnected. There exist, however, several highly prized and extremely rare early overseas publications, notably from Australia.

The first Australian annual was the Biers and Fairfax *Australian Cricketer's Guide for 1856-57*, which recorded the first inter-colonial match in 1856 between New South Wales and Victoria as well as offering instruction on the game. Published in September 1857, the inaugural *Guide* (see colour page xv) ran to 72 pages and cost half-a-crown [13p.]. Two further issues followed, retitled *Cricketer's Guide for Australasia* and *Australian Cricketer's Guide*, but poor sales and mounting losses brought about its demise. A copy of the first issue surfaced at Phillips in September 1980 when it went for £240 and the price climbed to £380 at the 'Winder' sale. The year 1877 saw the emergence of two new but also short-lived publications around the time of the inaugural Test match between Australia and England: *Conway's Australian Cricketer's Annual* from John Conway, a first-class cricketer who was to manage the 1878 Australian touring team, and W.O. Whitridge's *South Australian Cricketer's Guide*. Copies of the two *Conways* fetched £200 at Phillips in May 1984 and the first issue alone was bid up to £190 at the 'Winder' sale; while the first of the *Whitridges*, 1884-85, made £85 at the Sussex CCC sale in May 1980; a lot comprising all three issues achieved £280 at the 'Winder' sale, and the first two were knocked down for £150 at Christie's in June 1989.

Long-running by comparison at five issues was the *Australian Cricketers' Guide*, edited by Henry F. Boyle, an early opening partner of the "Demon" Spofforth, and David Scott; three years of this went under the hammer for £260 at Phillips in May 1982 and then a full set (1879-80 to 1883-84) in the 'Winder' sale pushed up to still higher levels at £650. After a decade virtually bereft of annuals the *Australian Cricket Annual*, edited by John C. Davis, who in the preface to the first issue (1895-96) referred to the lack of "an Australian Annual, after the style of WISDEN or LILLYWHITE". Sadly Davis's efforts ran to only three issues before going the way of their predecessors as collectors' items, for which £220 was paid at Christie's in October 1988.

In other parts of the world early cricket annuals achieved greater longevity. The *Barbados Cricketers' Annual* ran for 20 issues from 1894-95 to 1913-14. Taylor wrote of it in 1906: "The first number was sold out within a few weeks of publication", and it was only through the ransacking of one of the Government offices that he could complete his set. We have, though, observed no set for sale, although 14 issues made £280 at the 'Winder' sale.

In South Africa the *Natal* (from 1888-89 *South African*) *Cricketers' Annual*, edited for all but one number by J.T. Henderson, ran successively for eight issues from 1884-85 to 1891-92 and then resumed for a further two, 1905-6 and 1906-7. Winder, in a fierce contest with McKenzie, secured the full run for a fantastic £1,510 when Phillips offered them as three lots in May 1982; but "McKenzie's revenge", as it was described by David Frith in *Wisden Cricket Monthly*, came at the 'Winder' sale when the dealer scooped them all as a single lot for £440.

Also worthy of note is *The American Cricket Annual*, compiled and edited by Jerome Flannery between 1890 and 1901. Taylor noted that "a conflagration has ... made them valuable" and the full set which made £130 at the 'Winder' sale rose to £340 at Christie's in June 1988.

County annuals

The most collectable of the English county annuals, mainly published by the county clubs, are from Hampshire, Kent, Surrey and Yorkshire. The Phillips sale of June 1987 was a good indication of demand and Hampshire led the way, with a remarkable £780 bid for 75 plus a few duplicates of the various *Hampshire Cricketer's Guides, County Cricket Club Guides* and *Handbooks* between 1885 and 1985. The Christie's sale of October that year included seven of the *Guides* between 1923 and 1934, which fetched £120.

The early years of the *Yorkshire CCC [Annual]*, which is still published as a hardback although all other counties have long since been in paperback, are rare, so a lot containing the first 13 issues (1893-1905) and a further 40 up to 1976 commanded £500 at Phillips in the June 1987 sale, which also saw £160 bid for 50 Kent annuals between 1893 and 1975 and £150 for 63 Surrey yearbooks between 1888 and 1982. In 1972 McKenzie offered a near-complete run of 75 Surrey volumes (1886, the third issue, and 1888-1971) for £75. It is interesting to note, too, that Mike Marshall, the guiding light of the Essex cricket museum and library at Chelmsford, has a full set of the county's handbooks from 1927, but the county do not. Marshall, however, is doing his best to rectify that.

Periodicals

The best known of the early magazines is *Cricket*, often subtitled "A weekly record of the game" from the words on its title-page; this is not, however, strictly accurate, for although it was published weekly in April to September, i.e. during the English season, it was monthly during the rest of the year. *Cricket* ran from May 1882 to December 1913 at 2d. throughout its run of 949 issues and 32 volumes – for comparison the price of its post-First World War successor *The Cricketer* was 6d. in 1921, 1s.3d. in 1954 and, after the modern inflationary times, £1.20 in 1989 – and has become increasingly a target for collectors. Taylor wrote that a bound set of *Cricket* (to 1906) was "honestly worth from ten to twelve guineas, the earlier volumes being exceedingly difficult to meet with". In 1972 McKenzie offered the first 29 volumes for £300; and while at auction in the early 1980s it was possible to pick up the middle years at around £8-£10 a volume, the 'Winder' sale in November 1985 once again established new levels, with a complete bound run making £850. In May the following year at the Buckley sale a run lacking only, and a little surprisingly, 1909, made £580 and at Phillips the next month 19 volumes between 1883 and 1913 were bid up to £450, since when some of the middle years were going for over £40 each at Christie's in June 1988.

Precursors of *Cricket* were the *All England Cricket and Football Journal* (1877-79) and, more directly, the *Cricket and Football Times* (1878-81). They are exceedingly rare, but a lot containing two volumes of the first, with inscription from A.D. Taylor to Ashley-Cooper, went under the hammer for £220 at the 'Winder' sale and, writing in his own *Cricket Quarterly* in 1969, Rowland Bowen announced that, despite deficiencies at the time in the

Facing Page
The two established monthlies and two more recent additions to the newsagents' shelves.

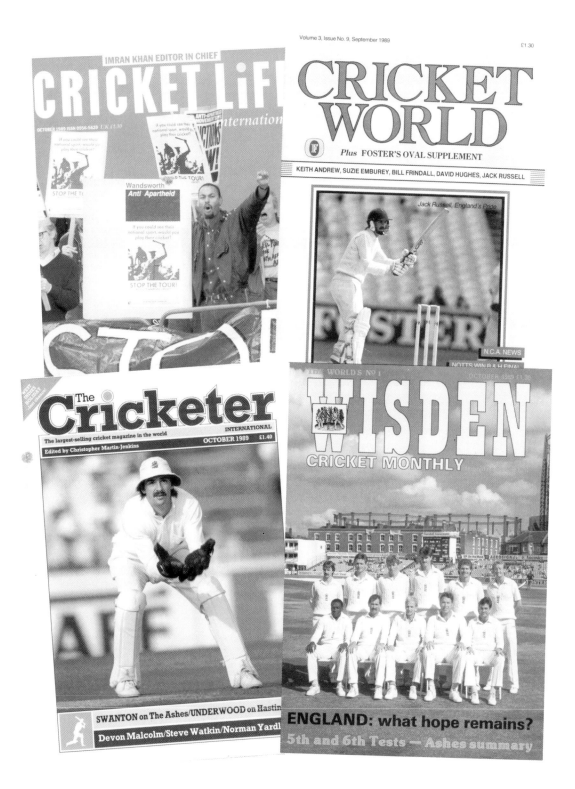

British Library and Lord's collections, he had assembled a full run of *Cricket and Football Times*. A short lived contemporary of *Cricket* was *The Cricket Field*, which survived for only four years (1892-95) but did include Gaston's articles on bibliography. In 1972 McKenzie offered a set for £25, which had climbed to £200 at Phillips in June 1986.

The longest-running periodical is *The Cricketer*, founded by P.F. (later Sir Pelham) Warner in 1921, though not until its 53rd birthday did it pass the previous senior, *The American Cricketer*. The latter was published in Philadelphia from 1877 to 1929 and Taylor, writing of course in 1906, said: "A complete run of the above is worth a considerable sum. I have never heard of a set changing hands either in England or America." The best we have noted, inevitably at the 'Winder' sale, was a collection comprising 36 of the 52 years, which was bid up to £480. As for *The Cricketer* itself, several runs more or less complete to that date have been seen: 1921-71 at £200 in McKenzie's 1972 catalogue; 1921-78 from McKenzie at £475; 1921-81 at the 'Winder' sale bid to £580; 1921-84 to £500 at Phillips in June 1986; and 1921-60 to £380 at the Buckley sale in Bristol the previous month.

From 1960 to 1973 *The Cricketer* had a rival in *Playfair Cricket Monthly*, which has not caught on among collectors, but a more recent publication, *Wisden Cricket Monthly*, has been more keenly pursued. The first eight volumes fetched £70 at Phillips in June 1987 and the price reflects the rarity of the first issue of June 1979, which is known to have changed hands for £25. Finally, and perhaps appropriately, for its editor, the unorthodox Rowland Bowen, liked to have the last word, we should mention his often scholarly *Cricket Quarterly*, which appeared from 1963 to 1971 and explored many areas untouched by the more popular journals. The *Quarterly* was available only on subscription and it is not now easily found. A complete run made £80 in the J.R. Batten sale at Graves and Pilcher, Hove, in July 1985 and the first seven volumes (what happened to the last?) went under the hammer for £120 at the 'Winder' sale.

CERAMICS AND SCULPTURE

Ceramics

Normal prerequisites for connoisseurship, central to the collection of pottery and porcelain – such as taste, instinctive "flair" and a constant study of documentary pieces – barely impinge upon cricketing ceramics, so limited are the most prized objects.

To see a 1955-56 display advertisement by Drury & Drury, well-known dealers in historical sporting objects, suggests that the range of precious and refined Old English pottery with a cricket theme in circulation three decades ago differs little from the better ceramics which leak on to the market today. In the Drury cabinet were those perennial favourites, the larger Staffordshire figures claimed to represent Parr and Caesar (see colour page xvi), now collectively valued at £1,600 for the pair, together with five blue-ground mugs of various sizes with raised white figures of Box, Clarke and William Lillywhite, plus the same figures in white enriched with silver lustre on a buff ground, all dated c.1847.

For the best part of a century, primarily up to the outbreak of war in 1939, cricket has been associated with china and pottery designs. To pick a figure out of the air, there must be about 2,000 different pieces known, the great proportion of them genuine junk of impeccable provenance.

Symbolic of their era, Box, Pilch, Lillywhite, Clarke and Cobbett appeared in such profusion that they set the scene for a virtual cottage industry. Based on Charles Hunt's 1841 engraving of these cult figures, they were to be found on glazed earthenware cream jugs, mugs, tankards, tea caddies and tobacco jars. As they passed into the shades, so the industry turned to W.G., Ranjitsinhji and Giffen, joined eventually by Hirst, Rhodes, Hobbs, Barnes, Sutcliffe, Bradman, Verity and Woodfull. As prime examples of this genre, that great collector Rockley Wilson picked up for 6d. in Sheffield in the 1930s two china jugs decorated with portraits of Sutcliffe and Kilner. The Sutcliffe jug was filled with apricot jam and the Kilner with raspberry.

The bewildering diversity of commemorative pottery available to the collector was shown at the May 1984 Phillips auction, when lots were disposed of featuring Box, Lillywhite, Pilch, Grace, Giffen, Ranji, Fry, Barnes, Richardson, Haigh, Denton, Kilner, Sutcliffe, Wood, Verity, Bradman, Woodfull, Greig and (Greg) Chappell.

Time, however, has taken a fearful toll of the best pieces, and "fakes" – artificially aged by having the pieces removed from the kiln too quickly with glaze crackle effects, augmented by the application of liquid Vandyke Brown, and some of the colouring worn off with an abrasive like wire wool – can still fool the unwary buyer. The search and joy of possession or the discovery of a long sought-after rarity are ingredients which influence the collector, but in so narrow and rarified a field, as much depends on condition as on boom periods when abnormal prices rule, and the whims of richer buyers can send the price up to a level out of all proportion to normal value.

Cricket and the artistic traditions of the eighteenth century are seen to best advantage in one of the very first known examples of porcelain ever manufactured in England. This is a *sucre* (sugar) bowl with a cricket scene, dated 1745-60, illustrated in *Glorious Innings* (Melbourne, 1987) and annotated "one of the mysterious 'A'-marked group of English porcelains". Its delicate rococo ornamentation is derived at a remove from the Hayman scene familiar to cricketana collectors, but, sadly from an English point of view, this historic souvenir forms part of the marvellous Tony Baer collection housed at Melbourne Cricket Ground.

The same collector, who may be said to have cornered the ceramics market, was the underbidder for a unique punch bowl, made in Jingdezhen around 1786 and purchased by MCC in 1984. Rated by Tony Baer as even more important than the sugar bowl, it bears three copies of Hayman's 'Cricket in Marylebone Fields' and is unique. No other piece of Chinese export porcelain showing cricket is known. As purchasers or recipients of the MCC Christmas card which used this bowl for illustration purposes will know, on the inside appears a fighting vessel flying the pre-1801 Union Flag, and, it is suggested, the name "Thirks" on the poop may be an error by the Chinese copyist for Thirsk, the birthplace of Thomas Lord. It is a romantic and attractive notion that the bowl was commissioned by Lord himself.

Another celebrated Melbourne acquisition is a Leeds creamware jug showing the frequently reproduced depiction of the match between the Earls of Darnley and Winchelsea at Lord's c.1790. Founded in 1774, Leeds pottery is a deep cream in colour and typical subjects were prize-fighting, horse racing and any scene of general conviviality. Leeds ware is often difficult to distinguish from Staffordshire.

Staffordshire ware

The merging of porcelain and earthenware styles in Staffordshire factories produced a cheaper porcelain containing bone-ash, representing a great practical and commercial advance for English pottery.

Underglaze blue printing was a favourite English decoration in the first half of the last century, especially fashionable after about 1820, and Staffordshire earthenware so decorated forms one of the largest classes. One of the alarmingly few remnants which relate to cricket is a pottery set of a soup tureen (which also has a fishing theme), a China teapot, and a white and

cobalt blue large oval meat strainer dish, decorated with a transfer in blue of the scene taken from a picture entitled 'A Game of Cricket at Windsor Castle'. Better known to collectors as 'Windsor Castle with Cricket in Eton Meadows', this 19¼in.x15¼in. dish, dated c.1820, carries no maker's name but is stamped with the words "Metropolitan Scenery, Windsor Castle". An example fetched £440 at Phillips in April 1979.

Staffordshire pottery mugs, symbolic of their time.

As the entry from the official MCC catalogue indicates, an example of the dish was presented by Henry Ling in 1946. Descriptions of this choice piece by Ron Yeomans and Rockley Wilson tally, except that Yeomans preferred to call it octagonal. Wilson, in turn, claimed that his "gravy dish" was identical to a china teapot in the pavilion at Agar's Plough, Eton College.

Goodwin and Harris meat dish.

A dish which sounds uncannily similar formed part of the Tony Baer collection, and at Christie's in June 1988 a "Goodwin and Harris shaped oval meat dish", 19in. wide, embellished with the same scenery, just made the lower estimate of £500. Regarding the date of manufacture, it may not be inappropriate to mention that J.E.Goodwin, art director at Wedgwood from 1902 to1934, issued a variety of designs, some based on 18th-century originals and, in 1908, reproduced the powder-blue of the Ch'ing period as ground colour on blue porcelain.

A genuine rarity is the mug by Fletcher and Co. of Shelton, the putative date for which coincides with the revival of hard-paste porcelain at the end of the 18th century in Staffordshire. The setting is again the Darnley-Winchelsea match, and when sold in July 1914 for 43 guineas [£45.15] it was then, according to Ashley-Cooper, the largest sum ever paid for a single cricket item. Tony Baer procured either this or a very similar mug at the Lord's sale in 1987. Slightly cracked, but now expertly restored, it is a beautiful piece, not inordinately overpriced at £1,100.

The ending of the Napoleonic Wars in 1815 marked the start of an unblushingly commercial period of vulgar taste, the market swamped with pieces made and sold on a local basis at fairs, sporting fixtures and other gatherings. This, the heyday of Staffordshire ornaments of a homely nature, has been frequently portrayed as the last true English folk art – art for the people rather than for galleries and museums – naïf, colourful and essentially peasant in style.

Those most in demand are the flat-back figures of the middle and late Victorian period. These hollow, press-moulded, earthenware pieces, with their simple oval bases and distinctive flat-backs, were intended for viewing from one side only, and, as such, slotted neatly into the vogue for chimney pieces in Victorian homes. Cheerful and endearing in their simplicity, they were produced at inordinately low cost, the painters often children aged seven or eight, working long hours under dreadful conditions.

Queen Victoria's wedding in 1840 prompted a surge in the public demand for pottery portrait images of heroes of the day, and the choice of subjects offers a social history of the last century in a robust and quaintly happy way. Cricket was only slowly becoming popular with the class of people likely to buy these anonymous, mass-produced figures, which may partly explain their paucity. Cricketana collectors also have to compete with the wider spectrum of Staffordshire collectors, many of them from the United States.

Production of similar, though inferior, figures continues to this day. Among the earliest known is the set of three spill-holders depicting members of the All England XI (see colour page xvi), taken from engravings of the three cricketers which appeared in the *Illustrated London News* of 1843, accompanying a report of the Kent and All England match; Lillywhite, the outstanding exponent of round-arm bowling, batsman Fuller Pilch of Kent, and behind the stumps, Thomas Box of Sussex, the best of his day.

Among a number of pieces comprising a pair of cricketers, two of the most desirable are the duo generally known as the 'Non-Striker' and 'The Batsman', both 6½in. high (see colour page xvi). Simply modelled, but brightly coloured, the bowler wears pink trousers, a pale orange jacket with red braiding and button, and the non-striking batsman a dark blue jacket and bright orange cap. 'The Batsman' has a yellow hat, white trousers and a brightly coloured red check jacket. The wicketkeeper is clad in pink trousers and white jacket.

The *Price Guide to British Pottery* (Antique Collectors Club, 1979) notes that "Cricketing subjects are always popular even when, as here, unidentified", and gives a guide of £160-£200 for a single figure and £400-£500 for a pair. The manufacturer responsible for the pair was Thomas Parr of Burslem, between 1840 and 1850, and all evidence suggests that while condition is crucial to value, these prices are obsolete.

In his excellent article in the *Essex CCC Handbook 1983*, collector Mike Marshall discusses other Staffordshire figures for the period c.1850-65, remarking that they are generally single figures of batsmen and bowlers, varied both in size and colouring and unidentifiable as particular players. The figures stand square-on, the wicket to their right and to the left a discarded jacket. Drury & Drury had a couple of these figures for sale 30 years ago at well under £50 a pair.

In keeping with the Victorian tendency towards sentiment, other designs use children, either as a boy and girl pair, or single figures of the boy holding a bat and the girl a ball. One of these companions to the boy figure, size 6¼in. and dated c.1850, in a colourful glaze with gold leaf decoration, was included in a Burlington Gallery catalogue at £145. The young lad, in grey glaze, the same size, but dated c.1860, rated £5 more. In Mike Marshall's collection 'The Boy Batsman' sports a yellow bonnet, a blue jacket braided in gold and pink trousers. His bat is green in colour and the stumps orange. Also 6¼in. tall, 'The Boy Bowler' has pink trousers, a royal blue jacket and a green wide-brimmed hat. The catalogue from First Impressions takes it a stage further: "He is standing beside a black set of stumps ready to bowl underarm. For some obscure reason the ball ... is coloured green." Today the pair would probably fetch around £400, whereas a rarer figure of the batsman, smaller in size, has been known to sell for more than £500.

Possibly the rarest grouping of all was made c.1860. The pair of batsmen are dressed in military uniform reminiscent of the officer corps in the Volunteer Rifles. Both figures are standing to one side of the stumps, bat in hand, while one also has a ball. Estimated at £150-£200, one lot, 26cm. tall, realised over £2,600, despite restoration, in November 1984. The single figure of an officer in a similar uniform is equally rare.

As any illustrations demonstrate, a suspension of credibility is imperative when contemplating the rare and cherished figures widely believed to represent George Parr, of Nottinghamshire, and Julius Caesar, the diminutive Surrey batsman. Two sizes are known, 13in. and 10in., but since not all catalogues indicate size, valuation can only be tentative. Suffice it to say that they are rare and, if authenticated as mid-Victorian, fetch high prices.

The bowler, Parr, is modelled standing, ball in hand, wearing a red and blue peaked cap and orange sash, backed by a jacket, stumps and cricket bat. Replicas of both of them, or even "fakes" purporting to be originals, have been produced for many years now, sometimes catalogued "Staffordshire style", although even modern copies have a certain value. Replicas of the bowler are much harder to find, and word has it that they were only made for a few years by a single small pottery.

A pair (no size given) realised £290 at Sotheby's in October 1976 (dated c.1865); another pair, same limitation, £420 in May 1982, while an advertisement in July 1976 quoted an asking price of £500. The larger-size pair went for £600 in April 1979 and for £1,600 at a non-cricketing Christie's auction in 1988. Julius Caesar on his own was worth £360 in 1981 and a Parr (c.1865 and damaged) went for £100 at Phillips in October 1988.

Five plaster reproductions of Caesar and a small version of Parr found a buyer at Christie's for £190 in June 1988, and among a number of Staffordshire-style reproductions, a pottery figure of W.G., 24cm. high, managed £22 at Phillips in June 1986. First Impressions produced a strange hybrid figurine, 9½in. tall, the head of W.G. modelled on the body of Caesar.

Cylindrical Staffordshire mug with village cricket match.

"The Champion" wears an MCC cap and, for all we know, this may yet become a collector's piece as an "illustration of the way potteries had to scrape the barrel".

Earlier Staffordshire cylindrical mugs and bowls vary in size and colour. One of two examples recently to appear was printed in puce with vignettes of a village cricket match, 6in. high and 6¼in. in diameter, the handle printed with cricketing symbols (Christie's, October 1988, £750). The other, less than 3in. high, has two separate views of a village match and is printed in black, heightened with splashes of green, black and puce; it sold for £130 at the same sale.

Modern Staffordshire cricketing tankards, with transfer-printed scenes can be had for £30, while 'Another Six', supplied in a box, was advertised at £4.95 in 1988. A pair of hand-painted earthenware figures of a batsman and bowler, believed to depict W.G. and one of his brothers, was marketed by Hesketh Concept in December 1979 at £70.

Most voguish, however, retaining a strong hold on fancy yet still surprisingly cheap, are the Staffordshire jugs and mugs decorated with relief figures in white of Clarke, Box and Pilch, all dated from the 1860s onwards. Two colours are known: cream and silver lustre on an ochre ground and a dark blue glaze background. The jugs are infinitely the more rare; two have been noted for sale, both dated c.1860, 7in. high, one in each colour and both from Burlington Gallery at £275.

Notwithstanding private sales and the inevitable non-disclosure, when it comes to mugs we question whether many more than two dozen exist. Fewer than twenty silver lustre mugs have been auctioned in the past decade, and depending on size it would be fair to argue for £85-£100 as an average price. The waisted blue shape has details of its handle more frequently itemised – either strap or scroll – and again there are two sizes. Based on realisations since the Phillips auction of 1978, only a gravely impaired specimen would slither much below £200 at the asking.

Royal Doulton ware

Florid in colour and opulent in shape, Doulton stoneware is seen by some as Victoriana carried to excess, but the jugs and vases have long been a favourite with collectors (see colour page xvii). Granted a royal warrant in 1901, the firm of Doulton of Lambeth and Burslem was founded in 1815 and has since then produced a steady stream of vases and the like which show an astonishing taste, with elongated and distorted forms embellished with bizarre decoration.

Terracotta was extensively used for figures, ornamental flasks and jugs from the 1830s, while from the 1860s particular attention was paid to stoneware, with decorations conceived, carved and modelled by students from the Lambeth School of Art. Their products were unique and invariably signed by the artist, either by name or monogram. A feature of Doulton stoneware and other Lambeth ceramics is that, seemingly, fakes are non-existent.

A veritable "Rembrandt in clay", the name of George Tinworth is inseparable from Doulton. Born in 1843, the son of a drunken wheelwright and victim of a repressed childhood, Tinworth was in many respects illiterate, his reading confined to the Bible and related texts. He was the first artist employed by Doulton and worked from their Lambeth factory, seated on an upturned chimney pot with a battered table to support his modelling board. From this unprepossessing background, he became a prominent modeller in red earthenware, turning out captivating religious decorations, canoeists, mice chessmen and "frogs at cricket", two male figures.

Highly intricate designs were produced, often for quite mundane objects, a notable example being the 'Cricketana' vase by Tinworth (see colour page xvi). Its cylindrical body stands some 15in. high and is adorned with medallions in relief of cricketers, including W.G. It was purchased from Phillips for £2,200 by a private buyer in 1979, and its reappearance was set to be a highlight of the Pilkington sale at Phillips in September 1989. One of

Tinworth's truly exquisite creations is a pale brown silicon figure of a boy cricketer, 8½in. high. Silicon was a Doulton patent, featuring a matt, high-fired body and special impressed mark, "D.S. Lambeth". The process was in use between 1880 and 1912 and the figure has been dated c.1900. Two were snapped up at a Sotheby's Billingshurst auction in 1988 for between £800 and £900 each.

Boy cricketer by George Tinworth.

The characteristic swollen, barrel-like body shapes, Art Nouveau decoration and ribbed strap handles render Doulton stoneware jugs and vases unmistakable. Strongly coloured shades of brown with either blue/green or brown/blue ornamentation on green or brown bases predominate. Three cricketing figures stand out in white relief, assumed to be trios of Ranji, Grace and Giffen and of MacGregor, Woods and Abel. Mike Marshall's copy has a family connection in that his wife is a distant cousin of Giffen, while another collector, Ron Harries, avows that his jug, of a true elliptical shape, has portraits of William Gunn, Woods and M.C. Kemp (wicketkeeper).

They are attributed to the period 1890-95, and, dependent on the degree of distress, auction prices have ranged from £85 in May 1982 to a current expectation of £380. About ten have been noticed on sale in the past decade, usually given as about 8½in. high, with an occasional smaller version. One "in perfect condition" (6¾in.) was advertised in 1973 seeking offers over £45, and another, marred by a hairline crack to the handle, realised over £170 in May 1984, just below estimate.

A step outside the norm, Burlington Gallery had a Doulton stoneware ewer for sale at £495, printed in black and featuring Giffen, Ranji and W.G. contained within medallions, their names inscribed below a decorated border.

Doulton mugs have the same applied mouldings in white surrounded by stylised floral designs, but the shape takes on a slimmer, more waisted form. They are highly important and infrequently seen, so that even in a restored condition, as the June 1988 Phillips auction revealed, the realisation can be in the £260 region.

A complete departure in style is typified by the W.G. Grace "in full cry" set of jugs, beakers, and rounded three-handled loving cups or tygs. Common to most of them are cameos of batting, bowling and fielding, showing a direct hit on the stumps. The handles are usually modelled in the form of a cluster of bats, stumps, shoes and a ball, the whole surmounted by a hat. The loving cup shown in Stephen Green's booklet, *Cricketing Bygones* (1982), is dated 1880 and has completely different handles from the one sold at Phillips in October 1986. The latter, a salt-glaze three-handled silver-rimmed loving cup, designed by John Broad, had applied white relief figures against green

Left An unmistakable and unique Doulton item, the Surrey vase, designed in the floral style of the period (1902), engraved with the initials of eleven Surrey cricketers, probably by the players themselves.

Far left Royal Doulton tobacco jar.

backgrounds, the remainder of the cup brown in colour. Imperfections reduced the price to £260, but for anything else like this, registered at the Patent Office in 1880, one would be hard put to find a vendor prepared to relinquish ownership for under £500.

Likewise, a Doulton marked tobacco jar with a blue, grey and brown lid, showing six cricketing scenes depicted again in white on brown glazed backgrounds, dated c.1890 and 5in. high, would today attract bids around £220.

The first cricket mug in the modern Royal Doulton Collection is the hand-painted and decorated Hampshire cricket "character" piece, a celebration of the centenary of county cricket at Southampton. Priced at £25 in a limited, numbered edition of 5,000, it became available on 21st June 1985, the day before the county match against the visiting Australians. What we would all regard as a true limited edition is represented by the cream-glazed stoneware tankards commemorating Surrey's 1952 championship victory. They were inscribed "Surrey County XI Cricket Champions 1952 captained by Mr. W. Stuart Surridge", with facsimile signatures, and apart from those given to members of the team, only a dozen others were made.

Bisque and Parian figures

Biscuit pottery, from which Parian ware evolved, was itself an imitation of marble, and this dead white, brittle and thick-walled, rather granular porcelain allowed the upper middle classes the illusion of marble statuary in their homes.

Bisque figures of batsmen and bowlers resemble glazed Staffordshire but are finer in detail. Production continued into the 19th century, mainly at the works around Derby, but also on the Continent. Nevertheless only a handful have been seen at auction in the last few years. Amusing small bisque figures of youthful cricketers (5in.), heightened with wash colouration and entitled 'Out First Ball', realised £45 in 1978 but fell to £32 in May 1982. W.G. Grace, wearing an MCC cap, pads, and holding a wooden, detachable blade, the whole 23.5cm. high, was worth £160 in June 1988. German coloured figures of a young bowler and his female companion trailing a bat (11in., but no date given), realised £180 at the same date.

Parian ware

More ivory in tone than biscuit porcelain, lighter and more pleasing on the eye, unglazed white porcelain was a deliberate imitation of the Elgin Marbles from Paros, a Greek island in the Aegean Sea, designed to cater for those unable to afford true marble. It has the same silkiness in feel and appearance.

Introduced in the mid-1840s, following researches after the formula for creamy Derby biscuit, its allowance for free modelling enabled makers to produce remarkably lifelike portrait busts of people in the public domain. New technical resources of science and machinery further encouraged potteries to keep abreast of fashion changes, one of which seems not to have been cricket, as relatively few pieces are known to posterity.

The statuettes of a batsman and bowler, modelled by T. Fowke in 1867 for the Staffordshire firm of Minton, adorned the cover of a Brighton Museum publicity leaflet in 1989, while a pair of Continental coloured figures of another batsman and bowler, 8in. high, were sold at Christie's in October 1988 for £110.

For some, however, the *pièce de résistance* is the beautifully worked figure of a boy reading, leaning back against a tree stump, his bat beside him, cast by the sculptor George Halse and manufactured by Copeland in 1874. Some 16in. tall, 'Young England' is breathtakingly detailed, right down to the pages of the book, and, with his sister figure, must assuredly fetch over £1,000 today. Several have been located – one in the Memorial Gallery at Lord's, a couple in the Pilkington collection offered by Phillips in September 1989, while one more is the pride and joy of Mike Marshall. The figure of a young batsman by William Kent, of Kent and Parr, potters at Burslem from c.1880 to 1962, is another exquisite piece. It forms part of a boy and girl duo,

'Young England'
manufactured by
Copeland in 1874.

W.G. Grace figurine, without bat.

Robinson and Leadbetter bust of W.G. Grace.

the boy with a bat in his left hand and a ball in the right, while the girl symbolises tennis. Its auction price in 1983 was £360.

Manufacture of Parian ware diminished in the 1890s, although some production continued well into this century, notably by the firm of Robinson and Leadbetter. Works from this Stoke-on-Trent pottery are often underestimated by the general collecting public, possibly because they did not specialise in Parian until 1865, a decade after it came into existence. This specialisation gave their work an extra refinement and fidelity to the subject, and few characterisations of W.G. have as much punch and vigour as the full-length figurine (12in.) made about 1880 of the "Old Man" standing at ease, left hand on hip, bat held casually with the right. Anything about Grace prior to 1890 or very soon after tends to be rare, and its value shifted from £650 to £750 in the years 1984-87, achieving a dramatic £1,000 at Phillips in October 1987, even allowing for the absence of the bat.

Robinson and Leadbetter busts are 7-9in. tall, stand on an integral square base with a recessed neck between portrait and base, and enjoy a cream, fine surface, soft to the touch. The name of the person is usually impressed on the base, generally to the front. Their bust of W.G., overall 29cm. tall, is magnificent, well worth the £440 it made at auction in May 1984.

Belleek ware

A singular use of iridescent glazed Parian is a feature of products from the Belleek factory in Co. Fermanagh, Ireland, founded in 1857 and still with us today. Perforated decoration and basket-like strips mark their products, and it was said of them in 1878 that they "have an almost unearthly appearance of liquid beauty". Whether this tribute stands the test of time is a matter for personal opinion, but based on a viewing, the spill holders with a cricket theme, dated about 1880, have undeniable appeal. Besides the one at Lord's shown in Stephen Green's booklet, few others are known in private collections.

Royal Worcester

Irrespective of their cricketing context, the sensitive and lovingly fashioned treasures created by Royal Worcester would, by any standards, rank in the *premier grand cru* class. First among equals could be the rare and splendid 6¾in. high tyg, dated c.1890, which exceeded £2,600 at the Geering & Colyer auction of March 1979.

Aspects of collecting
Left Victor Trumper in an imagined pose at Sydney Cricket Ground, a Roger Marsh painting specially commissioned by John Hawkins. **Below** Masonry from the Oval perimeter and the old Lord's Tavern, rescued by David Frith. **Bottom** The life and times of P.G.H. Fender (Sussex, Surrey and England) from the collection of Mike Smith.

Above 'Schoolboy's Treasure' by Rupert Dent c.1890, cricket and other pastimes.
Right Portrait of a young boy with a cricket ball in his hand rather than the more usual bat, by John Russell, pastel c.1800.
Below Mid-19th century match in Sussex, signed Wm. Drummond, oil.

Above Not a Riviera café but the tea gardens at Trent Bridge, Nottingham, in its centenary year, 1938, as depicted by Arthur Spooner. The young autograph hunter studies his latest capture, perhaps the figure at ease in the centre; this is almost certainly Sir Julien Cahn, president of Nottinghamshire CCC and wealthy patron of cricket.
Left A modern view of the Trent Bridge ground by Roy Perry.

Above Critical eyes from 'The Boundary Bench', a 1901 watercolour by James Mathews.
Left 'Caught Out!', another village scene, by W. Bennett, 1907.

Facing Page
Top A scene from the 1882 'Ashes' Test match at The Oval adapted and reproduced in a vivid, three dimensional effect.
Bottom A more recent Australian touring team in a rural setting: Jocelyn Galsworthy's 'Gemini v IZ (Australia)' at Sunningdale, June 1988.

Above Rural cricket scene by James
Stark (1794-1859), a member of the
Norfolk School.
Left 'The Veteran Bowler'
by Alexander Hohenlohe Burr
(1837-99).

Facing Page
Modern art
Top 'Caught and Bowled' by LeRoy
Neiman, a rare excursion by an
American artist into the English
national game.
Bottom Lawrence Toynbee's
'Catch at First Slip' captures the
split-second activity of cricket.

Above The distinctive features of
C. Aubrey Smith, cricketer and
Hollywood actor, by Bill Prosser.

Left Sunil Gavaskar, the record-
breaking Indian opener, in William
Bowyer's 1989 Royal Academy
portrait.

Facing Page
David Gower, captain of
Leicestershire and England, in
repose and action, by Mark Ferrow.

Below N.B.F. 'Tufty' Mann, the
South African left-arm spinner,
captured at his typewriter in a
painting by Dr William Craib.

Naïf School
Above 'Douglas Jardine playing Yorkshire CC 1934' by Joe Scarborough.
Left Larry Smart's 'Cricket Match at St Mary's Grange, Wiltshire'.
Below 'A Summer at Riverfield' by Jean Stockdale: Grace, Gower, Botham and hot air balloons in an Edwardian time warp.

'Out for a Spin'
Ranjitsinhji, F.S. Jackson (centre), C.B. Fry and the parrot, Popsey,
in a Lanchester, as imagined by Roger Marsh.

Above 'Village Cricket', chromolithograph by John Ritchie, 1855, of a village match in southern England, once thought to be Hambledon.

Above An unusual hand-coloured lithograph, c.1835, of a village match with, apparently, a wicketkeeper at each end.
Right Print of Fuller Pilch (the Kent and England batsman), engraved by Adlard.

Facing Page
Top left Gilbert Jessop, famous for his fielding as much as his fast scoring, as seen by Albert Chevallier Tayler.
Top right E. W. Dillon (Oxford University and Kent), one of the latest and rarest cricketing prints from *Vanity Fair*.

Below William Clarke (the Nottinghamshire bowler), another Adlard engraving.
Right A selection of prints from the vast range of cricketing subjects.

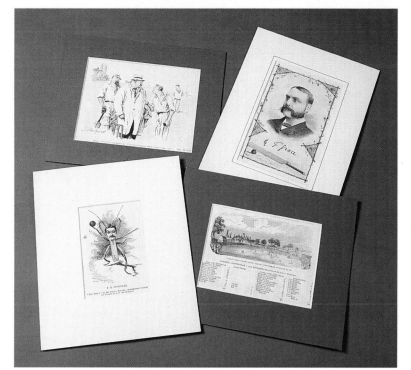

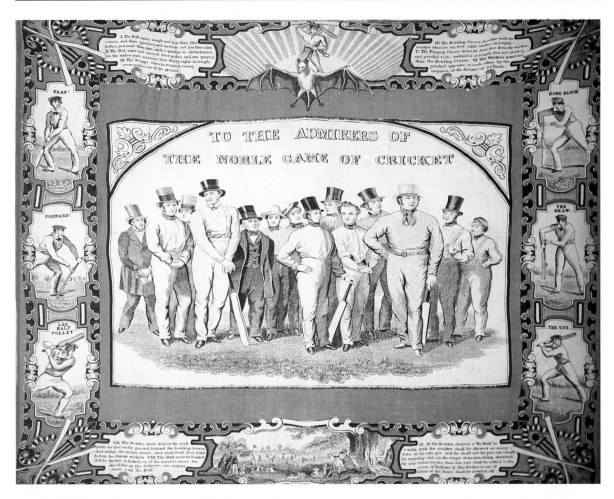

"W. G."

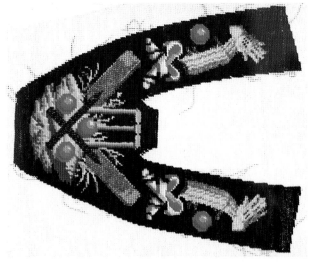

Top Cotton handkerchief depicting the All England XI of 1847, based on a watercolour by Nicholas Felix.
Left The rare Stevengraph ribbon of W.G. Grace, 1896.
Above Slipper design with cricket motifs embroidered in beads and wools.

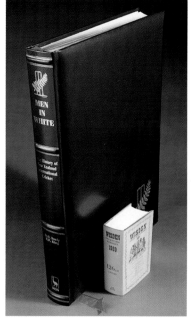

Above The largest cricket book in the world, the special edition of the New Zealand work *Men in White*. **Left** Rare early Australian annuals. **Below** *Felix on the Bat*, the first cricket book with coloured prints.

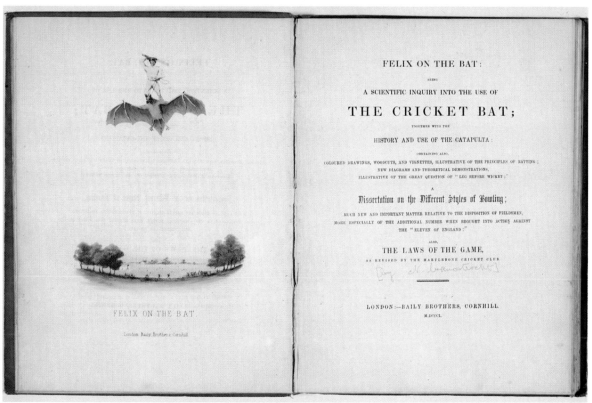

Valuable Vases
Above Royal Worcester gift to Don Bradman in 1938, marking his three consecutive double centuries against Worcestershire.
Below The Royal Doulton 'Tinworth' adorned with cricketers.

Staffordshire ware figures
Above right Batsman and bowler, believed to be Julius Caesar, of Surrey, and George Parr, of Nottinghamshire.
Right Spill-holders depicting William Lillywhite, Fuller Pilch and Thomas Box.
Below right 'The Batsman' and 'The Non-striker'.

Above Count André d'Aquino's
1983 portrayal of Dennis Lillee.
Above left A group of popular Royal
Doulton stoneware.
Left The set of six porcelain figures
based on E.P. Kinsella's much
reproduced urchin.
Below Crested china miniatures.

Above Minton tile from the
'Elizabethan' series.
Right Ceramic plaques showing
Duckworth, Hobbs and Chapman.

Right A modern collage, in wood and
paint, 'Ranji and the Champion' by
Howard Carter.
Below E.P. Kinsella's comic
character seen here, unusually, on a
plate.
Bottom Minton pieces for MCC's
150th anniversary.

Above Stained glass window from the home of R.G. Barlow, the Lancashire and England batsman, rare among first-class cricketers as a collector. It depicts Barlow at the crease, accompanied by his colleagues, A.N. 'Monkey' Hornby and wicketkeeper Dick Pilling, and is now located at Old Trafford.
Left Enamel box commemorating the MCC Bicentenary.

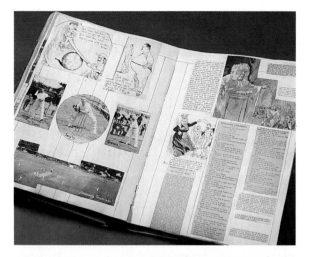

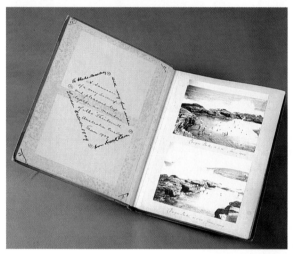

Top left Scrapbook kept by A.E. Stoddart during the 1894-95 tour of Australia.
Above left Photograph album presented by Frank Laver, manager of the 1909 Australians, to each member of the tour party, in this case, Charlie Macartney.
Top right London Transport poster advertising the last Test match before the Second World War.
Centre right Autograph albums, part of nearly every cricket collection.
Bottom right Admission tickets, membership passes and other cards.

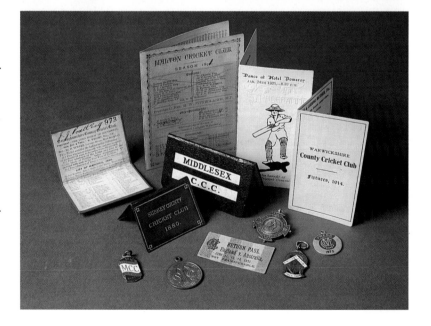

BRYLCREEM

keeps **your**
hair **right**
in the
picture

For soft, lustrous hair, use Brylcreem! For handsome, healthy hair, use Brylcreem! Brylcreem makes your appearance a smart one, wherever you go, whatever you do. Massage your hair with Brylcreem every day and see how its pure oils give your hair that vital, well-cared-for look. Brylcreem controls the hair without excessive oiliness, because the oils in Brylcreem are *emulsified*. That means *clean* grooming. That means lasting hair-health. Ask for Brylcreem — in tubs 1/8, 2/6, and 4/6 or handy tubes 2/6.

BRYLCREEM is *emulsified* for clean grooming

Cricket has been a popular theme for advertisers of a wide range of products over the years.

Times are changing and so are we. *K* Shoes.

Sumptuous menus – and dinners too, no doubt – in honour of Jack Hobbs (left) and (below) the 1896 Australians, guests of the Earl of Sheffield at his Sussex country seat.

Facing Page
Victorian belts and buckles, a feature of the MCC Bicentenary sale.

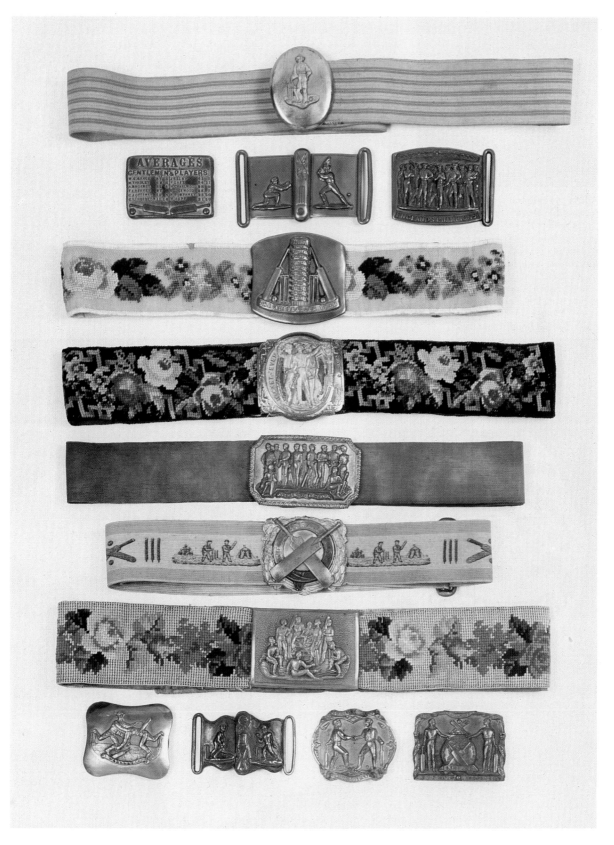

Above Sweatband worn by the formidable Dennis Lillee.
Right Limited issue ties: (from left) journalists on 1946-47 tour of Australia; '25 club' tie for journalists covering at least that number of Tests; 1935-36 Australian tour of South Africa.
Below Cricket merchandising by Kerry Packer, including the white ball used for floodlit matches.

Above and below Cufflinks and boot bag belonging to J.R. Mason, of Kent and England.

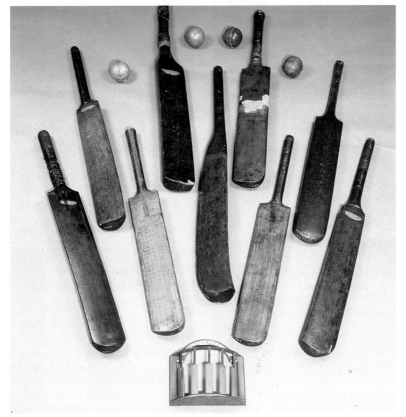

Above left Balls with which the legendary Tom Richardson, of Surrey and England, took all 10 Essex wickets in 1894 and eight Australian wickets in his last Test in 1898.

Left Bats spanning three centuries (and scoring many more) featured at the MCC Bicentenary sale.

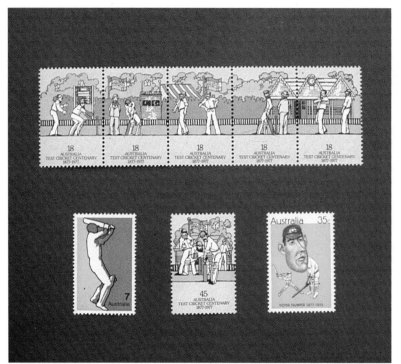

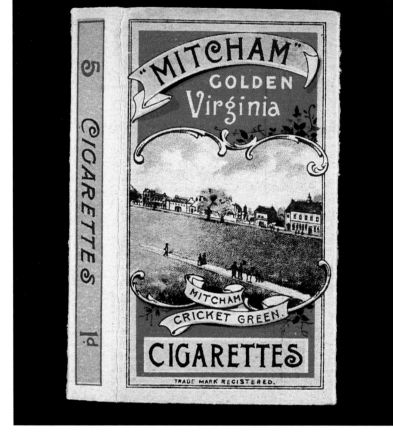

The growing field of cricket philately
Top left Australian stamps including Centenary Test commemoratives and the peerless Victor Trumper.
Top right The first cricket stamp, from a Portuguese colonial post office, and (above) its earlier 'Cinderella' counterpart from a German football club.
Left and below Cigarette pack art.

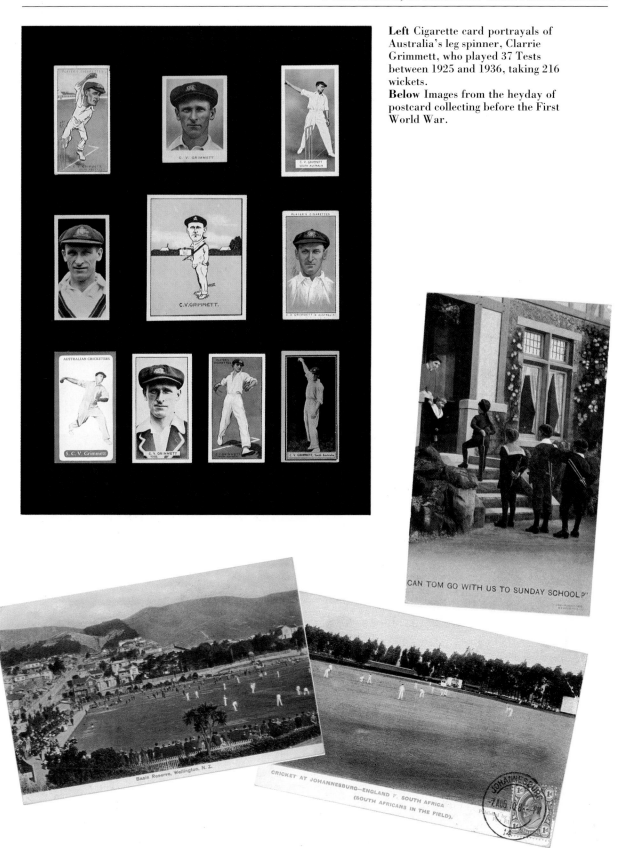

Left Cigarette card portrayals of Australia's leg spinner, Clarrie Grimmett, who played 37 Tests between 1925 and 1936, taking 216 wickets.

Below Images from the heyday of postcard collecting before the First World War.

Right Indoor cricket: a bagatelle game.
Below The 'Creation' of a cricketer by Michael Brownlow – with apologies to Michelangelo.
Bottom Detail from the 7-foot square Howardswood ground developed with full amenities, including treatment room, museum, art gallery, library and floodlights, over 30 years by Peter and Mark Coombs.

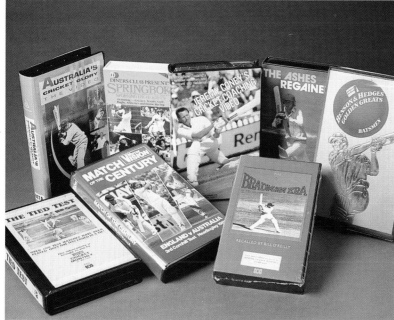

Above Not all cricketing records are statistical.
Left A new collecting avenue: video cassettes from home and abroad.

Above and right Expressions of greeting, modern and Victorian. **Top right** Imaginative packaging combining cricket and chocolates. **Centre right** Not quite what it appears ... a replica of the Ashes urn sold at the MCC Bicentenary auction.

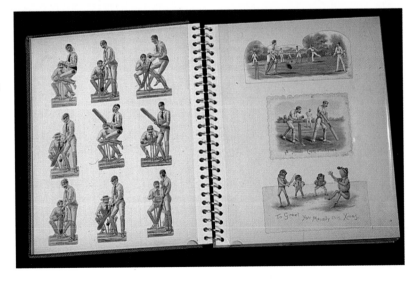

Right Dr W.G. Grace on a
fantasy banknote/admission ticket
to Birnbeck Island, near Weston-
super-Mare, with Sir Frank Worrell
on a 1976 Barbados banknote.
Below Vintage cricket wine.

Above Illuminated address to
A.J. Webbe, of Middlesex, from his
Winchester College opponents in
1910.
Left The sounds of cricket, privately
and commercially recorded.

Right A fan presented by
leading perfumiers Eugene Rimmel
to ladies at Eton v Harrow matches
in the 1870s.
Below An array of blazers and caps
from the Roger Mann collection.

The choice of Edward Salter, principal artist at the factory from the 1880s until his death in 1902, to decorate this singular piece of porcelain was inspirational, but, sadly, no records survive in the Dyson Perrins Museum, Worcester, to indicate who actually commissioned it. Not a word familiar to most of us, 'tyg' is derived from the Anglo-Saxon word 'tigel', meaning a tile or brick, or indeed, anything made of clay. The tyg under discussion, a wide, double-curved cup with loop handles, is further ornamented with motifs of crossed bats and stumps, gilt and cream patterned vine leaf and bunches of grapes as border decorations. Like so many other outstanding pieces, it migrated to Australia.

The late Frank Lees, a leading antiques specialist dealer in Worcester, supplied Don Bradman (as he then was) with a confidential valuation reckoned to be quite staggering even in those days, for a most handsome gift to the greatest batsman of them all from the Royal Worcester company in 1938 (see colour page xvi). The vase ($13\frac{1}{2}$in.x$6\frac{1}{2}$in. wide) commemorates his three consecutive double centuries in opening matches at Worcester in the 1930s and is said to be "beyond price". It is predominantly royal blue in colour and the central picture, based on a photograph published in *The Times*, is a painting of the famous view of the county ground with the cathedral in the background and "The Don" at the crease. The vase was designed by C.B. Simmons, the company's art director, and the panel was painted by Harry Davis, a company artist now looked upon as one of the greatest ceramic painters of

Royal Worcester tyg.

this century and a pupil of Edward Salter. A few years ago an earth tremor almost shifted it over the edge of the shelf on which it was standing at Bradman's home in Adelaide on to a brick hearth below; the vase is now on display at the South Australia State Library.

Harry Davis is also linked with a Ranjitsinhji dinner and dessert service of Indian scenes associated with his seat, Jamnagar. Said to be part of a planned 200-piece dinner service, only seven dessert plates ($9\frac{1}{2}$in. in diameter) are believed to survive and these had not been heard of since Davis completed the commission in 1925, although they had been in regular use in the Ranji household in England. This Harlequin service was ordered in 1923 and a trial plate of this date, depicting La Khota Khota, is in the factory still.

It is regarded as one of the greatest and most important commissions ever undertaken by Royal Worcester, yet in a specialised sporting auction at Christie's in 1988 three different dessert plates failed to find a bidder at estimate of £1,500-£2,000. A corresponding set of English scenes was shipped out to India to remind him of the countryside around Staines, of which he retained fond memories. We have to assume a more hectic scramble were these ever to come up for sale.

Royal Worcester were also behind two other major commemorative items. The 150th anniversary of Thomas Lord's third ground in 1964 was marked with a presentation bowl, designed by Neal French, painted by Harry Davis and gilded by Ivor Williams. This unique piece was presented by Lord Cobham, Lord Lieutenant of Worcestershire, to MCC in a Long Room ceremony on 5th October 1965, and Lord's has also one of only three wine coolers specially made to commemorate the centenary of Anglo-Australian cricket in 1977. Dyson Perrins Museum has one other, while the third, appropriately enough, forms part of the Melbourne Cricket Club collection.

Casket designed for the Derbyshire CCC Centenary.

Royal Crown Derby

Information about the Royal Crown Derby bone china casket, given to Derbyshire County Cricket Club to raise funds in their centenary year of 1970, is inordinately difficult to find. Copies of the promotional literature alone take some digging out, yet the casket took six months to produce and has some particularly fine raised gilding by John McCloughlin, the head gilder.

The county club colours of brown, turquoise and gold are used overall, with the background colour the distinctive Derby mazarine blue. On the lid is the inscription "Derbyshire County Cricket Club Centenary 1870-1970" and emblazoned on either side are the club badge in gold and the Derbyshire coat-of-arms, also in gold. Designed by the Royal Crown Derby art director, Brian Branscombe, it measures 11½in.x8½in.x8½in. and features also vignette scenes and cricketing symbols on the panels. Sold publicly at Chatsworth on 9th August 1970, it failed to reach the £1,000 estimate and was bought privately at a lower figure. A limited edition of 500 'Duchess' sweet dishes was also issued at the time, priced at £15.15s. [£15.75] and a five-petal trinket tray limited to 100 and priced at £2.5s.9d. [£2.29].

Kinsella and Continental pottery

As cricket's popularity spread, and aping the British became a fetish among certain classes, European potters seized on this and capitalised also on the English market.

An acquired taste for some and effortless favourites with others, the set of six porcelain "cute" figures based on the Irish artist E.P. Kinsella's comic 'Cockney' boy cricketer (see colour page xvii) can be awkward to complete. Authentic in detail and made in Germany in the early 1900s, of the various cricket postures 'Out First Ball' and 'The Hope of his Side', both approximately 13cm., are the most commonly seen, and at Phillips in October 1985 averaged, according to condition, around £50 each. Three of the figures were adjudged a good buy at £65 in late 1961, and 'The Catch of the Season' is still considered to be the hardest to come by. Another German figure, plagiarised after a Kinsella design, entitled 'The Boss' (14cm.) realised £32 at a 1982 Phillips auction.

Unlike the Kinsellas, though, Continental figurines in cricket attire are only moderately well received. The clothing is too garish and the shots are not to be found in any of the coaching manuals. A boy and girl pair, decorated in colours upon oval bases, she holding a bat and he with cap and ball, attracted £160 at Phillips in June 1986, while a smaller, 19cm. figure of a boy batsman, chipped, made only £30 at Bonhams the following year. Burlington Gallery, on the other hand, had an unusual 19th-century batsman (10in. high), in blue glaze, shown with cap, scarf, waist-kerchief and holding a bat, for sale at £285. A W.G. Grace spill vase, produced on the Continent c.1890, copied from English period pieces and showing three studies of him batting, 6¼in. high, was to be had for £395 from the same gallery.

Transfer-illustrated shaving mug.

Transfer-printed pottery

Pre-First World War transfer mugs are always in demand. Heavy and rugged-looking, they have a feeling of solidity so typical of that era. A most agreeable example is a Campbellfield Pottery Company cylindrical mug in brown and red, with a full length portrait of W.G. at Lord's, and, as the catalogue notes, bust portraits of Ranji and (probably) George Giffen. This appeared at Christie's in October 1988, and for an extremely well known collector to have been agog over it suggests a rarity in keeping with its realisation of £580.

An especially fetching item also seen recently was a transfer shaving mug with lid, depicting two scenes printed in red on a bulb shape, one of cricket, the other of soccer, with cricket repeated on the lid. Marked F&R Sports, dated c.1865 and 5¼in. high, it was one of several transfers with a cricketing

Transfer-printed mug,
1905, depicting
George Hirst and,
on the reverse, his
famous partner
Wilfred Rhodes.

theme from Burlington at between £150 and £370.

A uniquely Yorkshire flavour is attached to a trio of notable items. Burlington had on offer at £245 a very rare white glaze mug, dated c.1906, with transfer portraits of 'David Denton, Always a Favourite' and 'Schofield Haigh, one of Yorkshire's Heroes'. Ron Yeomans had a two-handled pot mug struck in 1933 by W. "Potman" Ellis of Leeds, with on one side a picture of Hedley Verity and on the reverse some of his records up to that date, while a Royal Falcon ware mug, $4^3/_4$ in. high, marking Verity's 15 wickets in the 1934 Lord's Test, realised £100 at Christie's in October 1987. Another Yorkshire item recorded by the same enthusiast was a mug made in Hunslet in the early 1920s. It showed Herbert Sutcliffe and his father W. Sutcliffe. Herbert had no inkling of its existence when shown it, and one wonders how many exist.

Prices between £220 and £270 were paid in 1981 for blue ground pottery jugs, printed in colours, bearing portraits of Bradman, Sutcliffe and Woodfull (13.5cm), while a set of Minton cream glazed commemorative pieces prepared for the MCC 1787-1937 anniversary (see colour page xviii) have been tipped by a top-flight collector to set new levels of value. Adorned with MCC colours, few appear at auction, and Henry Ling's advertisement in *The Cricketer* (1949) of the set of three, together with the glass goblet issued at the same time, all for £8, sets one to thinking furiously, for at Phillips in June 1987 the jug made £150, the tankard £130, the mug £140 and the ashtray £60.

Goss china

William Henry Goss and his son Adolphus were the first to capitalise upon the Victorian urge in the 1880s for day trips and excursions producing inexpensive souvenirs in the shape of miniature china ornaments painted with exact heraldic crests. Production ended in 1939 when average prices were around the shilling [5p.] mark, and Gossware is easily identified by the firm's name and distinctive trade mark of a goshawk with outstretched wings.

Although higher prices are now being signalled, they are still underrated except for the small china ornament bearing the Hambledon crest, crossed bats and the date 1750. More widely known are the miniature china cricketers' bags, about which some dealers tend to get a mite sniffy. Ron Harries, a leading collector in Hertfordshire, has augmented his Gossware with an extraordinary array of these tiny bags from Griffin China and elsewhere (see colour page xvii). They vary in size, but all bear the crests and insignia for towns, villages and hamlets across the land, and beyond the confines of the British Isles to some obscure French resorts. A group of five fetched £30 at Christie's in October 1987.

Plates, Plaques and Tiles

Coalport plates

Massive tomes have been devoted to Caughley and Coalport china, yet any cricket connections, although important, are provocatively minimal. Local pre-occupations and country sporting roots normally ordain the choice of any commissioned factory decoration. Where cricket was never prominent, as in Shropshire, and there were no major Victorian landowners to underwrite appropriate pieces, then leading Caughley and Coalport factories seem not to have bothered.

By the end of the century, however, non-local money and management became involved at John Rose's Coalport factory, and the intrusion of the name of W.G. Grace seems to have represented one facet of this. Unfortunately, no one can be absolutely definite about this, and nothing directly relevant to any other Coalport pieces apart from the legendary plate was ever seen or heard of by the late Chris Pilkington, whose enormous enthusiasm for both Coalport and cricket was just about equal.

The facts about W.G.'s 'Century of Centuries' plate are well known. In 1895, to mark this record, Grace commissioned a plate from the Coalport China Company. According to the company's archivist, only two of the original 16 are known to have survived; Lord's has one and the other is on loan to the Ironbridge Gorge Museum from a private collector. However, the display caption in the Memorial Gallery at Lord's states that 18 plates, the more usually accepted number, were manufactured. They were commissioned by S.J. Kepple & Sons, of Bristol, for a dinner given by Grace on 22nd January 1896, to 17 members of the Century Club in return for the hospitality given to him by the Club in June 1895 in honour of his hundredth century. Each diner retained his plate which bears on the reverse a seating plan for the occasion. Irving Rosenwater (*Journal of the Cricket Society*, Spring 1975) wrote that ten were still in existence, and the appearance of one on the

W.G.'s original
'Century of Centuries'
plate.

market, it was believed for the first time, caused a flutter of excitement at Christie's in June 1989. It was eventually knocked down to J.W. McKenzie for a worthy £4,200.

The plate, with slight modifications, and, significantly, the replacement of Grace's signature by his portrait, was later issued and sold commercially by Coalport until 1914. It is recorded that at the time of issue they were on offer at 10s. [50p.]. References to them appear in the factory records under a number of pattern numbers, X1661-3, X1670 and Z1965. Regrettably, none of these pattern entries provide any additional details.

As known to collectors, this influential dessert plate (9in. wide) has a semi-gadrooned rim decorated in gold, with a printed central portrait within a band of bats and stumps listing the centuries, the whole coloured either red, blue, green or "puce". Since 1978 somewhere around 30 have been advertised or sold at auction, where, inevitably, they provide an atmosphere all of their own. Ignoring the record price of £900 paid for a blue version in the genteel hysteria of the Bicentenary sale in 1987, prices vary according to the colour. Red is said to be virtually unobtainable in pristine condition, but a very reasonable specimen notched up £680 in 1980, and since 1986 prices have hovered around £400. At the Phillips sale in 1978 the blue soared to £800 but since 1981 has remained static around £500. One specimen described as "finished in puce" appeared at Phillips in July 1981 and picked up £380.

The reissue in 1983 by Nubern Products of a limited edition of 750 in blue was advertised at just under £45 in 1985, and whether these, too, will career off in value is a matter for conjecture.

Nubern commemorative plates

To be candid, the series of modern plates issued by the Royal Worcester factory are rather drab, adorned only with facsimile signatures, so it is not at all surprising that Eric Bernardes of Nubern Products sensed a sales vacuum of plates at reasonable prices to satisfy the vast amount of interest there is in cricket, and in so doing carved a useful niche. His timing was opportune in that while in conversation with Colin Cowdrey he discovered that he needed only three more centuries to match Grace's feat. Accordingly Bernardes set to and devised an updated, modern format of the original, which, as part of a fund-raising drive for Kent in 1973, raised £5,000, a considerable sum for that time.

The Cowdrey plate duly appeared in 1973 and was followed in 1978 by further bone china coupe-shaped plates with a single colour enamel transfer decoration for John Edrich and Geoffrey Boycott. The year 1973 also happened to be the centenary of the county championship, so, following prompting from Lord's, Nubern collaborated with Hampshire in commissioning the first of an annual series of championship winners' plates.

Nubern Championship-winners' plate for 1980.

These, too, are bone china, with a range of appropriate colour transfer decorations in the centre and, around the rim, the badges of the 17 first-class counties. The complete set will appreciate given time, but at the moment the county plates flutter around the £25 mark, the best selling item being the Hampshire plate. Originally £9, it has climbed at auction to £90 and is now reputed to be about £130. The slowest of all is probably the Edrich plate, and some might say this has something to do with the attitude of the Surrey membership. The Bradman plate characteristically tops the list at over £100; Hobbs touched £65 in 1984 but £40 would be more realistic at the moment, while £90 for Geoffrey Boycott, also in 1984, remains his highest score.

Royal Worcester plates

Royal Worcester have produced no cricket memorabilia for public sale, but their bone china plates bearing the reproduction signatures of the members of touring sides from overseas visiting Worcester were first presented to the 1938 Australians, and then consecutively from 1949 to 1973. A special plate was issued in 1953 for the Ashes victory with the signatures of both teams.

Each plate was limited in number to about 50-60, one given to each member of the team and a few made available to specialist collectors. The 1938 plate sold for £160 at Phillips in November 1985 and those for other years ranged from £95 for 1949, 1950, 1953 and 1955 to £40 for 1973. As observed in the Royal Worcester and Royal Crown Derby section, other Royal Worcester wares connected with cricket were private commissions.

Other plates

Half a dozen other pieces have caught our attention. Two of them, both gold-fluted, show action shots of Hirst and Rhodes, while the third, acquired by leading collector Roger Mann, is a plate given to Jardine by "Vizzy", the Rajkumar of Vizianagram, a great patron of Indian cricket, who ran his own XI and captained the 1936 side to England. It depicts his palace in the background, with a cricket match in progress within the grounds. The Hirst and Rhodes transfer portraits are also to be found in 4in. high mugs, dated 1905, and marked on the base H.H. & S. A fair expectation for the pair would be in excess of £150.

The Barnes mug from the Bicentenary auction.

Slightly less exotic, if we accept the fact that he is shown as a batsman, is an elusive plate dedicated to S.F. Barnes and captioned "Brilliant Bowling by Barnes. Obtained six wickets for 24 runs". The identical caption can, be found on the reverse of a mug showing Barnes the bowler, a specimen of which appeared in a lot at the Bicentenary auction. Three copies of the plate have been seen, insured by their owners for not far short of £300.

Burlington Gallery had for sale at £145 an unusual French piece, marked Hoissy le Roi, dated c.1890 and 9in. in diameter. The batsmen and two bowlers illustrated have a distinctly Chinese appearance.

Sponsors of modern plates have found sales slower than expected. A total of 96 transfer-printed 10in. plates produced for The Friends of Grace Road in 1986 to commemorate Leicestershire's Benson & Hedges Cup victory just about made a small profit at £10 each. Three years earlier, a local artist, Mildred Shearon, designed a plate for the centenary of the Kirkheaton Cricket and Bowling Club in a limited edition of 250. The design incorporates the White Rose of Yorkshire, cricket, bowls, the clubhouse and those legendary Yorkshiremen affiliated with the club, Hirst and Rhodes. Originally priced at £12.50, a fair proportion still remain unsold. Nor can we recall anyone going overboard for a Royal Spode china plate commemorating the 1977 Australian tour of England. Priced at £9.50, it is gilt-edged in burnished gold, and has a colour centrepiece of the Australian emblem and the signatures of the touring party.

On the flood tide of cricketana, Schweppes commissioned a Wedgwood bicentenary plate, to be presented to every cricket club which could prove continuous existence over 200 years as at 1983. The first and only one presented went to Sevenoaks Vine CC, founded in 1734, and it is interesting to note in passing that the club also has a bat dating from 1735, which was almost sold in the 1980s but withdrawn thanks to local pressure, as well as a silver snuffbox from 1818 and a film of their 1934 bicentenary match played out in period costume.

Plaques

New Hall Pottery plaques of Hobbs, Chapman and Duckworth with green or brown surrounds are avidly sought (see colour page xviii), while Mike Smith of Tunbridge Wells is the fortunate owner of a W.G. plaque made specially for that expert on all matters relating to Grace, G. Neville Weston. The asking price for a colour printed Bradman plaque (17cm.), with his portrait and facsimile signature, was £450 in 1988. A particularly cussed one to find is the Woodfull plaque made c.1930, for which £500 was being bruited about.

Christie's auctioned in October 1988 two Sandland earthenware plaques of a young cricketer, smoking a cigar and defending a wicket composed of a spade, umbrella and briefcase. The centre was printed in colours and the frame heightened in green and gilt, and the price realised was £280. For £9.50 in the late 1970s, one could have a 5½in.x7in. plaque showing an Edwardian match in relief made by First Impressions.

Tiles

Scarcely a Victorian building was complete without thin slabs of ceramic material, usually earthenware, known to posterity as tiles. In R.G. Barlow's house in the 1890s, "Old Ebor" (A.W. Pullin) reported that there was a representation in coloured tiles of Lord Sheffield's ground, flanked by portrait tiles of Hornby and Barlow to one side and Pilling on the other.

Pioneered in the Stoke potteries, the encaustic tile was hand-decorated from the 1860s, and lustre decoration was adopted in the 1890s. The Victorians had no "style" of their own, but borrowed indiscriminately from patterns of the past. Many hundreds of themes were manufactured, but only one cricket scene surfaces with any regularity, and it must be psychological resistance, memories of schooldays and hospitals, for even this tile has never really caught on among collectors. Made in blue and white by Minton in their Elizabethan series, the tile is decorated with a circular reserve of Tudor figures playing cricket and a motif of cricket bats to each corner (see colour page xviii). Six inches square – the normal Victorian size for wall tiles – and dating from c.1860, it bears a strong resemblance to a Malkin Edge tile of c.1895, showing boys playing a game of marbles. At the Phillips sale of 1978 it realised £70 and more recent lots are a sensible proposition at around £40-£50. An advertisement in *The Cricketer* (1925), placed by the Strand firm of Hassall, offered 60 blue/white 6in. tiles with two unique cricket designs at 1s. [5p.] each, or 18s. per dozen.

A Sobers ceramic tile in a limited numbered edition of 200, with explanatory text, was marketed by the Canberra branch of the Australian Cricket Society.

Miscellaneous

Space and sanity prohibit no more than a passing reference to samples from the mass of gew-gaws, souvenirs and mementos in pottery form. All collectors, be they ever so humble, have examples of them – ashtrays, potlids, matchstrikers, Royal Grafton, Burleigh and Sandland ware, thimbles, 'Sooty' eggcups, cricketing dogs as book-ends, hand-painted enamel lockets (some still with strands of the loved one's hair), decorative dishes such as 'Alletson's Innings' inscribed "W.P. fecit", old Sheffield tobacco boxes showing cricket on Broadhalfpenny Down. Some collectors were lucky enough to pre-empt demand with items fashioned exclusively for them. Ron Yeomans made much of a mug showing the Headingley pavilion that was created for his private delectation, and also enjoyed a colourful, glazed figure made by Alan Young of the Pickwick Pottery, showing the great man being bowled comprehensively as 'Mr Pickwick gets a duck'.

The china tankard commemorating the first Minor Counties tour abroad, to Kenya in 1979, stands out in a crowd, but for sheer size-impact nothing compares with that made by the Ashes Centenary Tankard, produced in 1982 by the Franklin Mint. As promised in their sales literature, sent to regular subscribers, the mould was broken and none is to be found anywhere on the company's premises when we tried for one. Handsomely adorned with a border of 22-carat gold, it has a graphic portrayal of Barlow bowled by Spofforth, Blackham is behind the stumps and W.G. a burly figure at the non-striker's end. For any commemorative piece at under £20 to break even, sales need to exceed 10,000, but, as reported, sales fell below target, highlighting yet again cricket's inability to sell on a multi-national basis.

Sculptures, statues and statuettes

Whereas ceramics abound, sculpted works are – for obvious reasons – relatively hard to find outside the established museums and galleries. In common with the much under-publicised bust of Sir Neville Cardus, created by Nigel Boonham to mark the centenary of the most garlanded critic of all, and placed in the Manchester Free Trade Hall for the Hallé Concerts Society (but still bereft of a cricket home for lack of funds), most major works are special commissions. Some of the smaller figures may have been aborted commercial ventures or objects of intense personal wish-fulfilment and idolatry, but the sheer amount of costly preliminary work prior to the actual mould manufacture tends to give them an expensive exclusivity.

The almost sensual Henry Rossi marble figures at Woburn Abbey are regularly illustrated in books on cricketing art, but we wonder how many people have actually seem them *en plein air* or delved into their creative heritage. Models for statues of batsman

The bust of Neville Cardus by Nigel Boonham and (left) Cardus's passport. It is interesting to note how he described his profession and also the inaccurate date given for his birth. His centenary was correctly celebrated on 3rd April 1988.

and bowler were exhibited by Rossi at the Royal Academy in 1819, followed four years later by a marble statue of a cricketer, and then again in 1824 by a model for a statue of a bowler to be carved in marble. Which of them is to be seen at Woburn is pure guesswork. Rossi moved in the same artistic milieu as James Dance (alias Love), so one can readily deduce the cricketing influences upon him.

'The Batsman' by William Meredyth Thomas (1819-77), a plaster figure on a wooden plinth, dated c.1840s, is not unlike Rossi's sculpted marble. Size 53cm.x25.5cm.x17cm., it is, however, more of a transportable nature and, in common with numerous other treasures, it has made the Melbourne migration.

The five bronzes by Joseph Durham (1814-77), seen at Lord's and formerly in the Pilkington collection, stand only a few inches in height, but one is clearly the basis for the lifesize reclining figure of Basil Edwin Lawrance entitled 'Waiting for Innings'. Originally presented to the Guildhall Art Gallery in 1893, it is now in the entrance hall to J.M. Brearley's old school, City of London, situated on the riverside near St Paul's Cathedral. The bat which reposes by the boy is particularly prominent, as are the studs on his footwear. To be candid, it is misplaced where it is. It requires attention and not of the sort liable to be offered by feltpen experts. Let the official school history speak for itself: "... a remarkable sculpture ... originally presented to the embarrassed Guildhall, which astutely sent it on to the school. The authorities apparently hesitated to look this piece of statuary in the mouth; but perhaps few tears would be shed if it could be removed to some more distant repository of the School" (1965). It was said to be insured in 1988 for £10,000, but is worth double that, and we can imagine a few more appropriate venues for it to be on view to a wider and more appreciative audience.

Life-size bronze head of Frank Woolley by Willi Soukop (b.1907).

Two other sculptures rarely seen by collectors are a statuette of C.B. Fry, bat lofted high above his head, playing off the back foot, presented to the *Mercury*, a nautical training ship. His association with this ship on the River Hamble, Hampshire, later in his life, was a key element in a 1987 BBC Radio 4 drama. In the Maidstone Museum is a lifesize bronze head of Frank Woolley, created by the Vienna-born Willi Soukop, and shown at a Royal Academy Exhibition. It was bought in June 1976 by Maidstone Borough Council, who raised the funds by public subscription and grant-aid from the Victoria and Albert Museum. Woolley's family came from Maidstone, though he was born in Tonbridge. The sculpture in bronze on a black marble base was made in the summer of 1974 from sittings given to the artist while Woolley was in England on holiday from

Canada. Lord's has a similar bust dated c.1960.

Arguably the finest piece of sculpture ever sold at auction is the white marble figure of 'The Young Cricketer', depicting a boy batsman in a forward defensive stance, his cap and coat behind him. Purchased for £2,200 at the momentous Phillips auction in 1978, this entrancing work, created by William Day Keyworth in 1875, stands almost 3ft. high on an octagonal base. It now forms part of John Gill's collection at First Impressions, carefully kept under wraps, the sad non-fulfilment of an initiative to have it reproduced in reconstituted marble, so as to look and feel the same as the original.

More than a decade later there appeared in Christie's June 1989 auction a similarly choice marble figure by Keyworth the Younger, dated 1895. It was 33in. high and said to have come from a country house in Yorkshire. A bid of £8,000 secured it for a buyer on the Continent.

The same lack of consumer response a decade ago stopped Gill from undertaking a faithful reproduction of a fast bowler in bronze, 18in. high, signed by Randle Jackson and dated 1923. Another bronze of a fieldsman, similar in scale and close enough in style to be also by Jackson, was reminiscent of that great fielder, Colin Bland; the wind-up to hurl the ball in from the covers is a memory of vintage years.

Between 1979 and 1982 First Impressions unveiled a parade of 20 individual portraits of players from the cricket pantheon, each one an individual work, framed and mounted on deep bottle green velvet. Made from cold cast metals, 10in.x8in., each had real gold leaf moulding and antique crackle finish. Whether the fastidious indifference of collectors to modern work such as this still applies has yet to be market-tested again; it may be worth a relaunch. The same goes for a twinkling specimen of athleticism in his action replica of a wicketkeeper in the Alan Knott mould. Although tiny in size, it is a symphony of movement, every sinew displayed.

John Gill's all-action wicketkeeper.

The awed devotion accorded W.G. Grace has haunted artists and given collectors three-dimensional images of him in every imaginable shape, size and distortion. Roger Mann, for one, has two wooden statuettes of him, featured as a batsman and a roundarm bowler, as well as a head and shoulders figure identical in all but colour to the imposing bust which stands guard in the Lord's Museum. Mann's bust, sculpted like its counterpart by W. Tyler in 1888, reached him from G. Neville Weston, the leading student of Grace. It previously belonged to E. Rockley Wilson, who had it standing in a bedroom at Winchester College. Equally arresting is a large, full-

Roger Mann's wooden statuettes of W.G. Grace.

Geoff Boycott's memorable on-drive.

length bronze of W.G. in a typical batting posture, his weight on the back foot, bat pointing upwards. This is a stance ridiculed today when the emphasis is on an even distribution of weight, but, as Mann points out, batsmen of that period preferred to attack off the front foot from the outset, so the pose is technically correct and apt.

Copies of a W.G. figure by Dennis Fairweather, creator of a full range of hand-painted "natural" golfing characters, county and professional types, can be found in a number of shops, but Keith Hayhurst, Curator of the Old Trafford museum and a leading collector in his own right, managed a coup of his own. He bought outright the only cold cast stoneware-resin statuette in existence by Fairweather of his fellow Lancastrian, A.C. MacLaren. While of dubious aesthetic appeal, it is guaranteed to produce at least a smile, being both quaintly humorous and a shrewd investment .

Sir Donald Bradman offers less opportunity for artistic licence, but nevertheless the bronze casting made of him for the Kensington District Cricket Club to mark his 80th birthday in 1988, is a brave attempt to capture the footwork and timing elsewhere enshrined now only on ciné film. Among lesser cricketing mortals, one to pick out is a leather covered portrait figure of Lord Dalmeny, captain of Surrey 1905-07 and later the sixth Earl of Rosebery. He is depicted standing with hands in blazer pocket and holding a cap, and this 19in. high tribute by D. Humphreys, signed and dated 1906, was sold at the Bicentenary auction for £220.

Modern sculptures

For those prepared to no-ball the obvious and the fashionable, cricket has received acclaim in clay from a wide variety of modern artists. A studio clay figure signed by R. Bradley of W.G., bat tucked under his left arm and standing upon a square wooden base, dated 1936, found a ready buyer at Phillips in October 1985 for £38.

John Atkins has in a limited edition of 100 a cold cast figure of Geoff Boycott playing the on-drive with which he completed his hundredth hundred at Headingley in 1977. The proposed figure was first cast in clay and after modifications and several blunt discussions between artist and subject, the actual casting was done by Pat Moore. Inclusive of the marble base on which it was mounted, just 9in. high, the price in 1978 was £165 and over half the edition was sold. Since then he has sculpted figures of Hammond playing his off-drive and Bradman square-cutting (both £450 in 1986) and Trumper jumping out to drive (£395 in 1981). All have been in small editions of 15-20 only and cast by the lost-wax method, a more costly process than the Boycott figure.

Austin Bennett works in the rural beauty of the Shropshire hills, and finds that the controlled power inherent in cricketing techniques suits his style, and the shapes made in space, by fielders particularly, are interesting material for sculptural development. He is represented in the National Portrait Gallery by a bronze cast of the noted ballet choreographer, Sir Frederick Ashton, and although he is happy to model strictly figurative pieces such as 'Cover Drive', it is not really representative of his work. His three 'Slip Catch' abstract bronzes are akin to Henry Moore in their serious artistic nature.

One of three 'Slip Catch' abstract bronzes by Austin Bennett, who was commissioned in 1989 to produce a cricketing diorama, believed to be the first of its kind.

Enid Bloom, on the other hand, is a leading sculptress in the classical tradition, with a long record of exhibitions both in Britain and on the Continent. Her cricketing figure, 'Four Runs', stands 26½in. high and was, says the artist, inspired by her family's passion for the game. Her son was used as the model, together with photographs of eminent cricketers and "memories of Imran Khan hitting out at Lord's". Available only in a limited edition of 12 at £550 each, 'Four Runs' was shown at a gallery in Pinner, Middlesex to complement an exhibition of cricket paintings.

Enid Bloom's 'Four Runs'.

The combination of art and sport drew sculptor, figurative artist and New Zealander, Bonar Dunlop, irresistibly to cricket. His first five cricket pieces – 'Batsman', 'Bowler', 'Wicketkeeper', 'Fielder' and 'Slip Fielder' – each one 5¾in. high, were cast in a white marble resin. They were later sold in semi-mass production by Arista Design of Hawick as a resin bonded ceramic at £27 each, but are, according to the artist, inferior in class to the originals. His larger series, 6½in. high, appeared as a *Wisden Cricket Monthly* exclusive offer in 1981 at £110 per set. The figures – 'Square Cut', 'Bowler' (Richard Hadlee), and 'Slip Fielder' (which takes up different positions by rolling it) – were widely admired and more than one noted collector asked for advance notice of anything by him.

Peter Hicks, of Seend in Wiltshire, has since 1971

Peter Hicks with his St
Ivel Trophy for the
WCA.

Richard Hadlee,
by Neale Andrew.

applied his talents in sculpting to the representation, in either cold cast resin bronze, bronze or silver, of military and civilian pieces, as well as sponsored trophies such as the Cricketeer Trophy for the Women's Cricket Association in its 50th year, 1976. This was the year when women cricketers first appeared on the sacred turf at Lord's, and the trophy was sponsored by St Ivel, a part of the Unigate Group, for which the sculptor then worked. Among his commemoratives, action pieces, entitled 'Sporting Figures', included a figure of a batsman, hand cast and reproduced in cold cast resin bronze. Hand-finished, on a mahogany plinth, it was available at £22.50.

Although hopeful of producing a series of statuettes of famous cricketers, because of the pressure of other commitments James Butler, RA created the single figure of 'W.G.: the Great Cricketer', which was exhibited at the Royal Academy Summer Exhibition in 1979. It was issued the same year by Cricket Fine Art in a limited edition of 250. Weighing over 15lb., this 11¾in. statuette was cast in solid bronze, not the cheaper substitute cold cast bronze. Each statuette carries the foundry stamp of the Meridian Bronze Foundry and No. 1 of 'W.G.' realised £350 at auction in April 1979. Among his many works Butler, a member of the RA Council, includes a figure of Jomo Kenyatta, commissioned by the Kenyan Government and now standing in the main square in Nairobi.

Two further representations of Grace are worth recording; a most impressive 2ft. high simulated bronze figure, actually only plaster beneath, which realised £300 in July 1983, and a cast-iron bronze head by Colin Miller, executed in 1973 and exhibited at Lord's and the Tate Gallery. It achieved £400 in May 1985.

Despite media hype, or possibly because of it, large busts of Boycott and Hadlee by Neale Andrew, son of the former England wicketkeeper, failed to captivate cricketana collectors, and a disappointing showing at auction in 1988 suggested a better deal by private treaty. A specialist in figurative sculpture, he does, however, have a large bronze of Sir George (Gubby) Allen at Lord's and was responsible for an intriguing 14in. bronze miniature of Viv Richards.

References in cricket's literature are made to a "remarkable" bust of Learie Constantine by Karen Jonzen and to an exhibition of the works of David Wynne, which included, *inter alia*, a bronze statuette on loan from the MCC of Alec Bedser and a "nude" sketch of Bedser loaned by Michael Pugh! Fleeting mention was also made at the time of his benefit of a 14in. high model of J.G. Binks, the former Yorkshire wicketkeeper. It was said to be the first and only known cricketing model among thousands executed by Professor Julian Maugsch, a Hungarian sculptor living in York.

As part of their 'Heirs and Graces' series in 1979, John Day Design Studios had a figure of a mid-19th century cricketer, said to reproduce faithfully the style and elegance of that era. Mounted on a wooden plinth and 8in. high, it was cast in an ivory finish and went on sale in a limited edition for £35.

Other modern pieces

Recent years have seen a revival of sorts in the production of cricket figures. Count André d'Aquino's initial set of 'Arlott's Immortals' in 1983 helped set the scene, full of character and movement.

Portrayed in painstaking detail, the ceramic sculptures of Hobbs, Constantine, Laker, Evans, Boycott, Lillee (see colour page xvii), Viv Richards and Botham were made individually in English bone china and hand decorated. The moulds required for the first three figures alone were reported in *Wisden Cricket Monthly* as necessitating over a thousand different assays, half a ton of plaster of Paris and, for each figure, seven firings to build up the colour.

On sale at £300 per single figure or £2,400 per set (50 were made), they are still available upon application, but were probably overpriced to begin with. Very little is heard about them, despite questioning among collectors and by collectors, so the assumption is that they are seen by their owners as rainy-day investments.

A fascinating craftsman is Essex-born Howard Carter, whose exhibition 'Carvings in Wood' at the Crane Kalman Gallery, London, late in 1987, displayed a range of work which, amid so much sobriety elsewhere, offered great delight. His affectionate descriptions of cricket's heroic figures have an honesty and independence as well as simplicity of vision. Painting is blended with wood carving in a modern-day version of those earlier naïf folk artists, the long line of Staffordshire figurine modellers of the last century.

Six cricketing themes were on show: 'Alfred Shaw', 'Cricket Icon', 'Ranji and the Champion' (see colour page xviii), 'Lord Hawke' (based on the *Vanity Fair* caricature), 'The Champion' and 'The Three Graces'. The cricket circuit believes that the last named, a wood carving 35in. high, was bought by Albert Finney, not otherwise known as a fan of the game, with the asking price

'The Three Graces',
by Howard Carter.

rumoured to be £5,000 or thereabouts.

Of a similar genre, though not financial bracket, we may also mention the distinctive plaques made out of pre-coloured, pliable clay by a Jersey schoolgirl, Clare Luke. They were featured on a set of postage stamps issued by Jersey in April 1989 and, among the children's games and toys depicted, on one of the 23p values was a batsman standing near to a wicket apparently in the process of being demolished by a ball.

The Century Collection by Sport in Miniature, of Derby, exclusive to *Wisden Cricket Monthly,* bestrides several sections of the book. The first celebrated the centenary of Hobbs's birth (1882) with an edition of 100 hand-painted pewter figures by Tim Richards at just under £40 each; the same figure was also available in polished pewter at £16.50. Then followed Trueman, W.G., Botham, Wisden, Rhodes, Evans, Hammond, Larwood, Compton and Laker, the prices rising by 1989 to £55 and £27 respectively. In addition to the normal set, a gold-plated centenary issue for Wisden's death appeared in 1984 in a limited edition of only 10 at £75.

ORNAMENTAL OBJECTS

Silverware and silverware trophies

Over the years sufficient silver-plated tableware of a cricketing kind has been produced to allay the anxieties of even the most jittery BBC props buyer confronted with the need to dress a dozen Bertie Wooster-type country house extravaganzas.

The Burlington Gallery alone could have happily provided silver-plated cocktail stirrers in the shape of cricket bats (c. 1900) for around £75 each, or an assortment of cruets from the 1910-20 period, original glass and silver-plate vessels with cricket ball feet and crossed bats as handles for, say, £235 each. Something slightly more antique, c.1860, a composition of bats and balls to form a two-bowl cruet, would carry a price tag of £350, whereas a silver menu holder with cricket associations would be a considerable bargain at £120.

No self-respecting house party would be complete without a silver-plated and copper egg boiler in the form of a cricket ball, supported by crossed bats and united by stumps (not forgetting the spirit lamp), sold at the Phillips auction in 1978 for £210, nor a silver-plated three-hole egg stand on a tripod of three cricket bats, each with a bat at the base which also made £210 at the same sale.

Toast racks would present little problem. Something with a mid-Victorian flavour, consisting of bat dividers, stump end pieces and ball feet would set one back about £200. Fairly abundant they may well be, but one at least had royal pretensions and would grace any table. Prince Christian Victor, nephew to Queen Victoria, and probably the best cricketer with royal blood, spent most of a short home leave from India in 1891 playing cricket while waiting for his parents' silver wedding day. Evidence of his enthusiasm for the game comes from a silver toast rack with three stumps and bails as end-pieces, with intermediate partitions of crossed cricket bats. The centre one is surmounted by the initial 'C' with the Garter and a non-British crown. Inside is a partly obliterated inscription which reads "From **** July 5th, 1891". July 5th happened to be the anniversary, and his father was a K.G., so it seems reasonable to visualise this as a wholly delightful and personal gift.

From the Yorkshire team of 1901, coffee jugs weighing over 30oz. each, such as the one presented to David Hunter, could also be procured. The entire team received silverware in celebration of a second County Championship win in a row. Appropriate to the occasion, R.G. Barlow of Lancashire had a

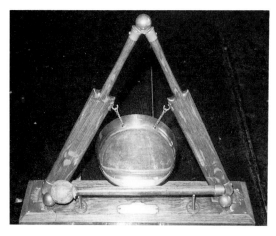

Mounted gong
presented to R.G.
Barlow by W.G. Grace.

W.G. Grace adorns a
silver ink stand typical
of its era.

mounted gong, with necessary striker, presented to him by W.G. Grace "for his fine cricket against the Australians, 1886". It was modelled in oak and plated metal, and fetched £400 at the Phillips auction of May 1982. On hand, too, would be ashtrays. Ron Yeomans had over 20 cricketing ashtrays, one in the shape of a cricket ball, all gifts from the manufacturers. Each time a new one was turned out a sample was sent to him, and among his later acquisitions was one made of solid silver, struck to commemorate the centenary of the first English team to tour Australia in 1861-62.

Silver presentation inkstands have always been *de rigueur* in the best households. One, a central inkwell in the form of a cricket ball supported by three bats flanked by stumps, presented by members of Swanmore Park CC in 1877, was borne away by Chris Pilkington from the 1978 Phillips sale for £3,200. The frenzied bidding on that occasion was put into perspective when a bid of only £680 secured the same piece seven years later. At Phillips in 1986, a silver marine type deskpiece inkwell, presented by Lord Ashton, President of Lancashire CCC to the captain, Lt.-Col. L. Green, to commemorate the county's third successive Championship, realised £260.

Examples abound of engraved silver lockets, cricketing spoons (often engraved with cricketers on the handles), silver match cases, stamp boxes and paper knives in the shape of cricket bats. Ron Yeomans also had a full-size cricket ball in silver, complete with seam, and dated 1933. In the January 1981 Geering & Colyer sale was a George IV silver rectangular, small (3½in wide) musical snuff box, the cover engraved with a cricketer, made in London 1824, maker's insignia "W.L.". It probably belonged to the former Kent and England player, A.J. Evans, as it came from the estate of his sister and was thus also possibly the property of his father, A.H. Evans, captain of Oxford University.

This is comparatively small beer, however, when set against an extremely

rare silver snuff box in the form of a cricket bat, just over 9in. long, made by William Dudley of Birmingham in 1850. Fitted with three lidded compartments and telescope handle, the blade is engraved with a picture of a cricket match and foliate scrolls and rosettes. It weighed 8oz., appeared at the Geering & Colyer sale of March 1979, and became the property of A. Baer, Esq. for £1,100.

Two silver snuff boxes, one musical and the other in cricket bat form.

    The majority of items under this collective heading are typically presentation pieces: cups, trophies and other personalia. So numerous are they that for any sort of cross-section indication we can only turn to a contrived form of recitative, and our debt to the many collectors who supplied details is great, most especially to Mike Smith. In list form then:

Robert Carpenter's loving cup.

R.G. Barlow: a silver cup presented to him in 1883 by friends in Australia for his tremendous performances that year. A further great innings the following year brought a claret cup from another admirer.

Robert Carpenter: a two-handled loving cup presented in 1864 to that outstanding Cambridgeshire batsman of the 1850s and 1860s. This was another Ron Yeomans treasure and the reverse side had an engraving of a batsman at the wicket; it formed part of a £450 Carpenter lot in April 1979.

David Denton: a pair of silver candlesticks, part of a miscellany acquired for £600 in October 1987.

K.S. Duleepsinhji: a silver cigarette case inscribed to "Billy", his former coach W.A. Woof, dated 1923.

Arthur Fielder: a penknife and inkstand (1979, £100 and £200); a paper knife awarded after Kent's 1913

Championship season (1986, £200); a handsome commemorative bowl for his 10th-wicket stand with Woolley (1986, £145) and a silver match-holder, inscribed for the Kent fast bowler in 1904.

F.R. Foster: an inscribed cigarette case from his Warwickshire professionals (1987, £320).

Wally Hammond: a silver cigar box, engraved on the lid with the names of his fellow 1928-29 tourists to Australia and presented to him on the occasion of his marriage (1980, £270).

Right Wally Hammond's cigar box.

Far right Silver card case and snuff box, among many items presented to Jack Hobbs.

Jack Hobbs: a silver card case, a gift from Enid Leveson Gower in 1910 (1987, £40); a snuff box from "Razor" [Smith] dated 1912 (1987, £130); a silver bowl with embossed floral decoration, 1912 (1987, £40); inscribed cigarette boxes (1979, £130 and 1980, £130); also a silver salver presented to him by his captain (Arthur Gilligan) after the 1924-25 tour to Australia (1979, £150).

J.R. Mason: Kent CCC presentations in the form of a paper knife (£100), inkstand (£200) and pair of candlesticks (£220), all sold in 1980.

Harry Moses: a tray presented by the New South Wales Cricket Association for his 297 not out v. Victoria in 1887-88.

Ron Yeomans delighted in a beautifully engraved whisky flask, presented in 1883 to E. E. Leatham, a cricketing celebrity in the Pontefract area of Yorkshire. The Leathams were very much a county household name in the decades around 1870 and ran their own team. Members of the family also linked up with a Mr R. Barclay to found a high-street bank to which doubtless a number of readers are presently indebted. A silver-plated heirloom,

"bought for a song" (actually £300) at auction in May 1982, comprises a five-piece tea service presented to Mrs W.L. Murdoch by Ranjitsinhji in 1896. Murdoch was the former Australian captain and then captain of Sussex. Mike Smith, the present owner, suggests that "either Ranji was protecting his place in the side, or had been getting out early to pay visits!" The tea service was in fact a Christmas gift. He also relishes a silver model of a batsman thought to be Felix and judged by some to be the most attractive piece in his collection.

Trophies

Part of the sumptuous Tony Baer collection includes a silver cup presented to John Lillywhite by the Sussex Club in 1871, recognising his magnificent service over 20 years, as well as the silver trophy shown in *Glorious Innings* (Melbourne, 1987), presented to W.G. for athletics on 10th April 1869, with silver wings on either side representing handles. Worthy also of mention, in what is again a heavily collected field, is the luscious campana form trophy cup, dated 1821, a presentation from Wargrave Cricket Club in August 1850 to one Frederick Sarney, Esq., which at Bonhams in April 1987 soared to £2,200. Then there is the Heavy Woollen District Cricket Challenge Cup, formerly the property of Dewsbury and Savile Cricket and Football Club, which only just managed bottom estimate of £1,000 at Christie's in 1988. It might well have exceeded that had it been appreciated that a decade earlier, in February 1978, it was valued at £4,000 and formed the subject of an illustrated letter in *The Cricketer*.

Heavy Woollen District Challenge Cup.

Above left Tea service presented to Mrs Murdoch.

Metalware

An early 20th-century spelter figure of C.B. Fry, wearing a cap and open-neck shirt, preparing to bowl, appeared at the Phillips 1978 sale, realising £210, but the· trio of Fry as a bowler, batsman and wicketkeeper, the latter surmounting a clock, are rare as a set. Anonymously lotted as an "interesting cricket garniture in bronzed metal", the set sold for £340 at Phillips in June 1988. Noted as c.1890, Burlington Gallery offered for £140 a gun-metal spelter candle-holder figure of W.G. wearing pads with bat in hand, in front of a tree, 5½in. high. A full measure of metalware exists for anyone not yet surfeited by three-dimensional objects at enormous prices. For £240 at Christie's in October 1988 there was an electro-plated six-division novelty toast rack in the usual configuration of wickets, bats and ball feet, but with the charming addition of a cricket belt handle and two miniature figures of batsmen in support. A similar, if not identical, item made £75 at Phillips in May 1982.

W.G. turns up in many guises, in this instance as a cast iron book-end, modelled as a seated portrait and decorated in colours, 17cm. in height, and at £65 from Phillips in 1985 a useful prop. To these the bibliophile could add

C.B. Fry,
the all-rounder.

book-ends in solid brass, weighing just under 2lb, set on mahogany, the stumps exactly the size of *Wisden*, £95 for a pair from First Impressions.

Pewter

A couple of sets of fascinating metalware formed part of Rockley Wilson's collection which he wrote about in *The Cricketer Winter Annual* of 1941. One was a set of six pewter pots, 4in. high, decorated with scenes from the Hayman picture. All were made about 1840 by the silversmiths, James Dixon

Rockley Wilson's six pewter pots.

and Sons of Sheffield, and differently engraved. Wilson understood they were a special commission, as the firm had no records of a large-scale order to these specifications. Beautifully worked, they would have been expensive at the time and were believed by their owner to be unique. In the light of this a realisation of £3,800 at the MCC Bicentenary auction is less surprising than many on that occasion. Cricket scenes also feature on five rare Scottish goblets, one 9in.x5in. and weighing a wrist-bending 4¼lb. These, too, belonged to Wilson.

Pewter tankards also emerged at the Bicentenary sale: one, salvaged during the demolition of the old Lord's Tavern in the winter of 1966-67, 5in. high and inscribed "Lord's", made £110 and a half-pint model with a spout, engraved "Lord's Cricket Ground" on the base, edged past at £120.

Medals and medallions

Modest testimonials to a player's standing among his *confrères*, or symbolic of some outstanding feat duly inscribed to mark the fleeting moment of triumph, medallions are probably as old as established cricket. Theirs is not normally the limelight until at Christie's, in October 1988, Bob Willis, the former Warwickshire and England captain, made the cricket world sit up when he found a welcoming home, with Mike Smith in Kent, for all the 45 gold, silver and white metal inscribed medallions given to him for Test, county and Prudential Cup achievements. By the time the auctioneers were able to recover their composure they were able to calculate an average realisation of £35 apiece.

Portrait medallions of popular cricketers – Grace, Ranji, Fry, Stoddart, Kortright, MacLaren, Mason, Jessop, Abel, Richardson, Hayward, Lockwood and Alec Hearne – were advertised in May 1901 at 3d. each, post free, from Merritt and Hatcher in Upper Thames Street, but there has been little sign of them since. On a more elevated plane, Goldman took particular delight in a copper medal given to all the players in the Gentlemen v. Players centenary match at Lord's in 1906, bearing on the reverse the match scores. Of his modern equals, Roger Mann has two of the very rare medals presented by W.G. to the members of both teams in the 1898 fixture. His two were awarded to J.R. Mason and William Gunn.

For an outlay of £10-£40 each, there is no great shortage of silver medals and medallions, some decorated with enamels of crossed-bat motifs or cricketers in action; gilt, brass and bronze reliefs of cricket scenes, or, come to that, 9ct. gold fobs, again with crossed bats and stumps. Over 60 alone were on show at the Phillips October 1988 auction, dated from 1894 to 1948. To be sure, some are more costly. A silver medallion, either a member's pass or an

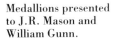

Medallions presented to J.R. Mason and William Gunn.

official's badge, for use at the Leicestershire ground, made in Birmingham by John Mole in 1877, was purchased over estimate for £75 within the past couple of years. Hereinafter probably to become known as the Swithenbank medallion after the winner's name, a gold pendant medal presented by the Englishmen of Jamestown, USA (6cm., 1885), realised £245 at auction in November 1986, and was later for sale at £495.

Highly esteemed by collectors are the medals struck to commemorate the first MCC tour to Australia in 1903-04 (earlier ones were privately organised). It was reported in 1967 that Ted Arnold's medal reposed in the safe keeping of his grandson, along with others of his cricketing souvenirs and trophies, but the medal awarded to George Hirst was reported as stolen from the home of one of Yorkshire's foremost collectors, indicative of the importance someone attached to this particular tour series. Dick Lilley's came up for auction in April 1987, was deemed "most desirable", and found a buyer at £280.

A beautiful product of the silversmith's art took the shape of a gold shield with the royal coat of arms at the top, an inner shield with inscription and initials, the latter studded with seven diamonds, and between the initials, silhouetted in bold relief, a sold gold cricket bat in miniature, and was the Prince of Wales's tribute to "dear departed Johnny" [Briggs]. In 1923, 21 years after Briggs's untimely passing, the medallion was presented to Lancashire CCC at a private ceremony during the North v. South Test trial match at Old Trafford; enigmatically, the medal marked the highest individual score (33) of the low-scoring match at Sydney between Australia and England in 1886-87, by Briggs, who was noted as one of the greatest slow left-arm bowlers. Its present whereabouts is, alas, unknown.

Medallions vie with plaques as the most felicitous manner by which hosts from developing countries, in the cricketing sense, can honour visiting sides, and their value depends, obviously, on the date, character and playing strength of the visitors. A pleasurable instance for someone educated in the "windy city" was the tour medallion engraved "1889 Port Elizabeth", signposting the first English tour to South Africa. On the reverse is engraved the name of the tour organiser, Major Warton, and it was worth £120 to a kindred spirit at the Bicentenary sale. Hopefully some of these medallions from Holland, Singapore and other far pavilions will find their way in time to the fledgling cricket museums in countries where cricketana will eventually find its rightful place. Featuring the late Sir Frank Worrell, an 18ct. gold medal marking the West Indies golden jubilee, sold from Trinidad in 1979 for £80. Sri Lanka followed suit with 500 silver medallions issued to mark their inaugural Test match in 1982 against England in Colombo. During the match 400 were reputedly sold, and a part of the remainder were earmarked

The Swithenbank medallion.

for readers of *Wisden Cricket Monthly* prepared to part with £18.50.

The medal issued in 1914 to mark the centenary of the third Lord's ground has shown the way for a group of modern-day variations on a theme. At the instigation of the TCCB, John Pinches had a medal designed to commemorate the centenary of county cricket in 1973, showing a game in progress at headquarters, and bearing on the reverse the engraved badges of the seventeen first-class counties. It was also marketed as a medallic stamp cover in a special presentation wallet. To mark the centenary of Anglo-Australian Tests, the MCC commissioned from Garrard & Company, the crown jewellers, a 1977 Silver Jubilee year hallmarked medallion, for presentation at the Centenary Test match in Melbourne. Large numbers were struck of the silver and silver-gilt versions (£22.50 and £30), but only 14 platinums were made to order at £675 each. Although the value of platinum has increased less than fourfold in the last dozen years, the scarcity value of these picturesque items should make them a sound investment. Each player in the Centenary Test received a replica of the gold medal presented by the Victorian Cricket Association a century before, in honour of the very first Test, both sure bets to leap in value. The Australian Cricket Board also chipped in with a Melbourne-based silver medallion, tastefully adapted on a specially stamped medallic cover.

As their contribution to the souvenirs for the 1980 Centenary Test at Lord's, Toye, Kenning & Spencer issued a hall-marked sterling silver medallion in a limited edition of 1,000 at £50 each. Also available in bronze, it bore a scene from the original 1880 match (played at The Oval) and the official anniversary emblem on the reverse.

Gordon Ross, writing in *The Cricketer* (April 1985), kept track of the increase in the cost to the company of the basic metals for the Gillette Cup man of the match medals. From 1963 to 1979 they were made in 9ct. gold by Garrard, during which time they had risen in price from £16. 7s. 6d to £202.50 each. For the last year of the sponsorship, 1980, it was decided to have them done in silver-gilt, representing a saving of around 600 per cent. Since there were only 22 of them, and only one can be detected as having turned up for sale, the silver-gilt medals will be *primi inter pares*, and collectors enjoying influential contacts within the Surrey and Middlesex camps are urged to keep their friendships well massaged.

From another one-day competition, the gold award medallion from the infamous Benson & Hedges Cup match, in which the Somerset captain, Brian Rose, declared against Worcestershire to ensure his side's qualification for the quarter-finals, fetched a remarkable £300 in September 1980.

Assorted pins, pendants and brooches.

Jewellery

Victorian and Edwardian silver and gold pendants, silver lockets, stick pins for ties and cravats, cricket bat brooches and rings pour into auctions and form part of the staple diet of most collectors. These items are often relegated to a shoebox or some similarly mundane container and few buyers would be prepared to go beyond £30 for pieces to be had in such profusion. We did hear, however, of a miniature jade cricket bat stick pin/brooch, with a gilt metal mount, for which £100 was being asked, and in this hail of memorabilia, personalised gold cufflinks, such as those engraved "R. Kilner, West Indies 1925-26" in a case (£190 at Phillips in May 1985) and a Kentish pair dating from 1906 inscribed "Champions" and "Invicta" come readily to mind (see colour page xxv), as does a Band of Brothers brooch. In recent auctions, better-than-average items have been a four-handled silver manicure set, the handles modelled as cricket bats, the leather case as a cricket bag (£120 at Phillips in October 1986), though a silvered metal cricket compass pendant/charm with symbols of the game, estimated at £100-150, failed to sell at the same auction. Again at Phillips, this time in October 1988, a 9ct. gold brooch, 3 cm. long, in the shape of a wishbone with stumps and bat, two small seed pearls and an imitation ruby formed as a ball was a charmer at £80, along with a gold pendant, inscribed "1882, Sydney N.S.W.", with a top of crossed bats and a ball, in the centre an incised figure of a cricketer and with tied stumps as sides, worth £140.

One of the great collectors of yesteryear, F.S. Ashley-Cooper, picked up in Winchester an ivory memento of the game, in the shape of a set of stumps (2in. high) joined together with gold links to a ball, and another legend, Joe Goldman, purchased "for a not inconsiderable sum" in the 1930s a perfect miniature of Lord Frederick Beauclerk set in a paste brooch, dated c.1805.

It was sold to him as a special favour by a reluctant dealer who happened to be a cricket fan and so was "overcome by zealous entreaties".

To satisfy what has been seen as an insatiable demand, womenfolk have over the years been offered a wide range of gift ideas. There have been Playfair cricket cufflinks in green and gold enamel showing an action shot of a batsman, obtainable only from the Dickens Press in 1964 at 18s. 6d. Stratton men's jewellery had tie retainers in lustre gilt of a batsman sweeping to leg from 5s. to 8s. and a presentation set of a tie retainer shaped as a cricket bat and cufflinks in the form of a half cricket ball for a round £1. That was back in 1959, and for something much more contemporary, Julie Crossland's beautifully finished, hallmarked 9ct. gold cricket ball cufflinks (£198 in 1989), tie pins or brooches (£134) and different-size cricket bat pendants at £73-£175 are appropriate gifts. Scale replica cricket bats, 4cm. in 9ct. gold (£69.50) and 18ct. gold (£140.50), shaped as pendants, were on offer in July 1981.

Below The photograph shown to the Cricket Memorabilia Society. **Bottom** Brass-cased mantel clock, auctioned by Christie's in 1988.

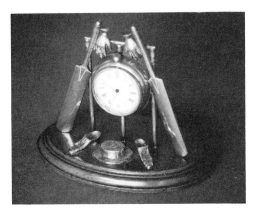

Clocks and watches

Clocks

A distraught collector attended a meeting of the Cricket Memorabilia Society at Trent Bridge in 1988. He offered to all present a coloured photograph of a prized possession, stolen from his house. It was a cricketing clock and he hoped that fellow members might be able to help him in his hitherto forlorn search. What sets the stolen clock apart is the delicate juxtaposition of gauntlets and shoes, giving it a vivacity of its own.

Its nearest approximation is a 12in. high, c.1890 clock within Arabic numerals, contained within stumps, two bats leaning against a set of stumps plus leather balls and batting pads decoration, which was offered at £475 by Burlington Gallery. This was consistent with the £400 realised in June 1988 for an interesting, 7³/₄in. novelty clock, with the usual assemblage of bats, balls and stumps, on an oval oaken base.

A 6¹/₄in. high brass-cased mantel clock, also wholly characteristic of Victorian taste, with crossed bats, wicket and ball on an oval naturalistic base, was auctioned at Christie's in October 1988 for £320. It proves an interesting contrast to the £190 for a 6¹/₂in.

brass and metal piece with similar accoutrements at the Phillips sale ten years before. Ron Yeomans had an interesting silver drawing-room clock, which formerly stood on the mantlepiece of Lord Harris's spacious country home. Yeomans also found in Edinburgh a 6in. brass clock, its face resting on two sets of stumps, completed by two batsmen and a ball.

Watches

Instead of benefit matches and testimonials, the majority of our parents earned their gold watches merely by enduring. Cricketers have to go one better and earn the admiration of a wealthy patron or their committee by some supercharged display of their skill. The tendency, therefore, is for inscribed presentation watches to be retained *ad infinitum* within the family (until they hear of the cricketana boom, that is), allowing descendants to bask in reflected glory. Few are seen at sales and references to them in the cricketing press are equally fleeting. In a lunch interval ceremony during the Gloucestershire v. Glamorgan match in 1927, Sir L. Goodenough Taylor presented Hammond on his 24th birthday with a gold watch and chain, along with a spade guinea (of George III) and a match-box, all highly collectable today.

Going back almost a double century, a tortoiseshell watch once owned by Rockley Wilson had Hayman's cricket scene painted on the reverse, and closely resembled the one given to MCC by T. Geoffrey Blackwell. One which realised £480 at the Bicentenary auction bears some similarity – a tortoiseshell veneered outer case with a contemporary cricketing scene, c.1740.

The thrill of ownership, especially when it rewards hours spent in tracking something down, triumphs over any damage to the wallet, and the intensely personal nature of presentation watches give them a special cachet.

Watch presented to Victor Trumper by Paddington CC.

More than perhaps any other cricketer, the mystique attached to the name of Trumper transcends time, and David Frith has graphically described the trepidation felt by all collectors awaiting the auctioneer's hammer blow, followed by the joy, when he acquired a watch inscribed "Paddington CC, presented to Victor Trumper by his club mates 1897-8". Under the purchaser's nuggety exterior dwells a heartfelt passion for cricket's memorabilia heritage, and while the transaction hurt, £700 in 1987 will quadruple given time.

Another devotee, Rockley Wilson, had a silver watch in 1941 made by Charles Newton of London, hallmarked 1756. It was inscribed "David Harris, King of Bowlers, Windmill Down, 1783", and was given to

Harris by a Mr. Parr. Harris played his first recorded match in 1782, for which Wilson also owned the scorecard. It had once belonged to Lord Harris, who sold it to Ranji, and then, to quote Wilson, it came "down in the world" when he purchased it at the sale of Ranji's home at Staines.

More recently, Keith Hayhurst chased hard for a solid silver pocket watch inscribed on one side "To Hammond from Fergie" [W. H. Ferguson] and on the other a kangaroo and the 1932-33 MCC touring crest. Open the lid and the watch still works.

Vesta cases

Vesta case by Hilliard and Thomason

In the early years of the 19th century, matches, the replacement for the tinder-box, were rough wooden chips of wood, topped with a blob of dangerous and noxious sulphur. A safer development, introduced in 1840, was the vesta, a small, friction, "strike anywhere" wax match, named after the goddess of the hearth. Even this had a tendency to ignite too easily, and the cylindrical containers then in use were considered too expensive at 2d. each. Manufacturers thus developed a suitably durable container, adapting tools hitherto used for snuff boxes and other objects of vertu.

By the 1860s the characteristic end-opening case had evolved, resembling a miniature cigar case with rounded corners. Either the lid or the side was the striking surface and a regular attachment was a small ring for the watch chain. Cricket was but one of a large range of subjects used to decorate the cases, which were made from a variety of metals, as well as wood, china, mother of pearl and vulcanite. Silver, however, was the most popular material and examples are unlikely now to be found much under £200. A prime specimen made by Hilliard and Thomason of Birmingham in 1881, enamelled with a picture of a batsman about to strike a ball, was bid up to £420 at Christie's in October 1987, while at the same sale £220 each was reached for an undated electro-plated case formed as a cricket ball. Generally, however, vesta cases from the late Victorian and Edwardian periods are less in demand, with realisations noted in the region of £20-50.

Enamels

English hand-crafted enamels were first made in Birmingham towards the latter half of the 18th century, and were in daily use in Georgian society as either snuff boxes, or patch and pill boxes. These original Birmingham enamels are now collectors' items, and, thanks to a generous benefactor, Melbourne can bask in a Bilston patch box of enamelled copper, transfer-printed with lid inscription "A Present from Sevenoaks" and "Sevenoaks Vine". It was originally thought to represent a match played at the Vine in 1782, and was described as such in May 1980, but *Glorious Innings* narrows it down to another permutation on the Hayman scene. It is a very early example of a "commercial cricketing souvenir", hailing from the period so graphically shown in the film 'The Wicked Lady', when artificial beauty spots and low necklines were all the rage, and its original owner, whoever that might have been, would be dumbfounded at today's valuation in excess of £1,000.

In 1980 Toye, Kenning & Spencer, also of Birmingham, produced a pair of enamelled copper boxes in celebration of a hundred years of Test cricket in England. Issued in a limited edition of 1,000 at £35 each, 2in. in diameter, the boxes had a handpainted nostalgic scene of the first Test at The Oval. Like the ordinary edition which showed the official 1880-1980 anniversary emblem in full colour, it was enamelled a deep red. Widespread inquiries suggest that these are not often seen, but the Crummles pill boxes, bearing impressions of Grace and Bradman, are sold at selected leading London shops in a presentation box at £31.50.

Glassware

When a "Glass goblet designed and engraved to commemorate the 150th anniversary of the Marylebone Cricket Club, 1937 . . . designed by Barnaby Howe, made at the Whitefriars Glassworks, diamond point engraving by W. Wilston. quatrain by E.V. Lucas" is sold for £85 as a *print*, 5in.x6in., on card with printed title, at the Bicentenary auction, what price then the Lord's Jubilee glass goblet made a century earlier? Engraved with a necessarily cruder version of the "Grand Jubilee match between the North and South of England" scene shown on the handkerchiefs produced for the occasion, it must surely be the peak of cricketing glassware. Its 1937 counterpart has not been seen at auction for many a year and would also break records. Any valuations we attempt can be mere surmise, but what about £500 and triple that for its splendid predecessor?

There are scores of glass tumblers and tankards, engraved with the faces and achievements of cricketers or reliefs of cricketing figures, and while in some cases their rarity is unquestioned, their impact is muted by ordinary physical problems of accommodation and display, and absence of visual appeal. The great majority are spin-offs prompted by notable events and landmarks, in most cases personalised presentation pieces, but a glass bottle bearing cricketing reliefs and another in the form of a cricket bat appeared as a lot at Phillips in May 1982, fetching £12. As it happens, glassware is less common than many another more unlikely material such as ivory or papier-mâché at auctions. The Bicentenary sale had an unexciting late 19th-century American cut glass lemonade jug commemorating P.F. Warner's English XI visit to New York in 1897 (£250), and a miniature model setting of a Victorian cricket match in a glazed case, with glass figurines on a flocked green pitch, 11in. wide (£450). A sampling of other auctions yields a pair of glass beakers, printed in gilt and green, with signatures of the 1955 South African side, seen at Phillips in October 1988 and sold for £30.

An exceptional commemorative modern set, to mark the centenary of Derbyshire CCC in 1970, was specially designed by Webb Corbett. It comprised a square spirit decanter, at 18 guineas, with associated sugar dredger and glass dishes, all with the county arms. The showpiece, a lead crystal chalice, did not reach estimate at the Chatsworth auction and in 1988 remained with the club.

Other decanters issued in the last decade must include 'The Catch', a lead crystal piece by Zaglo, 9⅝in. high, with a cricket design on all four sides, issued as a limited edition via *The Cricketer* in 1975 at just over £47 inclusive. A crystal decanter at just under £50, with crystal whisky glasses and tulip-shaped goblets, commemorated the two-hundredth anniversary of the first recorded match in Scotland in 1785. Yorkshire-based David Drabble has not been inactive, and John Arlott's tender poem 'The Old Cricketer' lent itself beautifully to a limited edition lead cut-crystal decanter at £49.50 in 1983. This was followed by 100 decanters of the same kind to commemorate Dennis Amiss's hundred hundreds (reached on 29th July 1986) and offered in a presentation box at £49. Drabble also minted a pair of French crystal goblets, 6¼in. high, to celebrate New Zealand's first Test victory on English soil, at Headingley, very reasonably priced at £9.25 in 1984.

Sportsman of the Year for 1976, David Steele's rise from obscurity was accorded fitting recognition with engraved goblets and tankards from the Harleston Engraved Glass Company, priced around £20 each. Then, at half the price, came rather more modest goblets commemorating Northamptonshire's Gillette Cup victory and Middlesex's County Championship triumph, also in 1976. The 1977 Test Centennial prompted the same company to issue a limited number of 903 (England's world record Test score) hand-engraved English crystal goblets, also designed by Tony Carpenter, with original Hambledon-type bats and stumps and appropriate lettering, 5½in. high, and priced at £14.45.

Andrew Glass Engraving chimed in with an "impulse creation", an engraved glass tankard commemorating the Centenary Test year and Jubilee Year Test. The original tankard is with the Hon. Andrew Lawson Johnston, and of 500 manufactured by the sand-blast technique, 50 at a time, about 300 were sold at £16. Derbyshire CCC reacted to Bob Taylor's world wicketkeeping record in 1983 by commissioning a limited edition of 250 Royal Doulton cut-glass tankards, available from the County at £25.

The Wombwell Cricket Lovers' Society of Barnsley, Yorkshire, is justly regarded with true affection by many outside the confines of the county, and one of their many pleasant ceremonies is the gift of a suitably engraved piece of glass to visiting speakers. These engraved glasses were introduced in 1951 (the foundation date of the society) by founder member, Arthur Johnson, who produced them himself by the air-sand blow method. They included cartoons and faces on a variety of glass items and went all over the world to guest speakers. Since his death four years ago, they have been produced by a local firm through Tudor Trophies of Barnsley, but restricted only to names and dates.

Stained glass

That redoubtable collector and writer, Ron Yeomans, owned a colourful piece of stained-glass, showing cricketers and cricket scenes. It formed part of a panel in one of his doors, and was the only piece of cricketing stained glass he knew of in 1963. It was made in 1948 for the Decoration of Inns exhibition in London, and came to Yeomans via a Mr E.R. Payne, a resident of the Stroud area, and two of the scenes in the glass are based on Stroud village cricket, with the centrepiece taken from Horace Hutchinson's book, *Cricket* (1903). Since then, one of a series featuring a variety of sports, a stained glass panel of a cricket scene, 16in. x 28 in., dated c.1938, leapt to £440 at Christie's

Stained glass cricket scene, c. 1938, sold at Christie's in 1988.

Mike Marshall's stained glass portrait of W.G.

in June 1988. Another redoubtable collector, Mike Marshall, commissioned from a local craftsman a unique wall-mounted stained glass figure based on the Wortley picture of W.G.

The *Jewish Chronicle* of 16th October 1987 gave word of a series of stained glass windows at the North Western Reform Synagogue in London dedicated to the memory of the Reverend Philip Cohen, minister of the congregation from 1958 to 1972. The spiritual side of his life was enhanced by a love of cricket, and in the upper part of the final completed window is a "red sphere resembling a sun which is in fact a cricket ball in full flight towards the stripes of a wicket".

It remains to mention the work Keith Hayhurst, curator of the Lancashire CCC museum, has done to restore to its former glory the Barlow window. Richard Gorton Barlow lived and died cricket. His gravestone, with its unforgettable legend, "Bowled at Last!", in Layton Cemetery, Blackpool, is eloquent testimony to this. In his house in Raikes Parade, also in Blackpool, in addition to walls covered in pictures, there were tiles by the fireplace portraying Hornby, Barlow and Pilling, while another lot in the dining room depicted Lord Sheffield's ground. A gas lamp in the hall showed the names of Barlow's Lancashire colleagues and W.G., and it is fitting that some of his other souvenirs have found their proper resting place in Hayhurst's care at Old Trafford. The ground also glories in a stained-glass window which once stood in the vestibule of Barlow's house, ready to greet all-comers (see colour page xix). The same trio are illustrated and the story of the peregrinations of this window since Barlow's death in 1919 speaks volumes for Hayhurst's persistence in pursuit. It also says much for Lancashire durability, typical of Barlow at the crease, for the glass survived moves from its original home via a summer house location, onwards in 1948 to the Stockport home of his illegitimate son, Reginald Gorton Barlow Thompson, prior to its present setting in one of the new hospitality suites at Old Trafford. An ardent collector himself, Barlow would approve of this.

PRINTED EPHEMERA

Autographs

A swift swirl of the pen is just about the only truly personal act the first-class cricketer can do for us lesser mortals. Although long gone are the days when Jack Hobbs, gold pen in hand, could marshal schoolboys into an orderly queue before putting pen to paper, many modern cricketers are similarly patient with their admirers. There are instances – as doubtless there always have been – of players unwilling to sign, but a further source of angst to collectors are fraudulent signatures on touring team sheets. Many worry about this, for it demeans both giver and receiver, and one hears dressing-room stories of persons who can rip off signatures of notable cricketers as and when asked. Short of having items personally signed in one's presence, there can be no absolute guarantee of authenticity.

A pity this, as autograph collecting reflects an enthusiasm going back well into the last century. This is corroborated by Stephen Green's reminder in *Cricketing Bygones* of the autographs he was shown of the All England XI collected by a Victorian enthusiast. For every book collector there must be many more whose short-term preoccupation has been with autographs in one shape or another (see colour page xx). As David Wells, one of the leading modern collectors, has so engagingly written when reflecting on his hobby, it is something taken up in schooldays but which rarely lasts through life. His own collection grew in excess of 13,000 items, mainly team groups, on photographs, signed letters and greetings cards, housed in large loose-leaf albums, the contents mounted in chronological order and covered in tissue paper. G. F. Grace eluded him, but not the bunch of letters sent by J.T. Brown to his parents describing the matches of Stoddart's 1894-95 tour to Australia, nor a collection of postcards sent by Rhodes to an Australian friend describing his first overseas tour. Wells's review, in the *Journal of the Cricket Society*, of Ray Rawlins's *The Guinness Book of World Autographs* (1978) drew attention to some of the basic rules, such as "never cut an autograph down" and "never stick autographs directly on to books and mountings", self-evident truisms unfortunately lost on our forebears. Goldman wrote how as a small boy he camped around the nets at Lord's to watch practice sessions, then badgered the players for autographs. These he later cut from an exercise book and pasted into more permanent album form. The strange (and surprising) gaps in what could well have been his collection can be judged by the desiderata listed in an advertisement in *The Cricketer* in August 1936. It coincides with the period when he was writing for that journal on

Dear Mr Johnston

Enclosed please find the promised autographs of 3 of the 'once upon a timers".

The tinkers think it ought to be worth an o/d free of interest.

Yours sincerely
D.R.A. Gehrs.

The value of autographs – an interest-free overdraft is the price requested of his bank manager by Mr Gehrs, 28 years after his last Test appearance for Australia.

The elaborate signature of John Small.

cricketana and the prominence of the advertisement argues inside influence. Missing were Shrewsbury, Lohmann, Briggs and Lockwood, all well-known names, but also wanted were Paul, Rice, Cunliffe, Mee, Milligan and Marlow.

A constant endeavour of autograph-ologists is how to display their collection to best advantage, be it chronological, by theme, event or acts of individual brilliance. Derek Blanchard, for example, has a section devoted to hat-trick performances, but at last reference had yet to obtain New Zealand's Peter Petherick.

In the 1930s persistent autograph hunters had become such a nuisance that county grounds posted notices threatening expulsion. Freed from constraint, however, the lively Lancashire spinner, Cecil Parkin, once sold his signature at 1d. a time during a charity match between a Hobbs XI and Wimbledon. When the coppers were counted, it was found he had written his name 1,471 times and collected £6.2s.7d. Current observation, however, suggests a decline in juvenile fascination on that scale, more than compensated for by mature mania. The Bicentenary sale at Lord's in 1987 saw estimates exceeded tenfold. A group of 145 autographed postcards of early 20th-century cricketers, including Hobbs, Hayward, Fry and several Fosters, offered as three lots, soared to £5,200 and an F. Gardner drawing surrounding autographs of the 1926 Australians was a winner at £3,200. Many of the same touring side signed a George V one pound note and this achieved a not ignoble £500.

"Probably a record for a signature" was how *Wisden Cricket Monthly* (November 1987) greeted £120 paid for the autograph of John Small, one of the original members of the Hambledon Club. The most prized autograph in J.W. Goldman's collection predated the first (1772) minutes of the Hambledon

The 1926 Australians
and F. Gardner
drawing.

Club. Co-signed by Richard Nyren, Thomas Brett and Small, and dated 25th September 1771, it refers to "Shock" White of Reigate who turned up at Hambledon with a bat wider than the stumps. Two days later "ffour [sic] and quarter inches shall be the breadth forthwith" became law. Goldman's other autographs were procured by gift, purchase, zeal and "last, but not, I hope, least, tact", and the reward came with letters by George Parr (22nd March 1859) and one from Alfred Lyttelton to Sir Spencer Ponsonby Fane in 1908 in which he inclines himself "to the opinion that this office so greatly honoured among sportsmen shd. be reserved for those who are more able to devote some time to it", and that Lord Balfour could not possibly fit in the Presidency of MCC offered to him.

W.G. Grace is dealt with at greater length in the section on Letters so it suffices to note that a postcard realised £48 in April 1979 and at a Sotheby's auction the same month, autobiographical statements by him on a questionnaire sent in by Henry Cust, MP and journalist, together with four related autograph-signed letters, warranted £350 to someone interested in the subject under discussion.

Irving Rosenwater has written[1] of A.J. Gaston's massive compilation of signatures and letters, 18in. thick. By contrast, most of Goldman's 2,000

Two pages from *The Cricketer's Autograph Birthday Book*.

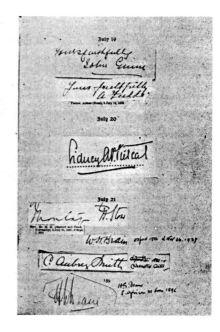

Footnote:
[1] Irving Rosenwater, *Alfred J. Gaston: a Study in Enthusiasm* (1975).

autographs were pasted into T. Broadbent Trowsdale's *The Cricketer's Autograph Birthday Book*, published in 1906 by the Walter Scott Publishing Company. This had on the left-hand side the names of many hundreds of cricketers, giving their birthdays and in some cases the date of death, together with a potted biography. On the right-hand side, under the date, in addition to 103 facsimile signatures, was a space for the autograph to be written or stuck in. Here Goldman would add data culled from *Wisden*'s 'Births and Deaths' section.

David Frith and Derek Blanchard are two of many who have impressive collections, while Srikantan S. Ramamurthy's miscellany claims just about every Test player to have taken the field, from Lillywhite and Alfred Shaw onwards. With Ben Barnett's personal autograph book, inscribed by every player involved in the 1935-36 Australian tour to South Africa and enlivened by original cartoon sketches of the major players by Arthur Mailey, plus every signed Australian tour brochure since 1906, Canberra-based Ramamurthy must be one of the few to rival Roger Mann. The latter has the autographed team sheets – not made-up sheets of separate autographs – of every team to have left English shores this century, and all but two (at the last count) to complete the set of visiting teams. In total number of pre-1939 first-class cricketers from all countries, only about 20 are missing, and, to quote Mann, "patience is a virtue, and virtue is Grace".

Close on 12,000 autographs methodically and carefully laid out in a series of scrap albums formed lots 151-172 at the Phillips sale of October 1988, the property of one collector. Some were on team sheets, and included the rare 1937-38 Lord Tennyson tour to India pleaded for in the *Journal of the Cricket Society* back in 1979. The great majority, however, were individually stuck in, together with related photographs and press cuttings. The material was primarily from c.1930 onwards, but included earlier names such as Fry, Faulkner, Jessop, C.W. Alcock and Walter Brearley, and the scrupulous care given to its alphabetic listing and arrangement by county and country evinced tenderness on the scale accorded by philatelists to their Penny Blacks and Twopence Blues and well merited a total return of £3,670.

Bidding for the Earl of Sheffield's visitors' book containing some great cricketers' signatures of the 1890s was strongly contested, reaching £150 in May 1981. Team signatures, too, have had their moments: the 1904 England and Australian teams at Sydney realised £160 in 1987; there was a respectable £75 in 1985 for the 1907-08 MCC team to Australia and £160 in 1987 for a tour programme signed by both factions on the 1932-33 Bodyline tour. Victor Trumper carries all before him, the major stalking point for an album, one leaf of which, dated 31st August 1899, was signed by 15 members of that summer's Australian team,

An impressive collection.

plus other autographs probably collected at Scarborough during the match against C.I. Thornton's XI. With the addition of cut-out signatures of W.G., Fry, Warner and several other luminaries of that generation, it proved a notable purchase at Christie's in June 1988 for £520. Trumper and the 1905 Australians also figured with a host of contemporary Test and county players at the same auction for £380. Without Trumper, autographs of the 1902 Australians fell to £90, at Phillips in October 1987.

It was suggested that an offering at Phillips in April 1988, a large white Victorian tablecloth, c.1900-10, signed in pencil by approximately 100 cricketers of the Trumper and Trott era, might have come from a hotel much frequented by senior cricketers. Finding for it atmosphere-friendly accommodation may well prove as much a poser for the buyer as the price of £150. The signatures of the 1893 Australians, carefully embroidered in silk by Mrs W.L. Murdoch, who either shared or suffered her husband's passion for the game, reached £450 at Sotheby's major Gleneagles sale in 1980. Cheques are said to be valid wherever signed, but what to say about the stump signed by Don Bradman and Len Hutton, "England v. Australia at Leeds, July 1930", commemorating Bradman's record-breaking 334, except that it is a singularly valuable bit of timber, uprooted at Phillips in June 1988 for £220.

A recent letter from Ray Lindwall, received in response to a query regarding Tufty Mann.

Letters

An amusing account written by Lord Byron touching on his part in the Eton v. Harrow match of 1805 was purchased by Messrs Maggs on behalf of a syndicate of Old Harrovians for £350 in July 1927, for presentation to the school. No sum like that has been attained ever since, not even when Harrow was linked with another historic name, that of John Wisden. This was during his coaching days at Harrow, when in a letter from the Harrow captain he was refused permission to play for Sussex in 1856. This, with the Sussex reply, realised £120, at Bonhams in November 1987.

Letters signed by or about famous cricketers of long ago have become of great worth, and a purely subjective table for autograph letters, with approximate valuations based on known prices, could look like this (W.G. Grace is discussed later in this section):

£150: Spofforth

(especially when, as in a letter to Ashley-Cooper, he dismissed the slightest merit in taking 20 wickets in a match).

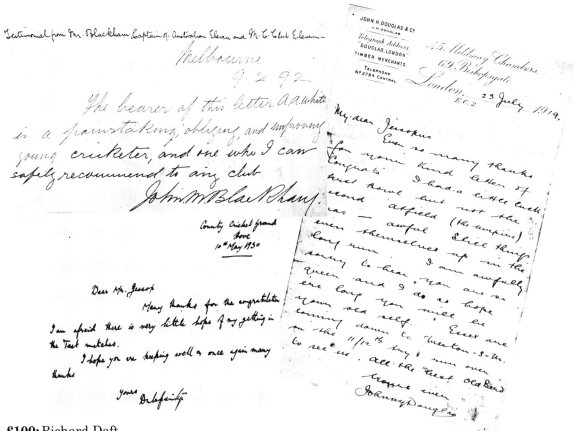

Assorted letters with valuable signatures.

£100: Richard Daft.

£80: J.B. King of Philadelphia.

£70: Hobbs
(even though 35 letters written to his friend Norman Pilleau from 1928-63 realised only £50 at Sotheby's in November 1972).

£60: Ferris and Carpenter
(Carpenter was obviously a favourite son in his native Cambridgeshire: a smoker's compendium presented to him in 1864 drew £450 in April 1979).

£50: Jardine
(unless when writing on Hammond in 1936: "for so great a player he is far from strong on the legside. I have never understood why leg theory was not tried on him - this time *O'Reilly* (our italics) must surely try it"; this soared to £180 in November 1984).

£40: Lords Harris and Hawke, Murdoch.

£35: Warner, Humphreys.

£30: Stoddart, Fry.

£25: Sutcliffe, Bradman.

£20: Oldfield.

Stoneyridge,
Warley Rd.,
Gt. Warley,
Essex.
19. Feb.

Dear Sir,

Many thanks for your invitation to play for the Buccaneers at Lord's on the 31st. I am very sorry that I shall not be able to play. Sorry, too, not to have been able to speak to you on the phone on Saturday but we were due out on the field & I'd only just started changing.

Yours truly,
Kenneth Farnes.

Kenneth Farnes regrets....

W.G. asks Sewell to stand by as reserve for Ranjitsinhji.

LONDON COUNTY CRICKET CLUB.
CRYSTAL PALACE.

"ST. ANDREW'S,"

Telegraphic Address
"GRACE, SYDENHAM."

LAWRIE PARK ROAD,
SYDENHAM, S.E.

4 May 1899

Dear Sewell

Will you bring your bag down on Monday, so that if "Ranji" should be unable to play I should like you to take his place. I enclose ticket for Pavilion. I am

yours truly,
W.G. Grace

Obviously the identity of the writer affects valuations, as can be seen with Carpenter, Daft and Spofforth, but that extra something, such as modest disclaimers of their own ability, expressions of opinion on playing contemporaries, reasons why laws should be amended, the benefit of the tea interval (Hobbs waxed forth strong on that subject) or personal rejoinders to press criticism, can add anything up to £100 to the figure. The comment "You and I got out of the game at the right time . . ." probably pushed up the asking price for an undated Hobbs letter to "My dear Doctor", as much as any references to "Struddy" and Tate. Antiquity, too, plays a part, and the earliest letter in the Roger Mann collection is from John Smith, the actor, who played for Eton v. England in 1750 and writes about the match.

A collection of letters sold at Phillips in November 1984 for £320 is worth exploring, for as well as notes by Jardine and Hammond – not to mention Mountbatten, Attlee, Wavell and Bader – there was a rare Farnes letter of 1940, a year before his death. A Bosanquet letter of 1935 regrets how he was "buried in the country" (Dunsfold) and how his visits to London depended upon the weather. Hugh de Selincourt pleads inability to meet an engagement because of ". . . a book to be finished by the end of the month on top of it all", and Bill Edrich, writing in August 1943, excuses himself from a match as he was at the Staff College, Camberley, and "they won't even give me time off to play for the RAF or England".

E. V. Lucas, writing in the *Sunday Times* in 1936, very rightly observed that "an autographed letter brings you very near to the writer" and letters can afford fascinating glimpses into character. In retrospect, some of the older professionals reveal unsuspected ability in expressing themselves in good, well-mannered English. Purple prose, however, was never a W.G. Grace forte. His letters are rarely more than memoranda or fixture confirmations, brisk, professional and businesslike. Roger Mann has two albums of W.G. letters and pre-stamped cards, some 300 in all, mostly ex-Neville Weston and probably the largest collection in private hands. Embracing most of his adult life and covering matters other than cricket, the collection includes a couple of diverting letters to the South African, C.O.H. Sewell, whom Grace was hoping to entice into playing for his side, and suggesting that to get round his father he play under another name. A letter to the Charles Pardon cricket reporting agency, in 1891, concerning a proposed tour, with two others and one from E.M. Grace, auctioned at Phillips in May 1982, gave some indiction how his name lingers on, a solid tribute at £140. An unusually long letter was offered as part of a mixed lot, which made £260 at Christie's in November 1981, but Grace letters are beginning to feel less rare, reflected in an average price of £70, the figure which dealer John McKenzie was asking in 1983 for a two-page letter to Henry Cust: " . . .I send you a biography of myself by post . . . I am too tired to write answers to all your questions . . ." G.W. Beldam of Middlesex, the best sports photographer of his day, was asked by W.G. why he had not paid his London County subscription for the season, and for this screed Burlington Gallery were expecting £275 in 1987.

Writing in January 1884 to a Mr. Shew from Thrissle House in Bristol, W.G. is at his abrupt best: "Dear Sir, I hear from Mr. Eaves that you are a fast bowler, if you can get down here on Saturday next at 3 o'clock, I shall be pleased to see you bowle [*sic*]. I have a good wicket here . . ." A decade ago, the Rev. Peter Brook, a former chaplain at Clifton College, was loath to part with a London County CC postcard, addressed to A. Podmore of the London and Westminster Bank, postmarked 19th December 1899, and equally terse: "I find we cannot play you at Norbury on May 5th, as we play Surrey here. Would April 28th suit you and would you like to come to us on a Bank Here are hundreds more in this vein, with nothing exceptional about them, beyond the simple fact that the man called by his team-mates "Sir" or "W.G." according to seniority, and partial to his whisky and seltzer, holds us in thrall.

Murray Hedgcock has a notable letter in which Felix writes to try to sell a painting owned by his wife. The letter forms a nice pair with a second-edition copy of *On the Bat*, bought by the collector's wife from Leslie Gutteridge of Epworth Books in 1954 for £4 – the equivalent for her of an average weekly wage. The late James Coldham had an impressive array of letters, enhanced by the acquisition of part of the Charles Pratt Green collection. This enabled him to add early names like Caffyn, Daft, E.M. Grace and Walter Humphreys to those written to him personally by Fry, Hirst, Jackson, C. Aubrey Smith and Townsend. A rich harvest of well over 400 of these letters and cards, including also MCC Presidents and cricket authors, descended on Phillips in October 1988 and yielded almost £3,500. Among them was Tom Emmett's letter written from Rugby to Pratt Green in 1891 regretting that "I gave the only old bat I had away the other day" to some East End schoolkids, "one I had a right to be proud of and at the same time be thankful that at my time of life I could do so well". In reply to a letter from Coldham about his ranking as a quick bowler, C.J. Kortright (1871-1952) showed that the passage of years had done little to dull his abrasiveness:

"The question (personal) you ask me is an impossible one for me to answer as I have never played my own bowling . . ." Written over 40 years ago, this letter is a beauty, if only for its comments on Australians.

Scrapbooks

The dividing line between albums and scrapbooks is so blurred as to need recourse to *The Concise Oxford Dictionary*. A "Picture, paragraph, etc., cut from book or newspaper for keeping in a collection; **~-book** (for pasting these into)" is the singularly unromantic definition for books of personal keepsakes which can develop by the inclusion of relevant material into an impressive symposium of memorabilia.

Five telegrams, 12 photographs, eight cheques and five scorecards are the garnish to 630 letters and nearly 800 individual signatures described by Percy Francis Thomas (usually known by the pseudonym H.P.-T. [Hippo Pott-Thomas or, more likely, Hypotheticus]), in an unpublished manuscript, when speaking of a friend's "funniest-looking bulgy volume that you ever clapped eyes on". In it is the Rev. R.S. Holmes's offer to MCC of his cricket library for £91.15s., including 90 calf-bound volumes at 2s. 6d. each, and letters from Ashley-Cooper, Noble, Shaw, Lord Harris, Fry, Ranji, E.V. Lucas, Relf, Bettesworth, James Lillywhite and many others. Robert Thoms, W.G.'s favourite umpire, gives a detailed description of Richard Daft's benefit match and Ranji called for a copy of his own *Jubilee Book* by "Saturday Morning". From such stuff are dreams made.

Self-assembled books such as these are often the result of years of devoted labour and there is a great fascination in keeping them. Repeatedly one hears regret about newspapers thrown away 20 years ago and now priceless and difficult to replace. That formidable Australian collector, P.J. Mullins, compiled one covering the period from the 1890s to the 1930s, but firm and binding decisions have to be made from the start as to what to exclude and how to classify the contents. Should the scrapbook be devoted to one year's doings? Are the minor or privately-organised matches, which are nevertheless often chockful of the character of cricket, in the shape of toothsome menus and unusual membership credentials, worth the expense of patience, energy, money and grief? Several of these appeared at the MCC Bicentenary auction in April 1987, generally albums of bound newspaper clippings and related documents, often embossed on the cover with details of the contents, which can embrace anything from inclusive periods, tours or particular club memoirs.

The lot to engender most competition was a 500-page scrapbook, which apart from material connected with Lord's between 1925 and 1952, contained such earlier gems as a manuscript scoresheet of MCC v. Oxford University

1841, carte-de-visite photographs of cricketers c.1860, scorecards of MCC v. Australians (including the famous single-day match of 1878) and Eton v. Harrow (1869-79), and, touching and perhaps unique, a family snapshot of W.G. Grace with his son and infant grandson. It took a bid of £1,200 to secure these treasures. Also worthy of note were a 100-page scrapbook compiled by the former Kent player, Francis Marchant, featuring prints, newspaper cuttings and photographs associated with the county's cricket in 1883-1909 (£550); and L.H. Gay's 103-page scrapbook for the 1894-95 tour of Australia, including a list of the 245 animals and birds he shot and, a different sort of wild life, the ladies he danced with in Melbourne (£480). To make clear, however, that the more mundane type of scrapbook, consisting largely of cuttings is in a rather lower price range, at the same auction most 20th-century material was knocked down for £40-£70 and realisations would almost certainly have been lower on a less heady occasion.

"The pride and joy" of the great Geoffrey Copinger collection is A.C. MacLaren's scrapbook, containing, *inter alia*, congratulatory telegrams sent to him in 1895 after his record 424 against Somerset. Available to historians and archivists is a handsomely bound scrapbook presented by the family of C.H.B. Marsham to Kent CCC on permanent loan in 1986, recording the county's championship-winning summer of 1906. As part of his watching brief over the Kent collection, E.W. Swanton wrote that, in addition to reports and photographs, there were telegrams and letters of congratulation from such variegated sources as workhouse inmates and the Viceregal Lodge, Simla. David Frith has a scrapbook kept by Archie Jackson's fiancée, and a separate volume dedicated to correspondence between Jackson and a Hampshire farmer, Harry Mills, until the former's untimely demise in 1933. A rather forlorn note from Michael Mervitz in the *Journal of the Cricket Society* (Autumn 1976) wondered what had happened to the collection of scrapbooks assembled on an international scale over more than 25 years by G.W. Paren of Winchmore Hill, London. Mervitz had ensured that envelopes full of South African cuttings crossed the seaways and airways to Paren at regular intervals for many years.

Two large cricket albums, the handiwork of John Loraine Baldwin,

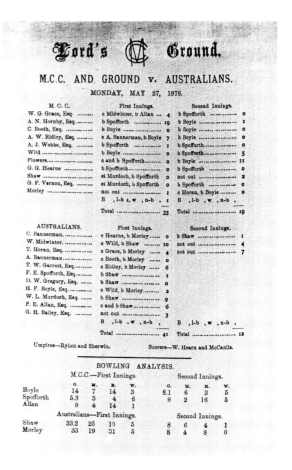

subject of a *Vanity Fair* caricature, for over 50 years linked with the Canterbury Week and a founder member of I Zingari, fetched £56 at Sotheby's in 1928. Although the albums were adjudged less complete than those maintained by Sir Spencer Ponsonby Fane over a longer period, the price paid for albums recording the dominating themes in his life and the MCC Centenary Dinner of 1914 was thought to be unreasonably low. Described in the Sussex CCC auction of May 1980 as "artistically compiled", A.E. Relf's album of his tours to Australia (1903-04) and South Africa (1905-06), with menus and invitations, some autographed, realised £110 and, judging by the extracts subsequently published in *Wisden Cricket Monthly* of an album still at Hove, was worth every penny of it.

A rare item which has survived from overseas: a Lisbon CC subscription receipt of 1861.

Assorted ephemera

The survival rate of printed ephemera never ceases to astonish, and to dip into any of the folio albums constantly under revision by Roger Mann, the leading collector of ephemera today, and his fellows is to sense the bottomless

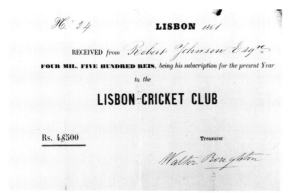

depths of cricket ephemera. Besides tour itineraries, tour brochures, match programmes, handbills with wood engraved vignettes and window bills for novelty fixtures, one is as likely to find John Small's autograph accompanied by a picture of the Bat and Ball inn at Hambledon to make him feel at home, as the front page of *John Bull* showing a picture of the Lord's pavilion burnt down.

The same album might contain pages from actual scorebooks from an 1840s University match with printed ancillary items; theatre programmes with a cricketing theme; Alfred Mynn's admission ticket to his own testimonial match at Lord's in 1847; documents on the formation of Gloucestershire CCC in 1863 and the same for Middlesex, with letters from such county founding fathers as the Walker brothers; railway concessionary tickets; and railway and banquet memoranda from early MCC tours to South Africa.

Gaston's outstanding collection relating to Sussex cricket and cricketers included window bills from 1839, the original Sussex circular red seal (1839), subscribers' tickets from 1841, scoresheets, benefit cards for John Lillywhite and others, and early newspapers with cricket reports from 1772. One Sussex item that somehow eluded him was the proof books of Baxters, the Lewes printers, dated 1814-18, retained in the library of the Sussex Archaeological Society at Lewes, which have several intriguing items connected with cricket. To proofs of handbills for early matches and for Lambert's 'Art of Playing the Game of Cricket' (1816), price 2s. to subscribers, could be added prints of a cricket match with "mediaeval-like tents" for the spectators, other engravings and a scorecard for the last day of a Nottingham v. Sussex match. In the same library there is reference to a sepia wash drawing by T. Henwood of a cricket match in the Dripping Pan, Lewes, dated 1833, the original of which was (in 1966) in the possession of the Rev. C.G.H. Dicker in Bath.

Although the original, of course, is in the Guildford Museum, the price of one shilling [5p.] in 1969 was an excellent bargain for the first certain mention of cricket in English. It came in the form of a double-sided quarto sheet, containing on one side a facsimile reproduction of the three relevant passages bearing on a court case involving one John Derrick in 1598. The other side has a transcript of the manuscript into modern English. Another very rare item, a broadsheet called 'The Princely Way of Sabbath-breaking', a true account of the Duke of Marlborough disporting himself one Sunday afternoon on a village green near Windsor with another peer of the realm and a couple of local lads, playing a game of single-wicket cricket for 20 guineas, is preserved in the British Library, and we hope this book will summon many others of this vintage from obscurity.

Good scrapbook material....

Stephen Green's illuminating article, 'Archives and Cricket' (*The Cricketer*, November 1970), cited several useful examples of documents entrusted to professional care and he signposted the important role which can be played by archive repositories in the preservation of club and personal records. Kent Record Office, for instance, has the "schedule of receipts and expenses of Alfred Mynn, cricketer, bankrupt".

Whether the cricketing world will actually deposit material is quite a different matter. The scattered and fragmentary nature of deposits across the country finds expression in the Sports Council publication, *Sport – a Guide to Historical Sources in the UK* (1983). Although it is nowhere near complete, its author, Richard Cox, does try to include existing manuscripts and archive collections, covering book collections, club records, fixture lists, governing bodies, legal documents, museums, news cuttings, photographs, plans, prints, rules, scorebooks and scrapbooks. Chippenham, for example, has the E.P. Awdry collection of cricketing literature, and there are deposits of cricketing relevance in the Greater London Record Office and Nottinghamshire Record Office. Cumbria Record Office has the Ballantine-Dykes scrapbooks (1877-93); Greater Manchester has the Bolton CC cuttings books and photographs from 1875, and also to be found in this survey are documents from the Belfast Cricket League (1907-70), Hendon CC ledger-book records for 1852-92 and West Kent CC papers (1876-1967).

Cricket ephemera's other more colourful "peeps into the past" include the programme from a smoking concert in 1897 at the Paddington (Sydney) CC, during which a presentation was made by the club to Victor Trumper and several well-known cricketers were among the concert performers, especially one A.C.K. McKenzie, "who sang a sentimental song". Each member of the English team visiting South Africa in 1888 received a "Memorandum for Members of Cape Cricket Team", written with great verve by the tour organiser, Major Warton, and a delightful reminder of a more leisured age. Caps and ribbon were provided for members of the team, but ties and coats were personal problems; details were also on tap about what to wear, the weather prospects, the baggage allowance, money and customs duty ("Guns are heavily charged"), and each member was asked to bring the equivalent of a ukelele for "general amusement".

The old established firm of wine merchants, Messrs Williams, Standring, Sandeman and Heatley of Duke Street in London's West End, had, in 1942, a book, presumably in Benjamin Aislabie's own handwriting, relating to MCC accounts from 1826-42. Aislabie was the first official Secretary of MCC, and the entries make clear something about which many are curious – the extent to which cricket was patronised by the outside public in the years 1820-30. Although they were not first-class fixtures, the "'door-money" for popular matches such as Winchester v. Eton and Harrow, on successive days in July 1830, amounted to £7.13s. and £5.19s.6d. Members and a host of society friends were admitted free, so even if we double the figures, at the known entrance fee to Lord's at this time of 6d., it still argues an attendance of around 600 each day, somewhat lower than recognised figures of 3,000 persons. For a more important match in 1827, the Players' XI v. XVII Gentlemen, the gate-money over three days came to 679 sixpences, or, if preferred, £16.19s.6d. This rather suggests that members would have been liable for entry in what was known as the "match book", a fund collected to meet the deficit on such occasions.

Each overseas tour throws up a selection of memorabilia, and the MCC tour to Australia of 1924-25 was no exception. One lot, including a signed souvenir brochure, menu card, invitation cards and photographs, all formerly the property of Roy Kilner, realised £130 at Phillips in June 1988. A truly exceptional quantity of ephemera of every description, including autographs, silk scorecards, letters, cards, cartoons and photographs, estimated at £40-£60, went for a remarkable £750 at Phillips in June 1988; there was rumoured a strong E.V. Lucas element therein.

Mike Smith has, among a vivid assortment of A.P.F. Chapman ephemera, a telegram from the Prime Minister, Stanley Baldwin, couched in typical statesmanlike jargon: "Hearty congratulations on victory after a most gallant fight of which both sides may feel proud." Also a further one in 1931, foreshadowing trouble in Pakistan yet to come: "Much appreciate your kindly reference in Press regarding Umpires – our task is now made easier by fine sporting spirit of both sides." In a trunk used by P.G.H. Fender on his tours are many of his personal documents, including his regular unemployment book giving as his address the RAF Club in Piccadilly, several posters reflecting his political aspirations as a Conservative candidate, and a letter thanking his host for a photograph of himself taken at the dinner: "My only regret is that I did not make a greater impression on the very charming young lady on my right. I did what I could but it would seem that I was carrying too much weight by comparison with other competitors. Weight for age in reverse!" His cricketer's diary for 1914 has some lovely entries: "Train to Bradford 4.10am, arrive 9.30am, return at 4.50am – arrive at 10.45am". Food for thought for our modern professionals as they roar up the motorway in their sponsored cars!

A final, ephemeral thought: has anyone felt the need to retain a specimen of the old cricket pools coupons, discontinued by Littlewoods and Vernons in the summer of 1971?

Club records and archives

Books of minutes and scorebooks have an unfortunate habit of disappearing, even in the best regulated circles. In 1970, according to Rowland Bowen, an old manuscript account book, one of several assorted ledgers and other financial records, came to light in an old bread oven in Green Lane, Hambledon. In it were details of payments made by the old Hambledon Club from May 1808 to 1826, when matches had to be abandoned or curtailed owing to rain. It is valuable for showing contemporary rates for the job: the Froxfield players of 1809 were paid 5s. each for a day's lost play, the home team 3s.6d. each, and the umpires and scorers a total of 7s.6d. The Hambledon gentlemen received 5s. for another game, their opponents 4s., and one can only speculate about these pay differentials, unless a gate was usually taken and the visitors guaranteed the lion's share. "Players belonging to the Club" were paid for their services. In 1782, on practice days, players were paid 4s. if winners, a shilling less when on the losing side. Reductions for unpunctuality went into a kitty for extra grog.

If we have over-elaborated this example, it is because preservation of the game's records is so important and what a wonderful world it would be for cricket's historians if the game's authorities at every level copied the South Australian Cricket Association, which in 1923 handed over its earliest minute-book for safe-keeping in the State Archives.

One club record which did get away, and found a safe billet with David Frith, was the minute book for Albert CC (1875-80), together with a scorebook, which fetched £26 at Phillips in September 1980.

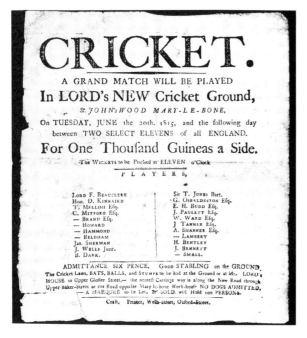

Handbills and posters

Advertising in Britain is as old as the tiny handbill promoting a William Caxton publication in 1477, *The Pyes of Salisbury*, the only extant copy of which is in the Bodleian Library, Oxford. Given the ephemeral nature of the beast, early cricket handbills are almost, if not quite, as rare, especially in good condition. Among the early, choice items is a playbill commemorating a performance at The Theatre, Leeds, on 12th June 1780, of a new drama, 'The Cricketers, or the Sports of Chapel-Town'. There is a copy in the British Library and one known to be in private hands, once in the possession of F.S. Ashley-Cooper. In 1968 Irving Rosenwater published a short monograph, *The Story of a Cricket Playbill*, in an edition of 25 copies, itself a collector's item.

Window bills and broadsheets linking various theatres with cricket appear with a degree of regularity at auction. A window bill of 1823, advertising performances at the Theatre Royal, Birmingham, under the patronage of the Birmingham Cricket Club, realised £55 in 1988.

Much more pertinent, in 1895 Gaston picked out from his collection of early Sussex window bills, dating back to the 1830s, one heralding a benefit match for William Lillywhite on the High Constable's Ground at Brighton, with Sussex (plus Pilch) taking on All-England in 1842. Melbourne has a series from the Goldman collection, again courtesy of Tony Baer, which include "A Match of Cricket . . . England against the County of Sussex" (1836); "Sussex v. Kent, 7 June 1841" and "Kent against England . . . August 1 1842". The anouncement of this match on the Beverley Ground, bearing the names of players who appeared such as Felix, Mynn, Box and William Lillywhite, went for £145 in June 1988 and the survival quotient of advertising for this famous game seems better than most, in that at least four bills have been seen.

An estimate of £50 - £80 was wildly exceeded at the Lord's sale in 1987 for a handbill devoted to an 1852 match at the Oval, between One-Arm and One-Leg Greenwich Pensioners, announced as "Great Novelty!" How and why so callous and bizarre a spectacle could be enjoyed then is outside our brief, but bidding was eager, sufficient to take the realisation to £500. A handbill for the 1837 Eton v. Harrow match went for £200.

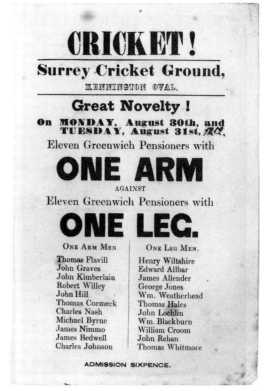

Ron Yeomans wrote with gusto of a memento in his collection which recalled an 1870 match when Scarborough cricketers defeated the mighty United South of England XI. The handbill forbade admittance to all dogs, and Yeomans wondered who vetted the canines. Roger Mann has a delightful pictorial billposter for the Gavrett Ground, dated 1844, for a match involving Twenty-Two Gentlemen of Lincoln's Inn, and an estate agent's handbill announcing the sale of Downend, otherwise "Grace-land".

Posters are probably the least considered of all trifles, and in the homes of cricket lovers are often to be found relegated to the smallest room in the house, usually at head height for gentle perusal. The 'Test Match Special' poster, illustrating the BBC team of commentators in cigarette-card style, designed by Gil Hiley and widely available in 1982, has been seen adorning many a loo door, and the same applies to the poster illustrating the history of Lord's. Slightly more grand settings have been found for the "Star" sketch of Boycott (1983) and the wall-chart marketed in 1975 by T. Bailey Forman with the somewhat lurid caption, "The Golden Years when Notts Cricketers led the World". It is an easy generalisation to make, and is possibly undeserved, but the awkward size of posters and their built-in obsolescence leaves little alternative. This is amplified by their humble origins, throwaway prices and low life expectancy. Advertising agencies and book publishers appear to keep nothing for more than a few months at best.

Try securing a pull of the "Texaco" dressing-room scenes, or the K Shoes advertisement which uses a line-up of pretty girls waiting for a slip catch (see colour page xxi). As for posters of the first Prudential World Cup of 1975, Corbet Andersons turn up with greater frequency.

It would be intriguing to know whether any of the posters designed and painted by Madeleine Marsh for *The Cricketer* survive. They were seen at Lord's and The Oval and at neighbourhood stations in 1929, but where are they now? The same, but even more so, applies to posters advertising a comic cricket match at The Oval, in 1901. Of course there are exceptions. The *Daily Herald* news vendor's bill dramatically announcing "W.G.'s SON DROPS DEAD AT CRICKET", auctioned for £35 in October 1985, not only survives but has found a very good West Country home indeed. This son, youngest of the great man's three, was Charles Butler Grace, a hard-hitting, tail-end batsman and lob bowler in his handful of first-class appearances for London County in 1900. The fateful event occurred in a club match at Bexhill, Sussex, on 6th June 1938, when he was aged 56.

Three Graces: W.G., C.B. (who died at the wicket) and the next generation.

Admission tickets and tokens

The entrance ticket to the Artillery Ground – about 3in. square, probably the work of L.P. Boitard, the well-known book-plate engraver, and dated for 18th June 1744 – is undeniably appealing. A cricket match is shown in progress, based on the artist's 'Exact Representation of the Game of Cricket' (1743), over the name "SMITH" in a laurel wreath. The ticket owned by MCC came from Julian Marshall, author of books on tennis, while Rockley Wilson obtained his as a book-plate. They are believed to be the only two of their kind known. A signed ticket by M. Lambert to the Oxfordshire Cricket Club, a late 18th-century engraving, admits the reader to the magnificent Cardus-Arlott book, justly entitled *The Noblest Game* (1969). Admission checks of this kind (see colour page xx) became less popular and less easily mislaid when membership cards or their equivalent were brought in. The MCC red pass was introduced in 1880, but admission tickets in the form of brass discs resembling coins, used for the Darnall and Hyde Park grounds at Sheffield, are prize captures.

Mike Smith's Darnall disc is especially interesting in that it is dated 1825-29 and bears the initials "WHW". The first ground on which the great matches in the north of the country were played was opened by G. Steer at Darnall in 1821 and the new one in 1824. Steer's son-in-law, W.H. Woolhouse (WHW), became proprietor, and, in true property speculator manner, it was he who in 1829 took over the Hyde Park ground which displaced Darnall. These initials also appeared on a smaller token, with initials "G.H." cut into it, and on one side reads "Payable for refreshment 3d". Another example of these tokens is marked "3d." and admitted persons to the Thornbury CC. It was possibly a ticket for the match, Bristol v. Thornbury CC, on which W.G. dwelt in his book *Cricket* (1891).

Admission disc to the Darnall cricket ground.

Sussex CCC led the way at their sale in May 1980 with original admission chits, two for the John and James Lillywhite benefits of 1871 and 1881, plus a framed photograph of John, all for £75. Another ticket for the same John Lillywhite match at Brighton, 1871, between Gentlemen and Players, made £30 at Phillips in July 1981, though bidding had reached £50 in April 1979.

Although fairly common, these tickets are never to be under-rated, especially those for earlier testimonial matches, such as the one granted to Alfred Mynn in 1847; that he ended as a bankrupt makes it more poignant. Those for the 1880s – as with the Harry Phillips benefit, and the match at Chichester between Lord March's XI and the Australians, played for the benefit of the local professional, Charles Howard (both 1886), which in the same lot realised £22 at the Sussex auction – are also highly admired captures. A fragrance of the social order between the wars lies over a Lancashire County and Manchester CC car park and chauffeur's ticket for 1926, sold at Phillips in July 1981 for £18.

When spring-cleaning the county ground at Southampton in the mid-1950s, the Hampshire secretary Desmond Eagar found hundreds of discs in a large sack. They were circular and in two sizes, and a hole in the middle indicates they were kept on metal rods for use as pass-out checks. A number were sold on behalf of Hampshire CCC funds for 2s. 6d. When offered one by a dealer for 10s., "as they are very scarce", Eagar counter-offered 2,000 at 2s. 6d. each. Collapse of dealer, followed by unforgiving silence.

One of the greatest Compliments ever paid to a Cigarette

The Australian Cricket Team Smoke Only Army Club CIGARETTES

CAVANDERS Ltd. Est. 1775 Pioneers of Hygienic Cigarette Packing PLAIN or CORK TIPS

Men whose prowess depends upon eye, nerve and wind smoke only Army Club

20 for 1/-

Advertising campaigns featuring the Australians tourists are nothing new.

Advertising ephemera

Advertising ephemera is gaining in recognition and price at a startling pace, albeit largely unknown to the cricketana collector. Prices for original artwork or free-standing display material now start at three figures and the product advertised is completely immaterial. Based on recent gallery exhibitions and not on the prices paid at cricketana auctions, we would expect cigarette display cards for 'Players Please', which show Woolley, Hammond and a very youthful F.S. Trueman, to be classed in the £150 bracket. A mounted and framed picture of the England and Australian players for 1928-29 shown on a Robin cigarette display card would start at £200. The firm of Cavenders Ltd., who sold Army Club cigarettes, used advertising pieces centred on a character called "The Major". Among the items on a display put together by the Royal Doulton company was an advertising plaque captioned "The Australian Cricket Team Smoke Army Cigarettes", c.1921-31. These display cards would be on a par with the Robin in value.

A pair of Gunn & Moore advertising panels featuring vivid colour portraits of the 1884 England and Australian teams almost doubled the estimate of £40-£50 in July 1983. A print of the Australian cricket team captained by Woodfull advertising fresh laundry realised £32 at Phillips in May 1982, and a Fry's Cocoa advertising sheet depicting W.G.

TESTS PROVE AUSTRALIANS WOULDN'T GIVE A XXXX FOR ANYTHING ELSE.

Grace, entitled "The Finest Cricketer and the Finest Cocoa of the Century", £18, also at Phillips, in October 1985. A poster of Denis Compton's shining coiffure (see colour page xxi) realised £18 in November 1983; original artwork from Royds advertising agency for Compton and Brylcreem may not yet reach sums equivalent to the 3,816 runs he scored in the golden summer of 1947, but we are getting there!

Advertising agencies and their clients have long seen in cricket a medium for the message. When cricket is not a scenic backdrop to lushly imaginative visions of the conditions under which mid-summer beverages are drunk, its earlier cult personalities came to symbolise all that was good both in the national character and the product. Bovril managed to link up with the Pope in one infamous advertisment for beef extract before advertising standards were imposed, so, naturally, Colman's Mustard saw in W.G. an immediately recognisable focus for their product. Between the wars Hobbs and Sutcliffe as a partnership typified solidity and resolution and as such were also utilised by Colman's for press advertising. John Walker and Sons had their symbol, an 8ft. tall striding figure of Johnnie Walker raising his hat, and slogan "Born 1820 - Still Going Strong", on ingeniously devised scoreboards positioned in cities and holiday resorts around the country during the Test matches of 1930 and 1934. "How's Johnnie Walker? – You're the

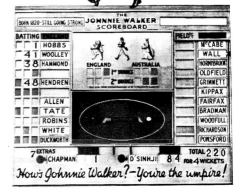

Umpire!". Our adjudication has to be in their favour; they created immense interest and the manner in which discs interchanged and the ball moved according to each delivery anticipated the electronic scoreboard.

After Compton, Brylcreem used Keith Miller, Arthur Milton and John Arlott in the mid-1950s, and Arlott's warm voice and presence were later inseparable from St. Bruno tobacco advertisements. Magazine pages were filled with endorsements for energising, masculine imagery: Dextrose used Peter Loader; Dextrosol, Brian Statham; Lucozade, Tony Lock in 1956; and Ian Johnson, Miller and Ray Lindwall were in close touch with Remington Razors from 1956-57. How Brian Close's dog reacted to the tinned food, Clean Bowl, which the label assured us he was fed on, has not been vouchsafed to us; Ian Botham, whose dog was similarly fed, has been associated with a host of other products.

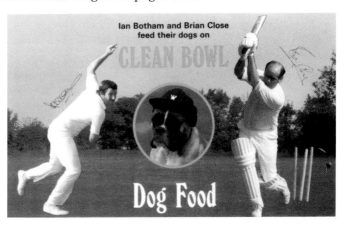

Cricket has not been used for brand-name packaging as much as might be expected. Perhaps two dozen are known, one of the more obscure coming from the Bristol firm of Holloway & Son, who used on their paper bags a gummed picture of an imaginary "Close Run" thing, with W.G. and Blackham involved in a possible run-out incident.

Victor Trumper's agreement with Edwin Geach.

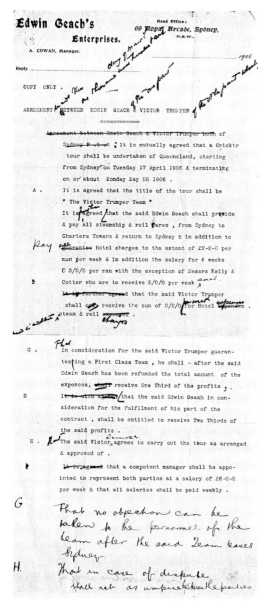

Legal documents

Signed agreements, contracts and indentures bearing on international tours come as close as most collectors ever will to Test selection. From the 1873-74 tour to Australia Roger Mann has a contract signed by W.G. and the agreements sent to G.F. Grace, Jupp, Humphrey and McIntyre for their signatures and/or amendment.

In 1965 Tony Baer had the original hand-written indenture for the 1884 tour by the Australians, counter-signed by many of the greats, together with documentation on the tour manager, George Alexander, who had a separate agreement with the publishers of *The Age* and *The Leader*, the David Syme Company, to supply their own correspondent with daily news bulletins and tour facts. It now reposes in Melbourne.

Victor Trumper's 1906 agreement for taking a team to Queensland, partially annotated by himself and offered with the tour souvenir booklet, was surely worth more than the £150 realised at Christie's in October 1987, although, on reflection, Grimmett's signed copy of a duplicated contract for the 1934 tour by Australia, which kept the press resolutely at bay and restricted players from appearing "at any Theatre, Music Hall or Picture Theatre", managed only £85 in June 1988. Theatrical appearances were freely granted the participants in the Spiers and Pond England adventure to Australia in 1861-62. Already contracted at £150 for the trip, players were also allowed to dispose of photographs on their own account, and to give coaching sessions for profit. Spiers and Pond, an enterprising firm of Melbourne caterers, did, however, retain publication rights for any biographies. When Gordon Ross wrote in 1981 about the original contract for the tour, it was in private hands, and the owner, Mr J. Barnett, had no intention of parting with it. Ross did, however, make the valid point of asking why a century elapsed before commercial sponsorship re-entered the game with the Gillette Cup in 1963.

Menu cards

Liebig's, of Fray Bentos and Extract fame, supplied gratis on application lithographic reproductions of strikingly good photographs of celebrated cricketers, with short biographies, on attractive menu cards issued in April 1897. Five menu cards, printed in sepia with portraits and biographies of Grace, Stoddart, Hearne, Ranji and Richardson, appeared at the MCC Bicentenary sale. We like the cautionary warning, "Imitations, which do not taste so nice, are not so carefully manufactured", almost as much as the winning bid of £420.

Two particularly succulent early masterpieces are a fan-shaped menu, created by Melbourne CC for their special dinner to Lord Harris and his amateurs at the end of the 1878-79 tour, which regaled a buyer to the extent of £260 at Christie's in November 1981, and the menu card of the dinner given by Melbourne CC in honour of Ivo Bligh's 1882-83 team, containing possibly the earliest known representation of the Ashes. This card resides at Lord's.

Resplendent with gold tassel is the special two-sided silken menu in the colours of the Earl of Sheffield, for a banquet marking a fixture at Sheffield Park between the Earl's XI and the 1896 Australians (see colour page xxii). One of very few made, it contains the names of both sides plus officials and is decorated as only the Victorians could with intricate cricketing designs. The menu for a dinner complimenting Ranji on his ten centuries in 1896, devoured £32 at Phillips in May 1982. The becoming splendour of G. Hillyard Swinstead's menus are special favourites. The

Two Hampstead menus, by G. Hillyard Swinstead.

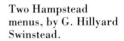

workmanship associated with his name lifted the design for the Hampstead CC Annual Dinner menu at the Trocadero in 1904 into aesthetic and financial orbit. Spofforth, the chairman, is depicted in white tie and tails toasting "the Hampstead warriors", each of them holding a shield with his own initials. A copy, framed and signed by the artist, 15cm. x 21cm., and inscribed to Ashley-Cooper, was for sale from the Burlington Gallery for £225 in 1987.

Whoever collected the card for the farewell dinner at the Guildhall, Cambridge, to Ranji on 17th October 1908, with autographs by W.G., Sir Arthur Conan Doyle, Ranji and others (£38, May 1980), could have paired it for £40 with a Grosvenor Hotel dinner in the dying days of 1912, autographed by Ranji again, Fred Tate and county celebrities, part of a lot which also included the MCC Centenary Dinner card for 1914, Lord Hawke in the chair. The seating arrangements conjure up a glittering assembly of officials and

Right A modern dinner menu, designed by Mike Tarr in 1988. **Far right** Menu card of the dinner given for the victorious MCC tourists of 1903–04.

members, headed by the young princes, Edward and Albert.

The prescience of the person who placed a classified advertisement in *The Cricketer*, as long ago as 1926, for the signed menu card given by MCC to the team which recovered the Ashes in 1903-04 has to be admired. Printed menus for this team, again designed by Swinstead, met with a gourmand's approval at the Bicentenary auction, and when offered with several of the four-page menus for the 'Dinner to the M.C.C. Australian Team, May 1st, 1912', 12 in. x 10 in., with cover design, averaged £140 a lot. An associated lot, the 1912 menu together with the original zinc plate used for the illustration, mounted on wood, went under the hammer for £120.

A 1948 menu card, decorated with an Arthur Mailey cartoon, was very fairly priced at £18 in a Christie's November 1981 sale. Almost 30 years later, among several souvenirs of the Centenary Test in Melbourne, one brought back by Alec Bedser must be unique. This was a menu for the Australian Cricket Board dinner, signed by Sir Donald Bradman and the four surviving bowlers who had taken a hundred wickets in Anglo-Australian Tests – Bill O'Reilly, Ray Lindwall, Clarrie Grimmett and Bedser himself.

Scorecards and scoresheets

For many true believers scorecards come close behind love letters and those written by cricketing immortals as the most revealing evocation of nostalgia, especially if self-completed and annotated. They have, however, never been a sole major collecting field, and it is questionable whether they are as fervently collected today as they were in more leisured, pre-limited-overs times. By the end of the day in many hands they tend to be a crumpled discard, and unless two are bought, one to be completed at leisure and perhaps autographed, how can a spectator be sure of retaining a tidy record if he has witnessed history in the making? Fully printed cards are, of course, a partial, though less personal, answer.

The first scoresheet to record details of individual scores is of a match on 2nd June 1744 at the Artillery Ground, London, but the second earliest is of far greater historical interest. Played also on the Artillery Ground, the match was between Kent and All England on 18th June 1744, and it gave not only individual scores, but also how batsmen were dismissed and by whom. It is also famous as the subject of James Love's *Cricket. An Heroic Poem.*

In what was Colonel Butler's house in Hambledon in 1893 there was a screen covered with the original paper scores of Hambledon Club matches from 1777 down to the club's break-up in 1788. The majority of the sheets had been printed by T. Pratt, the Kent scorer from Sevenoaks. In an advertisement in a Kent newspaper of 1776 he promised "a correct list of the ensuing game at Sevenoaks" between the Hambledon Club and Kent "within half an hour after the game was finished", price 1d. Typical of the 18th century, the scores were printed on thin sheets of paper, so when were the first scores printed on less fragile cards? According to Ashley-Cooper, scorecards at Brighton were first issued in 1823, and, of the other great collectors of yesteryear, Rockley Wilson recorded a card printed by T. Orton of Sheffield dated 1827, and Gaston advertised for sale original cards, printed on cricket grounds, for 1837, 1838 and 1839.

Illustrations of scorecards of 1803, 1817, 1824, 1840 and 1843 have been published, the last priced at 2d. In 1772 scorecards carried asterisks and other printer's rules to indicate the method of dismissal: out of their ground, run out, catched out [sic] and bowled out. The next year scorecards specified who were the bowlers, wicketkeeper and that most indispensable of fielders, long stop, as well as the earliest use of the word "byes", instead of

Right 2d. scorecard of
1864, issued by
Frederick Lillywhite
from his familiar tent.
Far right 1893
scorecard, still without
space for the bowling
analysis.

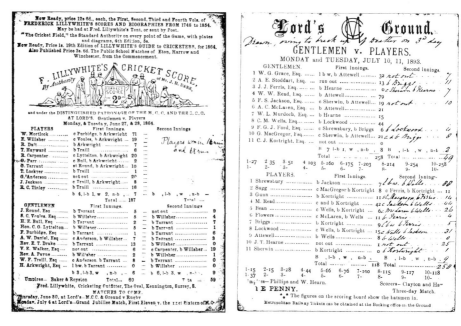

the older "bye-runs" or "bye-balls".

Not until 1836 did MCC scores credit the bowler with any wickets
caught or stumped off his bowling. To gain recognition one had to bowl the
stumps over. Cards produced in London did not carry the bowling analysis
until after 1893 at least, although it was being done in Yorkshire by Billy
Whittam. Surrey began the practice in 1903.

A rare silk scorecard of the match between Kent and All England, 1839,
size 7½in. x 5½in., framed and with a decorative border, is one of very few
as early as this to have come on sale. Burlington Gallery also had another,
for All England v. Narborough in June 1868, priced at £150. First Impressions
offered at £4 a replica silk scorecard for a Kent v. All England match of July
1841. Fuller Pilch, Box and Mynn are among the illustrious names, and the
original was the property of J. R. Mason.

Rev. Robert Stratten Holmes, a noted early collector, had in one frame
cards for Kent v. England, 1839 and 1841, and Sussex v. England, 1847,
played on the "Royal Cricket Ground". The first was for the benefit of Fuller
Pilch and was printed on the ground, West Malling, by G. Windsor from
Gravesend, who was also responsible for another scoring card, that of 1840,
giving the final score in the Kent v. England match, at Town Malling: "a full
statement published at the end of each innings and at the conclusion of the
day's play; 2d. each". Holmes's card measured only 4½in.x3in., and has
a footnote worth treasuring: "Printed for G. Mant, at his Fruit and
Confectionary [*sic*] Stall, and published every hour, at the end of each day's

play, and at the close of the game. To be had as above, a hot dinner at 2 o'clock, 2/6d. Carriages admitted. Good stabling on the ground . . ." Is this early evidence of sponsorship?

An innovation in 1924 was the announcement on these cards as to the side winning the toss. Following as it did soon after the identification by asterisk and cross against their names of captain and wicketkeeper, it was felt that even the most exacting critic now had every detail to hand, and cheaply too. At 1d. the official scorecard for the West Indian fixture over two days against the Civil Service in 1928 was the first for many years to be priced so low. The pre-war price had been 2d. and in the previous century 1d. Whittam, the well-known matchcard printer in Yorkshire, reduced the price of his card for the first day's play only for the Yorkshire v. Kent fixture at Dewsbury in July 1895 to ½d., headlined "Whittam's Official Cricket Card, One Halfpenny each".

Tony Baer in 1965 had the New South Wales v. Victoria scorecard of December 1926, when 352 from Ponsford and 295 from Ryder made up part of Victoria's world record total of 1107. Once again, it is hard to avoid mention of Roger Mann. In addition to a printed scorecard of the Non-Smokers v. Smokers match played on the East Melbourne Cricket Ground in March 1887, recording the "largest score in the world" (803), he has a framed silk recalling the great eighth-wicket stand between Lord Hawke and Peel against Warwickshire in 1896, when Yorkshire amassed 887, then the highest score in English first-class cricket. He needs just four more to complete his collection of every Test match played in this country since the beginning in 1880 to the outbreak of the Second World War. His 14 albums trace cricket from the late 18th century to 1939, and many are signed, and on the cards is noted their source; since many of them are from the collections of deceased cricketers and collectors, a record such as this allows for the genealogical tracing of each item.

Framed commemorative scorecards in silk can share equal billing with ordinary card impressions. As suggested by the figures below, their relative value is ordained as much by age as by historical associations.

1878: the legendary MCC v. Australians match, when a crucial Australian victory dictated cricketing history, a modest £48 (November 1984).
1887: Smokers v. Non-Smokers, at East Melbourne, when Non-Smokers compiled the then world record total of 803 for nine, on printed silk, £220 (April 1987).
1890: Original English Lady Cricketers, Red XI v. Blue XI, at Preston Park, Brighton, on printed silk, £100 (April 1987).
1892: Gentlemen v. Players, on printed silk, £80 (November 1984).
1895: a silk impression of the Somerset v. Lancashire scorecard when

JB Hobbs

Hammett & Co., Printers, Parade, Taunton.

COUNTY CRICKET GROUND, TAUNTON.

Saturday, Monday and Tuesday, August 15th, 17th and 18th, 1925,

SOMERSET v. SURREY

	FIRST INNINGS.	SOMERSET.		SECOND INNINGS.	
1	J. C. W. MacBryan	b Holmes	6	b Fender	109
2	Young	c Sadler b Lockton	58	c Strudwick b Sadler	71
3	T. E. S. Francis	b Sadler	0	c Strudwick b Lockton	12
4	J. C. White	b Sadler	1	c Strudwick b Sadler	30
5	P. R. Johnson	c & b Lockton	30	c Peach b Fender	16
6	E. F. Longrigg	b Sadler	5	run out	4
7	R. A. Ingle	b Fender	22	c Shepherd b Peach	23
8	Hunt	b Lockton	4	b Fender	59
9	J. Bridges	c & b Shepherd	25	b Fender	26
10	R. G. R.-Glasgow	c Jardine b Lockton	4	c Sadler b Fender	5
11	M. Ll.-Hill	not out	0	not out	1
		b, 1-b8, n-b, w4	12	b9, 1-b5, n-b4, w	18

Total ..167   Total ..374

1-11 2-12 3-16 4-93 5-110 6-112 7-118 8-126 9-163 10-167
1-184 2-203 3-228 4-262 5-268 6-268 7-310 8-352 9-373 10-374

	FIRST INNINGS.	SURREY.		SECOND INNINGS.	
1	Hobbs	c Hill b Bridges	101	not out	101
2	Sandham	c Longrigg b Bridges	13	not out	74
3	D. J. Knight	run out	34		
4	Shepherd	b White	0		
5	D. R. Jardine	run out	47		
6	E. R. T. Holmes	c Hill b Glasgow	24		
7	P. G. H. Fender	st. Hill b Young	59		
8	Peach	b Young	20		
9	J. H. Lockton	absent			
10	Sadler	c Johnson b Young	25		
11	Strudwick	not out	10		
		b15, 1-b8, n-b3, w	26	b7, 1-b1, n-b, w	8

Total ..359   Total ..183

1-50 2-146 3-148 4-170 5-221 6-260 7-322 8-325 9-359 10-
1- 2- 3- 4- 5- 6- 7- 8- 9- 10-

Scorers—Trump & Boyington.   Umpires—Draper & Young.
Lunch Interval 1.30 p.m.   Tea Interval 4.15 p.m.   Stumps Drawn 5.30 p.m.

BOWLING ANALYSIS.

SOMERSET.

		First Innings.				Second Innings.			
		O.	M.	R.	W.	O.	M.	R.	W.
P. G. H. Fender	...	13	3	39	1	35.5	6	120	5
E. R. T. Holmes	...	6	2	12	1	17	—	56	—
J. H. Lockton	...	16	4	36	4	9	2	15	1
Sadler	...	16	4	28	3	21	5	58	2
Peach	...	9	2	21	—	20	7	46	1
Shepherd	...	6.3	1	19	1	21	5	60	—

Sadler bowled 2 wides.
Mr. Fender and Mr. Holmes bowled 1 wide each.

Mr. Fender bowled 3 no-balls.
Mr. Holmes bowled 1 no-ball.

SURREY.

		First Innings.				Second Innings.			
		O.	M.	R.	W.	O.	M.	R.	W.
J. C. White	...	29	13	51	1	14	6	34	—
R.-Glasgow	...	25	1	144	1	6	—	42	—
J. J. Bridges	...	37	5	115	2	11	3	27	—
Hunt	...	4	1	14	—	8	1	15	—
Young	...	5.3	1	9	3	15.5	1	39	—
E. F. Longrigg	...	—	—	—	—	3	—	16	—

Mr. R.-Glasgow bowled 3 no-balls.

Creating Two Records by J. B. HOBBS.

126th and 127th Centuries.
13th and 14th Centuries in One Season.

MacLaren made 424, £70 (May 1984).

1896: dismissal of the Australians by MCC for 18 (with another), £25 (November 1983); on silk, £50-£70 (November 1984).

1898: W. G. Grace's Jubilee match, on printed silk, £260 (April 1987).

1922: Hampshire v. Warwickshire "miracle" match (Hants all out for 15, but still winners), on silk, £34 (Hampshire CCC sale, 1984).

1925: Jack Hobbs at Taunton, when he equalled and surpassed W.G.'s 126 centuries, £38 (Sussex CCC sale, May 1980).

1926: Victoria v. New South Wales, when Victoria compiled 1107, £38 (September 1981) and £130 (June 1988).

1928: Warwickshire v. West Indians, signed, £4.50 (Worcs CCC sale, September 1980).

Test matches

1880: (silk) presumed to be an original and not the one issued by Lord's in 1968, £130 (Sotheby's Gleneagles, August 1980).

1882: the "Ashes" match, £40 (December 1981); printed silk, £80 (November 1985).

1884: first Test at Lord's (with another), £20 (November 1983).

1905: a printed silk of England v. Australia at Trent Bridge, £130 (April 1987).

1926: the Oval Test, signed by both teams, £50 (Sussex CCC sale, May 1980 and again in 1981).

1956: "Laker's match", signed by Laker, £17 (September 1980).

The scorecard for the first day of the Headingley Test in 1984 listed the England team under the West Indies heading and vice versa, and with Cowans instead of Allott. By mid-afternoon the revised scorecard was on sale, with the price raised from 18p to 20p. Will this "rogue" card become a collector's piece?

Scorebooks

A. J. Gaston accumulated among his ephemera every Sussex scoresheet from 1830, but Gerald Brodribb's succinct survey in *The Cricketer* (27th June 1953), based on a national tour of discovery, dwelt on the lamentable situation then prevailing. The paucity of tour scorebooks he found was disgraceful, and for a sport so fond of statistics, the *fons et origo* upon which

Facing Page
Jack Hobbs's record-breaking second innings.

The Harrow innings – 65 *exeunt omnes*.

fact is established and myth dispelled, the state of affairs was incredible. Many county scorebooks have gone adrift or been lost in the process of "storage", so it is welcome news indeed that since 1975 the Association of Cricket Statisticians have been engaged in an exercise to "log" all existing scorebooks of this rank.

During the University match in 1949 a scorebook of Magdalen CC dated 1827 was presented to MCC, and it was said to be then the earliest scorebook known to the club. It is, however, superseded by the scorebook for the first Eton v. Harrow match in 1805, which resides in the Museum of Eton Life but was loaned to MCC during its bicentenary year. The pencil scores on the first page of an original book covering the match between the All England XI and 22 of New York, played at Hudson City in September 1868, was part of the estate of the late E.A.C. Thomson, as reported in 1941. The next fixture written up in the book was 22 of Sleaford against the United South

Another big score for A.E. Stoddart against a St. Vincent XI who had travelled to Barbados to meet the tourists.

of England itinerant side in June 1870, with the brothers W.G. and G.F. Grace opening for the visitors. Another genuine rarity is the original scorebook of the 1896-97 tour by Sir Arthur Priestley's side of the West Indies, during which Stoddart made several centuries. This surfaced at the November 1985 'Winder' sale and brought back echoes of early Caribbean languor at £190.

Five manuscript scorebooks compiled by a New Zealand compatriot, Phil Bevan, "from cabled reports of the games as they were in progress of the 1926 team in England", and presented as a memento of the occasion to Clarrie Grimmett, are a bit of an oddity, and one suspects the £240, accorded the lot of which this formed a part at the Christie's sale of June 1988, was more for the inscribed ball used by Grimmett to take his 100th wicket on that tour.

EQUIPMENT AND CLOTHING

Bats

Aged bats and those either signed by the great and the good, and preferably pre-Second World War, or associated with epic achievements and events, are still sought after, despite problems of finding a suitable billet for them en masse in the ordinary household (see colour page xxv). There is, however, another criterion of peculiar interest, and that is just how the giants of the past were actually judged by their own audience. Not everyone was as well connected as A.J. Gaston, to whom his old friend, W.L. Murdoch, presented the bat with which he scored 286 not out against Sussex in 1882. Compare, for instance, a Mr A.J. Farrants of Ye Olde Spotted Horse pub in Putney High Street, London S.W., who in the early years of this century apparently expended huge sums to acquire bats used by famous players.

The pub still stands, but the most strenuous search of the Wandsworth Brewery's archives tells us nothing relating to any such person working as licensee or proprietor. Farrants enters the tale because a somewhat confusing advertisement in *Wisden* for 1903 (which, unaltered, was published for several years afterwards) refers to an auction of "record blades" in aid of the Cricketers' Benevolent Fund Society on "September 15th"; no year was given. The text relates that bids crowded in for a Wisden's Crawford Exceller bat presumably used or signed by W.G. A telegram and telephone messages raised the price to £40, before finally, at 10pm, time was called and Farrants had the bat for £50. The list of prices below the text shows that he also picked up, among others, a Ranji bat for 13 guineas, those of Lord Hawke and Fuller Pilch at £5.10s. each, those of Brockwell, Hayward and Trumble at £4 apiece, and Clem Hill's for £3. If genuine, these scales of values at the turn of the century are intriguing.

To plagiarise song-writer and singer Roy Harper, the sting in the ale may have been an incentive to bidding, but these are prices much on a par with or superior to the great majority of today's winning bids. The list also shows that Trumper was a good runner-up to Grace with £42, followed by Ranji, Jessop and Shrewsbury (£8 each), and at the bottom of the heap, Billy Barnes, J.H. Board and Major W.C. Hedley (£1.15s. each). A Mr Mottram of Johannesburg, over in the UK on holiday, chose judiciously to collect W. Gunn (£3.12s.6d.) and Monty Noble (£2.5s). A.S. (Arthur Shelton?) of Nottingham snapped up W. Scotton of Nottinghamshire for £2 and Messrs A.W. Gamage, of whom mention later, thought C.B. Fry well worth 5 guineas.

By comparison, it may be enlightening to see how we moderns rate the personally signed bats which have come on the market in the last decade.

In strict alphabetical order, then, with no heed paid to proficiency with the bat: a John Piggott bat used in 1896 by Bobby Abel, which *Wisden Cricket Monthly* found particularly fascinating in that the "odd little Surrey man", branded as not at his best against quick bowling, was said, in an attached note from his son, to have used this bat to score a double century against Kortright, the fastest of them all. At the MCC Bicentenary sale, this scored £550. Three bats from R.G. Barlow's own collection, one inscribed with his principal scores of 1881-82, realised £120 at Phillips in May 1982. Charlie Barnett's bat from 1934, inscribed and signed, attracted bidding as fast-moving as his batting, to reach £240 at Bonhams in June 1988. A.J. Dixon's bat of 1877 was sold at the Trent Bridge sale of August 1984 for £220. A C.B. Fry bat, with a Training Ship *Mercury* inscribed plate, raised £90 the same year. The bat used by Norman Gifford in his last season as captain of Worcestershire was sold for a figure just in excess of his batting average in 1980, £20, in the county's auction of that year.

One of W.G.'s bats, inscribed in 1906 that he had scored 120 with it against Kensington, sold for what was a record figure for an autographed bat in 1984 of £500, while another signed bat went for £120. The bat donated by Tony Greig to the Sussex CCC sale in May 1980, used in his last innings for the county, picked up sentiment along the way to touch £200. William Gunn (plus one of Barlow's) limped in at £50 at Phillips in November 1983. At the Trent Bridge sale, one of Nottinghamshire's more recent favourite sons, Richard Hadlee, added £70 to the county's funds for a bat with which he had scored 99 against England at Christchurch. Tom Hayward's bat, inscribed after his 1899 season, realised £300 at the Bicentenary extravaganza.

And then we come to J.B. Hobbs. An inscribed bat with whch he made his only century in 1921 (172 not out v Yorkshire), was a snip at £30 in 1981, but over double the figure ever paid for any bat previously was achieved at Phillips in May 1985 for the willow with which he passed Grace's record aggregate of 54,896 runs – £1,200, sidelining W. G.'s £500 in the process. W.L. Murdoch's bat, signed and dated 1902, went for £85 in November 1984, and Sutcliffe's bat, formerly his own property and inscribed in his own hand with details of the 1934 season, accumulated £360 at Phillips in April 1988. A bat inscribed on the face by Victor Trumper during the 1905 tour delighted a new owner to the tune of £450 at Christie's in October 1987.

The weight of any bat is entirely a personal concern and can vary from the average of 2½lb. nowadays to the massive weapons of wood used in previous centuries. Dimensions are, however, now sacrosanct - a maximum of 4½in. in width and 38in. in length. In 1840 the first so-called "spring handled bat", costing 10s.6d. [53p.], was made by a Salisbury cutler who inserted a steel bar in the middle of the handle; credit for the invention of the cane handle bat in 1853-54 is normally given to Thomas Nixon, a useful professional slow bowler. By 1884 a bat with a cork core in the blade was advertised, and Crawford's Exceller bat had two vertical crosscuts down the handle into which strips of rubber were inserted. From at least 1866 bats used by all grades of cricketers were kept in covers of green baize; others

An 1855 receipt from W.H. Caldecourt, umpire and bat manufacturer, and subject of a John Corbet Anderson lithograph.

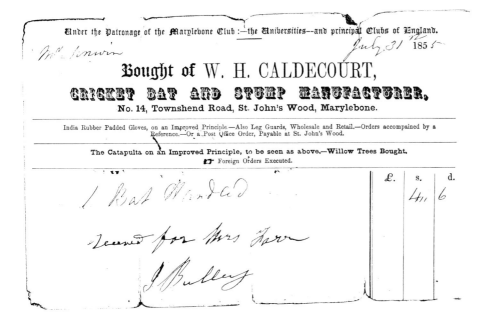

were housed in leather cases, each with its lock and key. Harking back to the size of bats, an unusual cast-iron cricket bat gauge, inscribed "Chertsey 1827" with incised emblems of bats and stumps emerged at Phillips in June 1986, but, with an estimate of £600-£1,000, failed to find a buyer.

The earliest known bat is on display in The Oval pavilion, inscribed "J.C. 1729". Once wielded by James (sometimes given as John) Chitty of Knaphill, it is shaped like an enlarged hockey stick and weighs 2lb. 4oz. At its widest part it measures 4in. The so-called "Hambledon Bat", in the pavilion at Winchester College since 1931, is reputed to have belonged to John Osmond Miles, who, family legend states, used the bat in the first match played on Broadhalfpenny Down. This may have been the "bat of 1743" mentioned by Frederick Gale in his book, *The Game of Cricket* (1887). Mysteries such as this lend folklore to otherwise featureless bits of timber, and, according to G.B. Buckley in 1931, there was in existence a bat stamped with the maker's name – William Pett of Sevenoaks – which had an overall length of 37in. with a blade measuring 24in. long and 4in. wide. It weighed, after the depredations of woodworm, 2lb. 2oz. and was blackened all over,

The Addington bat of 1743.

making it difficult to discover from what wood it had been made.

Primitive curved bats, akin to hockey sticks to deal with grub bowling, and their immediate successors, are all highly prized. One (41in. long) made for a left-hander by T. Johnson of Southfleet, Kent, and rated the most historically interesting item in the Phillips April 1979 sale reached £550. However, that was left far behind when another left-handed bat, a mid-18th century oak, made by Thos. Edmonds, was sold to an Australasian buyer at the MCC sale for an astonishing £5,000 (estimate £800-£1,200). It weighed in at 5lb. 5oz. and its price stands as the all-time record for a single bat. A repaired, strengthened and wormed bat, inscribed "Addington XI 1743", weighing a mere 2lb. 7oz., totalled £1,600 at Christie's in October 1987, around the time that Sevenoaks Vine CC were embroiled in an internal dispute over their 1745 bat, valued at £18,000. The club's membership was divided over whether or not to sell the bat which, for insurance reasons, could not be kept in the clubhouse; proceeds would go to the improvement of facilities at the Vine. Happily, or unhappily, it depends on one's viewpoint, the club decided to keep it under lock and key, and we shall never know how close it might have come to its valuation, staggeringly high as it is.

Bats from the last century, manufactured in conformity with the first upright or straight bat with shoulders, introduced by John Small Snr in 1773, vary according to their significance. One went for £75 in August 1980, while another, dated 1868, with North American significance, vaulted over top estimate of £60 to a stupendous £1,000 at the Bicentenary sale. This same historic sale had a number of Cobbett of St. Marylebone bats from 1820 onwards, at between £75 and £260.

Deeply desirable are bats used in an historic match or by someone for whom the eternal flame flickers. Charles Ernest Green is not a name one knows instinctively, unless you happen to be an Essex buff. He captained the county side in 1882 and for many years afterwards was an inspiration behind the scenes, as well as serving as President of MCC in 1905. A bat of his, presented by MCC for his "brilliant innings" for Cambridge in 1868, was publicised in the Christie's catalogue for the Bicentenary auction. Mike Marshall, bidding on behalf of Essex, had been told that £180 would be enough, but it went (with a bat signed by the Oxford team of 1904) for £320 to a well-heeled Canadian buyer. Both Mike and Essex were undaunted, decided to pursue the matter, and eventually managed to purchase it from its new owner for the price he paid.

"Silver Billy" Beldham, one of the Hambledon men, was the leading batsman of the late 18th and early 19th centuries, and a bat of his was presented by Messrs Clapshaw of Brighton to an exhibition organised by W.L. Murdoch and collector-dealer A.J. Gaston in aid of Sussex CCC funds, held at the Hotel Metropole in Brighton, December 1894. This same bat reposed for years in a glass case at the home of Mrs Puddepha senior, a descendant of the Clapshaw family, until its rediscovery in all its blackened glory by Beldham's modern chronicler, Graham Collyer. The significance of "Silver Billy" to his home town of Farnham was indicated when a gingerbread mould with hall-marked plaque, referring to Harry Hall, Beldham's mentor and himself, was secured at the MCC auction by a local syndicate, happy to part with £400.

Dignified by numerous signatures of Golden Age players, a Shaw & Shrewsbury bat sold for £1,500 at the Bicentenary sale, while an A.G. Spalding Hayward Record blade, originally auctioned at Christie's for the Red Cross in 1915 (when it raised 70 guineas), did exceptionally well at Phillips in June 1986. Autographed by 65 cricketers with 786 Test caps between them, "in the memory of those thousands who were playing cricket at the Front", it was a magnificent purchase at £950. At Phillips in June 1988 a between-wars bat, signed by the likes of Hobbs, Verity, Sutcliffe and Rhodes and presented in an oak display case with glazed frontispiece, managed only a middling £190. A Sandham, Strudwick & Bale bat, autographed by 12 of the Australians who toured North America in 1932, adorned with a caricature self-portrait by Mailey, holding a cricket ball in pouring rain, with signatures on the reverse of top England players and members of the MCC touring team to Canada in 1937, was a beauty for £220 at Christie's in October 1988. A well cared for and used Shaw & Shrewsbury bat, signed by both teams in the 1903-04 Adelaide Test, came with a £650 price tag from the Burlington Gallery – but when you can pick up six bats for £3 then, as a collector, you are in the Roger Mann class.

A few years ago Mann noticed that there were several lots of bats at an auction, many darkened with age and obviously the result of some sort of pavilion clear-out. At the time such lots were plentiful, but he noticed that something was written on one which could not be read with the naked eye. Out of a pocket came the magnifying glass and there were the words "This was Arthur Shrewsbury's last bat . . ." It was quietly replaced and instead of the glass out came the metaphorical prayer book we all carry on such occasions of serendipity. It turned out to be "one of the most satisfying things I ever bought", this from the owner of a collection which in private hands is in a class of its own. Along one wall of his cricket sanctum are eight specimen bats of various types, including a Nonpareil, which adjoin others owned by Sutcliffe, Hobbs, Shrewsbury, William Gunn (with which in 1890 he scored 228 for the Players at Lord's, then the highest score against Australian bowling in England), Major Poore, and the bat used by W.G. to score a century in 1891 on Lord Sheffield's tour of Australia. Mann also has Barlow's favourite bat, taken all round the world in the 1880s. Also in line astern are Tom Hayward's 1899 bat and Tom Walker's implement, possibly the one with

Bats used by Sutcliffe, Hobbs, Shrewsbury and other immortals stand like Napoleon's Old Guard at Waterloo in Roger Mann's sanctum.

which he scored 95 not out for the White Conduit Club v. Kent at Canterbury in 1786, and "acquired by a fluke" at the Lord's auction where it was wrongly numbered. If this is not enough, when last seen there were two flat-backed bats from the 1850s, a "Pod" from the 1840s (two were on sale at the MCC auction at £320 and £450) and one made around 1810 by H. Durtnal of Ickham, Kent. A Durtnal production from the late 18th century, which had once belonged to the Earl of Dalkeith, humped back, unspliced handle and all, was another part of the Bicentenary fling at £500.

Among mementos of Lord Sheffield's cricketing endeavours are bats, shared among a number of owners, including one used at Spitzbergen under the Midnight Sun in August 1894. Although David Frith has Archie Jackson's bat, used to score 73 against England at The Oval in 1930, many bats used by Australian giants have stayed in their home country, and ace collector "Ram" Ramamurthy counts among his bats a signed specimen, with brass plaque, used by Clem Hill in the 1897-98 series, one used by Trumper in 1907 (covered with the signatures of some 400 players) and the bat used by Doug Walters to score a century between tea and close of play against England at Perth in 1974-75.

Lord's houses in one display case alone sufficient bats to trace the evolution and development of bat manufacture, so lucidly discussed in Hugh Barty-King's *Quilt Winders and Pod Shavers* (1979), but, with over 130 bats on view, the finest collection of bats of famous players can be claimed by Trent

Bridge. One of the earliest curiosities was a bat made before the whalebone splice was introduced, but much more romantic is the bat made from the bough of a tree which overhangs Napoleon's tomb on St Helena, transplanted as a cutting to a Surrey garden around 1840, and fashioned from willow grown at Portslade in Sussex.

The majestic collection, formed by Charles Pratt Green and which originally comprised 149 historic bats, found textual expression in J.N. Pentelow's *Historic Bats* (1931), devoted exclusively to these willow wands. Such was the splendour of this array that every county was represented bar Glamorgan, with Nottinghamshire batsmen strongly mustered. A.W. Shelton, responsible for the transfer to Sir Julien Cahn of the collection accumulated since the late 1880s by Pratt Green, was able to repay the donor by passing to him the bat with which A.O. Jones made most of his runs, over 2,000 in all, in 1901. To anyone cognisant of the history of the game the mere list of names is thrilling: the Graces, Jessop, I.D. Walker, Thornton, Shrewsbury, and seven of the men who played in the great Test rubber of 1894-95 – Stoddart, MacLaren, Brown, Ford, Peel, Ward and Brockwell. There was also a clutch of mighty Australians – Giffen, Armstrong, Noble, Hill, Bardsley, Trumper and Murdoch. Possibly the most renowned bat was that used by Hayward to compile his 1906 record aggregate of 3,518 runs, though there was also one used by Alfred Shaw in the very first Test match of 1877. When Trent Bridge was glutted to overflowing with Sir Julien's benevolence, the balance was sold by Redmayne & Todd of Nottingham so that some of Pratt Green's armoury is dispersed across the cricketing globe. Nottinghamshire (how the donor was said to detest the abbreviation Notts) also have a bat donated in 1940 by Shelton to his lifelong friend, Sir Julien, bearing 252 autographs, collected by Shelton either personally or by letter. Only two of the names were those of men who did not play first-class cricket, Prince Christian Victor and A.E.J. Collins, whose world record score of 628 not out must have hung like an albatross round his neck for the rest of his short life. Spofforth appended his name only a short time before his death and the oldest cricketer to sign the bat was Sir Herbert Jenner-Fust (1806-1904).

More modern accessions to the collection include the bat used by Bradman to score a hundred in the Trent Bridge Test of 1938 and two historic ones from an adopted son of Nottingham, Gary Sobers, with which he made the world record Test score of 365 not out in 1958 and another with which he hit six sixes off an over in 1968.

Much is owed to that most likeable of Australian journalists, Murray Hedgcock, for his enterprise in penning a note in the *Journal of the Cricket Society* (Autumn 1973) on the 18 bats in Gamages department store, London, before it closed for the last time in 1972, whereupon Stephen Green was able to gather them unto the MCC bosom. How the collection came about no one will ever know, but Hedgcock concluded that it was a self-generating promotional exercise by the sporting goods department, which, like Topsy, just growed. Apart from a couple of comparatively modern signed bats – the most recent of 1953 vintage, signed by both England and Australian Test elevens, and the famous Gamage double-spliced bat (a longtime favourite of club cricketers) – the remainder were part of cricket history. Murdoch signed one, Grace a brace, while Fry and Hobbs were also represented. The greatest thrill of all, though, was to see the bat used by Rhodes to make the winning hit in the last Test of 1902, as well as the bat with which Hirst reached 58 not out in their epic last-wicket partnership.

The Basil D'Oliveira bat produced by T. Ives & Son Ltd.

Modern signed bats are the poor relations and, though popular as raffle prizes or at benefit dinners, rarely attract much interest at auction, if indeed they find a buyer. From any number of examples where the realisation fails even to match the retail price of the bat, we might select from the Phillips sale of November 1983 one signed by the 1976 West Indians, including a batting line-up of Greenidge, Fredericks, Rowe, Richards, Kallicharran and Lloyd, which made only £15, and another autographed by the England and Pakistan teams of 1971, which made £20. Time will doubtless lend them value, but, as already mentioned in the previous chapter concerning autographs, collectors are wary of the "substitute" signatures reportedly sometimes applied in the dressing-room. There are, of course, exceptions, among which we have noted bats offered for charitable causes and, recently, one from the MCC Bicentenary match of 1987, signed by the teams and reserves, which made £160 at Christie's in October 1988. Four months earlier Christie's had a bat autographed by the England and Rest of the World teams from that star-studded series of 1970 and it was bid up to £120.

Miniature bats are discussed in the next section, but we should mention some other novelties. A 4ft. 6in. Wisden Wonder bat, covered in autographs including Sussex and West Indies, was a qualified bargain to someone for £55 at Phillips in May 1980, while an even larger (5ft. 8in. high, 8in. wide) Newbury Excalibur, sold by Kent CCC and bearing the signatures of all the 1985 county teams, plus the England and Australia Test sides of that summer, was bid up to £260, somewhat below estimate.

A bat stamped with a player's portrait – believed to be the first time this had been done apart from the work of Australian cartoonists such as Arthur Mailey and Tony Rafty – was presented by Basil D'Oliveira to MCC in 1972, since when a thriving industry in bats bearing cartoon effigies by English artists such as Joan Redman and Mike Tarr has grown, many of them the result of private commissions.

Miniature bats

Presentation miniature cricket bats, be they Warsop, Gradidge, Gunn & Moore or Gray-Nicolls wooden blades, are warmly welcomed by collectors unblessed with palatial surroundings or living abroad, so that dispatch of the full-size equivalent is impractical and extremely costly. Such bats are often 18in. long, bear the signatures of touring sides or act as models of earlier types of bats; they are more than merely decorative, acting as agreeable conversation pieces. At auction they tend to average around £5 with facsimile signatures, from £15 upwards with the real thing.

The MCC Bicentenary sale had six lots, all bar one rather humdrum and carrying facsimile signatures (see colour page xxv); but one, the snugly mounted miniature bats made by trimmings from five old bats, including those of Grace, Gunn and Shrewsbury, framed in wood and brass, was an ornament so historically and aesthetically pleasing that it is remarkable that the authorities let it go. For all that, the donor, "E.A. Bennett, 1927", would have found solace that funds at headquarters benefited to the tune of £950.

There can be few earlier miniature bats than a model bat presented to Richard Nyren when he left Hambledon in 1791. Curved in shape, of uniform width and with shoulders, it belonged to Neville Weston. Its length was 5in., blade 3¼in. and width of blade ⅝in., and the speculation is that it was a model of one of Nyren's favourite bats.

The famous elm tree at Trent Bridge named after George Parr (1826-91), which stood for close on two centuries beyond the square-leg boundary but was rent asunder by a gale in 1976, surrendered enough timber for souvenir miniatures to be made and sold at the Nottinghamshire club shop. First on sale in January 1977 at £7.50, they are still to be had at much the same price. When another famous tree, the lime at the St Lawrence Ground, Canterbury, was pollarded, the bigger branches were kept at the insistence of club secretary, David Dalby. Bat and stump sets were then marketed as part of Kent's appeal year, 1985. They were beautifully made and, of course, a one-off production, but in three years only a dozen or so had been sold at a profit of around £1,000.

More in the nature of "advertiques", novelties or household gadgets, are ivory miniatures, probably designed as paper knives, to be had for between £20 and £35. Rowntree's miniature bat, a packaging gimmick for Cachous, appears with some regularity for sale but seldom sinks below £20. Another ivory miniature, inscribed "W.G.", 12 cm. along with a smaller version, estimated at £100-£150, failed to find a buyer at Phillips in October 1986, but two carved bone bats, 3¾in., made £35 at Bonhams in June 1988.

Batting and wicketkeeping gloves

The cricket bag used by J.R. Mason on Stoddart's 1897-98 tour to Australia contains his bat, cap, boots and batting gloves, the last of these claimed by the present owner, Roger Mann, to be older than any at Lord's.

That multi-talented cricketer, Nicholas Felix, is credited with the invention in 1837 of the first batting glove with plain rubber protection. It consisted of pieces of flat rubber glued on in different places. Prior to this batting gloves were made of leather, with inside finger stall padding, and made only to order. Tubular india rubber gloves manufactured by Robert Dark of Lord's were advertised in Denison's *The Cricketer's Companion* of 1844, and, after various modifications, by 1878 sponge rubber was tried in preference to tubular; in 1893 Frank Bryan's gloves had a flange by which they could be securely sewn on instead of glued. Both Lord's and Melbourne have pairs of gloves claimed to have been worn by Jessop, those at Lord's used in the 1902 Test series, while collector Mike Smith has one of the tubular rubber gloves used by Mason at the turn of the century.

Probably the first to wear gloves of any description was John Barnard of Eton, Cambridge, the Gentlemen and Kent, something of a dandy it is said, with a pair of kid gloves. Tom Box of Sussex was the only wicketkeeper who stood close to the stumps and about 1840 he wore a single buckskin glove on his left hand. Pictures show him either with no gloves or pads or more rationally attired with gauntlets (gloves) and pads.

According to Frederick Gale, E.G. Wenman kept wicket to the "terrific bowling" of Alfred Mynn without gloves or pads "until they were introduced in 1841". Normally ordinary, everyday leather gloves, or those used during hunting, were the only ones used, although many dispensed with them altogether. Long-stops did the hard work, being the equivalent of the modern wicketkeeper standing well back, and because of the rough state of some of the grounds, the less expert or valiant of them wore both gloves and pads, or at least wrist gauntlets.

Gauntlets – presumably of leather and possibly padded – were advertised by Duke and Son in 1848, and in 1851 Fred Lillywhite's gloves were perforated for ventilation. Ineffective as they probably appear to modern stumpers, it was suggestions by the best of their breed which led to ever more sophisticated refinements, aimed at lightness as well as self-protection, so that by 1888 The Blackham, rough rubber-faced gloves, became popular. This is, incidentally, believed to be the first occasion when a cricketer's gear was named after someone famous for his use of it. G. B. Buckley mentions that bats named after Ranji and "The Guv'nor" (Bobby Abel) were on sale in 1899, and W.C. Smith of Surrey was immortalised by a ball named Razor Smith in 1911.

Pads

G.B. Buckley's insatiable and rewarding researches into the *minutiae* of cricketing history reveal that the first attempt at a leg guard was the two wooden boards set at an angle, worn on one leg only about 1800 by "Long" Robert Robinson, the famous crippled left-hander from Farnham. The earliest pads in general use, necessitated by the legislation of 1828 permitting fast and erratic round-arm bowling, were small and flimsy, requiring an additional knee guard. Edward Wenman, who kept wicket for Kent from 1825-54, wore just a single short pad and, according to Buckley in *Cricket Quarterly* (Spring 1967), one of his, dated 1848 and signed, was still in existence in the Lord's Memorial Gallery. Cork pads were invented by Thomas Nixon in 1841, thus bringing pads into general use, and by 1844 Dark was advertising leg guards probably incorporating cork and india rubber. More open pads were the subject of much trial and error by Nixon and others throughout the 1850s. At the Great Exhibition of 1851, Lillywhite and Sons displayed new types of leg guards, stuffed with horse hair at 25s. [£1.25], compared with £6 for the best buckskin pads over a century later.

By 1857 cane leg guards appeared and ventilated pads were advertised as made to order by 1880. These became known as skeleton pads, and a pair of these ribbed lightweight pads forms part of the Lord's collection. Among private collectors, pads such as these are owned by Mike Smith and Roger Mann.

Alfred Mynn's pads, once the property of W.G. Grace as the only man in the realm fit to wear them, were believed by Buckley to be in the pavilion at Canterbury, but he may have confused them with the pair made of buckskin, with a cotton lining and filled with horsehair, which are housed there but are generally agreed to have belonged to Fuller Pilch, Kent's premier batsman of the 1840s.

Two pairs of old ribbed pads made £50 at auction in November 1983, and a pair of open-ribbed pads much the same sort of price in 1986. At Phillips in October that year, a pair of early 20th-century ribbed batting pads, estimated at £30-£40, reached £55. Another pair of skeleton pads came up for auction at Christie's in October 1988, a useful form of protection at £50.

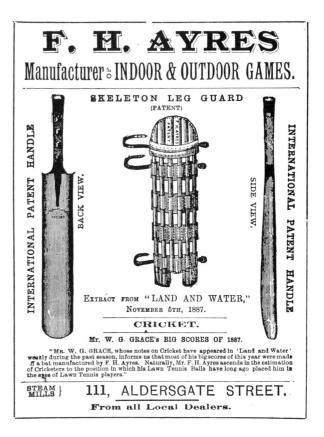

Balls

Presentation balls abound, usually mounted on a wooden or metal base, with appropriate engraved plaque or silver band saluting a noteworthy feat. For his illustration in *Cricketing Bygones*, Stephen Green made the particularly happy choice of an ornamental "hat", symbolising the top hat reputedly given in earlier days to bowlers who had pulled off the "hat-trick" of three wickets with three successive deliveries. Various examples of these tangible rewards for splendid endeavour have been noted across the years, and their value depends on who did what to whom. W.P. Howell's ten wickets for 28 for the Australians against Surrey in 1899 was hailed by the Surrey committee as worthy of ornamentation, as was the beautifully mounted ball presented to Arnold Warren of Derbyshire by his friends and admirers for his five for 57 in his only Test, at Leeds against Australia in 1905.

Many are in the possession of clubs, such as the historic ball which, as part of a set, was awarded a gold medal at the Melbourne Exhibition of 1881, mounted and presented to its maker, Isaac Ingram of the firm of Duke and Son, and bequeathed by Ingram's son in 1972 to Leigh CC, who play on Leigh Green near Tonbridge. The Duke family are reputed to have been making cricket balls in Penshurst, Kent, as early as the middle of the 17th century, but as Duke and Son were formally inaugurated in 1760. In 1921 they amalgamated with John Wisden and Company, and claim the invention of the treble-seam, hand-stitched ball, almost unchanged to this day. Some sense of continuity also emerges from the archives of the firm of Alfred Reader, established in Hadlow, 1808, by William Martin, and now deposited in the Kent Record Office in Maidstone. The inventory alone, comprising letters, testimonials, order books, wage bills and specifications, deserves a glance.

The earliest recorded ball manufacturer was more likely to have been John Small Snr, who played for Hambledon in the middle of the 18th century and was a leather worker in Petersfield, Hampshire. With less room to manoeuvre than with bats, 19th-century manufacturers had a threefold aim – to make cricket balls more attractive looking, more durable and less liable to go out of shape, and, naturally, less hard on the hands.

Since the first code of laws in 1744, the weight and circumference of balls have shifted according to the state of the game, the last regulation coming into force in 1927, but no ball earlier than the 1820 specimen at Lord's appears to have survived. It was off this suffering orb that William Ward made his historic 278 for MCC v. Norfolk. Roger Mann's collection includes a very early 19th-century ball, one of the first half-dozen known, and that ardent Sussex collector, Nicholas Sharp, has one used in the 1855 Sussex v. Surrey game when Sussex won by two runs. By 1865 a more expensive catgut seamed ball had been patented, and wire-sewn balls were advertised in 1885.

Not every ball had a leather casing. There was a wooden one with a thin layer of gutta-percha in 1849, Nicholson's well known composition ball in 1860 and the equally famous Eclipse back in 1881. There is, moreover, nothing new about the use of a white ball, greeted with such derision by sections of the media as part of the "circus cricket" of the 1970s. David Frith has one of the Kerry Packer World Series balls (see colour page xxiv), but we should bear in mind a smaller footnote in cricketing history, that the poet Keats was slightly hurt by a white ball while practising in 1819.

The prices of early balls seem amazingly steep. William Pett sold his cricket balls at 3s.6d. [18p.] each in 1766 and the price of Duke's best ball was 7s. [35p.] in 1811 and still the same in 1836. By 1858 prices had slipped slightly to between 3s.6d. and 6s. Reacting to market pressure prices by 1880 ranged between 4s. and 7s.6d. but even at that level, by comparison with a living wage a century ago, they still seem outstandingly high.

What must represent a fair average price for important unmounted cricket balls, generally with simple plaque inscriptions, is the realisation of £180 at Phillips in June 1986 for a set of three Test match balls, relating to the Anglo-Australian Test at The Oval in 1909, together with two other similar balls for 1921 and 1938. David Frith has the battered balls with which Tom Richardson took all ten wickets for 45 for Surrey against Essex in 1894 and eight Australian wickets for 94, his best analysis for England, in his final Test at Sydney in 1898 (see colour page xxv); the last ball used by the great Yorkshireman, George Hirst, on his formal farewell to first class cricket – at the Scarborough Festival of 1921 in a Gentlemen v. Players fixture – is the property of D.A. Stephenson of Kirkheaton, Huddersfield. The balls with which Sydney Santall, in 1909, took his 1,000th first-class wicket and then his 1,000th wicket for Warwickshire were each worth £150 at Phillips in November 1985. The ball used by Jack Gregory to bowl Hobbs after his century in the 1926 Test at The Oval caught the imagination at £250 in April 1979, as did the ball that spun like a top during Alf Valentine's mesmeric six for 39 to complete the West Indies' victory at The Oval in 1950. This signalled the coming of age of the West Indies as a force in world cricket, recognised by the late Chris Pilkington, who was prepared to bid £200 for the ball in November 1985.

Burlington Gallery asked £245 for F.R. Foster's 1912 Test match ball, with a silver hallmarked band inscribed "England v. Australia. At Adelaide. Third Test Match 12th Jan. 1912, 5 for 36 and Made 71". At first glance £17 for 17 deliveries seems a trifle over the top, but the betting is that the ball used during the controversially void Benson and Hedges Cup match between Somerset and Worcestershire in 1979 was a shrewd investment when bought in 1980, risible as it seemed at the time.

Few of the gods of the game seemed to be aware of the manna from

Heaven inherent in their own spoils, though Tom Hayward is said to have pensioned off his bats on a regular basis, dutifully inscribing them before they were given to suitable recipients. Hence the cordial reception at Christie's in June 1988 accorded any material clothed in the Clarrie Grimmett mystique. Two balls used by him on the 1934 tour in England and inscribed in his own hand failed, however, to make the impact expected of them. A return of £110 for nine wickets for 74 against Cambridge seems meagre, but much classier was the £200 paid for the ball with which he took his 100th wicket on the tour at Trent Bridge v. Nottinghamshire.

At a less elevated level, balls preserved for achievements in minor cricket have an interest of their own, though they are not always pursued with fervour by collectors. Thus a ball made by Thomas Twort and presented to G.H. Cornwall for seven wickets in seven successive deliveries at Cheltenham College in 1879, estimated at £100-£200, failed to find a buyer at Christie's in October 1988. We note the existence also of a ball prized for its excellent condition and workmanship with which W. Park accomplished identical figures, all bowled, for Noel Park CC on its home ground in June 1890.

The MCC Bicentenary auction, of course, knocked recognised values out of kilter, what with £750 paid for two balls used in the 1910-11 Australia v. South Africa series, for all *Wisden Cricket Monthly* suggesting that with this purchase the series "came back to life". "Ram" Ramamurthy's collection of Test match balls happens to have one used at Melbourne in that series, signed by the members of both teams. The auction nevertheless offered a couple of superlative catches for someone with an interest in Harvey Fellows: one, a ball hit over the stand at Lord's (occasion unidentified), for £420, and another, used when he was at his sharpest, the ball with which he took ten wickets in the 1849 Gentlemen v. Players match, for £450. Arthur Appleby, a left-arm fast-medium round-arm bowler from Lancashire, bowled throughout the 1867 Gentlemen v. Players match at Lord's, and the ball he employed to such telling effect for eight for 65, was worth £50 a wicket at the same auction.

In the same way as he caused the newsroom at *The Times* to erupt with euphoria during the fantastic 1981 Headingley Test victory over Australia, so Bob Willis set cricketana hearts fluttering with the auction of his personal memorabilia at Christie's in October 1988. The ball with which he took eight for 43 to overturn the odds of 500-1 was bid up to £1,150, as part of a lot also containing a medallion commemorating the feat and nine others. Another outstanding item at £300 was the ball with which Willis performed the hat-trick for Warwickshire v. Derbyshire in September 1972, now mounted on a stand with a white metal plaque.

In a showcase at Lord's are two unusual cricket balls. The first is the last-known example of a ball coloured blue, a remnant of a commercially disastrous venture by the High Holborn firm of A.W. Gamage in the 1890s. The contract was given to the firm of Alfred Reader on Gamage's assumption that carefully nurtured young ladies might suffer an attack of the vapours at the colour of blood – a factor most unlikely to disturb the makers of the other ball, made out of string and lovingly assembled by prisoners of war.

A Red Cross string ball of the correct size and weight, made by New Zealand POWs in north Italy, is a proud possession of New Zealand's first National Cricket Museum. The ball associated with the Earl of Sheffield's midnight match at Spitzbergen in Norway in August 1894 has also been preserved, as well as others associated with one of cricket's greatest benefactors.

Over the doorway into his cricket room, Roger Mann has an ornate display of 10 balls used in each match on Lord Sheffield's tour of Australia in 1891-92, mounted in the self-consciously aware style to which only Victorian tycoons aspired, and obviously from the Sheffield family home. Held in eggcup-shaped containers on a carved wooden rack, half with shields and the remainder numbered, they are described in the 1894 brochure for the exhibition in Brighton organised by W.L. Murdoch and A.J. Gaston.

Jim Coldham had an absorbing tale to tell in *The Cricketer* (November 1983) of the mystery surrounding the number of balls associated with Frank Cobden's famous winning hat-trick for Cambridge against Oxford at Lord's in June 1870, and inquired which of the *four* known inscribed balls was the actual one used by Cobden in that fateful over. A part-answer came (January 1984) in a published letter from Roger Mann, who owns the "least important" of the Cobden balls, the "Harrow" ball, presented to Cobden by I.D. Walker of Middlesex after an earlier performance in an Eton v. Harrow game of 1866. He pointed out that two balls were awarded to the bowler after the match, and went on to give the inscription on the ball actually held in the bowler's hand. A third ball, with different and incorrectly dated wording, was presented by Cambridge University CC, but the question was left open as to whether any more "fraudulent" balls happen to be in circulation. Whatever the case may be, should any of the genuine articles come up for sale, all those concerned could be looking at sums exceeding £350.

Finally, and in similar vein, we must not forget the most famous bowling feat of all time, Laker's 19 for 90 against Australia at Old Trafford in 1956. Here again there are rival claimants: Lord's has two balls, one from each innings and with appropriate plaque; but another emerged at Phillips in October 1987, of the same make and inscribed in ink and signed by Laker. This one had been the prize for a competition organised by the *Daily Express*, which entailed writing a telegram congratulating the bowler, and was advertised as the ball with which Laker took the 10 wickets in the second innings. Since England bowled a total of 150.2 overs in that innings, Laker himself delivering 51.2 in six distinct spells, there will have been at least two balls, so Lord's, the prize-winner and now the collector who bid £140 can rest a little easier.

Bowling machines

From 1883 to 1898 "the only Bowling Machine now in use" was the Wisden Catapulta, patented by Frederick Lillywhite and John Wisden in 1858 and

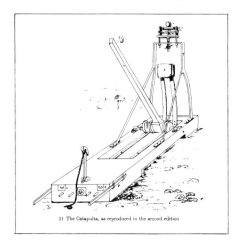

21 The Catapulta, as reproduced in the second edition

The dinosaur of bowling machines – the Wisden Catapulta.

priced latterly at 12 guineas [£12.60]. Basically it was an improved refinement of Felix's invention of 1837, and then given by him to W.H. Caldecourt, an employee on the ground staff at Lord's, whose shop on the ground sold his own bats and other cricket material. The Felix original was a crude iron affair, made by a local blacksmith, and given to his friend, J. Spencer, a fellow member of the Blackheath Dartmouth CC.

An appreciative description of a try-out with a Reginald Brooks-King bowling machine – patented in 1908 and still in production until the late 1930s, light and requiring no fixing to the ground – was given in *The Corner Stone of English Cricket* (1948) by the Hon. E.G. French. Unique in that the bowling arm was a compound one and capable of imparting every variety of spin, the machine cost 10 guineas in 1938, and a working model was in the possession of a Mr S.R. Chichester at his home, The Rough, Tilford, Surrey, at least as late as 1952. Scyld Berry in *The Cricketer* (September 1987) discussed the further evolution of these machines, advocating their wider usage for practice against unremitting pace bowling. He indicated that the earliest extant Brooks machine was en route for exhibition at the Science Museum in London.

Stumps and bails

Pitch invasions by spectators, yobs and cricketana collectors are nothing new, which probably explains the scarcity of saleable stumps and bails. Tony Baer pleaded with a local farmer to sell him the bails used on the final day of the tied Test at Brisbane in December 1960, but no sum within reason could move him. A stump used in the 1986 NatWest final realised £60 at the Bicentenary auction, and a pair of bails used in the Middlesex County Championship year of 1920, £55. A stump signed by England and South Africa after the Oval Test of 1947 and a hinged stump signed by England and India, also at The Oval, had fetched £35 at Phillips in September 1980.

According to G.B. Buckley, stumps made of teak, black with age, and believed to be over a hundred years old, were in use at Wollaton in Nottinghamshire in 1941, still nowhere near the seniority of the earliest stumps in the MCC collection, which Stephen Green believes date from 1798. Over a long period, the best stumps were made of ash or lancewood, the most desirable wood then in use, with examples, ebony-topped and brass-ferruled, noted in 1862. In 1864 ash came into use, followed in 1870 by solid brass capped and brass or iron shod. Steel stud stumps came much later, in 1895. A set of six brass-topped stumps with iron points made £55 at Christie's in June 1988.

A three-prong stump iron, for marking the holes the specified distance apart, was an unusual buy at £32 in the Phillips October 1986 auction. Bails were made of boxwood in 1835, or boxwood, ash or ebony in 1882, with other imported woods from 1888 onwards. During the last century iron and india-rubber bails were tried.

Mike Smith has three inscribed bails, authenticated as the former property of Robert Thoms by his grand-daughter, and for which he paid a total of £275 at Christie's in October 1987. Thoms was described by Grace as the "prince of umpires", and one of these bails is strongly believed to have been used in the first Test in England (1880), another in an 1896 Test between England and Australia, and the third was apparently in use during the match between Lord Sheffield's XI and the Australians at Sheffield Park the same year.

Three inscribed bails from the collection of the "prince of umpires".

Miscellaneous equipment

Nothing escapes the eagle eye of the collector. A cricket bat burnisher made of bone and dating from c. 1870, appeared at the Bicentenary auction (£85) as well as portable metal scales for weighing cricket balls (£280). Umpires' pocket six and eight-ball clickers, some made in Birmingham by the firm of Quaife and Lilley, are not uncommon, costing probably a pound a click. At the

'Tony Baer' sale of 1978, a 66ft. long cricketer's tape in a brass case, made by F. H. Ayres of Aldersgate Street, London, size 11cm. in diameter and inscribed with the various critical dimensions, reached £22 despite lacking the first 4in.

Belts and sashes

Belts and sashes are among the most attractive and eagerly sought-after accessories to dress (see colour page xxiii). Introduced in the 1850s the coloured and plain cotton canvas belts with brass buckles were first marketed by Edward Ade of Oxford Street, London, and soon became an integral part

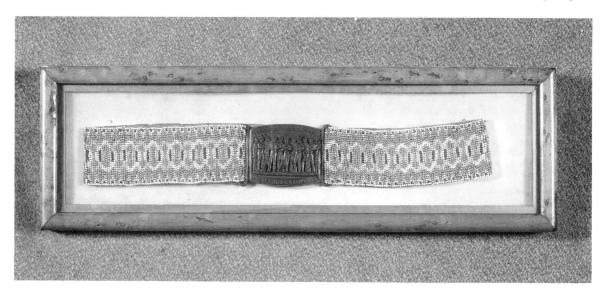

A suitable belt for 'England's Champions'.

of a cricketer's attire. The coloured webbing was often printed with a cricket design, or else a canvas belt was fitted to a buckle, embroidered in *gros point* by the ladies in their lives.

Tom Brown of literary fame wore the "captain's belt", for all we know something similar to the early Victorian cricketer's belt of white, grey, black and turquoise beadwork, with a bronzed clasp embossed with eleven cricketers, "England's Champions", which realised £180 in the Geering & Colyer sale of March 1979. A rarely seen All England belt with buckle from 1850 is displayed under glass in Roger Mann's collection. By 1868 belts were out of fashion and superseded by an elastic band at the back of the trousers, and this in turn gave way to a strap and buckle. Nonetheless, belts of appropriate club colours continued to be worn, long outlasting the knotted ties and scarves which came into vogue by 1860 and were worn by the first English team to Australia in 1862. Their sashes were of different colours for scorecard identification, and the style was later widely emulated.

Buckles

A fastening representing a bowler and batsman is known from 1854, and three years later Ade introduced two new figures to his well-known cricket clasp. There is a very nice embroidered belt at Lord's with a brass buckle bearing the names of George Parr's team in Australia, 1863-64, and Lillywhite Frowd advertised a variety of presentation buckles at 4s. 6d. to 5s. in the 1880s. No mention, however, is made in the stock-list of a buckle handed in by an Aborigine who had found it in the desert 1,000 miles north of Perth, possibly the last memento to a gold prospector who had perished in them, thar hills. Handed as a gift by the visiting Australians to the East Molesey club, Surrey, in 1953, it carried in addition to relief motifs of the lion and kangaroo, scores of the first Test match played in England and the lettering "Score of Great Match. England v. Australia". It might have been made for presentation to both sides in that 1880 match.

An assortment of buckles, either the mass-produced kind or those exclusive to touring teams, surfaced as Australians capitalised upon their national Bicentenary in 1988. Other buckles turn up in the oddest corners of the globe. During the Boer War, a patrol of British soldiers camped one night on a farm in the Orange Free State; after they had moved on, a farm labourer scavenged the site and found a belt buckle with an effigy of W.G. and the names of the players who accompanied him to Australia in 1873. The romantics among us would wish to believe that one of those players was on the patrol, but mathematics is against the notion, and in 1965 the buckle was one of the most prized possessions of Port Elizabeth CC's interesting little museum.

Eighteen lots of belt buckles from the last century caught the eye at the MCC Bicentenary sale (see colour page xxiii). Their total realisation was nearly £6,000 and the pick of them, a blue and white belt depicting a cricket scene and with gilt clasp, dated c.1860 and with the motto "We fear no foe" (estimate £100-£200) closed around someone's midriff for £1,300.

Gold and silvered buckles with cricketing motifs in relief, such as bats resting against a tree, stumps and scorer's tents, batsmen and bowler holding laurel over stumps and crossed bats, are fairly plentiful and for less spectacular items a fair expectation would be £30-£50. Vendors of brass and bronze buckles with identifiable players such as Grace and Spofforth (c.1882) or rural settings of an earlier vintage, sometimes with original belts, would feel hard done by at under £80-£100. Hallmarked silver buckles and belts with inscribed emblems, supported by batsmen and bowler figures, would be nearer £200. Expected to have been near the top end of the market was a mid-Victorian Philadelphian golden belt buckle, embossed with a large bald-headed eagle perched on three stumps, holding an array of cricket items, but it fetched only £55 at Phillips in April 1988.

The saga of Clive Williams's search for the provenance of a belt buckle found on the foreshore of the River Tweed in Scotland, and his thesis that the negroid features of the batsman with the background of windmill and canefield hut indicate a portrayal of 18th-century primitive cricket in Barbados, has been rewarded with the buckle's depiction on postage stamps from the Caribbean Islands, including Barbados, in 1988. The buckle is now accepted as the oldest known artefact relating to cricket outside Britain and Williams's dedicated researches into its possible links with the naval family of Hotham, who went to war in the Caribbean in the late 18th century, make a rattling good tale.

Clive Williams's
amazing find.

Blazers and sweaters

The admirable researches by Diana Rait Kerr, former curator of the MCC collection, suggest that blazers are of mixed origin. They owe much to the 18th-century waistcoats which continued well into Victorian times as tight-fitting jackets. The gaudy colours of the vagabond club sides, the subject of mirth from the hoi-polloi and admiration from those in the know, stem from the coloured shirts worn at the time.

In 1888 W.G. wrote: "Most leading clubs and counties have a distinguishing colour, and cricketers generally wear caps

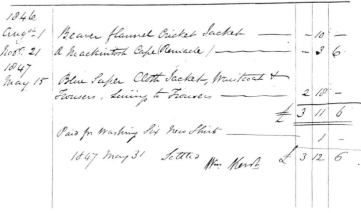

Generous credit offered by Wm. Kent to a young customer.

made of this colour. A jacket is often made of the same flannel and shade as the cap. The jacket can be used while fielding . . . but a jersey or sweater is preferable". Blazers for leading clubs such as Free Foresters and Cambridge Quidnuncs were conspicuous at the MCC Bicentenary sale, and an MCC touring team blazer of navy blue wool, trimmed with yellow and red striped braid, inscribed "P.F. Warner 1926" for the visit to South America, was highly prized at £550. Even his woollen tennis shorts were worth £140 at that mad sporting spree. G.O. Allen's Eton blazer fetched £180; the I Zingari blazer squeezed into with great cheer by Colin Cowdrey on the cover of the May 1987 issue of *Wisden Cricket Monthly* sported £160, and international rock music celebrity and serious collector, Charlie Watts, chose a green, black, pink and blue confection said to have been worn by Ranji at £230. An Indian touring team blazer from 1946, believed to have been Vijay Hazare's, went under the hammer for £280.

"Ram" Ramamurthy has a full set of Australian blazers from 1938 to the present day and among others too numerous to mention, Mike Smith will happily give an airing to Reg Simpson's Commonwealth blazer and Bob Willis's MCC blazer, while in a cupboard in Roger Mann's cricket room hang blazers from Essex, I Zingari, Northamptonshire, Australia, Lord Hawke's colours and those of Lord Tennyson's tour just before the last war (see colour page xxxii). No serious collection is complete without one, irrespective of size and shoulder width, and for those contemplating a new wardrobe, prices from some recent auctions show: Colin Milburn's Northamptonshire blazer, £90 (November 1984); Reg Simpson's England blazer, £140 (Trent Bridge auction, August 1984); "Garth" McKenzie's Australian blazer, £120 (November 1984, another Charlie Watts purchase).

When Bob Willis sold his England and Warwickshire blazers, ties, sweaters and caps at Christie's in October 1988 for prices between £50 and £600, while collectors rejoiced, there was also a degree of sadness about so final a dismissal, perfectly captured in a phrase in the *Daily Telegraph* reflecting that "one fears his memories now mean nothing". No tinge of melancholia, though, attached to the sale of C.V. Grimmett's effects and a 1932-33 Australian XI green wool blazer, with label inscribed with his name in ink, which held a packed audience at Christie's in thrall four months previously until it was knocked down at £600. His Test woollen jumper by Farmer's of Sydney went for £130, and sundry pairs of trousers for between

£40 and £80, the last with a receipt addressed to Grimmett at the Langham Hotel, London, in 1934. Prices for other sweaters have oscillated wildly: four sweaters (England, Yorkshire, Nottinghamshire and Derbyshire) worn by Brian Bolus realised £90 at Trent Bridge in 1984; a Roly Jenkins England sweater, £16 at Worcester in September 1980; one which belonged to Wilfred Rhodes, with his name stitched in, £280 at the Bicentenary auction, and David Sheppard's MCC touring sweater, £45 in May 1982.

Wilfred Rhodes's sweater.

Boots, shoes and slippers

As Diana Rait Kerr nimbly put it, the shoes worn by Felix resemble dancing pumps, although spikes appear to have been worn as early as 1812 and were advertised from 1844. Spike soles, attached to ordinary shoes, appeared in 1851. On the sole of the boots were five steel spikes, fitted into a collar of brass, each one attached to the sole by three small screws. There was also a solitary spike on the heel.

Brown and white shoes or boots, when they did come in around 1872, were buttoned or elastic sided, and were worn up to the season of 1880. A colour plate entitled "Famous Cricketers of 1880", issued in a monthly copy of *Boys' Own Paper* (1881) shows that all are wearing shoes or boots of this colour. Some time in the 1880s, brown and sometimes black boots superseded the part-coloured version and were worn until the end of the decade. More in tune with modern taste, a photograph of the Cambridge University side for

1891 shows that with one exception – the captain, Gregor MacGregor – all are wearing white boots, probably with good, honest hob nails. Canvas boots cost up to 16s.6d. [83p.] and, *à la mode* from 1882 onwards, buckskin from 18s.6d. to 26s.

That monied amateurs of the day ensured due care was taken of their gear is evident from the pair of bags, beautifully embroidered with his initials and date, in which the Kent captain, J.R. Mason, kept his cricket boots (see colour page xxv).

A pair of cricket slipper designs, embroidered with cricket motifs woven in coloured beads and wool, c.1880, $12\frac{1}{2}$in.x$10\frac{1}{2}$in. each, both in perfect condition and unusual to say the least, would have been easy on the feet but not on the pocket at £645 from the Burlington Gallery (see colour page xiv).

Boxes (protective)

In 1851, the year of the Great Exhibition at Crystal Palace, our forefathers had a body guard which so completely protected the person from injury "that the most timid can play without fear". Lillywhite's *Guide* for 1855 refers to "private guards", though as John Burnett pointed out in *Wisden Cricket Monthly* (October 1985) Pycroft mentioned at a slightly earlier date "a cross-bar india-rubber guard" which may have served the same purpose; but it was also suggested at the time that stuffing a handkerchief down the front of a long jacket could do no harm to the family heritage. Selkirk's definition of pads in *Guide to the Cricket Ground* (1867) includes "protectors for the abdomen".

These typically Victorian euphemisms lingered through "improved private pads" until by 1880 personal or private protectors were all freely advertised in the cricketing annuals. By 1890 all discretion had been abandoned and there for all to see and admire was Palmer's Patent Groin Protector at 7s.6d. [38p.] and 10s.6d. [53p.].

The Hampshire auction of 1984 raised several thousand pounds for the county, but the quaintest lot in the sale, made widely known through local radio and television coverage, was a box worn by Brigadier Michael Harbottle for almost three decades. It was bought at the last minute for £50 by a member of the family "presumably unable to face the future without the family heirloom".

Buttons

Sets of early buttons, such as those issued by the Islington Albion Club, are eagerly sought, though like the 14 'Cameo Cigarettes' metal buttons issued by the American Tobacco Company which have extraordinarily well defined portraits of the 1901-02 English team to Australia, these are more badges than buttons (button is the American idiom for such things). Blazer buttons as such, like the group of seven brass buttons with coloured enamel centres, featuring batsmen, bowler, fielder, catcher and wicketkeeper, c. 1910, sold by the Burlington Gallery for £35, are more true to type. Sets of six celluloid buttons depicting a player executing the basic skills of the game, and sometimes still in a presentation box, would expect a figure in the region of £80, but by far the great majority are to be found in dealers' rummage boxes and should cost no more than a pound or two.

Caps and hats

Changes in the 18th century by gentlemen players ousted from the cricket field the tricorn hats and practical jockey or postillion caps, so that the majority of players wore the conventional "topper". A gossamer hat of 1841 was advertised as similar to the beaver top hat, but lighter and much cheaper. By 1850 the top hat had been replaced by a variety of headgear. There were boaters, billycocks, David Copperfield tasselled caps and the tartan cap worn by Felix. Later fashion turned to bowler hats, in white felt, but these were generally relegated to off-the-field wear for professionals.

MCC pill-box cap.

The "pill-box" which followed, enjoyed only a brief vogue with the Australian team of 1878 and among amateurs of that date, although only W.G. is regularly portrayed wearing one. An early MCC pill-box type cap in red and gold capped a frenetic spell at the Bicentenary sale to amass £750, and a later, peaked version made £120.

Winchester School adopted a cap in 1851 and a dark blue cap the next year, Harrow a narrow striped cap in 1852 and their present cap in 1853. The universities came next, Cambridge in 1861 and Oxford in 1863, so that soon everyone wore cloth caps which, apart from the small peak, are similar to those we sometimes see today. At one time a county cap betokened the professional cricketer's calling and was an essential part of his self-esteem. The peaks have frequently altered in shape, "the Australian model cut on more generous lines" (Diana Rait Kerr). Ian Peebles pointed out in *The Cricketer* (April 1980) how rare was the MCC cap, despite W.G.'s example, and that the most famous of all caps were the elegant four-panelled Harlequin cap worn by Warner and then by Jardine on the notorious Bodyline tour of 1932-33.

The first caps were made of striped, printed flannel, but generally they have been made of worsted material, usually plain blue or green with a cricket motif embroidered on the front panel. Country house cricket was an excuse for a rainbow display of coloured jazz hats, and often these carried more clout than the people wearing them. This cannot be said of the cap which once belonged to the Australian captain, W.L. Murdoch, and is now a talking-point in the Old Trafford Museum. In admiration of R.G. Barlow's feat in hitting a century for the North against the Australians on a fiery Trent Bridge wicket and also taking ten wickets for 48 runs in the match, Murdoch removed his cap and handed it to the Lancastrian, uttering the immortal words, "I take off my cap to you".

C.L. Townsend, the old Gloucestershire cricketer, sent two caps to *The Cricketer* in June 1949 as evidence that when he was asked to play for England at Lord's in 1899 there was no such thing as an England cap, and one was only produced due to the efforts of A.C. MacLaren, Ranji and several other forceful personalities within the team. It was of dark blue with the crest of a single lion rampant surrounded by a circle of lighter blue, with the word "England" worked into the crest. He maintained further that a second cap, with a crown and three lions of England, was presented to him at The Oval that season. He was equally certain that no blazer was awarded.

Whereas a Yorkshire cap made £160 and Nigel Haig's Middlesex cap £150 at the Bicentenary sale, club or minor counties caps of the likes of Lincolnshire, Butterflies CC, Free Foresters and Cambridge Quidnuncs might make a tenth of that figure under normal circumstances, in contrast to the £30-£70 price range achieved on that day of Lord's. That pre-Second World War headgear not unexpectedly caps all is obvious from a short list of auction prices over the past few years:

Grimmett's cap from the 1924–25 series.

> Chapman's MCC touring cap, £130 (October 1987).
> D'Oliveira's MCC touring cap, £30 (September 1980).
> Duleepsinhji's 1929-30 MCC cap, £60 (1984).
> Greenidge's West Indian cap, £30 (1984).
> Grimmett's Australian Test cap of the 1924-25 series, £260, and another for the 1932-33 series, £400 (June 1988).
> May's MCC touring cap, £39 (September 1980).
> Page's New Zealand cap, £60 (October 1987).
> Sheppard's Sussex cap, £15 (September 1980).

"Ram" Ramamurthy has a full set of international Test and Australian state caps, while another top-flight Australian collector, Denis Tobin, includes among his more recent purchases Richard Hadlee's Test cap. Mike Smith can never be left out of any such compilation: his collection includes caps belonging to Len Hutton and Norman O'Neill, as well as H.J. Butler's Nottinghamshire cap, Malcolm Hilton's MCC touring cap and Dirk Wellham's New South Wales "bluey". Nor, come to that, can David Frith. He has Duleepsinhji's England cap and, one of cricketana's more esoteric items, a yellow headband snatched "still dripping" from the brow of Dennis Lillee (see colour page xxiv). "Hey, that's got my original sweat on it," Lillee exclaimed – which prompted Frith to wonder where you might obtain second-hand Lillee sweat.

We await with some trepidation the sale of the first cricketers' helmets. Patsy Hendren wore some measure of ad hoc protective headgear before the last war, but they were made more manifest first by a type of skull cap adopted by the former England captain, Mike Brearley, before Dennis Amiss promulgated the version which others have followed. It was, incidentally, proposed before the First World War that a word should be coined to signify the capture of four wickets with successive deliveries, and the expression "helmet trick" was tried out on a non-receptive audience.

Costume

Hints as to the style of costume in which 18th century cricketers were accustomed to play come from prints and pictures, but also from tantalising references in verse. An inkling of the dress worn by Winchester College boys comes from:

> "Cricket, nimble boy and light,
> In slippers red and drawers white."

In *Surry Triumphant*, published in 1773, we are told not only that "Young Dorset...ran foremost of the company, clad in a milk-white vest", but that Sir Horatio Mann sported azure sleeves, down which "the sweat ran thickly like a flood".

Whether representatives of Kent were the first to wear all-white is a question often posed. In the *Kentish Gazette* of 1782, the poem 'The Cricketers: a Catch', has the lines:

> "See the Cricketers of Kent,
> All in white, with delight,
> Play before the shady Tent."

Two historical showcases at the Lord's Memorial Gallery, presented in

1976 as a memorial to Henry Grierson by the XL Club, display a man's outfit of c.1820, as worn by Henry Daw of Christchurch. According to the Victoria and Albert Museum this is probably the only complete sporting outfit for any English game to have survived so long. The other costume on display was given to MCC on long loan by the Women's Cricket Association and shows the very sensible gear used by the Original England Lady Cricketers, who as a team flourished around the 1890s.

Shirts and trousers

In the 1840s colour on the field took the form of a shirt or perhaps a straw hat with ribbons. William Clarke's All England team adopted a white shirt with polka dot pink spots in 1847, Cambridge a light blue shirt from 1861, some years after the famous light blue shirts of the Rugby School XI which came into existence around 1843. *Bell's Life*, the principal sporting paper of the day, reported that "The Rugby boys, all habited alike, presented an exceedingly pretty field of miniature cricketers." When Grace – never an elegant sartorial figure – started his career in the tough school of the 1860s, white trousers were worn by the better-dressed players, but shirts were coloured, striped or checked according to fancy.

Fashion dictated pantaloons or trousers for men quite early in the 19th century, but they were not immediately popular. The latest-known cricket picture in which breeches were worn is an aquatint by Robert Cruikshank dated 1827. Round-arm bowling, fast and unpredictable, hastened the wearing of trousers under which leg-guards could be worn. "Pads would do for practice, but how unfair for the bowler if they were used in a match," said Lord Frederick Beauclerk, but extra stockings were rolled down to protect shins and ankles.

There is not much new about transfer prints on T-shirts. Shirts were sold in 1850 showing likenesses of Box and Lillywhite, six for 42s. [£2.20], while The Cricketer's Flannel Shirt for 1857 combined portraits and "exact positions of some of the present celebrities in the cricketing world". Ron Yeomans owned one which sounds rather like one of these – an oversize cricket shirt, hand-stitched and made of lawn, pleated and covered in transfers of long-ago cricketers, some top-hatted.

T-shirt from the Caribbean, 1985-86, when England's tour itinerary excluded Guyana.

Ties

After touring Australia with A.P.F. Chapman's victorious team in 1928-29, S.J. Southerton fostered the idea of forming a club for journalists who had reported on at least 25 Tests. The "25" club emblem had to be worn throughout every Test match between England, Australia and South Africa, no matter where the contest was in progress. The groundwork colours of black and blue stood for the reporter's pen and sub-editor's blue pencil, and the stripes flanking the green centre defined the peculiarities of the national blazers - blue with red and gold braid for England, green with gold edging for Australia, and green with gold trimming for South Africa. Green also represented the field of play, yellow the stumps and bats, and red the ball (see colour page xxiv).

Vic Lewis is the undisputed maestro of the cricket tie scene, and his collection of some 4,000 or so and book *Cricket Ties* (1984) says just about all there is to be said.

Rather like the reported promptings by members of the Test Match Special radio commentary team to buy the Primary Club tie in aid of blind cricketers (all those who have been dismissed first ball are eligible), Castells of Broad Street, Oxford, urged the wearing of a "hat-trick" tie in a 1960 advertisement. Incidentally, it was that firm who, in 1958, gave their informed opinion on MCC's colours as buttercup and marigold rather than the more prosaic red and yellow or more derogatory tomato and custard.

When one of Don Bradman's MCC ties sells for Aus $6,000, but fails to reach estimate and remains unsold at the Trent Bridge sale in August 1984, one does not know what to tip for a wants-list. Those that are desirable are "former" ties, now little or no longer seen, such as the very attractive pre-1939 Sussex tie, or its post-war variant. Some which will surely become elusive in years to come were those worn by the Australian, West Indies and Sri Lankan "rebel" tourists, advertised at £15 for the three a year or two ago. As part of a collection of thousands, Denis Tobin has one worn by Kim Hughes on one of the Australian tours. Another minor rarity could be the tie for the aborted 1970 South African tour of England, and while there are probably many around, a year's search located only three definites and one possible.

POSTCARDS, CIGARETTE CARDS AND STAMPS

Postcards

After years in the wilderness, when postcards of interest to cricketing deltiologists were more the province of junk shops and fusty corners of secondhand booksellers, the trade in cards is as buoyant now as it ever was during the Edwardian era.

The stagnation of the 1920s has been replaced by a boom in postcard collecting which started in the mid-1960s; even so, during the 1970s a good base for a collection could be had with cards around 40p. plain, 75p. coloured. Teams even then were more expensive, and have always claimed higher prices when autographed. According to the International Postcard Market price index, postcards generally had their largest price growth in 1976 (59 per cent) and luxuriated in an overall 48 per cent growth in 1979. For cricket cards, dealers at all levels report incessant demand and rapid turnover. The latest IPM *Catalogue* index for cards grouped thematically under cricket/county teams/players is most revealing: 30p. (1975), £2 (1980), £5 (1985), £8 (1989), an increase of more than 2,500 per cent over 15 years. Despite this build-up, in cricketana circles postcards still tend to be the supporting cast on a bill topped by pictures, prints and ceramics; but with a wide range of albums now available to suit every need, they remain neat, easy to store, colourful and still comparatively cheap.

The noted English collector, Bob Jones, has many thousands in albums, and a lot of people are hoping that he will carry out his threat to emulate Derek Deadman's superlative catalogue of cigarette cards with a comparable listing of postcards, as hinted in his *Wisden Cricket Monthly* profile of September 1985. The immense Geoffrey Copinger collection also runs into thousands, and dates back into the last century, to cover teams, individuals, counties, overseas players and grounds, many of them autographed, and the solid bedrock for any catalogue.

Although widely used on the Continent as early as the 1870s, pictorial cards in Britain only received Post Office sanction in 1894, and not until 1902 did the floodgates open, when the 'divided back' card (message on left, address on right) we all know today gave publishers scope to issue material on every imaginable topic. For a mere 1d., idolising schoolboys could make flesh of their heroes in a handy cardboard medium, and the close parallel in date between the golden ages of both cricket and card collecting has been frequently noted in print. Grenville Jennings, author of *Cricket on Old Picture Postcards* (1985), makes the point that "Cricket was well-represented on postcards during the early days, and became one of the few themes that can claim a continuity of production through the century." After the Great War, the postage rate was doubled to 1d., newspapers carried enough pictorial matter to satisfy even the most besotted followers of the game, social values and priorities altered, and the range, artistry and number of cards slumped accordingly. Those endearing messages so often seen on cards of that period, travel plans and meetings arranged, pleas from club secretaries to make up the eleven, were eradicated by the telephone. This means that pre-1914 cards, churned out by national publishers such as Raphael Tuck and Valentine's, as well as smaller operators – Foster of Brighton and our old friend, E. Hawkins – are most common. Other local publishers, such as the rival Tonbridge companies, Flemons and Mockford, rode on the backs of the perennial county championship contenders, Kent, to have their share of real photographic cards, showing county teams and personalities, sold in shops everywhere, even on county grounds. Although one or two of the latter have cottoned on to the sales potential of postcards

MAURITIUS CRICKET CLUB

Owing to insufficient players the game proposed for Saturday 12ᵗʰ inst has had to be abandoned.

"La Caverne" Vacoas,

H. H. ASPINALL, *Hon. Sec, M. C. C.*

10/9/03

Postcard of 1903 calling off a match in Mauritius: the fact that it was printed suggests that this was not an uncommon occurrence.

Above right Albert Craig, 'The Surrey Poet', here shown hawking his cricketing rhymes in Kent.
Above A bound collection of Craig's verses.

once again, those displayed are strangely unimaginative and limited.

After the collapse of the trade post-1918, a small number of commercial studios struggled on, joined by sports dealers A.G. Spalding and Gunn & Moore in featuring touring sides. *The Star* newspaper and Waterman's Ink used Jack Hobbs a lot and a modicum of further sponsorship crept in with the team advertisements for Jaeger's sweaters and shirts. But there is little heart in them, and none of the lush, velveteen feeling we get from the best Edwardian creations. Nevertheless, with the notable exceptions of cards for the 1921 and 1926 Australian tourists, cards for the 1920s onwards are less

PRINTED PAPER RATE

Sir Donald Bradman is
here to write on
the Tests EXCLUSIVELY
in the DAILY MAIL.
    All who follow
cricket will want to
read what Bradman
has to say about each
day's play.

Pat Reelve

Sports Editor-in-Chief

TO ALL
CRICKET
LOVERS

The 1929 South
African team in Jaeger
sweaters.
Above left Card of an
unusual display, in
butter, from the
1924–25 British
Empire Exhibition at
Wembley.
Left Don Bradman,
as announced by the
Daily Mail.

common. Brylcreem used Denis
Compton soon after the last war, and
the *Daily Mail* a reflective study of Don Bradman
in his new role of sports writer, but until the surge of
contemporary cards, those by photographers Morley Pecker, F. C. Dick
(sold through the bookshop at The Oval) and a succession from Lord's are
worthy enough and sometimes hard to find, but insipid.

The MCC Bicentenary auction did no good at all for the average
collector: 145 signed photographs, the majority pre-1914 England and
county players, including Hayward, Relf, Hobbs, Tarrant and an assortment
of Fosters, sold in three lots for a dizzying £5,200, and £35 per card can in no
way be the norm; even unsigned cards of the same and slightly later vintage
averaged nearly £8. This "over the top" approach is proving cruel to ordinary
collectors now that auction houses rule the hobby and bargains elsewhere
have decreased. For the moment anyway, county team groups sell for £3-£5,
with the exception of less fashionable sides, such as Derbyshire, Hampshire,
Leicestershire, Gloucestershire, Northamptonshire, Warwickshire and

Country cricket in Papua.

Worcestershire, where £10 upwards is regular. Cards of Glamorgan, a late starter, are rarely obtainable. Individual players are still spasmodically cheap, £2-£5, unless autographed, while touring teams start where individuals leave off. Minor clubs and village sides do not rate highly, as cheap as 30p., unless there is a name on the card when specialists in topographical cards make their broader interest felt. Grounds and scoreboards are keenly sought by some, but even these can be found for under £1. A striking exception was a chromolitho card of Melbourne Cricket Ground, by McCarron, Bird & Co., posted to Austria in 1899, which realised £60 at a Stanley Gibbons postal history auction in March 1989.

Comic cards and those best described as "cute" or of marginal cricket interest oscillate wildly from dealer to auction. Comic cards by Lance Thackeray attract some devotees, and a set of his 'At the Wicket' Tuck Series 955 (1903), postally used but in reasonable condition, could be worth about £40. Louis Wain is best known for his bizarre cats, but a cricket comic, 'No Play at Lord's', sold for over £50 at a Specialised Postcard Auctions, Cirencester, sale in December 1988, another ominous portent of things to come. Reproductions by Chisholm Fine Arts of 19 Tom Browne cards of the Edwardian era were on sale at the Lord's shop for 5p each in the late 1970s, consolidating the lasting hold he has on some collectors. The same is true of

Comic cards with cricketing links.

SUMMER SPORTS

the "Kinsella kid", the creation of Edward Patrick Kinsella, a genial Irishman who was primarily a poster rather than a postcard artist. The boy appears in six cricketing scenes and in a cycling series of six. His "sister" figures in another two series – tennis and diabolo. The first two Kinsellas were issued by Langsdorff, a London company, in 1906, the remainder following shortly afterwards. They are also becoming scarce, even secondhand.

With cards of peripheral cricketing interest it is hard to know where to draw the line. At pictures of trams with Test match grounds on their headboards, or the gasometer at The Oval transformed into a gigantic glass of Guinness? An otherwise ordinary street scene of Middleton Cheney, with the public house in the foreground, suddenly turns into a different shade of pound notes when the dealer spots the sign showing A. Mold as landlord and connects it with a former Lancashire quick bowler. Buddy Holly and the Crickets (with a set of stumps fully in the picture), photographed during their tour of England in 1958, as a postcard finds itself auctioned at Sotheby's, Belgravia, with a reserve of £95-£115!

Jennings ranks the best cards as those described as real photographic ones, and the worst, the printed examples of the *Star* series, by Gottschalk, Dreyfus and Davis. When we turn to auction realisations, a few specimens must suffice. A set of six postcards of Australian players, National Series 829, including Gregory, Trumper and Cotter, sold at Specialised Postcard Auctions in 1983 for over £25. Bob Jones bid £400 for a wide-ranging lot of some 150 cards at the 'Winder' sale in November 1985, while Jennings tells us that he derives as much pleasure from a battered card in his collection of the 1907 South Africans, with 10 autographs on the reverse, as from a multi-autographed Yorkshire album with approximately 275 cards, for which he paid £750. Some 46 pre-First World War cards sold at £480 in November 1986, but all else pales when set against artist-signed sets of proofs, occasionally done in the Edwardian era for dedicated collectors, for which a putative asking price must be in excess of £500.

Collectors of modern cards are well catered for. We have to dodge them in pavement display racks; the magazines *Picture Post Card Monthly* and *Collect Modern Cards* keep dealers and customers in regular touch, and the subject is amply documented with annual catalogues. A rarely seen modern card is the one issued with *Cricket Quarterly* in 1966, a colour picture of women's cricket in Nouméa, New Caledonia, and now worth at least £10. Pamlin Print cards are still very cheap, 50p-£1, and among many new issues are cards advertising Colman's Mustard and the London Transport Museum. Reproductions of Patrick Eagar photographs and Steadman cartoons are matched with the sets of famous cricketers and grounds from Stamp Publicity (Worthing), supplemented by Morphot's 'Grounds for Pleasure' colour cards. Reflections of a Bygone Age is well known in this field, and among the most prolific of modern issuers is J/V Cards of Leicestershire. One of their more unusual contributions (published for Willow Stamps) must be 'Cricketing Rarities', an enlargement of the label issued c.1908 by the Nuremberg Football Club and depicting a batsman.

Cigarette cards

The exact origins of cigarette cards remain imprecise, the best likelihood being that the earliest was an American tobacco card dated 1877, which was discovered in the Metropolitan Museum of Art, New York; but as internal stiffeners for pre-wrapped tobacco they were the dream advertising medium. Cheap and adaptable, they made their mark in the grey, drab streets of newly industrialised towns toward the end of the last century, offering scraps of colour to rootless, half-literate men and their families. The cards appeared first as singles, then, once the consumer was hooked, as sets in series.

Entrepreneurs were quick off the mark to meet the great male interest in sport. The first known issue to portray cricketers turned up in Australia, c.1886, packaged by a New York firm, Goodwin & Company, under the brand name Old Judge and entitled 'Celebrities'. In-depth research was evidently not a strong point at Goodwin's, for there are some strange aberrations in the naming of players: R.C. Barton, Billing and J.E.K. Stud. The same company produced Old Judge Cigarette Factory base cards of an assortment of other celebrities around 1890, among them Blackham, Bonnor, Boyle, Giffen, McDonnell and Walters. Three of these were snapped up for £155 at a Caxton Hall auction in 1975, a percentage only of their value today. Another trans-Atlantic company, the American Tobacco Company, was responsible for Bonanza and Dollar brand name sets, and again the choice of people in the public eye included cricketers – S.E. Gregory, Trott, Ford, Philipson, Richardson and Ward.

Aided by the mechanisation of printing and the spread of cheap colour lithography, W.D. & H.O. Wills were quick to learn from the impact made in America by pictorial cards, and their printers, Mardon's, are thought to have run off a pioneering set in 1887, soon to be followed by the first of many runs by John Player & Sons in Nottingham. As part of the "tobacco war" of 1899-1902, Ogden's of Liverpool introduced their Guinea Gold photographic cards, then their 'Tabs', and, prior to their sale to Imperial Tobacco in 1902, so rampant in size were their issues that they are still commonplace. The Imperial Tobacco Company dominated the market in the first years of this century, but there were still about 150 other companies, usually very small, quietly doing their own thing in the way of cards.

The printing of cards ceased in 1917, not to begin again properly until 1922. During this period, one of the most celebrated firms issuing high-

A selection of cards
from Wills and Taddy.

quality cards went under. This was James Taddy & Company, founded in
1750, whose first series of cards came out in 1887. Originally purveyors of
tobacco, tea and snuff, they were one of the earliest companies to introduce
packet tobacco, with beautifully produced cards whose dual purpose was to
act as stiffeners and to encourage brand loyalty. The abrupt demise of the
company, brought about by industrial strife, ended a great era of cigarette
cards. The low survival rate of their cards has led to their issues becoming
exceptionally desirable rarities. As someone was overheard plaintively to
remark, "Where would I be without my Taddys?"

However, they were but one of the many series of cigarette and trade
cards, both monochrome and coloured, international in coverage, which have

been assiduously collected for many years and auction prices for the earlier issues are stratospheric.

Between the wars, ornate printing styles and rather stilted textual notes gave way to more functional modes. Print runs by the great manufacturing companies – John Player, Ogden's, Ardath, Churchman's, Carreras, Godfrey Phillips, R. & J. Hill and J. Millhoff – became ever more gigantic and could be counted in hundreds of millions. On the principle of "lick and stick", special albums were provided by local tobacconists at the cost of a few pence. As the collecting habit grew, and to fill the gap for an organisation prepared to acquire, sell and store the cards, the London Cigarette Card Company was founded in 1927. Along with Murray Cards (International), its comprehensive reference sources, catalogues, handbooks and auction catalogues were the collectors' standby until the first of Derek Deadman's superb compilations. His extended listing of *Cricket Cigarette and Trade Cards* (Murray Cards International, 1985) merged into a single volume his two earlier publications, both of which included thousands of 20th-century cricketers plus many earlier. It is ideal as an index for collectors, and embraces peripheral matter, including matchbox labels.

The value of Deadman's work is magnified by a separate listing of cricketers portrayed within a wide range of other activities, either as politicians, actors, golfers or footballers. For the beginner its bulk is intimidating and for those who felt quietly smug about their own albums it can be soul-destroying. The given figure of 12,000 cards includes varieties, and while Australian issues are second to Britain, many have come from unlikely countries, Italy and Belgium being two of the 14 nations mentioned. Despite this, there has not yet been a series of West Indies cricketers issued in the Caribbean itself, but the game has received a passing nod from B. & J. B. Machado, of Kingston, Jamaica, in cigarette pack form and in three 1927 cards featuring Hammond, Lowry and the New Zealand team.

From 1900 to the 1930s few first-class cricketers failed to appear, as well as virtually every member of Australian first-class touring teams to Britain since 1899, and some from even earlier sides, as noted with the Old Judge sets. Some faces have been overlooked, and John Wheeler, in the *Journal of the Cricket Society* (Spring 1977), recorded his wife's disappointment that her uncle, Alfred T. Cliff, who played as an amateur for Worcestershire from 1912 to 1920, did not appear on any card. Probably represented on more cards than any other cricketer, Jack Hobbs received a centenary appreciation in the form of cards in *Wisden Cricket Monthly* (December 1982). Bradman features on more than a hundred cards, but W.G., for once, is well down the field with only about half that many, coming on the scene a little too early for this form of tribute (see colour page xxvii).

Quite apart from pictures of the players, there have been grounds, old

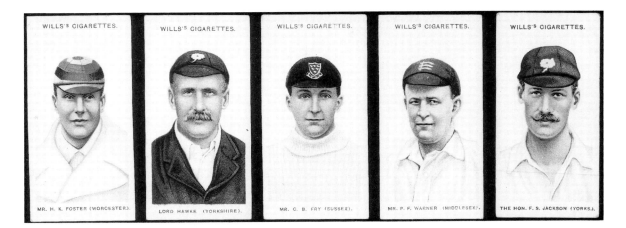

cricket prints, umpiring tips, puzzles and games, crests, ties, statistics, comic cards by Phil May, *Punch* cartoons, as well as comic characters such as Bonzo and Billy Bunter. The 1926 caricatures by "Rip", part of the Player's 'Cricketers' series, are remarkable for their likenesses, characteristic postures and mannerisms.

Few of the cards pretend to a genuine artistic appeal, and perhaps among the most attractive are those that are earliest and most rare – the delicate lithographs produced in Germany for the Wills 'Cricketers' sets of 1896 and 1901. By comparison their later issues, 1908, 1928 and 1929, seem garish. Other catchy early sets are the 1902 'Vanity Fair' issues – three series, each of 50 cards – and the 'County Badges' set printed on silk for Godfrey Phillips. Their 'Pinnace' sets issued between 1923 and 1925 have a dignity of their own, especially the larger size "brown backs" available from the Godfrey Phillips stand at the British Empire Exhibition held at Wembley in the summer of 1924.

Others look amateurish beyond belief, and a particularly striking example is the series produced by J. Baines of Bradford. These would date from the 1880s to 1914-18 or thereabouts, with some 40 cards shaped as shields, hearts, ivy leaves and so forth. Generally monochrome, with a band across the shield in different colours, and distributed through local shopkeepers, they need to be seen to be appreciated fully.

The price of cards has moved sharply upwards in recent years and shows no signs of abating. Most issues between the wars are relatively easy to find, less so those from overseas. Issues pre-1914 are an entirely different matter – even in 1962 figures of £5 per card were mentioned, with 2s. [10p.] the bottom line for less rare items, and some of the scarcer issues had not changed hands for 20 years or so. Rarity and price do not depend on age alone and some comparatively recent sets, especially those issued with confectionery,

Above A Barratt card of 1933 featuring the Warwickshire team led by R.E.S. Wyatt. **Below** Arthur Mailey, from the Pattreiouex series.

such as the famous Barratt's issues of the late 1920s and 1930s, which include several lesser known players, can be extremely elusive. Cards issued up to 1905 are always heavily in demand, even in only fair condition. The classic sets such as the 50 cards of the Wills 'Cricketers' of 1896 and 1901 will always command a premium, even though they may not be as rare as the Pattreiouex photographic 'Cricketers' series of 96 cards, which is nigh impossible to find complete, despite its being as recent as 1922. A single Wills card from the 1896 set (Lockwood) was bought for £18 in November 1984, while the 1901 set was valued at £250 in 1983, and single cards a year later at £5 each. The 1896 set now stands tall at £1,500. As for the Pattreiouex set, they now average around £30 a card.

A prime attraction at a November 1984 auction was a full set of 25 D. & J. Macdonald's 'Cricketers' (1902), estimated at £500-£800, which reached the astronomical figure of £2,600. A decade earlier a similar set realised £285. Fry, Grace, Jessop, MacLaren and Ranji are among those portrayed in this set issued from Glasgow, with the Winning brand of cigarettes. Most collectors find the greatest challenge lies in acquiring long series of cards such as Taddy's 1908 series of 238 county cricketers. Being a white background card they are not easy to find in clean condition, added to which they appear to have been issued on a regional basis, which makes certain counties harder than others. A portion of the set, 195 in all, realised £2,400 at Phillips in November 1987, and a total of 228, sold by county, soared to £5,828 in May 1989, with the 15 Northamptonshire cards making double any other county at £850.

Another favourite is the Godfrey Phillips series of over 200 cards from 1923-25, with just two or three cards awkward to pin down. Other sets appeal because of their outright beauty, a good example being the Australian issue of 40 cards of cricketers in action by Sniders & Abrahams (1906) in full colour and recently reprinted. Naturally enough, there is a swelling demand for these cards, which are based on the well known drawings of Chevallier Tayler. They are all action portraits, as opposed to the head and shoulders shots most commonly seen on cigarette cards.

Seventeen of the 20 cards issued by Charlesworth and Austin in 1902 (missing Hayward, Jackson and Richardson) sold for £815 at a postal auction held by Albert's of Kensington in 1986, with a group of 16 soaring to £1,400 at Phillips in November 1987. A singular set of "Rip" caricature cards, issued by Player's, and signed by all 50 subjects, was acquired for the Bradman Museum at the Lord's sale in April 1987 for £900, against estimate of £80-£140. A part-set of 15 Player's 'Australian tourists, 1934', each card autographed, reached £180 at Christie's in June 1988. A large lot at auction in May 1984 found a buyer at over £700, a very satisfactory price indeed for the Wills 1901, some of the Smith's issue of 1912, a blend of Ogden's, Player's, Pattreiouex, Carreras and 14 of the Kinnear 'Australian Cricketers' issue of 1897. At the time the Kinnears were listed by the London Cigarette Card Company at £50 each; they now stand at £120.

To reiterate, all pre-1914 cards sell well, but those from the 1930s, printed in millions, find a slow market. The famous Player's issues for 1934 and 1938, usually about 10-20p per card, are regularly to be found in certain shop windows, framed and mounted and selling for around £14.50. Since 1982-83 the 'Nostalgia' reprints by Murray Cards of facsimile issues of the two early Wills sets, accordingly lettered at the base and framed in brass, are often to be seen as office displays, an elegant addition to wooden panelling in VIP corners. Facsimiles, perforated so that they could be detached, also appeared in *Classic Cricket Cards* (1980) and *More Classic Cricket Cards* (1981). The range of 314 cards in all included Wills, Phillips, Player's and Millhoff.

Complete sets are always desirable and most sets up to the value of £50-£60 are available, given time. Beyond that it becomes a question of patience, and the dilemma is whether to acquire odd cards in a series or wait for the set. More often than not, the sets are in better condition than the singles, although this is not always the case, and it is still possible to upgrade as time goes by. Card collectors are very pernickety about condition and tend to buy where the price reflects their value for money. Mint condition cards can often be worth three or four times the value of one in inferior order, and dealers nowadays are only too aware of the value of their stock. The hobby has come a long way since the early 1970s, and plastic sleeves have replaced the old slotted ones, specially made for easy retention and examination, and which fit a wide range of albums.

The task of further research and updating of Deadman's catalogue lies with Geoffrey Seymour, who suggests that a good start to the hobby might be to buy a set of 50 Player's 'Cricketers, 1938', at a catalogue price of around £7. Despite its low cost, it is a colourful set, and if these fail to stimulate the collecting urge, then it is unlikely one would wish to proceed further. To collect every cricket card extant requires an uncommonly healthy bank balance. As Seymour wrote to us: "There is an alike series of 20 cricketers issued by seven different manufacturers which, if available, would easily run

Above Four "Rip" cards, from the set signed by each of the subjects.
Below J.J. Kelly, from the Kinnear series.

into five figures. Nevertheless, anyone compiling a comprehensive collection will probably have the finest picture library of cricketers known".

That is the happy lot of one of the world's leading cartophilists, Edward Wharton-Tigar, a former President of Kent CCC, whose collection of cards presented to the Lord's Memorial Gallery, and displayed on pivoting panels, represents a tiny fraction of those housed at home in special cabinets, all closely indexed and cross-referenced. Other leading collectors such as Tony Woodhouse and Bob Jones must be quietly staggered by the upturn in the market, from pence to many pounds. The former has the rare Wills sets of 1896, 1901 and 1908, while Jones can claim two of the extremely rare 1902 Macdonald's teams, of which only 11 are known. His many other treasures include a couple of the 1920-21 McIntyre's chocolate set (Hendry and Macartney) and the Kinnears.

Two cards from the 'Chums' collection.

Trade cards

Trade cards – sometimes referred to as tea cards or modern cards – appeared before the tobacco variety. Liebig's made the initial move, distributing cards with their meat extract c.1880, and since then there have been literally hundreds of issues each year. They have been given away with boys' magazines, confectionery, tea, chewing gum, soap, table salt, breakfast foods, charities and newspapers, and are generally taken together with cigarette cards for collecting purposes. Since the Second World War, when cigarette cards almost vanished, their popularity has grown. In the 1950s the absence of "pictures" with cigarettes encouraged manufacturers of other commodities to produce an ongoing stream of alternative cartophilic material and its continuing production in various guises has served as a stimulant to collectors.

Some of those to feature cricket have been modern sets produced for Kent CCC (the cost of which was underwritten by Wharton-Tigar) and for Northamptonshire's celebration of 80 years of cricket with illustrations by local artist, Robert Billingham. Private enterprise on the part of C.B.S. Ironmongery Ltd. ensured that comparative rarity, something uniquely Glamorgan. Inadequately advertised, at one stage the cards were unobtainable outside the Principality. Publishing houses are notorious for rather spineless self-promotion, and collectors need to resemble greyhounds or Ben Johnson, with or without drugs, to keep abreast of their one-offs. As part of their publicity for the book, *Bodyline: The Novel* (1983), Faber and Faber sneaked out a postcard with three reproductions of 1934 Player's cigarette cards (Bradman, Jardine and Larwood), and we can only guess how many flew through the slips. Initially, only book reviewers saw them, the rest some way behind in a very sharp race.

The inspiration for 'Shelley's Ice Cream Picture Cards' (MCI Ltd.), a set of 25 for £4, lay as much with the ardent Essex support of the managing-director as with the county's Championship win in 1983. It is a charming set, consisting of four coloured photographs and 21 tinted caricatures of the players by Dorrien, a West Country cartoonist, and deserves to be better known. The cards were given away with purchases of ice cream throughout the summer of 1984 and aroused much local interest. The original drawings were donated to Ken McEwan's benefit fund held that year. John Brindley & Associates have concentrated on Hampshire and other cricketing greats, using old photographs in vignette form.

Publishers promotional card for *Bodyline* by Paul Wheeler.

Prior to their 'World of Cricket 83', Panini Publishing had been producing sticker collections in the UK for six years. With TCCB approval, the photographs were commissioned and Graeme Wright, since the 1987 issue editor of *Wisden Cricketers' Almanack*, was asked to write the copy. Sales never quite came up to expectations, but this was not altogether a surprise. There are precious few self-centred cricket magazines aimed at the youth market, unlike football, and success depends on high-volume sales to offset high colour printing costs. Given the flimsy nature of the product and its targeted field, possibly these will never come into their own, and so far as can be ascertained none of these small ventures has won more than mixed success. Perhaps the best investment potential lies in the fugitive Glamorgan issue, and they may yet crop up in specialist journals such as *Collectors Mart*, on a par with the Cryselco Electric Lamps set of 1955, advertised in the September 1988 issue. Issued to mark the company's diamond jubilee, and illustrated with events of 1895 such as the Jameson Raid, the special wallet of 12 numbered cards, size 3½in., black and white with white outer borders, was estimated at £50 and just happened to include as No.5, W.G. Grace.

Cigarette packs

Amid the furore that attaches to cigarette cards, the packets that house them are easily overlooked. We forget that popular brands such as Wills Woodbine, five for 1d., did not achieve packet status of tens until 1916 and twenties did not appear until 1930. None which have a cricketing theme as decoration are common, disconcertingly so for embryonic collectors, who find bids around £30 nowhere near the mark.

The Bowlers, dating from the mid-1930s and manufactured by Walkers Tobacco Company of Liverpool, cleverly appealed to a broad public by

featuring two sports under one title. A lovely play on a famous set of initials is the M.C.C. packet of five Virginia cigarettes issued c.1893, although, strictly speaking, the initials apply to the Moslem Cigarette Company Ltd. W.A. and A.C. Churchman's Top Score pack was intended from its title to appeal to the cricket world. They were issued in sliding boxes of twenties in 1898, costing 3d., and the top cover portrayed a smiling Ranji, bat over his shoulder, raising his cap, with a pavilion and scoreboard in the background. On the reverse is a cricket ball in red. It does not appear to have endured beyond c.1905, and Hilary Humphries, of the Cigarette Packet Collectors Club of Great Britain, has seen it only in trade press references. In June and July 1899 Churchman's issued several booklets with Top Score, which, when the series was completed, formed a miniature cricket library for the year.

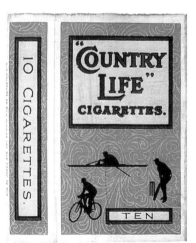

Churchman's also issued Olympic cigarettes in 1960, the packets carrying results up to and including the Games of 1956; 1960 results were then added, and as interest in the Olympics dwindled, general sporting records were substituted. Test match records of England against Australia, South Africa and the West Indies were listed back to 1924 and County Championship winners from 1933-67. Some earlier issues included the Player's Country Life from the 1920s and 1930s, showing country pursuits including a batting stance design; a bat, pads and stumps motif appears on packets of 10 by B. & J. B. Machado of Kingston, Jamaica. Sports cigarette packs by Godfrey

Phillips, c.1950, with a card-size packet illustration, are extremely rare to come by. The only one seen so far shows an unsmiling Ray Lindwall.

In the late 1940s and 1950s, Turf brands sold on a par with Weights, Woodbines and Park Drive, and in 1950 Carreras put out a series of 16 slides featuring cricketers in their Turf packets (see colour page xxvi). Series such as these tend to find themselves in a 'Catch-22' situation, shunned by card collectors as they are not strictly cards, while packet collectors often prefer the hull of the pack to the slide.

Quite outstanding is the colourful Mitcham packet by I. Rutter and Company (see colour page xxvi). It was probably only issued in a pack of five for 1d., aimed at those with lesser resources, and depicts an artist's impression of a cricket match on Mitcham Green.

Matchbox labels and book matches

The need to strike a light has existed since the dawn of man and the pioneer methods of doing so before the introduction of the "friction" match were complicated, usually tedious and frequently obnoxious. The first recorded sale of a matchbox was on 7th April 1827, and some authorities have it that label collecting dates from that period, which gives it a history 13 years longer than postage stamps. The first genuine pictorial matchbox label appeared in 1830, but it was not until 50 years later that pictures supplanted flowery script and carefully etched lines and swirls. Book matches in the form

Six matchbox covers
from the 19th century.

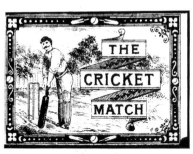

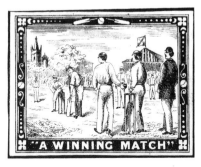

of paper advertising matches were first made in the USA and soon crossed the Atlantic to Britain. Since anyone can have their own printing on these covers, their number and variety are infinite.

Nineteenth-century advertising on matchboxes was nothing if not extravagant. Collard and Co., of Boundary Street, Liverpool, featured a play on words for their Cricket Match, using the insect and a weirdly dressed cricketer, with scorer's tent in the background in case we missed the point. These are undated but are c.1888, and something of the same came from Anneberg in Sweden, c.1903, calling itself The Cricket Match. A number had Continental origins, with, again, The Cricket Match series, by the Vulcan Globe Company, made both in Sweden and England just before the First World War.

Before 5th April 1916, match labels rarely showed contents figures. After that date customs and excise duty made it mandatory. This enables approximate dating, before any attempt at research in depth. Present-day labels, carefully preserved and written-up in albums, have a certain value, but those before 1890 have the greatest value of all. It is easy to say that labels should be pristine, clean and undamaged, but in many cases, those that survive need tender, loving care and a preservation order put upon them. If a wrap-around label, it should be uncut and, most prized, be still adhering to the box. Test Match from the Diamond Match Company of London and Liverpool, dated c.1899, in label form is valued around £7-£10, but, as a box, £40-£50 depending on condition.

In *Cricket Cigarette and Trade Cards* Derek Deadman includes in his comprehensive listing a number of labels and covers which illustrate first-class cricketers "as cricketers". These embrace G.F. Duncan and Company of Melbourne's 1938 set of 16 top Australians, while for

M.M. Walford, one of 25 county players featured by 'England's Glory'.

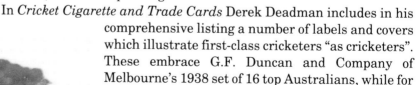

Britain, S.J. Moreland & Sons, of Gloucester, relied on the English love of the game as an advertising forum for their England's Glory set of 25 county players, issued in 1953. J. John Masters & Co., of London, issued a titled series, Test Match Winners, in 1980, as well as Winners Against the Odds, probably 1981. The Ashes urn appears on Australia "Murder" England from the same period. Shell issued a book-match cover to commemorate Colin Cowdrey being the first man to win a hundred Test caps, and Shepherd Neame, the brewers, brought out a set of 14 Kent cricketers in 1968 for Alan Dixon's benefit year.

For the real rarities, however, one has to turn to the Continent again. Of the "non-poisonous", Czechoslovak-made Test Match (1925), coloured black on yellow variety, showing a batsman square-cutting, there are only a handful, while only two copies have been seen in 45 years of Leicestershire Matches, issued in 1905, also black on yellow. The "How's That" caption is outmatched by the Belgian conception of an underarm bowler, batsman and wicketkeeper.

This is a sorely neglected field, and as a *vade mecum* the quite superb *Match Box Collectors Handbook* (1972), by David van der Plank, is unbeatable value. There are some 5,000 known collectors, specialising in themes, countries, manufacturers or series, and the point is well made that England's Glory and the sets from Duncan's are eagerly collected in their own right.

Philately

Modern stamps and covers

Philately, the collection and study of postage stamps, is a comparative newcomer to the field of cricketana, pushing to the fore only within the last twenty years. However, research has revealed that collectable material is available from as early as the mid-19th century, far predating the modern starting point of 18th January 1962. It was on that date that the then Portuguese colony of Cape Verde, a windswept group of islands 500 miles off the west coast of Africa, issued an insignificant, diamond-shaped stamp depicting a batsman standing awkwardly at the crease and gripping his bat in a way which would at the very least inhibit stroke-play (see colour page xxvi). Like most prototypes, the stamp was modestly priced and little heralded but it is now not easily found, even among specialist cricket stamp dealers.

Part of the appeal of cricket philately is that collectors can quite easily, and at not too great cost, attain a basic type of completeness, i.e. an example of every stamp featuring cricket issued by the world's post offices. Some are single stamps issued alone or as part of longer sets comprising other topics;

First day cover from
New Caledonia.

some are whole sets of two or more stamps all featuring cricket. The stamps, now numbering over 280 in some 90 separate issues, are well documented in both the cricket and stamp worlds; the price of most sets is in the region of £1.50-£3 and no issue should cost more than £7. Condition of the stamps, whether mint or used, is of paramount importance. The range of subjects or events commemorated is wide and the list of issuing countries, while mainly British Commonwealth and dominated by the West Indian islands, includes such exotic locations as Tokelau, Christmas Island, Surinam (formerly Dutch Guiana), New Caledonia, Tonga and Niuafo'ou, as well as Cape Verde.

Cricket stamps fall roughly into three categories: (1) the game itself, (2) special events (cricketing and others), and (3) famous players. Designs are, in the main, attractive and brightly coloured, though in some cases betraying an ignorance of the game – even allowing for the artistic licence incumbent on a designer attempting to encapsulate an area the size of a cricket ground on, literally, a postage stamp. A fully descriptive listing belongs in a specialised catalogue, which could soon be forthcoming, and space here permits only the briefest details by category, as follows (one stamp per issue unless stated):

Category (1): Cape Verde (1962); Pakistan (1962 – 2 stamps); Grenada (1969 – 4); Dominica (1969); Samoa (1971); Sharjah (1972 – 2); Australia (1974, 1989); New Caledonia (1975, 1987); Tokelau (1979 – 2); Singapore (1981); Surinam (1984); Guernsey (1986); Nevis (1986); India (1988).

Category (2): Guyana (1968 – 3); Jamaica (1968 – 3, 1976 – 2); St Lucia (1968 – 2, 1976 – 2); New Zealand (1969 – 2); India (1971); Antigua (1972 – 3, 1975 – 3, 1976); Great Britain (1973 – 3, 1980, 1988); Fiji (1974 – 3); Barbuda (1975 – 3); South Africa (1976); Barbados (1976 – 2, 1981, 1983); St Christopher/Kitts (1976 – 2, 1988 – 2); Dominica (1976 – 2, 1979, 1985); Grenada (1976 – 2, 1979 – 2); Guyana (1976 – 2, 1981 – 2, 1983 – 2, 1988 – 2); Bermuda (1976 – 4); St Vincent (1976 – 2); Trinidad and Tobago (1976 – 2); Belize (1976 – 2); Australia (1977 – 6, 1988); Isle of Man (1980); Sri Lanka (1982); Turks and Caicos (1982, 1983); Christmas Island (1984 – 4) Malaysia (1986 – 2); Anguilla (1987 – 4); Tonga (1988, 1989 – 5), Niuafo'ou (1988 – 3); Bangladesh (1988 – 3); Jersey (1989).

Category (3): Barbados (1966, 1977 – 2, 1988 – 5); India (1973); Turks and Caicos (1980); Australia (1981); Tuvalu (1984 – 8); Nukulaelae-Tuvalu (1984 – 8) Nanumea-Tuvalu (1984 – 8); Grenadines of St Vincent (1984 – 24, 1985 – 6, 1988 – 8); Union Island-Grenadines (1984 – 16); Nevis (1984 – 16); Niutao-Tuvalu (1985 – 8); Nukufetau-Tuvalu (1985 – 8); Nui-Tuvalu (1985 – 8); St Vincent (1985 – 8, 1988 – 8); Guyana (1985 – 7, 1986); Jamaica (1988 – 5); Trinidad and Tobago (1988 – 5).

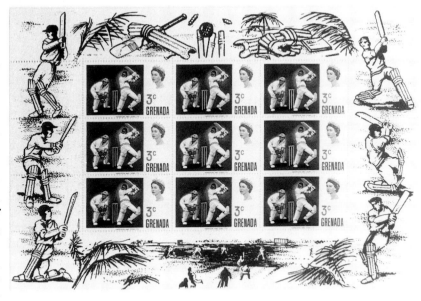

To these should be added items from Surinam (1975) and Norfolk Island (1981) depicting cricket not on the stamps themselves but on the sheets within which the stamps are printed. The sheet from Surinam, one of three containing ten stamps each, in a set commemorating independence from the Netherlands, is one of the more elusive philatelic items and, when found, likely to cost £25-£30. In a similar or slightly higher price range, and equally

One of the Grenada sheets of 1969.

hard to find, are the complete sheets of nine stamps each of the 1969 Grenada set of four; the margins have decorative borders showing batsmen, cricket gear and a game in progress, but few of the sheets have survived intact.

As the rate of issues has shown a sharp increase in the past few years, so it has been slightly disturbing to find cricket stamps, in a few countries, following the regrettable modern philatelic trend of issuing stamps bearing little or no relation to their place of origin. Post offices have handed over their issuing rights to agencies, some of whom are apparently concerned more with the exploitation of thematic collectors than with the philatelic well-being of the countries they represent.

Thus, as in category (3) above, while the appearance of Garfield Sobers on three separate Barbadian stamps (1966 and two in 1977) and of Viv Richards and Andy Roberts on two issues from Antigua (1975 and 1976) was welcome and entirely legitimate, the presence of contemporary cricketers from Kent and Yorkshire, and even of giants of the game such as Grace, Barnes, Hobbs, Larwood and Hammond, on stamps from the Pacific islands of Tuvalu (several sets in 1984 and 1985) could hardly be viewed in the same light. The latter issues – there were similar ones from certain West Indian islands in a total of 13 sets numbering 118 stamps – were part of a series called 'Leaders of the World', which also featured cars, cats, flowers, railways engines, pop singers and the Queen Mother. These issues caused much controversy and we know of many established collectors who steered clear of them. We know of others who put them into their albums, pointing out that all of these stamps, even the ones relegated to appendix status in the stamp

Richard Hadlee's world record number of Test wickets was commemorated philatelically in his native country. Many collectors pursue autographed covers, which do not always bear signatures as relevant to their subject as this one.

catalogues, were postally valid (we have seen several examples used on ordinary mail, which are highly collectable) and that they were produced with approval from the Test and County Cricket Board in England.

The choice, as always, must rest with each individual collector, who should also be aware that time is a great healer of philatelic reputations. Even the Penny Black, the first postage stamp, was criticised when first issued in 1840; now it is universally acknowledged in its position of primacy.

Most collectors also go for the first-day covers (envelopes) which accompany all new issues, either with the cricket stamps alone or with the full set. Most of the more recent Commonwealth covers are quite readily obtainable, but many of those from before 1980 are difficult to obtain and before 1970 still more so. The Fiji issue of 1974, commemorating the centenary of cricket in the islands, is one of the hardest to find, and we have not so far heard of, let alone seen, a first-day cover for the Cape Verde stamp. Covers, often with special postmarks, are issued for Test matches and other big events, particularly in England and Australia, and here again the earlier items are the most elusive. To be noted are covers for county centenaries – Kent, Gloucestershire and Derbyshire in 1970, Sussex county ground 1972, and Essex 1976 – and the early postmarks for the Gillette Cup (from 1970) and Benson & Hedges Cup (from 1973, though not in 1976).

For the Great Britain issue of 1973, three stamps depicting W.G. Grace based on the Harry Furniss cartoons and marking 100 years of county cricket, an album was issued containing covers and card-insert photographs for MCC and the 17 first-class counties; this was originally available for £12.50, but we have seen it valued in 1989 at well over £100. Scarce postmarks associated with this issue were struck at Hambledon and at the British Forces Post Office in Munich, where a special exhibition was being held. In connection with the issue we might also mention that it was accompanied by two special items from the British Post Office: a postcard (or PHQ [Postal Headquarters] card) depicting the 3p. value, which was the first of the cards that now accompany all British

Munich postmark to commemorate an exhibition in 1973, used with the county cricket centenary stamp issue.

commemorative stamps, and a 24-page souvenir booklet, containing the three stamps, illustrations, and text by John Arlott. Prices for the card in mint condition range from £30-£50, but the booklet can be had from stamp dealers for less than £5.

Far more highly priced, and sought by general philatelists as well, are the exceedingly rare printing errors, which slip past the stringent checks applied to modern stamps. From that Great Britain set of 1973 are known examples of the 3p. with the Queen's head omitted. It was listed in the Stanley Gibbons stamp catalogue in 1981 at £550, but by 1989 had soared to £2,500, making it by far the most expensive – if virtually unobtainable – item in the field of cricket philately. From the Grenada set of 1969 a 3p. missing the yellow (caps and wicket) went under the hammer for £160 at Stanley Gibbons Auctions in 1980.

It is, however, in the areas beyond the staple stamps and covers that much of the appeal of cricket philately lies for the specialist collector: in the discovery of 19th-century envelopes with cricket motifs or names; of postmarks used in those times bearing cricket ground names; of postage stamps from earlier than 1962 with strong cricketing links; and of stamp-like labels, the so-called Cinderellas of philately, which date back to the early years of this century.

19th-century covers

The oldest cover we have encountered was dated 1851 and featured on the flap an embossed motif of ball, wickets and crossed bats. It was posted at Charing Cross and sent a short distance across London to Thomas Geary at 43 Hunter Street, Brunswick Square. The cover fetched £250 in February 1987 at a Western Auctions stamps sale in Bristol and was one of seven 19th-century items with cricketing interest, which brought a total realisation of £750. The rest emanated from the eastern United States and the source should not cause total surprise. Cricket was being played there at least as early as 1737 and it was to there, with Canada, that an English team under George Parr made the very first overseas tour in 1859. It was, moreover, the view of at least one leading cricket historian, Rowland Bowen, that had it not been for the American Civil War, the United States rather than Australia might have become England's main cricketing opponents.

Be that as it may, the earliest among the group of American covers was dated c.1870 and sent to Steubenville, Ohio; it too had the familiar bat, ball and wicket design, but at the top-left, front corner. The price for this was £140, while £85 each was successfully bid for an 1889 Philadelphia cover inscribed "1853 CRICKET 1889" (possibly connected with the Young America CC or the 1889 Philadelphian tour of England) and for an 1893 Germantown CC, Philadelphia printed cover with accompanying notices about a football match and the bowling alleys at the club's Manheim ground. There were also two printed covers from Merion CC, Haverford, Pennyslvania, which realized £70 and £75, and another from Philadelphia, advertising "Jos. Parker . . . Importer of Cricket Goods", which brought £45.

The field of early covers or postal cards (as opposed to picture postcards) with cricketing connections is boundless but low survival rates make them extremely hard to find. As examples, we will mention some items we know to be in private collections: a postcard calling a meeting of the Metropolitan

CC of St John's, Newfoundland, postmarked 2nd August 1878; a cover sent to England on 10th June 1887, bearing the name of Melbourne Cricket Club across the top, the address of the secretary's office at the bottom-left corner and the club's monogram on the flap; a card sent from forwarding agents in London (based, appropriately in the light of modern Test cricket sponsorship, in Cornhill) to Batavia CC, Java (now Indonesia), on 15th February 1889; another card, of 7th March 1894, to C. Clift Esq. at the English College in Lisbon announcing the annual general meeting of the local Victoria CC; and, nearer home, a cover with a Kent CCC design on the flap, postmarked 25th July 1898 in Canterbury, sent to a member, C.E. Cheetham, in Sevenoaks, and containing two tickets and a notice relating to that summer's Canterbury Week events. There will be many others – and collectors would be advised to spare from the wastepaper basket any envelopes they receive in the mail from cricket clubs or organisations. One day those too will be sought after.

Cricket ground cancellations

Apart from the modern cricketing postmarks there exists a far older breed, those which were applied at English Test and county grounds to stamps which were affixed to telegram application forms to prepay the cost of transmission. So far as is known, however, they were not used on items of mail. Telegraph offices, either permanent or temporary ones manned by a special staff from London, were established at these venues for the dispatch of press reports and other urgent messages; they remained in use at least until 1909, by which time the telephone had taken over. Searches in the Post Office's archives have unearthed samples of these cancellations, recorded before the handstamp was dispatched to the ground. From 1884 onwards the following grounds have been noted: Birmingham, Bradford, Brighton, Bristol, Derby, Dover, Halifax, Huddersfield, Hull, Leyton, Liverpool, Lord's, Manchester, Nottingham, Sheffield, Southampton, Taunton and Tonbridge.

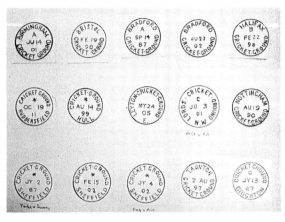

By chance – or, more likely, breach of rules – a few examples of these cancellations on stamps, usually on part of a telegram form, have survived. Post Office regulations ordered the destruction of all forms once the message had been sent, but some slipped through the net, perhaps smuggled out by clerks with contacts in the philatelic market. The late Desmond Eagar, once captain and secretary of Hampshire and a pioneer in cricket philately, had stamps cancelled at Taunton (2nd August 1897), Bristol (19th February 1898, when rugby was played there), Lord's (3rd June 1901) and Bradford (23rd June 1902). Noel Almeida, an indefatigable cricket stamp enthusiast from Australia, who has produced his own labels and stationery connected with the game, has an example dated 4th July 1902 at Sheffield, the occasion of the only Test match played at Bramall Lane. It was bought at auction in Sydney during 1975 for Aus$198, including commission, and this is the only specific valuation we have encountered for this type of material, although we do know of a fortunate collector who acquired one for a comparative song at a Phillips auction in London in October 1987 as part of a large lot of modern philatelic material.

Noel Almeida's own adhesive label.

Stamps with cricketing links

In addition to the stamps already discussed, which actually depict some aspect of cricket, there exists a separate class of those issued to commemorate or display some other feature but having some cricketing association. Many items in this category also predate the Cape Verde stamp, the earliest being a set from St Kitts of 1923. This small West Indian island, wishing to mark in an appropriate manner the tercentenary of its foundation as a British colony (incidentally, by Sir Thomas Warner, a direct ancestor of cricket's Sir Pelham) decided to build a recreation/cricket ground and to raise the funds for it by the sale of stamps.

A set of 13, ranging in value from ¹/₂d. to £1, was issued and proceeds from their sale were £3,916. Fourteen acres of land near Basseterre, the capital, were bought for £1,400 and the remaining money paid for preparation of the site and the building of a pavilion. The stamps, which bear a design representing Sir Thomas's ship, were catalogued at £1,500 for a mint set in

1989, with the £1 alone at £1,200, but cricket collectors should be able to obtain one of the low values for a few pounds. To complete the story, the ground was named Warner Park and it appeared on two later non-cricketing St Kitts stamps (1952 and 1954), as well as the cricket issue of 1988.

Several other grounds have appeared on stamps, ranging from the grand Melbourne Cricket Ground (in its guise as the main 1956 Olympic stadium on stamps from Liberia 1956, Romania 1979 and Haiti 1960) to Albert Park, Suva (Fiji 1942, 1954), the Esplanade, Galle (Ceylon 1967), the Padang (Singapore 1971, 1976), the Queen's Park Savannah, Port of Spain (Trinidad and Tobago 1935, 1938, 1953), Staten Island CC, New York (Bermuda 1973), Nehru Stadium, Delhi (India 1981), Victoria Stadium (Gibraltar 1987), Selangor CC (Malaysia 1972) and even a corner of a the old Hong King CC ground (Hong Kong 1941) and The Oval, as a venue for football (Sharjah 1966). There must be others awaiting discovery, which makes this a fruitful area of study.

Then, too, there are personalities who made their marks in other fields, such as Edmund Barton, first Prime Minister of Australia and a first-class umpire (Australia 1951, 1969); Sir William Henry Milton, captain of South Africa in what are now regarded as her first two Tests and later Administrator of Southern Rhodesia (Rhodesia 1969); and Lord Portal, Chief of the British Air Staff for much of the Second World War and President of MCC in 1958 (Great Britain 1986).

Cinderellas

Another fascinating area is provided by the so-called Cinderellas of philately, which for our purposes here may be termed stamps or stamp-like items not issued by national postal authorities; nearly all are extremely scarce. It is here that we find the oldest known cricket "stamp", a perforated publicity

Nawanagar stamp carrying the portrait of Ranjitsinhji.

label produced by Nuremberg Football Club in Germany, it is believed around 1908 (see colour page xxvi). Only nine examples are known to us and its appeal was confirmed in October 1988 when one made £270 in a postal auction run by Willow Stamps.

From the inter-war years come a whole range of stamps issued by the Indian state of Nawanagar, depicting the ruler who is known throughout the cricket world as Ranjitsinhji, and others from Porbandar, whose Maharaja led the first Indian side to England in 1932. Then there is a label for the state of South Australia's centenary in 1936, purporting to depict Don Bradman (examples of this were fetching Aus$210 at auction in Australia in November 1986), and another from 1938, engraved and printed to their highest standards by Bradbury Wilkinson, to raise funds for

Cheltenham College's centenary appeal. An example sold for £36 in a Willow Stamps auction of June 1985.

Among post-war items we note a sheet of 12 labels produced by the English Schools' Athletic Association depicting sports stars including Peter May and the late Jim Laker (one realised £47 at a Willow Stamps auction of January 1987); a sheetlet of six stamps from the printers, Harrison & Sons, in 1966 to mark their cricket match against Crown Agents (£41); a set of three membership recruitment labels from Hampshire CCC c.1966 (£18 in June 1985); and a small label to celebrate the centenary of the now defunct Hull Railway Clerks CC, of which only 300 were printed. There was also a total of 13 postal labels issued by four of the officially licensed private services which operated during the seven-week British postal strike of early 1971.

The eight issued by Barnard's Stores of Attleborough, Norfolk, were until quite recently still available from the shop, but the other five – produced by Gloucester Emergency Postal Service (2), London Express (2) and Norwich Local Post (1) – are highly elusive. A mint pair of the Gloucester issues were bid up to £24 at the Willow auction of January 1987; mint examples of the London Express service are known to us only in the MCC collection at Lord's.

Stamp printers Harrison & Sons' own commemorative sheet.

MISCELLANEOUS

Badges

Enamel and metal members' badges for home and overseas grounds, cricket lovers' societies, and clubs great and small are keenly sought. Ivory MCC life-member badges, issued in 1888 to help pay off the debt incurred when William Nicholson loaned the club £18,000 to purchase the freehold of the present Lord's ground, were, until the Bicentenary auction, rarely seen and richly coveted. Two hundred life members were eventually elected at £100 each, the last two in 1892. At the auction nine of these appeared, including one which belonged to Life Member No. 1, George Cecil Ives. This made £300, the other eight around £150 each.

Stoddart's team to Australia, 1897-98. **Above right** MCC life member badges.

A set of 14 cameo badges showing Stoddart's 1897-98 team to Australia, still on the original backing card issued by the American Tobacco Company, was one of the major prizes at the Bicentenary sale, roaring past estimate to reach £1,400. These pin-backed badges (the American name is buttons) are of special interest, being one of the very early sets issued with cigarettes in the same way as were cards. Part of the bric-a-brac of most collections, lapel badges rarely appear as separate lots, but two of some significance were highlighted at Phillips in October 1986. A 1934 pin badge of C.V. Grimmett was bid to £20, but neither of the two examples of the enamelled metal, official 1938 Australian team badge, estimated at £40-£60, found a buyer.

A 32in. square, embroidered with the badges of all the cricketing counties and Test match countries, except India and Pakistan, with the personally signed autographs of 150 leading cricketers, ranging from Warner to Sobers, later woven over in order to preserve them, was completed around 1960, and why it subsided below estimate to reach only £140 at Phillips in June 1988 is an enigma.

Julia Coote, a scorer in Sydney first-grade cricket, has an outstanding collection of cloth embroidered badges. These cover not only local clubs such as Cumberland and Gordon, but also English clubs such as Cheadle, Cleckheaton and Ventnor, and an assortment of English county badges, umpires' pocket badges and others from the Netherlands, Barbados and Signapore.

Familiar to generations of children through Robertson's jams and marmalades are the brooch-type badges featuring gollies. In earlier days they had a strong cricketing content. The first on the definitive Golly Brooch checklist to be directly relevant is No.24, 'Cricketer. "G.S.C.C." (i.e. "Golden Shred C.C.")'. No.25 is 'Cricketer. Plain bar joining feet,' and No.26, 'Cricketer. Larger rounded bar. Metal hands/feet. (Graham Products)'. Nos. 27-42 are all county cricketers, and Nos. 43 and 44 England and Australian Test players. No.45, Gloucestershire, was made in very small numbers and was probably not issued, nor was a Yorkshire cricketer with a green scroll. All these are pre-Second World War, and yellow, 'Golden Shred' waistcoat types; since Glamorgan is included they must post-date 1921.

After the war, brooches made by Fattorini, Miller, Gomm and others appear, without county connotations and all with subtle differences in eye alignment or appearance. The 1980s saw the acrylic "new look" types, with just two cricketers, differentiated by the size of the ball.

Lest we snort at them, a "team" of 12 enamelled batsmen lapel badges for Surrey, each pinned to a card, was bid up to £140 at Phillips in October 1986. The realisation argued scarcity, for in June 1988 "teams" of Sussex, Middlesex and Essex jointly made £170, but where are the other county batsmen representing "The World's Best Marmalades"?

Calendars and diaries

In a throwaway world, in which calendars can be foremost, the ingenuity of the advertising agency Deighton and Mullen's calendar for 1988 transfixed us. Robert Deighton's father played for Combined Services and Lancashire between 1947 and 1962 and manifestly the game is in the son's blood, as the company notepaper indicates. His team of creative artists was let loose to interpret cricket in a highly personalised way, and the end-product is a

'Unexpected Deliveries'

MULLEN

DEIGHTON & MULLEN
Practitioners in Advertising
KEY PLAYERS
A SERIES OF 2

KEN MULLEN, M.A., M.Litt. (Oxon.)
(Creative Director)

Born most *unusually and precipitately*, late one August *in the fog*, K.J. Mullen, of the *"49" Club* and the *Boxbusters* was, from the *first ball of his innings in life*, familiar with the *unexpected delivery*. Having been made to face one this *early*, he promptly, in the *spirit of rebelliousness* that has always enlivened his character, *seized the ball himself*, and has been *unleashing* unexpected deliveries at *motley recipients* ever since. The *figures returned*, over 14 seasons, attest to *some penetration*: he remains the *only cricketer* with 5 entries in the *Penguin Dictionary of Modern Quotations*, and 47 entries in the *Design and Art Direction* Annual, the advertising man's *Wisden*.

41 GT. PULTENEY ST., LONDON W1R 3DE.
TELEPHONE: 01-434 0040.

'The Dependable Opener'

DEIGHTON

DEIGHTON & MULLEN
Practitioners in Advertising
KEY PLAYERS
A SERIES OF 2

ROBERT DEIGHTON
(Chairman)

R.J.G. Deighton, of the M.C.C., I Zingari and the Free Foresters, *came to cricket early*. His father, playing for the M.C.C. against Australia in 1948, *bowled Bradman*. The *son*, showing a precocious respect for the *authority of excellence*, quietly took up batting instead; and was *filial enough to* delay his maiden century *some 30-odd years*. A *circumspect education* at Wellington and Durham introduced him to the *accumulative pleasure* of opening an innings; 10 years at DDB impressed upon him the *necessity of prolonging one*; and he steadfastly continues to *perfect the technique* of acquiring and retaining *sizeable advertising accounts*.

41 GT. PULTENEY ST., LONDON W1R 3DE.
TELEPHONE: 01-434 0040.

In addition to a calendar, Deighton and Mullen produced cigarette-style cards depicting their eponymous leaders.

hilarious and illuminating account of how outsiders see the game (cf. page 47).

The fact that the details were in Dutch in no way impaired the usefulness of the 1967 calendar from the firm of N. Leeftink in The Hague, the first calendar with any cricket symbolism for some time and warmly appreciated by Rowland Bowen. In the form of a linen banner on rollers, it depicted a batsman completing an on-drive, and there is an outside chance that this and the Rothmans cricket calendar for 1969 might be worthwhile acquisitions. Rothmans were then closely involved with cricket and their large and sumptuously produced calendar was sent only to the press, cricket clubs and certain organisations connected with the game. It was not available to the public nor was it obtainable for payment. Short and typically pertinent notes by John Arlott summed up the qualities and characteristics of the cricketers depicted in full-colour photographs.

Since *The Cricketer*'s 1981 calendar and *Wisden Cricket Monthly*'s 'History Makers', with 12 pictures in colour and 24 in monochrome, issued the following year, there have been reproductions from the *Lord's Taverners Fifty Greatest* book, the 'Duffer's Cricket Calendar 1987' with cartoons by "Gren", the 1988 MCC Cricket Calendar wall-hanger with 12 colour plates, and Rosalind Scott's 'Tea-Ladies' calendars for 1984 and 1985, both according to their producer, "Ladies' Lib" compilations, "born of 25 years' bitter experience!" The 1984 issue was completely sold out as "pressies for tea ladies at club annual dinners" at a very reasonable profit, but its successor lagged somewhat.

An attractive item, which escaped general notice, was the Oxford University Almanack for 1987. This wallchart featured, in addition to calendrical and university information, a print of the attractive cricket pavilion in the Parks from a watercolour by Terence Millington. Oxford University Press reported greater interest in this production than usual for the annual publication.

As objects of vertu, diaries were fashionable in the 19th century, when they became less of a private journal and more of an engagement book or *aide-mémoire*. The practice of inserting brief notes on important anniversaries, national events or holidays developed in the 1850s into useful tables of all kinds, thus adding to the diary some of the more useful elements of the old almanacks. With slim pencils housed in the spines, specialised diaries for various trades, professions (and sports) were being published by the end of the century, their informative notes in keeping with the vocation of the persons buying them.

Thomas De La Rue proudly claimed in 1938 the first pocket diary for cricket lovers. Bound in Persian leather and priced at 3s. [15p.] or 3s. 6d. with

pencil, it included 50 pages of cricket matter by E.L. Roberts, with an illustrated "supplement" on Australian cricket and "rare illustrations to delight the cricketer". De La Rue had overlooked that George G. Bussey & Co. had on sale in 1897 a 'Cricketers' Diary and Companion'. This was a waistcoat pocket diary, leather bound and gilt-edged. With full fixture lists, statistics, field placings for different kinds of

bowling, the latest revised laws and "tit-bits of useful information for cricketers", it would have been an agreeable stocking-filler at 6d. [3p.]. In 1928 there was also a de-luxe edition for 1s. [5p.]. It appears to have had the market to itself, unless the pocket-sized Cricket 'Diad', on sale at Lord's, The Oval, and principal county grounds for 6d. (1921), with seasonal results and statistics, also had a diary section.

Not until 1951 did the first 'MCC Diary' appear, published by Naldrett Press at 4s. [20p.] and later by Playfair Books at 5s. The 1959 issue was the first to cover the full year, January to December, and only in recent years has it had a challenger of any significance, apart from the diaries produced for the first-class counties. This is the 'Cricket Diary', published by Cricketana, of Bath, from 1984. On cream paper, with cricketers' birthdays on most dates, illustrations, quotations and pages of quick reference information, it is an attractive production. The group was joined by a 'Cricket Diary' for 1989 under the Marks and Spencer brand name, St Michael. 'The Club Cricketers Diary' appeared in 1982 and the first desk diary, the 'Wisden Cricketers Diary', compiled by Benny Green and bound in a deep green cloth, found a niche in 1986 as an augmented, if short-lived, version of the smaller counterparts.

Games

The heyday of games, puzzles and other indoor pastimes of family life was the late 19th and early 20th century before the advent of radio, cinema, television and the motor car stifled home entertainments such as the 'Grace Parlour Game', advertised in 1894. Many of these late Victorian games, designed for either the nursery or drawing room, have survived, their teaching or moralistic nature replaced by a more light-hearted tone, such as Halma (1880) and Ludo (1896). Games for the armchair enthusiast came in a multitude of forms, and it is not always easy to decide whether games of strategy and chance preceded mechanical games with bat and ball applications, or whether board games ran well behind games involving cards, dice or versions of tiddlywinks. Possibly they ran in tandem, but basically there were three components adding up to winter fireside pleasure - board games, card games and games inviting player participation on an active level. In between there were other diversions for the games addict, such as 'Dab-Cricket' (reading numbers from the pages of a book) and penny arcade games such as Miniature Cricket World Champion, auctioned at Phillips in October 1985 for £90.

The Wills's Woodbine Cricket Game from the 1930s used a rectangular tin-plate case, adorned with the promotional design of a Wild Woodbine cigarette pack, and enclosing a spinning wheel operated by levers, which registered runs and wickets through two operators. It crops up fairly frequently at auction in various states of disrepair, and averages around £50.

Among card games can be numbered Armchair Cricket, which adapts the principles of whist, with bats and pads as suits rather than clubs and spades. Launched in 1986 it offers realistic scores, and can result in a fascinating duel. There were also Googly and Run-it-Out, both with two packs of cards, scorebooks and book of rules (necessary adjuncts to all card games), examples of which have sold for £20; the 1964 product, Crickard; Oval, with a unique scoring method, every ball ensuring average innings and runs per over, and sold in 1965 for 8s.6d. [43p.]; and Gillette Cup, marketed in 1972 at £2.10s. and using cards and miniature figures. A new cricket simulation came from Lambourne Games in 1987 called County Championship, which does not use individual player cards, but grades each county for playing ability and uses a play system incorporating zonal weather, five batting modes and pitch conditions.

Succeeding older games with dice, such as Howzat, with its hexagonal dice, or tiddlywinks-style counters, a version of which, the Jack Hobbs Cricket Game was issued by the Chad Valley Company in 1922, there is a modern relative of shovehalfpenny and the winks, called It's Cricket. Using small red counters and a scorecard, it was launched in 1981 and some 2,000 sets were sold worldwide at just under £6. Pin Cricket, manufactured by St Michael in the form of a bagatelle board (see colour page xxviii), realised £65 in a December 1979 auction, but possibly the most complex sports replay games, serious simulations designed for quick playing, either solo or face-to-face, are One-Day International and the extension module Test Match Replay (1985), both by Lambourne Games. This has added complexities and variables, such as pitch and weather alterations, and is a blend of dice and cards, representing the Test-playing countries and allowing batting modes and tactical play. It features also a special set called Bodyline.

A general-knowledge quiz game, Cricketrivia, modelled on Trivial Pursuit and covering statistics and individual feats as well as literature, art and cricket phenomena, reached a wide audience in 1986. The brainchild of Anthony Miller, a former Commonwealth and Foreign Office advisor, it was marketed by Willow Enterprises and did not go unnoticed.

The Test Match, issued by Chad Valley, typifies the mechanical games so much part and parcel of the boyhood of most of the pre-computer generation. Many like Elec-Crickette by Ariel (£32 at Phillips in June 1986) appeared only as fugitive small classified advertisements, whereas Discbat Cricket (1953), which allowed fielders to chase or catch the ball through use of magnets underneath the table, percolated even as far as Rhodesia. Another was Family Circle Cricket, which even if the fireside atmosphere was lacking, still managed to recapture the "enthralling atmosphere produced by the broadcasts of the 1953 England v. Australia Test Matches", and all for 7s.6d. [38p.].

The older mechanical games incorporated plywood – or, in the case of Lamplough's Gold Medal Model Cricket (£75 incomplete, at Christie's, October 1987), tin-plate – figurines, bowlers with elasticated arms and fielders with catching positions in their bases. Mike Smith has a single-wicket version of Lamplough's game from the 1890s, still in working order,

Lamplough's Gold
Medal Model Cricket.

and the Test Match Game, to which Jack Hobbs lent his illustrious name. The Burroughs and Watts game, The Cricket Board, a rare complete example of which fetched £600 at the Christie's October 1988 auction, had lever-operated batsmen and bowler, and six painted composition fieldsmen on a green baize playing surface; encased in a varnished folding wooden box, it dates from around 1920. Its realisation puts it far ahead of Stumpz, which back in 1982, formerly the property of that renowned figure, A.W.T. Langford, climbed to £70. Stumpz was launched in 1934 by Thomas de la Rue and was endorsed by everyone from Bradman to Balaskas. For a cost ranging from 5s. [25p.] for the basic kit to the de-luxe set at 10s., owners had something in the cupboard over which Bill O'Reilly went to town in a big way: "Until 'Stumpz' there was no indoor cricket game, but 'Stumpz' is cricket".

Table cricket by
Burroughs and Watts.

There was, however, a table game which could also be played outdoors. *The Times* of 11th November 1903 reported that W.G. Grace and the inventor of "a greatly improved form" of table cricket, A. Weintrand, gave an exhibition of the game at Wisden's showrooms the previous day. Using a ball rather larger than an ordinary rackets ball the game could be played outdoors as well, when batsmen could run in the ordinary way. With practice, bowlers came to have the upper hand, not normally the case with the good Doctor, who, we are told, supplied the rules and "additions".

Subbuteo has been around long enough for it to become a household name, though more for table football than cricket. In 1970 the cricket version was available at prices ranging from 27s.6d. [£1.38] to 74s. [£3.70], with 00 scale miniature pieces, green baize pitch, sightscreen, groundsmen and rollers, spectators, deck chairs and scoreboard all available. Whether it will ever become a collectors' piece one cannot guess, and much the same applies to Table-Top Cricket, launched by Tri-ang in 1966 for £6, and Peter Pan Playthings' Test Match, endorsed at various times by Fred Trueman and David Gower. Mint early sets, given the hazards of children outgrowing and sometimes mishandling their toys and of a mobile, house-hunting community, cannot be common.

Computer games

A computer floppy disk or cassette is an unappetising collectible. Once catalogued and indexed by the collector, as opposed to the games player, it is fit only for the appropriate filing sequence, and we may add to that the problems of hardware/software compatability and fast obsolescence. Programs were often written initially for the creator's own amusement only, or that of his children, but their very "perishability" leads us to feel that the pioneering ventures ought not to be discarded.

Since the start of the home computing boom in 1982, advertisements for new programs have flowered, and while the various persons who tested the market have reported sales as far afield as Hong Kong and Zimbabwe, reaction in the main has been muted.

Early computer simulations tended to leave the user with minimal involvement in the game. All he or she needed to do was choose the team, answer simple questions and watch little stick figures swing stick cricket bats. The first traceable titles appear to have been Ashes and Test Match, but these were quickly followed by games which called for more awareness of tactical implications and a sense of strategy, such as Cricket Captain and Wyvern Software's Howzat. The latter was aimed at the 48k Sinclair Spectrum – the most popular home computer of the early 1980s – and came complete with a signed print of England's 1983 World Cup squad for lucky competition winners. Cricket by T.J. Owen was a more sophisticated version, and with high-quality graphics was for a time in a class of its own. It was highly addictive, had more player involvement, and a textual ball-by-ball commentary approach. Each game lasted an hour.

Expert reviewer D.N. Steel reckoned the real breakthrough came with

Tim Love's Cricket, which followed the game from "over the bowler's arm", but of necessity relied on comparatively simple graphics. Increasingly the computer became used to introduce random effects into a statistically predictable set of circumstances. Computer Cricket, by David Coates, incorporated most of the factors inherent in the games of that period, with sound effects to improve the sense of realism and, as in real cricket, the nature of the pitch is not known until after team selection. Audiogenic Software progressed along similar lines, their simulation allowing the player to choose his own team, plus an arcade mode creating timing and execution of the shot, with a facility which allowed variations in the bowler's speed and spin. The same company produced a 1986 version of Graham Gooch's Test

Cricket for the computer age.

Cricket for the newly emergent Amstrad PCW range. Cricket Master, by E & J Software, is one of the more recent simulations for mainstream home computers – the Spectrum, Amstrad and Commodore.

Non-graphic simulations, aimed at club secretaries and statisticians, enabling them to keep track of seasonal and career performances, had drawbacks in that they were not very user-friendly and errors were difficult to correct. In 1987 Spartan Averages, to name but one of many, was described as straightforward and user friendly, allowing the operator to create a database of career records to be stored for regular updating. A program by Stephen Fearnley allowed compilation of the season's averages.

Gramophone and other recordings

Should the sub-committee engaged on further updating of the Padwick *Bibliography of Cricket* ever need time off, a cricketing discography might be an agreeable diversion. Indeed, given time, it may become imperative. David Rayvern Allen has led the way with *A Song for Cricket* and supplementary material in *Wisden Cricket Monthly* in which he lauds the enviable cricketing ditties of Richard Stilgoe, the best known of which is probably 'Lilian Thomson'. Rayvern Allen reminds us, too, of fugitive numbers such as Colin Wilkie's German song commemorating the day 'Jim Laker took all ten', performed in 1981, and of another Englishman living abroad, David Hardy, whose group The Tickets provided a 'Centenary Rock' for Dutch cricket. Cy Grant's 1966 Tribute on a 45rpm disc (Pye) to Sir Garfield Sobers in 'King Cricket' and Sir Learie in 'The Constantine Calypso' is long forgotten, and did anyone think to preserve a pressing of 'How's That' by England fast bowler, Bob Willis, which went down the plughole with Splash Records? As a case in point, take 'The Cricketers of Hambledon', a 1929 song with music by Peter

Warlock. It is a genuinely tuneful melody, but is it on disc? A discography would tell us.

The cricketing press now carries almost as many review columns on latest audio releases as are devoted to videos. Apart from the spoken word, cricket has submitted to just about every texture and flavour of sound - one hesitates to use the word "music" (see colour pages xxix and xxxi). G.D. Martineau, himself a prolific composer of cricket "songs", wrote in *The Cricketer* in 1957 that it was "not wholly regrettable" that apart from calypsos no modern songs existed about cricket, and to hear them crooned, rocked and rolled would be an "excruciating experience". Instead we have enjoyed the tuneless, raucous 'Ashes Song' of 1971, a barbershop-style chorus of team members, since emulated by the West Indians, with Joel Garner quite unusually falsetto in his *sprechgesang*. Most of us can take Barry Gibb of the Bee Gees with good grace, but there has also been bouncy accordion music, tubular bells accompaniment, soul sounds in 'Soul Limbo' (1987) and the funky rhythms of 'A Perfect Action' (1986). Bles Bridges, a popular Afrikaans pop performer in South Africa, celebrated the 1985 Australian "rebels" with a rendition heard so often that according to Chris Harte in *Two Tours and Graeme Pollock* it drove the press corps quietly berserk. Other recent favourites are 'N-N-Nineteen', some delicious impersonations by Rory Bremner of Richie Benaud *et al* in 'The Commentators' (WEA Records, 1985) and the autumnal melancholy of Roy Harper's 'When an Old Cricketer Leaves the Crease' (EMI 1975). We have to agree with Rayvern Allen that this is the definitive cricket song, and even the album sleeve and lyrics sheet are hard to come by now.

Other records worthy of mention are: 'Victory Calypso', better known by its opening line, "Cricket, lovely cricket", and chorus, "with those little pals of mine, Ramadhin and Valentine", by Egbert Moore (Lord Beginner) on a 1950 78rpm; 'The Umpire Strikes Back' by F.S. Trueman (VJR Records, 1981), in which he "sings", entertains and keeps the bleep button operator in top gear; 'The Cricket EP' (by Percy Pavilion, Pavilioned in Splendour Records, 1983) may not be to everyone's taste, but is a blend of the cynical, the sexual, calypso and politics, with a "heavy down-beat number" on Basil D'Oliveira's exclusion from South African cricket; The Cricketers Jazzmen in a live performance of 'Stumpin' at The Cricketers' at a pub in Yateley, Hampshire; while the days of Tim Hudson, when he was Ian Botham's agent, and the great all-rounder's work for leukaemia research, are captured on 'Take Time Out to Care' and 'Ian, Viv and Me' (Spartan Records, 1986).

'Test Match Special' highlights have justly been snared for all time, usually on tape rather than record, but other mementos of the spoken word worth looking out for would include a broadcast by A.P.F. Chapman in July 1941, when, as part of an obviously escapist programme called 'When the

Crowd Roared' (famous sporting occasions recalled), the former England captain dwelt on memories of the MCC tour to Australia in 1928-29. The very next day Captain E.W. Swanton was scheduled to do a commentary from 'Somewhere in the Midlands' on the match between London Counties and Northamptonshire.

In the Ashes-winning year of 1953 a 10in. LP was issued giving scores, a short commentary, speeches by the captains and Bradman's impressions of play, all for 10s. [50p.]. How many have survived? Twenty years before that, Columbia produced a record (DB1140) on the Bodyline crisis, called 'Leg Theory' and giving the contrasting views of Harold Larwood and F.R. Foster on the recent furore. Quite apart from the subject matter, it was seen even at the time as something likely to be of great historical value in years to come. That year also Parlophone released 'International Cricket' and 'Yorkshire Cricket' (R1578) for 2s.6d. [13p.]. Lord Hawke revelled in his Yorkshire heritage, seeing cricket as a national asset and as a source for international peace. A recording by Jack Hobbs on 'How to Improve your Cricket' and a private 78rpm recording sent by David Sheppard from Australia in 1950-51 to his family, made memorable by his comments on the price of meat when it was rationed at home, form part of the Mike Smith collection. The Cricket Society had 500 copies made of speeches by Sir Robert Menzies and H.A. Judge at its 1968 England v. Australia Test match dinner. They were issued in 1971 at 27s.6d. and again we must wonder how many are extant.

A telerecording – in fact, a 33rpm record – entitled 'Cricket' was released on 1st July 1970 under the auspices of the Lord's Taverners (BBC Rec.86), and drew on a selection of BBC2 tea interval recordings made during the Sunday League matches. John Arlott opened by reading his own work, 'Cricket at Worcester 1938', and a formidable cast-list shows Brian Rix, Peter May, Graham Hill, Ian Carmichael, Leslie Crowther, Eric Sykes and the wrestler Mick McManus. The Welsh actor, the late Donald Houston, wrapped it up with J.C. Clay's 'More Reflections'. A pity the unforgettable Richard Burton voice was unavailable for the last named, but for 28s.9d. [£1.44] it would have been an acquisition well worth looking for.

Collector Don Rowan specialises in his own tape-recorded interviews with leading cricketers, and when he himself was interviewed in *Wisden Cricket Monthly* (April 1986) he had "captured" more than a hundred, whose playing careers spanned the period from Bodyline onwards. Among them are Graeme Pollock (recorded at Sutton CC in 1968, when he was playing club cricket in Surrey), Peter Loader, Frank Tyson, Tony Lock, Peter May, Colin Cowdrey, Godrey Evans, Jack Young (recorded at a railway station), and Keith Miller in the Gents at The Oval. Gil Langley was also captured along with players of an older vintage – Clay, Wyatt, Ames, Gubby Allen, Bowes,

Fagg and Bryan Valentine. Original vinyl discs make only fitful appearances at auctions and the prices paid for the recorded voices of Bradman, plus two piano solos by this multi-talented man (£32), and Hobbs (£20) at a September 1981 auction seem austere, so Don Rowan may yet be on to a good thing come the turn of the century.

Jack Hobbs on record.

Bradman was heard at greater length – several hours in fact – with fascinating reminiscences of his days in cricket in 'Bradman – The Don Declares'. The tapes were issued by the BBC in 1989 following their original production and broadcast in Australia.

Greetings Cards

Greetings cards for the Christmas season originated in England. The first card was published in 1843 at Felix Summerly's Home Treasury Office in Bond Street at the instigation of Henry Cole, and was signed by a John Horsley. Prior to the 1860s many cards were made and painted by hand. By comparison with the more popular Christmas notepaper with envelopes, their development was slow. Commercial cards were begun by the firm of C. Goodall & Son, helped by the progressive techniques of die-sinking and embossing. The introduction of new postal rates from 1870 onwards, which permitted transmission of postcards and printed matter at reduced rates, greatly increased the number of cards sent each year. This coincided with the growth of the Christmas trade in the United States and Europe, and by the end of the 19th century the custom was worldwide. The early 20th century was the heyday of sentimental and romantic cards, but, when cricket was used as a subject, it was almost inevitably some sort of exploitation of the jovial Tom Browne and Charles Crombie cartoons.

Although several collectors of note have built up albums or portfolios exclusively devoted to Christmas and other greetings cards (see colour page xxx), these tend really not to be so much collected as assimilated through the pores. Jim Coldham brought to bear his inimitable scholarship and lightness of style on the theme of 'Cricket at Christmas' in *The Cricketer*, December 1984. From this the collector learns that the first known Christmas card reflected an imbroglio between Lancashire and Nottinghamshire over the use of allegedly unfair bowlers: "... in December 1883, Lancashire sent Nottinghamshire a card entitled 'CRICKETING RULES drawn up by the Notts County Cricket Club, 1883-4', implying some very dodgy practices by the Nottinghamshire men and bias on the part of the umpires.

Between the wars there were MCC cards produced on the Gestetner Rotary, all rather nondescript, a blend of cricket impedimenta, sketches of imperial links and what Jim Coldham called "turgid verses". Cricket memorabilia "brochures" served as Christmas greetings for F.S. Ashley-Cooper and K.A. Auty of Chicago for their friends. Because of their bibliographical connotations and the uncertain numbers of those ever sent, the value of the survivors runs into dozens of crisp banknotes.

With the exception of the occasional pub sign, cricket was poorly served by commercial designers, and it was left to individuals such as the genial E.K. Brown and V. Pattabhiraman of Madras to break the mould of orthodox hearthside scenes with pictures of Fuller Pilch, cartoons and photographs embellished with cricketing play on words. Jack Russell's reputation both as wicketkeeper and artist was boosted enormously by his Christmas 1988 pen-and-ink sketch of the pavilion in winter at the Phoenix County Ground, Bristol, a festive robin adding the necessary seasonal touch.

Cricket clubs, associations and societies have also played a part, none more so than the Cricket Society which has for over 30 years supplied members with cards which have contrived to blend warmly affectionate festive cricketing themes with endearingly traditional scenes of holly, snowmen and Umpire Father Christmas. One of their first cards listed 11 well-known cricketers born on Christmas Day, most notably C.V. Grimmett and W.L. Cornford, but latterly inspirational flair has given way to the softer option of photographs of cricket grounds. MCC have tended to reproduce classical pictures and *objets d'art* from their own collection, with no overt Christmas connection but a useful art gallery in miniature. In September 1954, for instance, seven subjects in colour were available from the Curator at Lord's at 9d. [4p.] each, or nine in monochrome at 7d. each. In similar vein, the Association of Cricket Umpires has produced several attractive cards but without any Yuletide significance. The designs are chosen by competition between ACU members and sales average 3,000 a year. The one which featured Uppingham School issued in 1985 proved most popular and sold nearly 5,000. The ACU attitude is that, in the dark days of the year, a tranquil cricketing scene set in June acts as a tonic.

Aimed at local cricket clubs and individual cricket lovers, 'Christmas Cards with a Cricket Connotation' were issued from his Wellingborough home by book dealer Carl Howard. The set of five highly mannered cards produced in 1987 were drawn by a local Northampton artist, Simon May, and they show W.G. as a Santa, a village match, a dressing-room tableau, a cricket-playing snowman and an outfield catch at Old Trafford.

In an associated category are cards sent or received by cricketers, and it is a measure of the magic of the Trumper name that a Christmas card sent between members of his family in 1915, after his death, attracted a bid of £40 at Phillips in October 1986.

Close also to the hearts of giver, receiver and promoter are items such as Victorian Valentine and greetings cards. Included in the MCC Bicentenary auction was a Valentine with hand-coloured lithographic design and appropriate doggerel verse, and it was bid up to £200. Victorian greetings cards depicting men's and women's cricket featured at the same auction and achieved an average realisation of over £80, though a remarkable £400 was paid for just one card featuring a sentimentalised coloured lithograph of a boy cricketer with verse beneath.

Playing cards

These are not considered by Derek Deadman to be trade cards for the purposes of his exhaustive catalogue, discussed under the section on cigarette cards, but they do find a place as "they include some players for whom few trade or cigarette cards are known".

Victorian card with cricket theme and accompanying verse.

Colin Cowdrey in action against the Australians.

A boxed set, mostly black and white but some coloured, entitled Brearley's Batting Aces, was issued in 1978 by Wiggins Teape, but the company primarily concerned with the production of such cards has been Top Trumps. British Cricketers was issued also as a boxed set of 32 in 1978, followed by another set in 1979, and then International Cricketers, two different sets in 1978 and 1980, World Cricketers in 1979 and County Cricketers in 1980.

Pub signs, pub tables and other breweriana

Pub Signs

Of the public houses that have borne cricketing names from the 18th century, the oldest claimant is The Cricketers at Rainham in Kent, from 1763. The Bat and Ball at Hambledon may be older but, so far as is known, proof is lacking that it always had a cricketing name. In 1951 the owners, then Messrs Henty and Constable of Chichester, were prevailed upon by MCC to upgrade the image of the inn and a new signboard, painted by Ralph Ellis, had on one side John Nyren, chronicler of the Hambledon men, and on the other a typical game of the days when the club came into being.

By far the most regularly used name is The Cricketers, followed by The Cricketers' Arms, and in 1940, when G.B. Buckley sought refuge from the ferment of war, he was able to tally 237 existing hotels, inns, public houses, taverns and alehouses which could be linked with the game and another 113 that had disappeared. Apart from Grace, only the Fiery Fred, which opened in 1982 in Darnall, Sheffield, and the unaccountably situated Tommy Wass in Leeds (he was a leading bowler for Nottinghamshire before the First World War), are named after cricketers.

An illustrated letter in *The Cricketer* (June 1985) sought details of a carved pub sign bought in a local antique shop. Based on a *Vanity Fair* print of 1881 depicting Lord Harris, the carving measured 3ft. 6in. high and 2ft. 2in. along the base; no further details were apparently forthcoming. However, at the Phillips sale of May 1982, a pub sign for The Bat and Ball, with a central oval mirror flanked by painted scenes from a cricket match and inscribed "Kent v. Nottinghamshire at Tonbridge, 1869", realised £130. A painted metal public-house sign for The Cricketers Arms with portraits of Geoff Boycott, signed and dated T. Batty, 1981, was bought in at £160 in October 1986, well under estimate.

Geoff Wellsteed in the August 1985 issue of *Wisden Cricket Monthly* lamented the absence of cricketana in most of what are ostensibly cricketing pubs. But The Cricketers Inn at Meopham, Kent, whose sign changed in 1965 from top-hatted and whiskered cricketers to pictures of Hobbs, Strudwick, Ames and Woolley, had in 1984 a Grace handkerchief with its unambiguous inscription, "The greatest cricketer in the world", and Wellsteed himself cites, among others, a 1905 embroidery of autographs of English and Australian cricketers at The Bat and Wickets in Northampton and cricketers painted on the handles of beer pumps at The Cricketers at Littlewick Green, Maidenhead. By way of full redemption, the walls of the open-plan Black Horse in the little village of Grimston in Leicestershire are practically covered with framed portraits, scorecards, autographs, plates, bats and other memorabilia. Dennis Lillee is there, too, in the shape of a sweatband, and a Rest of the World XI blazer from Sir Garfield Sobers adds true class to an imposing collection.

Pub tables

Originals, as well as reproductions, of the cast-iron W.G. Grace table, which dates from the 1890s, are frequent visitors to auction houses. One appeared at the 'Tony Baer' sale of September 1978 and gathered in £280; the heady atmosphere of that seminal event was reflected in prices around £150 in 1979, when, ironically, a modern reproduction sold for £180.

The tables are usually found with a circular wood top, supported by three legs moulded with portraits of W.G. and a pierced apron of baskets of fruit centred by rosettes. Prices have stabilised at £350 or thereabouts. One with a marble top materialised at Phillips in June 1988 and found new and hopefully convivial accommodation at £400. No fewer than four raised £1,550 at the same auction house in October 1987, and Fleet Street gossip used to claim that there were about 50 of them propping up a merry throng in a certain public house known to everyone, but when questioned, memories failed.

An original W.G. Grace table.

Other breweriana

Surprisingly, in view of the game's close links with the tap-room, none of the older brewers utilised the cricketing theme. There was a brewery called The Bat and Ball, operated by Golding & Company, at Bat and Ball, just outside Sevenoaks until 1910, but Andrew Cunningham, the foremost authority on breweriana, has never seen anything bearing even their name.

Two of the small modern breweries – Chudley, which produces Lord's Ale, and Tate's of Kimford, who have adopted the trademark of a bowler in action (the owners are related to the Tate clan) – have issued small pieces of advertising such as pump clips, beermats and handbills with a cricketer emblem. Duncan Gilmour of Sheffield's 'Sheffield Shield Brand' includes cricketers as part of the necessary colonial allusion. Commemorative bottles of beer are now a popular specialist collecting field and cricket has not gone totally unrecognised, with issues for Worcestershire (Baileys 1984) and Nottinghamshire (Heritage 1988).

Bass issued a showcard depicting a cricket scene somewhere around the early 1960s. Theirs was in a vertical format, whereas a similar item from Guinness, probably issued around the same time, was horizontal.

Mackeson's 'Sports Series' had three cricket-related beer mats, using illustrations reproduced from *Punch* for a set of a dozen sports cartoons. Ind Coope's sports ground at Burton-on-Trent hosted the Rothmans Cavaliers XI and a National Hunt Jockeys XI, both occasions in 1968 marked by special mats. Fremlins Brewery issued a set of five different 'County Cricket Supporter' mats in 1965, for Middlesex, Sussex, Surrey, Essex and Kent, and 'Appeal for a County Ale' the following year with brief statistical details for the same counties. Newcastle Bitter entered the fray in 1982 for the David Bairstow Benefit year, but it was Whitbreads who really went to town in 1983 with five mats entitled 'Never a Dull Moment. The Astonishing Saga of the Whitbread Village Cricket Championship', imaginatively cartooned and

One of the Whitbread
mats.
Far right Poor
Malcolm Nash,
remembered once again
by Heldenbräu.

each "astonishing feat" genuinely good beerside reading. Quite a rare one, from a series of about 30-40 sporting achievements, is a 'Greenall Whitley-ism', mentioning 1886-87 when England were all out for 45 in their first innings at Sydney but still won. It urges the consumer to "Make it a certain score with a Groves & Whitnall Draught Beer".

The cricketing gentleman in Harp's 'Gentlemen Prefer Harp' was one of a set of four, three of which are sporting activities, but the fourth, for reasons best known to Harp, shows a saxophonist.

Souvenirs

We come not to bury cricket memorabilia but to praise it, though we are sometimes lost for words at the great avalanche of modern souvenirs. The sales list for the MCC shop begins to hint at a mail-order catalogue, while some new gift ideas from The Cricketer Shop leave the game far behind to embrace travel goods and executive playthings. Mind you, there are plenty of satisfied customers for their bookends and cricket bat pewter drinking flask.

The TCCB did their bit with the range of T-shirts, badges, rattles (now banned, praise be) produced with Walt Disney Productions to promote the Prudential World Cup in 1975. Who now remembers the motif figure of Jiminy Cricket? From 1979 onwards Wyvern Sports Marketing gave the public everything from 'Bionic Botham' and the 'Master Blaster' sweatshirts to car sunstrips and Ian Botham commemorative clocks at £26 a pair.

Like an ever-rolling stream, where will the ties, tie pins, lapel badges, shield-shaped plaques, on-the-spot inscribed plaques and ornamental figurines of batsmen and bowlers awaiting the buyer's own specifications, rosettes and the rest end? The Cricket Memorabilia Society might set up a committee of inquiry to ascertain whether they gather new converts, render established collectors ever more introspective or kill off interest altogether. To commemorate their centenaries, the counties merely act as tributaries to the flood of sweaters, umbrellas, sun hats (see colour page xxiv), mugs, cuff links, glassware, pens and penstands, specially labelled bottles of champagne and port, enamel and blazer badges, ashtrays, teaspoons, commemorative plates, silk scarves, key fobs, car badges, aprons, tea towels, jotters, notepads, bookmarkers, pennants, coasters and marcasite brooches. All the things you never thought you really needed!

Video recordings

The first game ever televised for the few thousand who then possessed a TV receiver was the Lord's Test in June 1938. It was the best part of half a century before viewers had the facility to record what was broadcast or before the television companies began to realise the sales potential of archive cricket.

In 1983 not every home had a video recorder so that the 'Benson & Hedges Golden Greats: Batsmen (1898 to the Present Day)' still seems a wonderful use of the medium. Produced by David Puttnam, presented by John Arlott and devised, created and masterminded by David Frith, at £19.95 it has not yet been excelled, and its sequel on the great bowlers should justify the faith of those who disagreed with the comment made by one reviewer that: "We are not weaned from the imperishable historical and imaginative writings of Altham and Cardus" to this complementary production. At all events, people with extensive libraries of cricket videos (see colour page xxix) are to be envied – the more so as the BBC keep only the edited highlights of cricket in their archives and not the full day's play.

Many collectors do their own taping on the same scale and fanaticism as confirmed bibliophiles, but what has not yet been disclosed is the genuine life-expectancy of video tapes. Early VCR tapes are of very limited usefulness in that the equipment necessary to transfer to VHS or Beta is obsolescent and firms prepared to undertake the work are not easy to find. Creeping fears are being expressed that even if tapes are handled with care, meticulously rewound after each playing, placed only on their sides and properly housed in the correct environmental conditions, hopes of post-retirement replay of hundreds of hours of viewing may prove to be a waste of time.

A small point admittedly, but do any of these *aficionados* collect commercials using cricketers to carry the message? Godfrey Evans was a good selling point to recommend milk in one of the first commercial television advertisments produced for the National Milk Publicity Council in 1957, but it is a fair wager that now it is as rare as any edition of Felix. Several rival enterprises have, since the early 1980s, serialised monthly compilations of all new commercials, so that Ian Botham's October 1988 commercial on not growing up as a ballet dancer is (reasonably) safe; but what about Craig McDermott's endorsement of a brand of crisps or Ian Chappell's demonstration of a rubberised golf tee as ideal training equipment for young batsmen?

Two Australian productions, 'The Bradman Era' as recalled by Bill O'Reilly in 1984 and 'The Tied Test' the following year, presented historic film sequences; the latter had supplementary comment by Alan Davidson, Colin McDonald, Lindsay Kline and the unforgettable Alan McGilvray. There are now about three dozen cricketing videos including those devoted to coaching, and the danger of over-production of items following the format of 'The Ashes Regained: the 1985 Cornhill Insurance Test Series' (BBC Enterprises) may jade the palate. Arcane specimens such as 'Great Moments of Indian Cricket 1932-86' (1987) and 'Springbok Sporting Highlights', volume 1, which has 24 minutes of Pollock's century at Trent Bridge, help redress the balance and satisfy the connoisseur.

'Jeremy Coney's Cricket Coaching Video' (1986) was highly rated by critics and commentators for its 130 minutes of dry wit and Martin Crowe at his effortless best, but how far down the road one wishes to pursue collecting ardour so as to covet the 'Prudential Cricket Coaching Clinic' (1985) is debatable. Even when backed by accompanying wallcharts, these mechancial demonstrations of the various techniques for self-improvement, backed by clips from big matches, are nothing new, the film version of the National Cricket Association's 'This Game of Cricket' having appeared some years before. The video version appeared in 1984 as a set of five, the price gradually reduced from £100 to £75 in 1987.

Films

The sounds of cricket have played many a part in cricket sketches and plays broadcast both on radio and television, but the fortunate few present at the first public screening of archive film footage can never forget the audible mass intake of breath when we glimpsed Grace in the nets, or the slow-motion parade past the camera of Stoddart, Shrewsbury, W.G. and a youthful Rhodes. Later we feasted on the floated, innocuous-looking bowling of Rhodes in his prime, and Tich Freeman, neither looking, frankly, much more than backyard bowlers to us chairbound batsmen.

The cordial reception accorded the series of Wisden Cricket Nights at the National Film Theatre and elsewhere, hosted by David Frith, plus his vigorous efforts to unearth, preserve and protect hitherto little-known or unrecorded cricket filmlets, has given fresh prominence to their historical value. Despite this, there must still be precious vintage 8mm and 16mm films offering a documentary record of great players and events, lurking in lofts and basements. That these may be on inflammable nitrate stock is cause for dismay. The dream of a national library of cricket films has some reality in the small store of National Cricket Association films, formerly housed at Edgbaston and now at Lord's, but much has gone adrift which should have been entrusted to headquarters, or actively sought out by the custodians of cricket's heritage.

The 'Wisden Cricket Film Show' travels to Leeds.

Film at Leeds Playhouse

Calverley Street, Leeds LS2 3AJ. Box Office Telephone: (0532) 442111

Sunday 13 November at 3.00pm
Wisden Cricket Film Show
Introduced by David Frith, Editor of Wisden Cricket Monthly

An afternoon of cricket film specially selected from the holdings of the National Film Archive. There are some short clips of WG Grace filmed in 1898 and 1899 and newsreel film of the 1926 Test series against the Australians and of the 1938 Test series. *The Life of Jack Hobbs* features the opening of the 3rd Test at Adelaide in 1924 and the scoring of his 126th century (Herbert Sutcliffe and Percy Fender also make appearances). Finally, there is an hour-long film about the 1950/51 Test series.

All seats are bookable in advance at £1.50. Book in person, by post or by telephone. Box Office: (0532) 442111. 10am - 7pm

Cricket and the cinema have been the subject of colourful articles and equally colourful follow-up letters in the cricketing journals. Rarely is the game itself the centre of attraction, usually relegated to bit parts or atmospheric outdoor decor. The National Film Archive (especially when Clyde Jeavons was on the staff) and other film archives and libraries do a professional job in offering proper environmental conditions for storage and cataloguing, but the appearance in October 1986 at a Phillips auction of two 16mm black and white cricket films provoked fresh thinking on what had happened to so many others. 'Edrich and Evans', nine minutes with sound, and 'Batting Strokes. Forward Defence', five minutes silent, were auctioned as a lot at £45. The assumption is that these must have been part of a larger instructional film, which used Jim Sims and others as models, called 'How to Play Cricket', made by Featurettes Ltd. of Wardour Street. This was made in 1948 – after a visit from the Australians which left the host nation sorely in need of guidance – and lasted 30 minutes.

But what, one asks, has become of 'Sussex v. Lancashire in Horsham Week', a film made in 1913, and seen by Plum Warner in the company of George Cox Jnr and Arthur Gilligan many years later? Cox recognised his father walking out to field, and also much in evidence was the heavily moustachioed figure of Albert Trott. A.C. MacLaren did the lecture circuit to schools in 1923, using films of players from both sides during his Australasian tour, showing games in progress and praised at the time as "undoubtedly the best lot of Cricket Films in existence". Where is it now? And where is the film written about in 1968 by Irving Rosenwater of S.F. Barnes bowling for Staffordshire against the Indians at Stoke-on-Trent in July 1932? He was then aged 59 and yet according to Rosenwater it hinted still at his greatness and was believed to be in his son's possession in Chadsmoor.

We assume that 'Cricket for Women and Girls', a 16mm. instructional film made by the Women's Cricket Association in 1938, is safe in their archives. Presumably, too, 'Cricket', the first 16mm. educational film, made by Kodak in 1930, still survives. Or have the players featured - Hobbs, Chapman, Tate, Freeman, Sutcliffe, Hammond, Strudwick, McDonald, Tyldesley and Gregory - been lost to some screen in the sky?

John Woodcock had available for hire copies of his film, 'Elusive Victory', made during the 1950-51 MCC tour of Australia, with E.W. Swanton as narrator and a useful supporting cast in R.C. Robertson-Glasgow, Rex Alston and S.C. Griffith. It ran for an hour, whereas Alec Bedser's 16mm. film in colour on the 1954-55 tour to Australia lasted 20 minutes more and would be enthralling to see, or even to own. Mike Smith is lucky enough to own six film strips made for the U.S. Peace Corps in the 1960s, the work of a female producer and prompted by "a need to get on better with the English", using cricket as a demonstration of all that is best in our national character.

A Miscellany

There is never a shortage of suitable material for the potential buyer; from cardboard cut-outs of Geoffrey Boycott and W.G. Grace to smaller collectibles such as a Baccarat ashtray from the 1930s for £50, a pair of glazed pottery book-ends from c.1940 for £40, or even a cricket compass, the mechanism crowned with metal crossed bats and ball, for £60. The problem for the compiler is how to bring about their fusion.

A prime necessity is currency with which to start out. David Frith has a George III penny alleged to have been used by the Hon. Ivo Bligh for the toss when he regained the Ashes in 1882-83. The story is that Bligh gave the coin to Spofforth, after losing a bet to the "Demon" that he could not uproot a single stump with the coin atop it two out of three balls. Spofforth promptly performed the hat-trick. When Spofforth later played for Derbyshire, the coin was passed to L.G. Wright, the county opening batsman. Among those whose cricket ambitions were encouraged by Wright was a Henry Henson of Reading. For years the coin was kept in a small box made by a Sydney jeweller, bearing the words, "From I.B. to F.R.S., May your descendants never win the toss with it against England", and it was from Henson that Ron Yeomans obtained the coin, virtually as a gift.

The Central Bank of Barbados paid tribute to Sir Frank Worrell on its new five-dollar bill in 1976. These are now priced by dealers at between £7-£10, but no value has been set for a W.G. Grace note, "issued" by Birnbeck Island, a tourist attraction just off Weston-super-Mare (see colour page xxxi). Of course it is more an admission ticket to the island than a bank note, but it is amusing to think of it as the latter.

Among articles classified as pure fun is a superbly fashioned and perfect miniature armchair, 3in.x2in., dated 1800-30. Two bats form the outer uprights, and it cost Joe Goldman 50s. [£2.50] over 50 years ago, but he was "assured the value is much greater". A real chair, one of W.G. Grace's own (a walnut-framed Dralon, round-backed easy chair), was disposed of at the Gloucestershire sale in 1982 for £270. His doorstep, incidentally, made £200 in 1985.

A large marquetry picture of a cricket match in Leeds on Boxing Day was in the porch of Ron Yeomans's home, while indoors there was a tapestry showing Father Time on the Grand Stand at Lord's and part of the scorebox.

Of a household nature we find a decorated pine chest, which reached £400 in October 1987, while a white-painted wooden bench from Lord's may have come in closer proximity to famous posteriors than its proud owner ever appreciated as he dragged it across London from Christie's in June 1988. The bench was one of those sold off by MCC as safety regulations dictated the substitution of tip-up seats.

Ron Yeomans had his front gate constructed from three stumps used in a Test match and officially "blessed" by Peter May, who must have appreciated the cricketing wallpaper used for the hallway and found for Yeomans by Len Hutton. He called it his "Griffin" paper, since the bowler had a distinctly bent arm.

Rockley Wilson had a green woollen hearth or bedside rug, 6ft.x3ft., with W.G. in batting stance at the centre and wearing his London County colours of red, yellow and dark green. It was a gift to Wilson at Christmas 1937 from his "man", whose wife probably made it. In a 1974 advertisement, £75 o.n.o. was asked for it.

Coming down to kitchen level, there are biscuit barrels, with handles made of entwined cricket bats, their tops surmounted by other cricketing symbols, and elusive cruet sets. A specialist collector of cruets knew of one of Crown Devon manufacture which he had never seen; another of German manufacture just before the last war has the figure's hands resting on a cricket bat and surrounded by cricket balls.

Where better to keep the cricket kit throughout the winter?

Silver-plated lamp with
cricketing figures,
1851.

From Portobello Road Ron Yeomans acquired a Victorian egg-warmer, contained in a massive cricket ball, mounted on stumps, with crossed bats at each side, surmounted by another bat. Underneath, and separate, was the warmer, made up of two small crossed bats and balls. A silver-plated lamp, dated 1851 and probably unique, with two cricketing figures at the base, was a more than handsome buy for £2,000 at the Burlington Gallery in 1989, about ten times its purchase price nearly a decade earlier at the Sussex CCC sale. Fringed silk place mats, each with a colour painted full-length portrait of a Golden Age cricketer, would add lustre to any dinner at £550 for 11 from the Bicentenary sale. Hayman's omnipresent picture of cricket on Artillery Fields features also on a splendid papier-mâché tea tray, 29in.x24in., given to Rockley Wilson by his brother, who acquired it in July 1939 at Whitchurch in Shropshire. Another papier-mâché tray, c.1785, reproduced anonymously after David Allan's painting of 'The Cathcart Family' and once part of the Joe Goldman collection, is now at Melbourne, part of the Baer collection. It depicts a game played for a wager between teams headed by Lords Cathcart and Palmer, and not, as so often described in the past, the first cricket match in Scotland.

A damask tablecloth, formerly the property of J.R. Mason of Kent, with white-work embroidered crest of Kent CCC at the centre, and the dates 1906, 1909 and 1910 (Championship-winning summers for the county) at the corners, 104in.x89in., was folded away for £65 at Christie's in October 1988.

Mrs W.L. Murdoch, wife of the former Australian and Sussex captain, obtained the signatures of players such as Giffen, Darling, Bannerman, Laver, McLeod and Murdoch, along with the umpires present at the match between Victoria and New South Wales in 1882, and afterwards embroidered over the writing on a teacloth in different coloured silks. Its ownership reads like a drum roll of collectors – A. D. Taylor, A. J. Gaston and J. W. Goldman. On another feminine note, printed paper fans, royal blue in colour, given by representatives of the firm of perfumiers, Eugene Rimmel, to ladies as they entered Lord's for the Eton v. Harrow matches in the 1870s are rare enough (£450 at the Bicentenary sale) for ostentatious display when acquired now (see colour page xxxii).

Golden Age heroes on
four place mats.

No collector is properly accoutred unless he can lay claim to the right props for his study/sanctum. Ron Yeomans told of his Victorian brass inkstand, composed of stumps, bats and balls. The tops of the balls unscrewed and the stumps were hollow to hold quills. Another small leather-cased ball opened to reveal an ink-well.

Around the walls would be hung pennants, MCC

boundary flags and picture frames decorated with cricketing scenes, and on the desk paperweights, such as the marble and ormolu one with a bronze of a half-length figure of A.E. Stoddart, which fetched £260 at the MCC sale.

A short, illustrated article in the January 1988 issue of the journal of the Cricket Memorabilia Society drew attention to yet another of cricket's little byways – the collection of book-plates. These Malcolm Lorimer felt added to rather than defaced books, especially those once part of the libraries of collectors of the calibre of Goldman, A.E. Winder, B.J. Wakley and Charles Pratt Green as well as the small blue book-plate of Epworth Secondhand Books.

Each member of the MCC touring side of Australia in 1928-29 had an illustrated address presented to him. A cherished memento, measuring $11^{1}/_{2}$in. x $10^{3}/_{4}$in., it was greatly prized by its owners and seen as a "veritable work of art".

Cricketing book-plates.

Another illuminated address has found a home with Mike Smith, this one on vellum and presented in 1910 to A.J. Webbe by cricketers of Winchester College who played against the XI he took there annually from 1875 (see colour page xxxi). Contained within a clasped calf box, the 86 signatures include Bonham Carter, Leveson Gower and J.R. Mason.

Tony Baer's umbrella stand.

No man in his right mind in England would go outdoors without his cricketing umbrella, perhaps the one in I Zingari colours which belonged to the one-time Kent batsman, Francis Marchant, and went for £70 at Phillips in October 1987. It might be kept in the hallway in a stand with the figure of a cricketer, which once stood in Tony Baer's London flat and which has been reproduced by the Burlington Gallery, selling at £220 in 1989. The stand might also hold a walking stick, carved with the head and various activities of W.G. Grace, likely to cost £100-£150, or an inscribed stick presented by Grace to a friend and worth £100 at the 1982 Gloucestershire sale.

Collecting involves hard graft, so life's little pleasures should also come in cricketana form. A foot-high wine ewer, by Hayne & Cater, inscribed to J.B. Warwick, Secretary of Nottinghamshire CCC, and presented to him in 1848, was the toast of all collectors at Sotheby's in December 1979, when it achieved an incredible £900.

Fortunately bottles of wine and other spirits come cheaper. Special labels on wine and port bottles are pictured elsewhere in this book, but a lesser known label shows a South African setting. A.F. Cricketer's Special Reserve Gin bore a cricketing label and Gilbey's Gin produced a mat with a cricket clock competition in 1983.

A suitable wine for the close of play.

Below The smoker might also like the attractive Victorian silver compendium, comprising a cigar-cutter in the form of a bat, with ball, bats, wicket and cricket bag match-holder, or the lighters presented to Jim Laker (below right) to commemorate the Ashes victory of 1953 and Surrey's county championship triumphs in the same decade.

A wooden box, captioned "The Right Spirit – Teachers Whisky", illustrated by two boy cricketers using Teachers whisky bottles as stumps, may now contain a dram or two after going for £50 at Christie's in October 1987. A cork bottle-stopper, with a silvered metal finial of a batsman, 10cm. high overall, sold at Phillips for £32 in 1978, when also a late Victorian brass bottle-opener, modelled as the head and torso of W.G. Grace holding a cricket bat, was bid up to £100.

Some might also wish to puff on a pipe. Clay pipes with cricket ornamentation are rarely seen, so one from c. 1895, modelled in the round with the head of W.G. and stamped "Gowland" on the stem, attracted more than a puff of smoke at £170 in the MCC Bicentenary auction. Others have been seen: one in vulcanite with cricket-bat stem and, of course, W.G. bowl made £45 at Phillips in September 1980, while a pair, one with a cap attached

by a chain, was drawn up to £130 in November 1984. It is also worth noting that in 1857 a 'Cricketing Colouring Pipe, Case and Tobacco Box', with cricketing figures on the bowl, was on offer by Lillywhite's for 3s. 6d. [18p.]; the pipe, without the case, was just 4d.

The only snuffbox Joe Goldman claimed to own was a cherry wood box of the Hambledon Club, showing a batsman at the crease, a seated batsman and crossed bats. From a scratch above the word "Hambledon" at the base, he deduced it was in use around 1835. He paid little for it and was uncertain of its value in 1936. Another of life's smaller pleasures were the rectangular 19th-century papier-mâché snuffboxes, the lids painted with cricketing scenes reminiscent of Hayman's Artillery Ground scene, or a "conflation" of 18th- and 19th-century period details. A pleasure, yes, but at the Bicentenary sale they cost £500 and £800 respectively.

Two toffee tins depicting the 1926 Australians, with the lid in the form of The Oval, exceeded £50 in May 1984, items sweet to the palate which rarely appear at auction, and one has to drop right down the ladder to find the "rarities". David Frith has a 1968 chewing sweet 'featuring cricket' still in its original wrappers, while Murray Hedgcock wrote to us in similar vein, suggesting that he had something that surely comes into the true range of collectibles as it may be the sweetest souvenir any journalist has of the redoubtable I. T. Botham. It is a sugar packet, thrown by him at a colleague on the eve of departure of the England team for Australia in October 1982, at Lord's Indoor Cricket School. Mind you, no one dared ask for it to be autographed.

There remain some unclassifiables:

A replica of the Ashes urn went to David Frith at the Bicentenary sale for £150, a gift from a grateful Charlie Watts for help in assessing and bidding on that historic occasion.

Ffteen MCC membership voting boxes, made of mahogany, which realised prices between £190 and £450 at the Bicentenary sale.

Telegraphic messages flown by carrier pigeon from Paris under siege to *The Times* in 1870 have survived, so there is no reason to suppose that full scores of all local matches carried by these birds which arrived at Wilkinson's tobacconist every evening in Stockton-on-Tees in the 1880s have not done likewise.

Motor car registration plate MCC 555 was offered for sale for £275 in 1976 (together with a trivial little number in the shape of a 1966 Sunbeam Talbot), but Colin Cowdrey had reluctantly to turn it down as he already owned a catchy number plate MCC 307 (cognoscenti will recognise that as his highest first-class score). In the end it was bought in June that year by a Sussex committee man, Spen Cama, to join the SC 555 in his "fleet". There will be many other similarly adorned vehicles and on one of them might sit a 13cm. silver-plated car mascot of W.G. Grace in batting stance, which brought £45 at Phillips in May 1984.

And finally. . .what might be described as the ultimate in cricketana, a ground complete not only with pitch, pavilion and scoreboard but also equipped with a playing strength of 150, tiered stands filled with a thousand spectators, floodlights, press and broadcasting facilities, a bank, a physiotherapy room and – of particular appeal in the present context – a picture gallery, museum and library. This remarkable item, otherwise known as Howardswood Cricket Ground (see colour page xxviii), is located not at a country house or, Packer-style, at an Australian football stadium but on a 7ft.x7ft. wooden base and is the proud creation of Peter Coombs and his son and fellow artist, Mark, who have developed it to a remarkable state of realism, if not Test match standard. Games are staged by them on one of three pitches of differing characteristics (the baize pile is shaved to assist spin or pace) and such is the precision of their handiwork that the figures representing well-known players are readily identifiable; the miniature bats, which are used by the human participants with padded fingers, carry manufacturers' logos; and the tiny books can even be taken from their shelves and read. Truly the last word.

The unique creation of Peter and Mark Coombs.

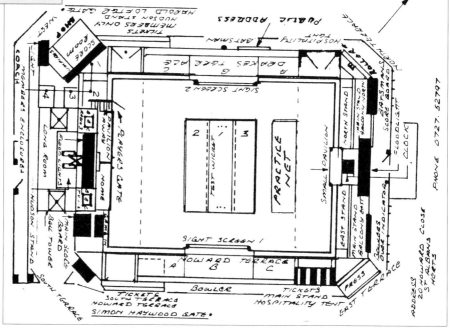

APPENDIX

The Collectors –
ancient and modern

The sea fret which Maurice Tate used to such telling effect at Hove seems also to have affected the beginnings of cricketana collecting in that Padwick, Ford, Gaston and Taylor were all Sussex men.

Alfred Lawson Ford (1844-1924) was the primogenitor of them all, one of the most enthusiastic and greatest, and those who could challenge him were few: the Rev. R.S. Holmes, Charles Pratt Green, F.S. Ashley-Cooper, Alfred D. Taylor and Thomas Padwick. Due homage is paid to them in Irving Rosenwater's *Cricket Books: Great Collectors of the Past*, to which, elaborating on the painstakingly researched series by James Coldham entitled *Collectors and Collecting* [1], he has added erudite monographs on G. Neville Weston, A.J. Gaston and J.N. Pentelow. Ford was a cousin of the cricketing Walkers of Southgate, and began collecting in 1861 (a year before Holmes). By 1906 he had some 500 books and ten times that number of prints, also a series of 80 large green-bound scrap-books. His bequest to MCC via Hugh Ford lent the collection at Lord's added dignity.

Where Selfridges now stands, was once a bookshop owned by the father of Robert Stratten Holmes (1850-1933), so it was axiomatic that this Congregational minister at Wakefield in the West Riding should become Yorkshire's first historian, a leading bibliomane and the supreme columnist of his day in *Cricket* from 1892 to 1895. Fifty years' collecting accumulated a library of some 1,800 volumes, considered among the most complete in existence, but at his death in 1933 the lacklustre state of the market allowed for its disposal cheaply.

Known to his contemporaries as a man of class and generous disposition, Thomas Padwick owned the first substantial collection to come on the market and the first major library sale handled by Alfred Gaston. The total realisation of £350, a not inconsiderable sum for 1898, seems more when one learns that some material was separately bequeathed to his son-in-law, Charles Pratt Green. An indefatigable researcher and omnivorous buyer, Padwick also copied out the whole of the sixth edition of Lillywhite's *Guide*; details of his collection, which covered most of the literature published before the turn of the century, were itemised by Rosenwater in another absorbing article in the *Journal of the Cricket Society* (vol.7, no.4).

Charles Pratt Green (1853-1950) of Malvern is celebrated elsewhere in this book for his extraordinary collection of bats. Like Gaston, a collector from at least 1882, he sold most of his books shortly before the Second World War to Captain F.B. Milne, founder in 1947 of the short-lived Cricketers' Club, but who lives on somewhere in a Hertfordshire loft, where Ron Harries thinks he has a cache of his correspondence.

A contributor to *Cricket* almost since its inception in 1882, Alfred James Gaston was not only cricket's first specialist dealer-collector, operating as a bookseller and librarian from Preston Road in Brighton, but one of the most painstaking and careful of the game's statisticians. A self-publicist of renown, he combined the sale of great libraries, including those of Padwick and Alfred Taylor, with an appointment as Publicity Agent for Sussex CCC, giving "charming and racy" lantern-slide lectures. His sumptuously printed 12-page *Bibliography of Cricket* as well as other more ephemeral publications issued for cricketers' testimonials, have almost vanished from circulation. The mammoth volume he compiled of signatures and letters bearing on cricket, begun in 1878, grew to a thickness of 18in., and, according to Irving Rosenwater [2], "some of this mighty collection still exists". For his contributions to cricketing lore, in April 1895 Sussex cricketers paid their homage, adding a cash donation of £80 to an address signed by Lord Sheffield, the Mayor of Brighton, his old friend and former Australian and Sussex captain, W.L. Murdoch, and one J.G. Blaker.

Deservedly known as the "The Cricketologist", Alfred D. Taylor (1872-1923)

Footnotes:
[1] *Journal of the Cricket Society*, vol.7, no.1; 7, 2; 7, 4; 8, 1 (Autumn 1974-Autumn 1976). Coldham also discusses the evolution of cricket bibliography and book dealing, and touches on other early collectors like E.B.V. Christian, J.B. Payne and Clarence P. Moody of South Australia, as well as a lengthy list of their inheritors.
[2] Irving Rosenwater, *Alfred J. Gaston: a Study in Enthusiasm* (1975).

was never a player himself, but supremely one of the great foundation collectors, a student of the game, researcher and writer. With 4,023 items, Taylor had the largest library on cricket assembled at the time and was the foremost Edwardian bibliographer. His *Catalogue of Cricket Literature* (1906), limited to 50 copies, was favourably received anew when it was republished in 1972. An original, formerly the property of C.I.S. Wallace, and then in the possession of E.K. Brown, has a note from Gaston, "Take care of this, it is scarce!" Like Gaston, Taylor's knowledge of Sussex cricket was all-encompassing, and writing under the pseudonym "Willow-Wielder" he edited and founded the *Sussex Cricket Annual*. He wrote the first history of Lord's and his histories of the Hastings and Cheltenham Festivals are much sought after.

Frederick Samuel Ashley-Cooper's obituary in *Wisden* (1933) is almost two pages long – a rare tribute to a non-player. He is seen by the best judges as cricket's greatest historian and statistician, an unrivalled authority on the game from his early teens. Much of *The Cricketer*'s early status was derived from his anonymous 'Notes and Comments' feature, and he was responsible for more than 30 years for *Wisden*'s 'Births and Deaths' section. Among his 103 books and pamphlets, recorded in G.N. Weston's *Bibliography* of 1933, *Cricket Highways and Byways* included interesting material on cricketana and collecting. His tremendous library of over 4,000 items was offered for £800 to Rockley Wilson in 1931, but in due course it was purchased by Sir Julien Cahn, after whose death in 1944 it passed into various hands.

With Joseph W. Goldman (1893-1978) we are in the modern era, and books bearing his bookplate are legion, as are stories of his enjoyment of barter and debate over sales. Jim Coldham saw him as a mellowed lion in retirement; visiting him at his Egham home was a stunning experience, though for some the huge range of items with only marginal interest and peripheral involvement in mainstream cricket caused mixed feelings.

Displaced only by Ashley-Cooper in the second wave of voracious collectors, Goldman's treasure house was long recognised as the finest private cricket library that existed, with many books ex-libris the great collectors

of the past, many unique and a great number inscribed to and from the famous. E.V. Lucas fans – and there are many – would love to own his "quaint but scarce" *Songs of the Bat* (1892), author-signed in 1936, with eight new lines in his own hand on the final page. In 1965, after 40 years' collecting, he offered his 4,700 items for sale, initially at a lump sum of £20,000. Almost unprocurable books and many limited editions notwithstanding, in the end part of the collection was sold at auction and the balance disposed of by E.K. Brown. The articles Goldman wrote on cricketana in *The Cricketer* during 1936, in tandem with his *Bibliography*, serialised in 1937-39 after publication as a limited edition of 25 copies, rekindled enthusiasm after the sorry demise of the Cricketana Society (1929-35), in which C.J. Britton and Dr T.R. Hunter were significant figures.

George Neville Weston (d.1984, aged 83) was once the doyen of collectors and the greatest authority on the Grace family. His limited edition, *W.G. Grace, the Great Cricketer* (1973) and its four supplements of only four copies each, are collectors' pieces, as are his early privately-printed brochures on his collection and bibliographies of Nyren, Ashley-Cooper, and *The Cricketer's Manual* by "Bat" (Charles Box). Weston collected Grace material with a single-minded dedication awesome to think about, and over the course of nearly 40 years of treading in the wake of the Champion he commissioned plates, tiles and china figures, each with a positive Grace theme, and, to quote another masterly Rosenwater appraisal, "each of course is unique" [1].

C. Ronald Yeomans (1908-80), a useful cricketer in his day, started collecting in 1919 and was, as prime founder of the Northern Cricket Society, Chairman of the Council of Cricket Societies until 1979, and as a journalist on the *Yorkshire Evening Post*, well placed to publicise trends in cricketana, largely based on his own discoveries, acquisitions and commissions. This was at a time when public relations was a phrase unknown to the counties and memorabilia scarcely, if ever, mentioned. In *Art & Antiques Weekly* (1968) he claimed paternity for the word 'cricketana' as applied to memorabilia, but it was in common usage much earlier for news in brief snippets much on the lines of today's sports diary inserts, and covering all aspects of

Footnote:
[1] Irving Rosenwater, 'G. Neville Weston - Collector Extraordinary', *Journal of the Cricket Society*, vol.7, no.2.

cricket. "Cricketania" has also been used occasionally, though now, mercifully, has fallen into desuetude.

One of the founder members of the Cricket Society in 1945, until his death in 1987 at the age of 63, cricket literati owed much to the knowledge, accuracy and genial company of James Desmond Bowden Coldham. His affection for Northamptonshire and German cricket was widely known and reached book form, but it was during his editorship of the *Journal of the Cricket Society* (1970-84) that it became a treasure trove of the unforseen and the unknown. His vast library included numerous unusual compilations, including 80 Ashley-Cooper pamphlets, and, as Geoffrey Copinger noted in his obituary tribute in *The Cricketer*, he also acquired part of the Pratt Green collection. While stationed in Burma on active service he wrote to many living pre-1914 cricketers and his collection of letters, eventually sold posthumously, can only hint at his widespread popularity.

By courtesy of the people concerned, *Wisden Cricket Monthly* has since April 1985 in the series 'The Collectors' invaded many a cathedral and cricketing house to view the major collections of today. By then John Arlott, who had assumed Goldman's mantle as the leading collector, was happily ensconced in retirement in Alderney and A.E. (Tony) Winder, who bought much of the Arlott collection, was about to put it on the market. So David Frith and Geoffrey Copinger opened the batting, with dear Jim Coldham at no.3, and at the time of writing we have been privileged to meet, either personally or through the pages of the magazine, Tony Woodhouse, Bob Jones (whose hoard of cards defies description), Mike Smith, Vic Lewis (author of the standard work on cricketing ties), tape cassette collector Don Rowan, lyricist Tim Rice, autograph specialists Terry Taylor and Derek Blanchard, Roger Mann and Glamorgan's own Ron Harries. Neither have Australia's mega-collectors been ignored – Pat Mullins, Srikantan Ramamurthy, Ken Woolfe, Denis Tobin and Max Atwell.

To say that Geoffrey Copinger and Tony Woodhouse are collectors is like calling Harrods a shop. At opposite ends of the country, for four decades they have been household names among collectors of cricketana, and to speak to Geoffrey in the pavilion at Lord's, one needs to join a queue.

Lovingly assembled over 60 years, the Copinger collection contains over 11,000 cricket publications, many still in their dustjackets, author-signed and systematically arranged in his own delightfully non-conformist way. No finer collection exists in the world, and on many counts he beats Lord's hands down. The oldest item is John Florio's *A Worlde of Wordes*, an Italian-English dictionary published in London (1598), containing the reference to 'sgrillare' (to play cricket-a-wicket), and thereafter, for Padwick you can virtually read Copinger. Add a remarkable collection of fixture and scorecards, multi-edition books, scrapbooks, a wealth of ephemera, postcards and cigarette cards, and you have the bibliographical equivalent of *Wisden*.

A born-in-the-bone Yorkshireman, Tony Woodhouse serves the county in many capacities, and more than any other book he owns likes the one by Richard Binns, because of its descriptions of village and league cricket in that often embattled county. He added his 9,000th book to stock in February 1988, and specialises in club histories, Scottish cricket and Yorkshire. Nearly 5,000 cricket trade and cigarette cards still leave him behind Copinger, whom he regularly threatens to raid with a pantechnicon – "something I would never do but I like to think that he thinks I might!" His best bargain was the purchase of 16 Lillywhite *Guides* from a shop in Cecil Court, London, for 50p each, and he has all the basic reference books, including a Lambert and a Bentley, but Epps, Britcher and Denison have (thus far) eluded him.

Editor of *Wisden Cricket Monthly* and the consummate all-round collector, David Frith has the greatest collection of photographic images in private hands and the signature of every major 20th-century cricketer. More than any of his contemporaries he has promoted the collection of cricketana in word, deed and print. Besides a library of 4,000 volumes, in a mountain of cricket clothing, equipment and

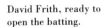

Ron Harries studies part of his ceramics collection.

David Frith, ready to open the batting.

Roger Mann, alongside a portrait of W.G. Grace commissioned from Gerry Wright.

Keith Hayhurst's loft.

ephemera there are items as unusual as masonry from the old Lord's Tavern and the Oval perimeter (see colour page i), an 1846 draper's receipt for a flannel cricket jacket and a lump of Bulli soil from the Sydney Cricket Ground.

For many people, Roger Mann is the best of collectors, in that he seems to have got it just right. Here is someone who can express his regret that he never saw his Hornby and Barlow of long ago actually in the nets, but can step across the room and with Barlow's bat demonstrate the whys and wherefores of Grace's back-foot technique, adjusting his

stance to that of a full-length statuette behind him. He talks with a cricketer's insight of the Hambledon men of 200 years ago shambling across the countryside, their "battes" in a saddlebag, all the while holding in one hand a great clodhopper of a bat of that period and in the other, specimens of letters, illustrations or documents relating bat to player to ground to the evolution of the game. He regards himself as the "interim owner" of precious relics, and insists that his material should never be disposed of in job lots, so that specialist collectors, with limited resources and unable to buy one or two specific items specially wanted, would have a decent chance.

Those as yet unsung include Keith Hayhurst, Curator of the Old Trafford museum, who has collected cricket material since boyhood and whose own loft has been converted into a cricket museum. Items from his collection strengthen the museum at Old Trafford, but he still finds room in built-in units for over 150 signed cricket bats of all sizes, ceramics, cigarette cards, brochures, posters, postcards, scorecards, clocks, books, prints and silk handkerchiefs. Others are Tony Sheldon, like Hayhurst an officer of the Cricket Memorabilia Society; that most discriminating of collectors, Tony Laughton; noted print collector Peter MacKinnon; Dr John Turner, self-confessedly once a very stodgy opening bat, but "we seem to have had a few of those around Yorkshire ever since Louis Hall", and now one of the finest collectors of books, memorabilia and cricket medals, "but I have no interest in bats as they take up too much room". Also waiting for the call are ceramic specialists, Andrew Johnson and Mike Marshall, the latter actively working toward the foundation of a museum at Chelmsford and an Essex devotee ever since he saw J.W.H.T. Douglas in action. Pieces from his ceramics collection adorn the pages of this book, and in his wide-ranging collection there is a complete set of *Wisdens* and uniformly bound Essex handbooks. Then there is London-based Australian journalist, Murray Hedgcock, who still has a 1955 Epworth catalogue "guaranteed to make any collector feel almost physically sick at lost opportunity"; Chris Harte, editor of the *Australian Cricket Journal*, another imaginative and far-ranging collector, and a driving force behind collecting far beyond his home base of Adelaide; and Australian-based Londoner, Tony Baer.

Playfair Cricket Monthly (January 1965) almost pulsated with admiration for the Baer collection, housed as it then was in a penthouse luxury flat a few hundred yards from Lord's. Even 20 years ago it was a collector's dream world, a cricket mecca, visited by Constantine and Sobers. Delicate porcelain, patterned and cut glassware, silk scorecards, music covers and postage stamps vied for attention, along with rows of books, including a complete set of *Wisdens* and his most valued item in the realm of books, a first edition of Boxall's *Rules and Instructions for Playing Cricket*. A collector from the age of six, his first acquisition was a mid-19th century mug, and the most eye-catching illustrations in Richard Bouwman's *Glorious Innings* (Melbourne, 1987) are those from his collection, now housed on loan to Melbourne CC. His *Wisdens* were sold in 1967-68 for £185 and he has basically lost interest in cricket as a game. He says he no longer reads books but remains, uniquely, Tony Baer.

Museums and collections

With some notable exceptions, the state of most public cricket collections in England is disappointing and calls into question the attitude of county and club committees. The year 1989 was designated Museums Year,

but did this impinge upon the collective consciousness of those within the game whose business it ought to be to care? Independent museums are springing up across the country, actively seeking (and getting) sponsorship, and, even in their embryonic state, putting on imaginative displays, with unprepossessing buildings artfully contrived to look appealing – and drawing the crowds. Have the counties thought to send someone to look at key collections in private hands from which to draw inspiration, or seen fit to approach the Association of Independent Museums for guidance on source funding? Or do they have other priorities?

Lord's

The largest, and justifiably most famous, collection is at Lord's. Lack of space dictates that only part of it can be put on display, either publicly in the Memorial Gallery or, with access restricted to members and their guests, in the pavilion. Stephen Green, the MCC's curator, used the columns of *Playfair Cricket Monthly* and, latterly, *The Cricketer*, for a number of wide-ranging and informative rambles along the corridors of Lord's, but nothing had prepared even the most seasoned of collectors for the quality of secondary items, "duplicates" and overflow remainders unearthed for the Bicentenary auction in 1987. It was as if virtually everything mentioned in this book was at Lord's – thrice over!

Thanks to the picture-book survey conducted by Tim Rice in *Treasures of Lord's* (1989) and to countless reproductions elsewhere, many of the game's finest paintings, trophies and *objets d'art* can now be viewed in the public domain. The art collection of the late Sir Jeremiah Colman lends richness and colour, and many cricketing countries have sent to Lord's paintings of their prinicipal grounds. The loveliest ground in the world, according to Sir Donald Bradman – Brockton Point in British Columbia – is there, along with St. George's Park, Port Elizabeth (showing "Tufty" Mann bowling), Selangor, Singapore CC and Penang Sports Club. All, oddly enough, were caught by a feminine brush.

The origins of the Memorial Gallery can be traced back to 1864, when Sir Spencer Ponsonby Fane expanded the art collection, and the following year, when R.A. Fitzgerald,

Left Mike Marshall, with a figure from his collection.

the Secretary of MCC, advertised in the national press for gifts of cricket bygones in order to form a museum. Many and varied were the objects trotted along to the club over the years as gifts, bequests or long loans, not necessarily all of cricket relevance. Green has pointed out animal heads, and cannon balls fired at Balaclava. During the First World War the treasures were sheltered by Lord Leconfield at Petworth, and for much of the second war at Stoke Hammond Rectory, near Bletchley, but by the end of hostilities space was at a premium. It was then that Diana Rait Kerr (about whose work a great deal could be written) became the first full-time curator, and subsequently the old rackets court at the rear of the pavilion was converted into a museum to serve as a memorial to the dead of the two wars. The Memorial Gallery was opened in 1953 by the Duke of Edinburgh, extended in 1959 and refurbished since to be a fitting home for all that countless thousands of cricket-lovers hold dear.

Gifts to the club over the years have not always been as dramatic as the bat used by W.G. Grace for his highest score of 344 for MCC against Kent, which arrived in the early 1970s under the terms of a legacy from a descendant of James Southerton. But Verity's cap, a framed silk scorecard from B.J.T. Bosanquet's family, framed vignettes connected with the 1907-08 MCC tour of Australia, and the ball used at Leyton in 1932 when Holmes and Sutcliffe amassed their record-making opening partnership of 555 mark useful stepping-stones to history.

The museum is light, bright and airy, reception is cordial, and the admission cost to a first-class exhibition very reasonable. It may seem churlish to find fault, but the atmosphere is curiously inert, with all the dormant apparatus of an art gallery, and bucks the modern trend of relating specialist collections to a wider socio-economic context beyond the playing field. A nod in the direction of new technology might attract the younger visitor, also those interested in the history of the game as much as its memorabilia, exquisite as that is.

The MCC Library is now one of the most complete cricket collections ever to have existed, its origin and early development startlingly casual for the headquarters of the game. It was started by a gift of books from a member in 1893 – more than 30 years after A.L. Ford began collecting – but not until 1944 could it claim to be properly representative of cricket literature. This was as a result of munificent gifts from Ford's nephew (1930) and the estate of Sir Julien Cahn. Since strengthened by Rockley Wilson's collection, the library has migrated from the pavilion into more spacious accommodation in the real tennis court building, with, since September 1985, ample seating for readers and researchers. The rarities are in locked glass cabinets, the balance on open shelves very much a working collection – and it shows. Librarians might quibble at the classification system, but that is a detail. Of greater importance is that unless and until Lord's acquires, say, the monumental Geoffrey Copinger collection, there is no national central repository for all known printed literature on cricket.

Trent Bridge

Standing second to Lord's in scope and size is the collection at Trent Bridge, Nottingham, whose museum was officially opened on 9th May 1987. The collection of bats housed in the pavilion is phenomenal, over 130, most of them from the Charles Pratt Green collection and overhanging the Long Room Bar.

Two of the most famous from modern times were donated by Sir Garfield Sobers to his adopted county: one was used to make the highest Test innings of 365 not out, the second for his onslaught on Glamorgan's Malcolm Nash in 1968, six sixes in an over. Notable oil portraits are those of James Grundy and Richard Daft, while hanging in the hallway outside the museum is Frank Batson's enormous canvas 'Playing Out Time In An Awkward Light'.

Also in the pavilion are a bat and walking stick which belonged to Alfred Shaw, the last pads worn by Arthur Shrewsbury, rare china figures, mounted cricket balls, and diaries kept by James Southerton on the 1876-77 tour to Australia, and by Edwin Browne, the county's secretary, of Richard Daft's expedition in 1879 to North America. There is also a map of Nottinghamshire – the pride and joy of its compiler, Peter Wynne-Thomas, the curator and a noted cricket historian and statistician – which shows the county origins of its notable cricketers.

Adjacent to the Long Room is the F.E. Gregory Library, largely the creation of A.W.

Shelton and, after Lord's, the largest at any English cricket ground, numbering well over 3,000 items. A particular favourite is the best-selling novel in its day, *Willow the King* (1899), written by J.C. Snaith, who played once for Nottinghamshire in 1900. The library is grossly overcrowded, and to the visitor's eye underfunded, so that in the circumstances the curator performs heroics. What are his chances of conserving material when, for instance, members of the Cricket Memorabilia Society had to tread warily to avoid an already distressed and fading sepia print of the Nottinghamshire side which played the Aborigines in 1868?

That such a situation exists harks back at least to the modernisation of the pavilion in 1956 when, in a false-roof section, Arnold Doxey (*The Cricketer*, March 1970) found six large sacks of documents, dating from the last quarter of the 19th century, awaiting the dustmen. Among the pickings were an astringent letter from W.G. Grace, written in April 1873, presaging the two-year estrangement between the leading county sides of the time, Gloucestershire and Nottinghamshire; a letter recommending Shrewsbury as a "fit person to play with the 22 Colts" in the annual trial match; account books and handbills; and letters relating to Palairet and Billy Barnes.

Old Trafford

Rebuilding operations at Old Trafford in 1982 incorporated a purpose-built museum, completed in the autumn of 1983 in the stand near the pavilion. From the start planning and implementation has been a concern of the curator, Keith Hayhurst, and it is still he who provides the momentum for the expansion of the artefacts on view. All members and visitors are welcome and there is free entrance on match days to see magnificent trophies from the 1830s presented by the Manchester CC.

There is cricket memorabilia associated with A.N. Hornby and R.G. Barlow, match balls from the 1850s, and old paintings and scorecards from the same period, together with the scorebook recording A.C. MacLaren's record English innings of 424. Early photographs from the foundation of the county club have been preserved along with autographs, menu cards, newspapers and a large silver tray presented by S.H. Swire (who played for the club and was its first secretary), splendidly inscribed with an engraving of the early pavilion at Old Trafford.

As well as modern mementos, the visitor will find turn-of-the-century scrapbooks, bats and plates relating to the Tyldesleys, Walter Brearley, S.F. Barnes and E.A. McDonald. Signed bats from county and international teams blend with handkerchiefs from the time of Grace to the Lancashire and Australian sides of the 1930s. A gem is the handkerchief presented to Eddie Paynter for his epic four-hour, Ashes-winning innings at Brisbane in February 1933. In typical Lancashire tradition it was presented by the Mercer Memorial Methodist and Sunday School, Clayton-le-Moors, as a permanent reminder of his "grit and determination under adverse circumstances in coming from hospital and placing the MCC in a favourable position". Old Trafford also has a growing library, under the watchful eye of the Rev. Malcolm Lorimer.

Hove

Luckily for Sussex CCC, increasing years have not wearied the club's librarian, H.A. "Ossie" Osborne. The inscription on a miniature silver bat presented to him by P.G.H. Fender reads: "Brighton Brunswick CC. Happy memories. Very many thanks. Percy George Fender."

Sussex, too, should render thanks, when one looks at the card index Osborne has organised over the past decade embracing all of the county's cricketers since 1780 and the immense wallcharts prepared for the 150th anniversary in 1989, which listed, in tabulated form, presidents, captains, position in the county championship, players' debuts, dates when caps were awarded, England caps, resignations and terminations of contract, and synopses of the seasons from 1839.

As it is, the library-cum-museum has minimal funds and depends on scrounging copies of books and selling bundles of duplicate periodicals. The previous incumbent, W.W.E. Melville, built the library with little help, if any, from the Sussex committee. The county has priceless old scorebooks, historical papers, souvenirs, photographs, the Gilligan albums of press cuttings and letters; it has also had in the past local collecting rivals of the calibre of Gaston, Taylor *et al*.

Other county collections

Surrey CCC has a large reference library and

collection of memorabilia rehoused in the Centenary Library, set up in 1980 in The Oval pavilion with financial assistance from the Chelsea Building Society. The club also boasts a useful assembly of paintings, scorecards and photographs in other areas of the pavilion, together with the oldest known cricket bat, dated 1729. A particular favourite of the curator, Peter Large, is the portrait of Alec Bedser. When the subject first saw it, he is reported to have remarked on the artist's perception of the size of his hands. The artist's riposte was: "You do have bloody big hands!"

Of the remaining English Test grounds, Edgbaston is well equipped with a range of Warwickshire memorabilia in the pavilion, but Headingley, owned not by Yorkshire CCC but by the Leeds Cricket, Football and Athletic Co., is poorly off – much to the chagrin of the late Ron Yeomans, who was prompted to appeal for Yorkshire-related cricketana in *The Cricketer* in 1978.

Among the other counties Essex's excellent collection of memorabilia, masterminded by Mike Marshall, has virtually outgrown its current location in the pavilion at Chelmsford and it is hoped that one day it will have a home of its own somewhere else on the ground. Famous Essex names such as Green, Douglas, Nichols and Russell are well represented.

Also well endowed are Kent, who have a small museum and, in the pavilion, Chevallier Tayler's well known and imposing canvas commemorating the 1906 Championship success.

Leicestershire keep their collection in the pavilion and long room. Hampshire use the office building and more recent squash and social centre. Symptomatic, though, of the ambivalent attitude towards memorabilia was the presence for many years, in a cardboard box on the floor of the press box at Southampton, of priceless old county scorebooks before the current scorer, Vic Isaacs, brought them into safe-keeping.

The latest county to join this group is Somerset, who launched a fund-raising appeal in late 1987, asking also for memorabilia relating to the game both in and outside its borders. The museum was opened in spring 1989 by Jeffrey Archer, the novelist, former MP and Somerset devotee, and it is housed in an historic building known as the Priory Barn. Among the treasures on display are one of Gimblett's bats and the blazer he wore when he began with the county, together with a scorecard, signed by Jack Hobbs, of the match in which he equalled and then broke Grace's record of centuries at Taunton in 1925.

Space prevents us from pursuing much further the collections to be found elsewhere, so we have chosen two examples from opposite ends of the social spectrum, two public libraries, and a mobile and a hallowed name.

Brympton d'Evercy House

Charles Clive-Ponsonby-Fane, great-great-grandson of the man involved at the birth of MCC's collection, has since 1978 been busily collecting artefacts related to I Zingari, and has already found an astonishing assortment of exhibits ranging from clothing, books and pictures to unlikely items such as a barometer and compass, toast racks and an egg cosy, all embossed with the club's familiar colours of red, black and gold. They are housed at the 13th-century Brympton d'Evercy House near Yeovil.

Church CC

A feature of the Lancashire League club, Church, for more than half a century was a handsome glass case, which contained the pads, wicketkeeping gloves and bag of the late Richard Pilling, used by him during tours of Australia in 1881-82 and 1887-88. On the opposite side of the room stood another handsome case with the bat, pads and bag of Frank O'Keeffe, the Australian professional to the club in 1922-23, who died at the age of 27 shortly before he would have qualified for Lancashire.

The demolition of Church's pavilion in 1980 meant the end of the showcases and, but for the intervention of club officials, might have seen most of the memorabilia thrown out with the old bricks. Happily Pilling's pads, along with photographs and accounts (O'Keeffe was paid £450 for the 1922 season and S.F. Barnes £25 for a single match) were rescued and are occasionally exhibited.

Mitcham and Plumstead public libraries

In contrast to the private collections are those assembled in public libraries. That in Mitcham, south-west London, lays claim to being the largest in any public library, with some 2,000 items. The precise origins of the collection at the library, which opened in 1933, are now apparently forgotten, but the accumulation of books, pamphlets and periodicals has developed, it seems, as a result of demand, probably spurred by an enthusiastic librarian in the past, local ratepayers and individual donors.

Several miles in a north-easterly direction, at Plumstead, is a less-known but similarly extensive collection in a library which is designated as the centre for sports books in the public library system for South-East England. It is a living collection, containing many of the latest volumes alongside such classics as Box's *The Cricketer's Manual* for 1849 and 1851; *St Ivo and the Ashes*; a third edition of *Felix on the Bat*; and many others from the 19th century, as well a nearly complete run of *Wisdens*. It is sadly closed to researchers because of fire safety, but its enthusiastic staff are more than happy to deal with inquiries.

Cruise Liner *Canberra*
Aboard the P & O cruise liner, *Canberra*, the willow wood-strip walls of the Cricketers Tavern reveal a fascinating collection of cricket memorabilia accumulated since its launch in 1961. The display of 500 ties from every type of club, signed bats, donated county and Test caps, bails, pads and scorecards was originally assembled by Margaret Redfern in consultation with Colin Cowdrey. Also in evidence are full-length portraits of Grace, Bradman, Ranjitsinhji and Constantine, but perhaps the nicest touch is that the bar shutters resemble a boundary fence.

Wisden Museum
For a great many years prior to John Wisden and Company's move from London to Robertsbridge, East Sussex, a feature of its showroom just off Leicester Square was a museum of historic cricket bats. The collection, numbering some 200 in all, was removed to Chiddingstone Causeway, Kent, the factory base for Duke and Son, acquired by Wisden in 1920.

The Co-operative Wholesale Society of Manchester purchased Wisden in 1944, and when it was sold again in 1970 to Gray-Nicolls, most of the bats went to a director of the CWS, G.W. Medlock. The Wisden Museum no longer exists and while some pieces from the original collection are now at Lord's, others

have flown the coop as far as Australia.

Australasia
The aggressive bidding of the Antipodeans was enjoyed by all at the MCC Bicentenary auction, glowering away at each other, but perhaps necessarily so, as it has not always been a part of the Australian make-up to preserve things. When collections are being built up at speed, material of real historical value actually on the spot must become scarce, and they will have to depend on the seemingly endless cash flow from Australia – and the Tony Baers of this world.

The Melbourne Cricket Club collection is largely the creation of the English enthusiast, Tony Baer, whose thousand and more pieces are the lynchpin of the assemblage of trophies, relics, paintings, pottery, china and silverware. *Glorious Innings* by Rick Bouwman presented some of the better-known Australian treasures, as well as hitherto little-known material. Original oils of Hobbs, Bradman and Sobers take guard against showcases filled with figurines and mugs, while the walls are hung with particles of history. Among the collection of mounted balls is one off which Trumper scored 166 in the fifth Test of 1907-08 at Sydney and the ball with which Boyle bowled W.G. in 1873.

It is good news for Melbourne that the majestic P.J. Mullins collection, one of the eight best in the world, is destined for Victoria rather than his home state of Queensland. Streets ahead of any other Australian private collection, and strong on local printed ephemera, he was also able to produce a typescript booklet, *Some the Bibliography May Have Missed*, a gentle bit of Pommie-bashing, listing some 700 of his books not in the first edition of the Padwick bibliography. His copy of Ranjitsinhji's *Jubilee Book of Cricket* is unusually inscribed "Ranji".

Australia's first national multi-sport collection opened as the Australian Gallery of Sport in November 1986, with permanent displays of artefacts, information and memorabilia on 20 designated sports. Located right outside the members' gate at the Melbourne Cricket Ground, but entirely separate from the Cricket Club, it furnishes a public showplace second to none.

Along with Ned Kelly and Phar Lap the racehorse, Bradman is one of the three great national heroes, and with grants from banks and other sources the local council of Bowral, New South Wales, has been given the go-ahead to lease land in Glebe Park, near to Bradman's old home. Plans to turn his old house into a museum were opposed by local residents, sensitive to problems of traffic in a narrow street, but the Bradman Museum has become reality, part of a £1.2m package.

The organisers were prominent bidders at the MCC Bicentenary auction and a New Zealand millionaire paid fabulous prices for an 18th-century cricket handkerchief and other memorabilia for the museum, the feature of which will be a film collection of the Bradman era, including early coaching films of Bradman himself. The first curator appointed was Richard Mulvaney, son of Professor John Mulvaney, author of *Cricket Walkabout* (1968) about the 1868 Aboriginal tour.

In Sir Donald's home state, Adelaide Oval was reported as having received from him the bat with which he recorded his first Test century in 1929; the one which reduced Queensland to a helpless heap in 1930 (452 not out); England to ashes at Headingley the same year (334), and the blade used for his hundredth hundred in 1947. To the South Australia State Library has been given the silver Warwick vase presented to him on the 1948 tour of England, the vase marking three double-centuries at Worcester and some newspaper placards, including one simply stating "HE'S OUT".

Situated beneath the old grandstand at the Basin Reserve, Wellington, the National Cricket Museum of New Zealand opened on 29th November 1987 and has attracted much favourable comment. Seagulls occupy cricket grounds as of right, and part of the sprightly character of this museum is the concession made to exhibits inseparable from one-day cricket: a transistor radio, suntan lotion and an assortment of crumpled beer cans. It is very forward-looking and progressive, and historical artefacts are acquired which reflect the evolution of cricket on a universal, as much as a parochial, scale; all is housed in a purpose-built and designed manner.

The 1743 Addington CC bat bought at Christie's for £1,600 in 1987 is a starting point in history, along with a Cobbett bat and one donated by George Parr in 1864 to the highest scorer in the Otago XXII. Lillee's infamous aluminium bat is on loan from the

Crowe family and the expanding range of memorabilia reflects 16 years of endeavour by the curator, Stanley Cowman, a Yorkshireman and therefore by definition a cricket addict. Behind him is the expertise of Roger Mann and the worldwide contacts of Christopher Martin-Jenkins, BBC cricket correspondent and editor of *The Cricketer*. A welcome addition came from Mann's successful bid for the New Zealand-born Clarrie Grimmett's Australian blazer at Christie's in 1988.

Warwick Larkins profiled in *Wisden Cricket Monthly* (April 1987) the "veritable museum" at the Albion CC, the "oldest continuous cricket club in Australasia". Based at Culling Park, Dunedin, its pavilion display has caps, jerseys, ties and blazers, bats used by New Zealand Test players, the shirt worn by Trevor Chappell during the underarm bowling fall from grace and a framed display of Glenn Turner's mighty 311 not out for Worcestershire, his hundredth hundred.

South Africa
South Africans have a woeful track record in the serious pursuit of cricketana. A sorry situation was thrown into sharp relief by a tepid response to an appeal launched by former Test umpire Hayward Kidson, aimed at former internationals, their families and descendants, as part of a project to establish a museum of South African cricket history, hopefully to be housed at the Wanderers Stadium in 1989.

Small collections exist at Durban, Port Elizabeth – where a showcase has the ball used in what is now regarded as the first Test match played in South Africa in March 1889 – The Wanderers Club and Newlands. Kidson himself has a large collection of cricket photographs and received much useful material from the estates of Louis Duffus and Herby Wade. He also has a selection of Springbok and provincial caps, scarves, sweaters, umpires' six-ball clickers, pocket-badges, cups, stumps, bails, balls and numerous important bats.

It needs missionary zeal on the part of the South African cricket authorities to reflect national pride and identity, unless it is to be left to collectors such as Trevor Chesterfield, John Landau and Brian Bassano, the last of whom has a bat signed by the three teams in the weather-ruined Triangular Tournament of 1912. The collection of the late Denys Heesom found its way to the state-run South African

Library, a worthy gesture but a mistaken one, since anything of a sideline nature left to a national repository becomes instant vegetation. Foremost among South Africa's book collectors are the brothers Duggie and Lennie Ettlinger, both of whom break the national mould of indifference and apathy.

Zimbabwe

The dire straits of South Africa are made to look even worse by the foundation in Bulawayo of a Zimbabwe cricket museum, created by Derrick Townshend. A former Rhodesian Currie Cup batsman and honorary librarian of the Zimbabwe Cricket Union, Townshend transformed his own collection of cricket memorabilia into a museum based at his home.

Of necessity, its strengths are indigenous caps, bats, blazers, sweaters, and all the paraphernalia associated with the game, but its acquisitions policy is outward-looking and international. Several mounted balls revive sad memories of the former Test opening bowler, Joe Partridge, who shot himself in 1988; but on a happier note, Townshend has Percy Mansell's cricket bag from the 1955 Springbok tour of England, and the bat with which Dave Houghton scored a superb century that all but defeated New Zealand in the 1987 World Cup.

Canada

The K.A. Auty Memorial Cricket Library at Ridley College, St. Catherines, Ontario, Canada, has a wide range of 19th-century books, including Woodfall's *Sporting Calendar* (1752), Hoyle's *Games* (1786), a complete set of *Wisden* and every Ridley College scorebook since the year of the school's foundation in 1889 (how many English schools preserve their scorebooks?). A catalogue of over 2,300 books, pamphlets and brochures has been published.

In addition to a remarkable collection of "flickers" and bats with the fading signatures of great names, its most spectacular asset is the scrapbooks kept by Sir C. Aubrey Smith. They offer complete coverage of a seminal event in the history of South African cricket, the momentous first tour of that country in 1889 which, if not already done, ought to have been microfilmed for the Wanderers Museum.

USA

The C. Christopher Morris Cricket Library and Collection, named after the famous Philadelphia and United States international cricketer, is housed in a "cricket alcove" extension of the luxuriously appointed Magill Library, Haverford College, Pennsylvania. Architect-designed and dedicated both to Christy Morris and over 150 years of North American cricket, its collection of books, journals, brochures, framed ties and memorabilia enjoys exemplary care in another cricketing outpost.

Galleries

The Burlington Gallery in Burlington Gardens, London W1, opened in 1981, and its exhibition, 'Double Century', in 1986 was claimed by Nicholas Potter, the managing director, to be the first commercial exhibition devoted exclusively to cricketana. Both it, and its successors, 'Second Innings' in 1987 and 'Following On' in April 1989, have been the results of years of hard work, combing the country via a network of contacts, dealers, private purchase and auction scouting. No catalogue compares today for splendour of material and wealth of illustration, and, as much as the auction catalogues, Burlington's illustrate the upward trend in the demand for cricketana at the highest level.

Bibliography

Books

Allen, David Rayvern.
> *A Catalogue of Cricket Catalogues, Booklists, Bibliographical Sources and Indexes Etcetera*. Privately printed, 1980. Limited edition of 75 copies, numbered and signed.
> *Early Books on Cricket*. Europa Publications, 1987.
> *A Song for Cricket*. Pelham Books, 1981.

Arlott, John.
> *The Picture of Cricket*. Penguin Books, 1955. (King Penguin Books)

Bailey, Philip, *and others*.
> *Who's Who of Cricketers: a Complete Who's Who of All Cricketers Who Have Played First-class Cricket in England, with Full Career Records*. Newnes Books in association with The Association of Cricket Statisticians, 1984.

Bailey, Trevor, *and others.*
  *The Lord's Taverners Fifty Greatest: Fifty
  Greatest Post-War Cricketers From
  Around the World.* Rev. Enl. ed.
  Heinemann/Quixote Press, 1984.
Barker, Dennis.
  Parian Ware, Shire Publications, Princes
  Risborough, 1985.
Barnard, Derek.
  *An Index to Wisden Cricketers' Almanack
  1864-1984.* Macdonald, Queen Anne
  Press, 1985.
Birkett, Sir Norman.
  *The Game of Cricket; Illustrated by a
  Series of Pictures in the Museum of The
  Marylebone Cricket Club Principally from
  the Collection of the Late Sir Jeremiah
  Colman, with an introductory essay by
  Sir Norman Birkett and notes on the
  illustrations by Diana Rait Kerr.* B.T.
  Batsford, 1955.
Bouwman, Richard.
  *Glorious Innings: Treasures from the
  Melbourne Cricket Club Collection.*
  Hutchinson Australia, 1987.
Burlington Gallery Exhibition Catalogues.
  *Double Century: Two Hundred Years of
  Cricket Prints.* 1986.
  *Following On: an Exhibition of Cricket's
  History.* 1989.
  *Second Innings: an Exhibition to Celebrate
  the Bicentenary. M.C.C. 1787-1987.* 1987.
Cardus, Sir Neville.
  English Cricket. Collins, 1945.
Cardus, Sir Neville, *and* Arlott, John.
  *The Noblest Game: a Book of Fine Cricket
  Prints.* Harrap, 1986. First published
  1969: reissued 1986 with a new
  introduction to cricket prints in history
  by John Arlott.
*Collector's Encyclopedia: Victoriana to Art
  Deco.* Collins, 1974.
Colman, Sir Jeremiah.
  *The Noble Game of Cricket; Illustrated
  and Described from Pictures, Drawings
  and Prints in the Collection of Sir
  Jeremiah Colman.* Batsford, 1941.
  Limited edition of 150 copies.
Cox, Richard.
  *Sport – a Guide to Historical Sources in
  the UK.* Sports Council, 1983.
Curtis, Tony.
  *The Lyle Price Guide to Printed
  Collectibles.* Glenmayne, Galashiels,
  1984.

Deadman, Derek.
  *Cricket Cigarette and Trade Cards: an
  Extended Listing.* Murray Cards
  (International), 1985. First published
  1979.
Frindall, Bill.
  *The Wisden Book of Test Cricket 1877-
  1984.* Macdonald Publishing, 1985.
Frith, David.
  Pageant of Cricket. Macmillan, 1987.
*The Game of Cricket: an Exhibition of Books
  Based on the Brockbank Cricket Collection.*
  John Rylands University Library of
  Manchester, 1986.
Green, Benny.
  *The Wisden Book of Cricketers' Lives:
  Obituaries from Wisden Cricketers'
  Almanack.* Macdonald, Queen Anne Press,
  1986. Reprint title.
Green, Stephen.
  *Backward Glances: an Album of 60 Early
  Cricket Photographs 1857-1917.* Newport,
  Isle of Wight: M.G. Richards, 1976.
  Cricketing Bygones. Shire Publications,
  1982.
Ireland, John.
  *Cricket Characters: The Cricketer
  Caricatures of John Ireland; text by
  Christopher Martin-Jenkins.* Stanley
  Paul, 1987.
Jennings, Grenville.
  Cricket on Old Picture Postcards.
  Keyworth, Nottingham. Reflections of a
  Bygone Age, 1985.
Lewis, Victor.
  *Cricket Ties: an International Guide for
  Cricket Lovers.* Ebury Press, 1984.
Lund, Brian.
  Postcard Collecting – a Beginners' Guide.
  Keyworth, Nottingham. Reflections of a
  Bygone Age, 1985.
March, Russell.
  The Cricketers of Vanity Fair. Webb &
  Bower, 1982.
Martin-Jenkins, Christopher.
  *Cricket – A Way of Life: The Cricketer
  Illustrated History of Cricket.* Century
  Publishing, 1984.
Matthews, Roy T., *and* Mellini, Peter.
  In 'Vanity Fair'. Scolar Press, 1982.
Padwick, E.W.
  A Bibliography of Cricket. 2nd ed. revised
  and enlarged to the end of 1979. Library
  Association in association with J.W.
  McKenzie (Bookseller), on behalf of The

Cricket Society, 1984. First published 1977.

Rendell, Joan.
  The Match, The Box and The Label. David & Charles, 1983.

Rice, Tim.
  Treasures of Lord's. Collins Willow, 1989. (MCC Cricket Library.)

Rosenwater, Irving.
  Alfred James Gaston: a Study in Enthusiasm. Privately published, 1975. Limited edition of 50 numbered and signed copies.
  Cricket Books: Great Collectors of the Past. Privately published, 1976. Limited edition of 200 numbered and signed copies.
  F.S. Ashley-Cooper: the Herodotus of Cricket. [The Author], 1964. Limited edition of 25 numbered and signed copies.
  J.N. Pentelow: a Biographical Essay. Privately published, 1969. Limited edition of 50 numbered and signed copies.
  A Portfolio of Cricket prints: a Nineteenth Century Miscellany. Spearman, Holland Press, 1962.

Simon, Robin, *and* Smart, Alastair.
  John Player Art of Cricket. Secker & Warburg, 1983.

Smith, J.H.D.
  IPM Catalogue of Picture Postcards and Year Book. Brighton: IPM Publications. Annual.

Stamp Publicity (Worthing) Ltd.
  Cricket Stamp Album. 1980 and supplements.

Stanley, Louis T.
  The Sporting Collector. Pelham Books, 1984.

Swanton, E.W., *and others.*
  Barclays World of Cricket: the Game from A-Z. Collins Willow, 1986. A new and revised edition to coincide with the Bicentenary of MCC.

Taylor, Alfred D.
  The Catalogue of Cricket Literature. S. R. Publishers, 1972. Facsimile of 1906 edition.

Tomkins, Richard.
  Classic Cricket Cards: 154 Collectors' Cigarette Cards Authentically Reproduced in Original Colours...; with an introduction by John Arlott. New York: Dover Publications and London: Constable, 1980. From the collection of M.A. Murray.

  More Classic Cricket Cards: 160 Collector's Cigarette Cards Reproduced in Original Colours; with an introduction by Brian Johnston. Constable, 1981.

Van der Plank, David, *and* Van der Plank, Rosemarie.
  The Match Label Collectors' Handbook. [The Authors], 1972. Loose-leaf format.

Van Lemmen, Hans.
  Victorian Tiles. Shire Publications, 1981.

Williams, Marcus.
  Double Century: 200 Years of Cricket in The Times. Collins Willow, 1985.
  The Way to Lord's: Cricketing Letters to The Times. Collins Willow, 1985.

Wisden Cricketers' Almanack. 1864 to date. Annual.

Wright, Gerry.
  Cricket's Golden Summer: Paintings in a Garden by Gerry Wright; with a commentary by David Frith. Pavilion, 1985.

Wynne-Thomas, Peter.
  A Brief Account of The Trent Bridge Pavilion and in particular Its Museum And Library. Nottinghamshire CCC, 1987.
  England On Tour: a Record of All England Cricket Tours Overseas, with Accounts, Results and Statistics. Hamlyn, 1982.

Periodicals

Australian Cricket Journal.
Cricket Memorabilia Society: *Newsletter.*
Cricket Quarterly.
Cricket World.
The Cricket Statistician (Association of Cricket Statisticians.)
The Cricketer.
The Journal of The Cricket Society.
Playfair Cricket Monthly.
Wisden Cricket Monthly.

Auction Houses

Catalogues issued by:
  Bonhams.
  Christie's South Kensington.
  Geering & Colyer.
  Graves Son & Pilcher.
  Phillips, Son & Neale.

INDEX

Page numbers in italics refer to illustrations

Abberley, R.N. 57
Abel, R. 15, 83, 90, 156, 186, 228, 236
Abell, R.B. 57
Aborigines: England tour (1868) 110
Ade, Edward 244, 245
Adelaide Oval 316
Adlard: prints 91
admission: passes 186; tickets 62, 214-15, 301; tokens 214-15
advertising 298; agencies: posters 214; ephemera 214, 216-18; see also handbills
A.F. Cricketer's Gin 304
Age, The (Melbourne) 218
Agnew's 30
AHS (cartoonist) 83
Aislabie, Benjamin 210
Albert CC 212
Albion CC, Dunedin 316
Alcock, C.W. 201
Aldin, Cecil 76
Alexander, George 218
All England Cricket and Football Journal 146
Allan, David 302
Allen, David Rayvern 19, 28, 95, 132-3, 288, 289
Allen, Sir G.O.B. 45, 176, 247, 290
Alletson, E.B. 170
Allott, P.J.W. 39, 225
Almeida, Noel 277
Almeida Books 19
Altham, H.S. 143
American Cricketer, The 147
American Tobacco Co. 249-50, 260, 280
Ames, L.E.G. 290
Amiss, D.L. 194
Anderson, John Corbet 58, 59, 77-80
Andrade, Cyril 30
Andrew Glass Engraving 194
Andrew, Neale 176
Andrews, Ruth 22
Anglo-American Sporting Club 110
Anglo-Boer War 102
Annaly, Lord 49
annuals: Australia 17, 144-5; Barbados 145; county 27, 145-6; South Africa 27, 145; United States 145
"Ape" (Carlo Pellegrini) 80-1, 84
Appleby, A. 240
Appleyard, R. 16, 17
aquatints 66
Archer, James 39
archives 21, 209-212
Argus (P.E. Reynolds) 138
Arlott, John 19, 27, 28, 32, 45, 59, 71, 75, 84, 100, 111, 129, 143, 194, 218, 275, 282, 290, 297, 309; collection 7

'Arlott's Immortals' 177
armchair, miniature 301
Armchair Cricket 284
Armstrong, W.W. 44, 233
Arnold, E.G. 187
Arrowsmith, R.L. 144
Art Society 84
Artillery Ground 32, 130
artists, cricketers as 56-7
artwork, commercial 47
Arundel 49
Ashes 50, 138, 219; urn 305
'Ashes Song' 289
Ashley-Cooper, F.S. 11n., 18, 26, 27, 32, 43, 58, 129, 131, 132, 134, 137, 141, 152, 189, 202, 206, 212, 220, 221, 292, 307, 308
ashtrays 300; silver 180
Association of Cricket Statisticians 137, 225
Association of Cricket Umpires 292
Athey, C.W.J. 20
Atkins, John 174-5
Atkinson, C. 70
Atwell, Max 309
auctions 11-13, 25-9, 231, 307
Audiogenic Software 288
Australia 44, 50, 54; tours: England (1878) 32, 118, 138, 207, 223, 250; (1880) 69; (1882) 104, 117, 138; (1884) 138, 216, 218; (1886) 215; (1893) 69, 202; (1896) 219, 224; (1899) 201-2, 238; (1902) 110, 202; (1905) 118; (1926) 109, 198, 199, 256, 305; (1930) 109-10; (1934) 218, 265; (1938) 168; (1948) 220; (1953) 234, 245; (1977) 169; North America (1932) 231; South Africa (1935-36) 201
Australian Cricket Board 188, 221
Australian Cricket Journal 310
Australian Cricket Society (Canberra) 170
Australian Gallery of Sport 315
autographs 197-202
Auty, K.A. 292; Memorial Library 317
Awdry, E.P. 210
Ayres, F.H. 244

badges 9, 280-1; see also buttons
Baer, Tony 16, 37, 42, 44, 59, 113, 114, 181, 183, 213, 218, 223, 242, 303, 310-11; auction (1978) 25, 28, 95, 116, 118, 133, 244, 294; collection 150, 151, 152, 302, 315
bags, cricketers' (china) 165
Bailey, Philip 137
Bailey, T.E. 144
bails 242-3
Baily Brothers 71, 72
Baily's Magazine 59, 69
Baines, J.: cigarette cards 263
Baines, Roland 91
Baker, C.S. 57
Baker, W. Bligh 70

Balderstone, J.C. 91
Baldwin, J.L. 207-8
Baldwin, Stanley 16, 211
Balfour, Lord 200
Ballantine-Dykes: scrapbooks 210
balls 238-42; blue 11, 241; oldest 238; silver 179, 180; Suffragette protest 11; unusual 240-1; weight scales 243; white 239
Bambridge, William 75
Band of Brothers: brooch 189
bank notes 198, 300-1
Bannerman, A.C. 118
Barbados, Central Bank of 300
Barclay, R. 182
Barclays World of Cricket 19
Bardsley, W. 233
Baring, Mark 54
Bark-Hart House Academy, Orpington 64
Barker, Thomas 32, 33
Barling, T. 15
Barlow, R.G. 16, 17, 169, 170, 179-80, 181, 228, 231, 251, 260, 313; stained-glass window 196
Barnard, Derek 123
Barnes, S.F. 24, 45, 109, 143, 149, 168, 300, 313, 314
Barnes, S.G. 15
Barnes, W. 227, 313
Barnett, B.A. 201
Barnett, C.J. 228
Barnett, J. 218
Barrable, G.H. 87
Barratt & Co.: cards 264
Barraud, Francis Philip 64
Barraud, Henry 88
Barrie, Sir James 28, 140-1
Barrington, K.F. 23
Barton, Edmund 278
Barty-King, Hugh 232
Basébé, Charles J. 63, 72-3
Bassano, Brian 316
Bat and Ball, Hambledon 208, 293
Bat and Ball, public house 294
Bat and Wickets, Northampton 294
Bath: cricket ground 51, 52; bats 9, 16, 200, 227-35, 315, 316; Addington XI (1743) 230, 316; aluminium 91, 316; burnisher 243; gauge 229; historic 169; illustrated 46, 234; miniature 235; miniature (silver) 179, 180, 181, 189, 190; modern signed 234; oldest 229, 314; "Pod" 232; record price 230; unusual 234
Batson, Frank 34, 312
Batten, J.R. 126, 132, 137, 147
Batty, T. 294
Baxter, "Honest" 95
Baxter, John 95
Baxters, Lewes printers 208-9
BBC Music Libraries 95
Beagley, T. 78
Beauclerk, Lord Frederick 42, 189, 253

Bedford Park 30
Bedi, B.S. 45
Bedser, A.V. 177, 221, 300, 314
beer mats; see breweriana
Beerbohm, Sir Max 100
Beeston, R.D. 138
Beldam, George A. 105
Beldam, George W. 9, 23, 84, 90, 105, 112, 205
Beldham, William 42, 230-1
Belfast Cricket League 210
Bellany, John 39
Belleek ware 160
belts 244-5
Bembridge Common 32
Benaud, R. 46, 144
Bennett, Austin 175
Bennett, Neil 102
Bénoist, Antoine 60
Benson & Hedges Cup: Somerset declaration 188, 239
'Benson & Hedges Golden Greats' 297
Bentley, Henry 26, 132, 133
Bernardes, Eric 167
Berry, Scyld 242
Bettesworth, W.A. 26, 137, 206
Bevan, Phil 226
Bickley, J. 78
Biers and Fairfax 144
Bigg, W.R. 66
Billingham, Robert 2666
Binks, J.G. 177
Binns, Richard 309
Birnbeck Island 301
biscuit barrels 301
bisque pottery 158
Black Horse, Grimston 294
Blackham, J.M. 118, 170, 218, 236, 260
Blanchard, Derek 198, 201, 309
blazers 247-8
Bligh, Hon. Ivo 100, 138, 219, 300
Bloom, Enid 175
Bluck, J. 65
Blythe, C. 83, 86
Bodleian Library 95
Bodyline: The Novel: cards 267
Boitard, Louis-Pierre 62, 87, 214, 219
Bolton CC 210
Bolus, J.B. 248
Bonhams 25
Bonnor, G.J. 81, 82, 83, 84, 260
book-ends 170, 184-5, 300
book-plates 214, 303
book matches 271
books 19, 20, 23, 26-8, 119-46; bibliographies 128, 129, 308; private libraries 307, 308, 309; statistical 130, 132-3, 138-9; tours 138; see also annuals, periodicals
booksellers 18-19
Boonham, Nigel 171
boots 248-9
Border, A.R. 51

Bosanquet, B.J.T. 204, 312
Botham, I.T. 20, 39, 45, 46, 56, 90, 93, 98, 101, 177, 178, 217, 289, 296, 297, 298
Botham, Kathy 93
bottle-openers 304
Bouwman, Rick 35, 311, 314
Bowen, Rowland 32, 146, 147, 211, 275, 282
Bowes, W.E. 290
Bowles, Carrington 66
Bowles, Thomas & Jno. 60, 61, 62
Bowles. Thomas Gibson 81
bowling machines 77, 242
Bowyer, William 44-5
Box, Charles 134, 308
Box, T. 73, 76, 78, 115, 116, 149, 152, 154, 236, 253
Boxall, Thomas 26, 27, 130-1
boxes (protective) 249
Boy's Own Paper 248
Boycott, G. 90, 91, 93, 102, 103, 123, 167, 168, 174, 176, 177, 213, 294, 300
Boyle, H.F. 145, 260, 315
Bradley, R. 174
Bradman, Sir D.G. 144, 221, 254, 257, 311; autographs 202, 221; bats 233, 316; batting 112; cartoons 101; cigarette cards 262, 267; clothing 20; figures 149, 174, 175; label 278; letters 203; music 97; photographs 104, 110; pictures 42, 44, 92, 93, 94, 193, 315; plaques 169; plate 167; pottery 164; recordings 290, 292; vases 161, 313
Bradman Museum 29, 35, 115, 265, 316
Branscombe, Brian 162
Braund, L.C. 85
Brearley, J.M. 172
Brearley, W. 201, 313
Bremner, Rory 289
Brett, Thomas 200
breweriana 295-6
Brewn, J. Ernest 22
Bride Head, Dorset 47
Briggs, J. 187, 198
Bright, Harry 76
Brindley, John, & Associates 267
Bristol Art Gallery 32
Bristow, T. 32
Britcher, Samuel 27, 114, 132-3
British Empire Exhibition 263
Britton, C.J. 129, 308
Broad, John 157
Broadbent, A. 15
Broadhead, Gerald 101-2
Brockbank, William 132
Brocket, Lord 42
Brockwell, W. 227, 233
Brodribb, Gerald 225
Bromhead, George 105
Bromley, William 42
brooches 189, 190
Brook, Rev. Peter 205
Brooke, Rupert 120, 122
Brooks, E.W.J. 101
Brooks, H. Jamyn 90
Brooks, Vincent, Day and Son 82
Brooks-King, Reginald 242
Brown, C. 78
Brown, D.J. 50

Brown, E.K. 18, 23, 292, 308
Brown, J.T. 197, 233
Browne, Edwin 312
Browne, Tom 258, 291
Browne, Tom, & Co. 65
Brylcreem 217, 257
Brympton d'Evercy House 314
buckles 244-6
Buckley, G.B. 29, 124, 127-8, 229, 236, 237, 243, 294; sale of collection 125, 146, 147
Bufford, J.H. 74
Bullock, W.J. 95
Burden, Clive 81
Burgess, W. 75
Burgschmidt, Ernst 128
Burlington Gallery 5, 37, 40, 46, 49, 58, 60, 61, 64, 69, 70, 71, 72, 73-4, 75, 76, 78, 90, 96, 108, 153, 155, 163, 164, 168, 179, 184, 190, 205, 220, 222, 231, 239, 249, 250, 302, 303, 317; catalogues 31-2, 36, 37, 40, 50, 65, 66, 70, 98, 317
Burn, Henry 75
Burnett, John 249
Burnside, I.H. 96
Burr, Alexander Hohenlohe 36-7
Burroughs and Watts: table cricket 286
Burton Court 49, 55
Bussey, George G., & Co.: diaries 283
Butler, H.J. 252
Butler, James 176
buttons 249-50
Byron, Lord 202

Caesar, J. 27, 78, 80, 149, 153, 154
Caffyn, W. 77, 80, 205
Cage, Lewis 42-3
Cahn, Sir Julien 27, 31, 129, 141, 233, 308, 312
Calcutta CC: painting 32
Caldecourt, W. 78, *229*, 242
Calderon, Philip Hermogenes 69
calendars 281-3
Calvert, artist 69
Cama, Spen 305
Cambridge University CC 72, 104, 106
Cameron, H.B. 16
Campbellfield Pottery Co. 163
Canada 311, 317
Canada: Toronto print 73-4
Canberra, cruise liner 315
candlesticks, silver 181, 182
Canterbury 75, 96
Canterbury Cricket Week 134-5
Canterbury: St Lawrence Ground 51, 64, 86; miniature bats 235
Cantle, Harold 41, 91
Cape Verde Is.: stamps 271, 277
caps 20, 250-2, 312; England 251
cards: cases, silver 182; games 284-5
Cardus, Sir Neville 7, 39, 143, 171
caricatures 97-102
Carmichael, J.W. 37
Carnarvon, Earl of 122
Carpenter, R. 181, 203, 204
Carpenter, Tony 194
Carreras: cigarette cards 262, 265; packets 269
Carrick, Robert 65
Carroll, Lewis, *pseud.* 81

Carter, Howard 177-8
cartoons 97-102
Castells of Oxford 254
catapulta *242*
Catton, J.A.H. 27, 122
Caxton, William 212
C.B. Fry's Magazine 47
C.B.S. Ironmongery Ltd.: cards 266
C.C. Morris Cricket Library 105, 317
Centenary Test matches (1977 and 1980) 25, 162, 194, 220; medallions 188
Centre for Cartoon and Caricature 101
ceramics 149-70
Chad Valley: games 285
Chandler, John H. 43
Chapman, A.P.F. 15, 16, 99, 111, 169, 211, 251, 289-90, 300
Chappell, G.S. 149
Chappell, I.M. 298
Chappell, T.M. 316
Charlesworth and Austin: cigarette cards 264
Charterhouse School *64*
Chichester: paintings 75, 76
Chichester, S.R. 242
Chitty, J. 229
Christchurch, Hampshire: painting 32, 86
Christian Victor, Prince 179, 233
Christian, E.B.V. 307n.
Christie's 13, 25, 84
Christmas cards 150; *see* greetings cards
Christmas Day: cricketers born on 292
chromolithographs 75-6
'Chums': cards *266*
Church CC 314
Churchman, W.A. & A.C. 262, 268
Cigarette Packet Collectors Club 268
cigarettes: cards 260-6, artwork 47; cases, silver 181, 182; packs 268-9
cigars: boxes, silver 182; cutter 22
City of London School 172
Clark, W.M. 134
Clarke, W. 59, 77, 91, 96, 149
Clay, J.C. 290
Clift, A.T. 262
Clive-Ponsonby-Fane, Charles 314
clocks 190-1
Close, D.B. 217
clothing, cricket 15, 244-54
clubs: historical records 211-12
Coalport China Co. 165-7
Coates, David 288
Coates, W.R. 62
Cobbett, J. 73, 76, 78, 115, 116, 149
Cobden, F.C. 241
cocktail stirrers 180
Cohen, H.M. 28
Cohen, Rev. Philip 196
coins: George III penny 300
Coldham, James D. 88-9, 205, 241, 291, 292, 307, 308, 309
Cole, Roland and Betty 18
Collect Modern Cards 259
Collectors Mart 267
Collet, John 66
Collins, A.E.J. 233
Collyer, Graham 231

Colman, Sir Jeremiah 28, 34, 42, 142-3, 311
Colman's Mustard 217
compass, cricket 300
Compton, D.C.S. 44, 55, 178, 217, 257
computer games 94, 287-8
Conan Doyle, Sir Arthur 220
Concanen, A.H. 97
Coney, J.V. 298
Constantine, Lord 51, 177, 288, 315
Conway, John 144-5
Cook 62
Coombs, Mark 46, 306
Coombs, Peter 306
Coote, Julia 281
Copenhagen House, Islington 62
Copinger, Geoffrey 27, 207, 255, 309, 312
Cornwall, G.H. 240
Cotes, Francis 42
Cotterell's, bookshop 18
county captains 104, 108
County Championship: plates 167
county cricket, centenary of 188; exhibition 22
Courtenay Studio 87
Cousens, C. 72
Cowdrey, Jeremy 49
Cowdrey, M.C. 45, 144, 167, 247, 271, 315
Cowman, Stanley 316
Cox, G., jnr. 45, 299
Cox, Richard 210
Craib, William Hofmeyr 44
Craig, Albert *256*
Crambie, Geoff 24
Crane Kalman Gallery 177
Crickard 285
cricket: first English reference 209
Cricket 32, 74, 88, 89, 90, 96, 105, 126, 128, 146, 307
'Cricket': lithograph 70
Cricket and Football Times 146-7
Cricket Field, The 18, 128, 147
"Cricket, lovely cricket" 289
Cricket Memorabilia Society 11n., 16, 29, 190, 297, 303
Cricket Quarterly 146, 147, 259
Cricket Society, The 290, 292
cricketana: collecting, 7-13, 15-29; prices 12-13, 14, 18, 25, 29; valuation 20, 24-5, 26, 28, 152; word derivation 11, 308
Cricketana, Bath 47, 65, 283-4
Cricketana Society 11n., 308
Cricketeer Trophy 176
Cricketer, The 11n., 16, 33, 40, 45, 59, 63, 69, 85, 98, 102, 103, 105, 122, 123, 128, 132, 133, 135, 136, 146, 147, 164, 170, 183, 185, 188, 194, 197, 209, 214, 220, 225, 241, 242, 250, 251, 289, 291, 294, 308, 309, 311, 313, 314, 316; calendar 282
Cricketer Cup, The 55
Cricketer Shop, The 296
cricketers, first-class: attitude to memorabilia 16-17
Cricketers, The: public house 294
Cricketers Inn, Meopham 294
Cricketers Jazzmen 289
Cricketers' Arms, Chertsey 34
Cricketers' Club 307

Cricketrivia 285
Crombie, Charles Exeter Devereux 76, 291
Crossland, Julie 190
Crossley, Don 16
Crowe, M.D. 298
cruets, china 301; silver 179
Cruikshank, Robert 66, 253
Crummles pill boxes 193
Cumbria Record Office 210
Cundall, Charles 32, 91
Cunningham, Andrew 295
cups: silver 181, 183
Curry Rivel Gallery 51
Curtis, W.F. 124
"Cushy", Hove cushion salesman 45
Cust, Henry, MP 200, 205
Cutler, Cecil 40

d'Aquino, Count André 177
D'eath, Eleanor Hughes 42
D'Oliveira, B.L. 234, 251, 289
Daft, R. 203, 204, 205, 206, 312
Daily Express 241
Daily Mail 257
Daily Telegraph 21, 248
Dalby, David 235
Dale, George 41
Dalmeny, Lord 83, 103, 174
Dance, James: see Love, James
Dark, James H. 34, 75, 78
Dark, Richard 236, 237
Darling, J. 85, 302
Darnall Ground, Sheffield 66, 214, 215
Darnley, Earl of 28, 38, 62, 83, 150, 152
David Messum Gallery 31
Davies, William, 'The Scorer' 34
Davis, Harry 161, 162
Davis, John C. 145
Daw, Henry 253
Day, Daniel 71
De La Rue, Thomas, & Co. 283, 286
De Lugo, Anthony Benitez 139-40
De Selincourt, Hugh 204
Deadman, Derek 255, 262, 270, 293
Deakins, Leslie 57
Dean and Munday 62
Dean, Charles 32
Dean, J. 42, 78
Deighton, Robert 281
Deighton and Mullen, advertising agents 47, 281-2
Denison, William 27, 28, 133-4, 236
Denton, D. 15, 86, 149, 164, 181
Derbyshire CCC 162, 194, 195, 257
Dewsbury Reporter 107
Dexter, E.R. 54, 100, 103
diaries 283-4
Dick, F.C. 257
Dicker, Rev. C.G.H. 209
Dickinson and Foster 64, 87, 88
Dillon, E.W. 81, 83
diorama, cricketing 175
Discbat Cricket 285
Disraeli, Benjamin 42, 81
Diver, A.J.D. 78
Dixon, A.J. 228
Dixon, A.L. 271
Dixon, James, and Sons 185
Dixon, John 47
Dodd, C. Tattershall 75
Doré, Gustave 62-3

Dorrien, cartoonist 267
Dorset Square, Marylebone 38
Dorset, Duke of 115
Doulton, Royal, ware 155-7
Down, Michael 80
Downend, sale of 213
Doxey, Arnold 313
Drabble, David 194
Draner: cartoon 102
drink labels 304
Drummond, W. 63, 72-3
Drury & Drury 149, 153
Drysdale, Sir Russell 35
Duckworth, G. 100, 101, 169
Dudley, William 181
Duff, R.A. 85
Duke & Son 236, 238, 239, 315
Duleepsinhji, K.S. 15, 181, 251, 252
Duncan, G.F., and Co. 270, 271
Duncombe, Rev. John 130
Dunlop, Bonar 175
Dunnell, O.R. 44
Durham, Joseph 172
Durtnal, H. 232
Dyson Perrins Museum 161

Eagar, E.D.R. 27, 143, 215, 277
Eagar, Patrick 107, 259
E & J Software 288
Earle, Thomas and William 43
East Melbourne CC 110
East Molesey CC 245
Eastman, Frank 43
Edmonds, Thos. 230
Edrich, J.H. 167
Edrich, W.J. 44, 55, 204, 299
Edridge, Henry 30-1
eggs: cups 170; stand 179; warmer 302
Ellis, W. "Potman" 164
Emmett, T. 93, 205
enamels 192-3
England v Australia 44
England: tours: Australia (1861-62) 105, 109, 117, 218, 244-5; (1863-64) 109, 117, 245; (1873-74) 218, 245, 315; (1876-77) 312; (1878-79) 219; (1882-83) 138, 219; (1894-95) 111, 197, 207; (1897-98) 280; (1901-02) 250; (1903-04) 187, 201, 208, 220; (1907-08) 201, 312; (1911-12) 23, 220; (1924-25) 211; (1928-29) 216, 303; (1932-33) 104, 192, 201; (1950-51) 300; (1954-55) 300; Canada (1937) 231; India (1937-38) 201, 247; New Zealand (1863-64) 316; North America (1859) 105, 137; (1872) 109; (1879) 312; (1897) 194; South America (1926-27) 247; South Africa (1888-89) 138, 210, 317; (1905-06) 208; West Indies (1896-97) 138, 226
'English School': paintings 38, 43
engravings 59-65
ephemera, printed 208-26
Epps, W. 27-8, 130, 131
Epworth Books 18, 303
Errington, J.R.F. 103
Essex CCC 146, 230, 267; handbook 153; museum 310, 314
Eton College 49, 64, 65, 70, 75, 76, 84, 86, 93, 97, 108, 141, 151, 202, 207, 210, 213, 241, 302; scorebook (1805) 225

Ettling, Emile 96
Ettlinger, Duggie and Lennie 317
Evans, A.J. 180
Evans, T.G. 177, 178, 290, 298, 299
Ewbank, George 138

F&R Sports: shaving mug 163
Fagg, A.E. 291
Fairburn & Co. 74
Fairweather, Dennis 174
fans 302
Farnes, K. 204
Farrants, A.J. 227
Faulkner, G.A. 201
Fearnley, Alan 91-2
Fearnley, Duncan 46
Fearnley, Stephen 288
Felix Rosenstiel's, art gallery 55
Felix, N. 56, 71-2, 77, 116, 117, 183, 205, 236, 242, 248, 250; books 26, 27, 28, 133, 134; pictures 38, 43
Fellows, H.W. 240
Fender, P.G.H. 16, 99, 100, 124, 313
Fenton, Roger 104-5
Ferguson, W.H. 192
Ferris, J.J. 203
Ferrow, Mark 46
Fielder, A. 16, 181
films 169, 298-300, 316
Finden, Edward 65
Finney, Albert 177
'First-Class Cricketers of 1893' 89-90
First Impressions 116-17, 118, 153, 154, 169, 185, 222
Fitzgerald, R.A. 74, 109, 311
Flannery, Jerome 145
Flemons: postcards 256
Fletcher and Co., Shelton 28, 151-2
Fletcher, K.W.R. 44
'Flickers' 112, 317
Florio, John 130, 309
Ford, Alfred Lawson 17, 28, 139, 307, 312
Ford, F.G.J. 233, 260
Forman, T. Bailey 213
Foster, F.R. 182, 239, 290
Foster, H.K. 85, 86
Foster, M.L.C. 54
Foster, Myles Birket 36
Foster's: postcards 256
Fowke, T.: statuettes 158
Francis, Mike 91
Franklin Mint: Ashes Centenary tankard 170
Freeman, A.P. 104, 298, 300
French, Hon. E.G. 242
French, Neal 162
Friend, D.B. 139
Friends of Grace Road 168
Frindall, Bill 9, 46
Frith, David 15, 19, 20, 23, 48, 51, 102, 105, 107, 110, 127, 135, 144, 145, 191, 201, 207, 232, 239, 252, 297, 299, 300, 305, 309-10
Fry, C.B. 82, 93, 98, 110, 149, 172, 184, 186, 201, 202, 203, 205, 207, 227, 228, 234
Furniss, Harry 41, 99, 274
furniture 301, 302

Gale, Frederick 71, 229, 236
Galsworthy, Jocelyn 47, 49
Gamage, A.W., Messrs. 227, 233-4,

241
games 284-7
Gardner, F. 198, 199
Garland, Henry 34, 38
Garner, J. 289
Garnsey, G.L. 17
Garrard & Co. 188
Garrett, T.W. 87
Garrick, David 37
Garrow, Simon 54
Gaston, Alfred J. 17, 18, 115, 122, 128, 129, 139, 141, 142, 200n., 208, 212, 221, 225, 227, 230, 302, 307, 308
Gavaskar, S.M. 45
Gay, L.H. 207
Geering & Colyer 64, 160, 180, 181, 244
Gehrs, D.R.A. 198
Gentleman, David 92
Gentlemen v Players: 88, 210, 215, 239, 240; centenary match 186; scorecard 223
George V, King: banknote 198
Getty, J. Paul jnr. 48
Gibson, Robin 45
Giffen, G. 149, 156, 163, 233, 260, 302
Gifford, N. 228
gifts 19, 39, 190
Gill, John 116
Gill, W.H. 43
Gillett, Frank 99
Gillette Cup: medals 188
Gillette UK Ltd. 32, 91, 219
Gilligan, A.E.R. 45, 182, 313
Gillingham, Rev. F.H. 83
Gimblett, H. 314
Gittins, Harold 99
Gladwell, Guy 53, 54
Glamorgan CCC 258, 266, 267
glassware 15, 193-5
Gloucestershire CCC 208, 257; auction (1982) 118, 301, 303; Grace Suite 41
gloves: batting 236; wicketkeeping 236
Godfrey Phillips 262, 263, 264, 265, 268
Goldman, J.W. 16, 27, 28, 32, 42, 63, 64, 70, 80, 103, 110, 114, 126, 128, 129, 130, 132, 134, 139, 141, 142, 186, 189, 197, 213, 305, 301, 302, 303, 308
Goldwin, William 130
Golly brooches 281
Gooch, G.A. 44, 90, 92-3
Goodenough House, Ealing 65
Goodwin, J.E. 151
Goodwin & Co. 260
Goodwin and Harris: meat dish 151
Gore, Spencer 31
Goss, Adolphus 164
Goss, William Henry 164
Goss china 164-5
Goupil & Co. 87
Gower, D.I. 20, 44, 46, 51, 56, 90, 93, 287
Grace, A.L. 92
Grace, C.B. 214
Grace, E.M. 22, 65, 112, 177, 178, 205
Grace, G.F. 177, 178, 197, 226
Grace, W.G. 17, 56, 87, 218, 219,

226, 224, 245, 247, 250, 267, 294, 300, 304, 308; 'bank note' 301; advertising 216-17, 218; autographs 200, 202; bats 227, 228, 231, 234, 312; books 22, 140; busts 160, 173; car mascot 23, 306; cartoons 41, 81, 82, 83, 84, 99; cigar 20; cigarette cards 262, 264; clothing 20; figures 22, 23, 149, 154, 158, 160, 173-4, 176, 177, 178, 184; films 298; furniture 301; handkerchiefs 118, 294; letters 40, 204-5, 313; medallions 186; memorabilia 21-2; obituary 122; photographs 104, 106, 108-9, 207, *214*; pictures 21, 22, 32, 39, 40-2, 48, 74, 85, 86, 88, 89, 90, 91, 93, 193, 196, *310*, 315; pipes 16, 22; plaques 169; plate 165-7; poster *214*; pottery 156, 163, 170; rug 301; sheet music 96; silverware 180, 183; stained glass 196; stamps 274; Stevengraph 113; table game 286-7; testimonial 21, 97
Grace Parlour Game 284
Graf, C. 71
Gravelot, Hubert 59
Graves, Son and Pilcher 23, 101, 126, 137, 147
Great Exhibition (1851) 237
Greater Manchester Record Office 210
Greaves Art Gallery, Sheffield 32
Green, Benny 284
Green, C.E. 230
Green, Lt-Col. L. 180
Green, Stephen 19, 32, 58, 59, 105, 107, 157, 160, 197, 209, 233, 238, 243, 311, 312
Greenidge, C.G. 46, 251
greetings cards 291-3
Gregory, J.M. 239, 300
Gregory, S.E. 85, 110, 260
Greig, A.W. 45, 149, 228
Grenada: stamps *273*
Grierson, Henry 253
Griffin china 165
Griffith, G. 78
Grignion, Charles. 60, 61, 62, 114, 115
Grimmett, C.V. 15, *16*, 99, 104, 112, 218, 221, 226, 240, 248, 251-2, 280, 292, 316
Grose, Terry 93
grounds: model 194, 306
Grundy, J. 312
Guildford Museum 209
Guinness: postcards 259
Gunn, W. 156, 186, 227, 228, 231
Gunn & Moore 216, 256
Gutteridge, Leslie 18, 121, 122, 123, 126, 135, 205
Guy, J. 78
Guyana: T-shirt *253*

Hackney School 64, 65
Hadlee, R.J. 45, 46, *101*, 175, 176, 228, 252, *274*
Haig, N.E. 251
Haigh, S. 85, 149, 164
Hall, Frank 97
Hall, Harry 231
Hall, W.W. 49

Hallé Concerts Society 171
Halse, George 158, 159
Hambledon 34, 198, 200, 211-12, 221, 288, 305; bat 229
Hamilton, I. 21
Hammond, W.R. 93, 101, 174, 178, 182, 191, 192, 203, 204, 216, 262, 300
Hampshire CCC 46, 145-6, 157, 167, 215, 257, 267, 279; auction (1984) 100, 249; museum 314; v. Warwickshire (1922) 224
Hampstead CC 220
Hampton Court Green 30
Hancock, Tony 135
handbills 95, 208, 212-13
handkerchiefs 61, 114-18
Hankey, R. 78
Harbottle, Michel 249
Hargreaves, Harry 99
Harleston Engraved Glass Co. 194
Harper, Roy 95, 227, 289
Harries, Ron 16, 120, 156, 165, 307, 309
Harris, D. 191-2
Harris, Lord 83, 84, 86, 109, 191, 192, 203, 206, 219
Harrison & Sons: labels 279
Harrow School 64, 75, 84, 93, 97, 108, 141, 202, 207, 210, 213, 241, 250, 302
Harte, Chris 289, 310
Hastings Town Hall 32
hat-tricks 238, 240
hats 250
Hawke, Lord 83, 103, 177, 203, 223, 227, 247, 290, 294
Hawkins, E., and Co. 105-6, 256
Hawkins, John 19, 23
Hawkins, Kathleen 94
Haygarth, Arthur 7, 8, 27, 115, 129, 135, *136*, 219
Hayhurst, Keith 174, 192, 196, 310, 313
Hayllar, James 37
Hayman, Francis 32, 33-4, 38, 59-62, 91, 114, 115, 150, 185, 191, 193, 302, 305
Hayne & Cater: wine ewer 304
Hayward, T. 83, 84, 186, 227, 228, 231, 233, 240, 257
"H.B." (John Doyle) 102
Headley, G.A. 93, 101
Hearne, A. 186
Hearne, J.T. 88, 219
Hearne, T. 78
Heartaches CC 141
Heavy Woollen District Challenge Cup 183
Hedgcock, Murray 205, 233, 305, 310
Hedley, W.C. 227
Heesom, Denys 316
Hekel, August 62
helmets 252
Henderson, J.T. 145
Hendon CC 210
Hendren, E.H. 100, 104
Hendry, H.S.T.L. 266
Henwood, Thomas 34, 87, 209
Herald, The, Melbourne 69
Hesketh Concept 154
Hesketh-Prichard, H.V. 85
Heslop, Michael 46, 91

Hick, G.A. 20
Hicks, George Elgar 22, 23, 32
Hicks, Peter 175-6
Higgs, K. 91
Hiley, Gil 213
Hill, B.J.W. 144
Hill, C. 85, 227, 232, 233
Hilliard and Thomason 192
Hillyer, W.R. 78
Hilton, M.J. 252
Hirst, G.H. 84, 85, 86, 149, *164*, 168, 169, 187, 205, 234, 239
Hobbs, Sir J.B. 38, 44, 83, 100, 104, 109, 118, 167, 169, 177, 178, 182, 197, 203, 204, 224, 228, 231, *232*, 234, 256, 262, 286, 290, 292, 300, 314, 315
Hodgins, Henry 32
Hodgson's, auctioneers 27, 123, 128, 129, 130
Hogarth, William 60
Holesch 39
Holloway & Son 217
Hollowood, Bernard 57
Holly, Buddy 259
Holmes, P. 312
Holmes, Rev. R.S. 135, 206, 222, 307
Hope, Thomas, of Amsterdam 42, 86
Hornby, A.N. 51, *53*, 97, 169, 196, 313
Horwood: London survey (1794) 62
Hove County ground 110
Howard, C. 215
Howard, Carl: cards 292-3
Howardswood Cricket Ground 306
Howe, Barnaby 193
Howell, W.P.
Howzat: game 285
Hudson, E.F. 18
Hudson, Tim 289
Hughes, K.J. 15, 20, 51, 254
Hull Railway Clerks CC 279
Hull Town CC 95
Hulton Picture Library 107
Humphrey, R. 218
Humphrey, W. 115
Humphreys, D. 174
Humphreys, W.A. 203, 205
Humphries, Hilary 268
Hunt, Charles 73, 149
Hunt, G. 63
Hunter, D. 179
Hunter, T.R. 308
Hurst, John 93
Hutchings, K.L. 83, 103
Hutchinson, Horace 195
Hutton, Sir L. 15, 92, 202, 252, 301
Hyde Park Ground, Sheffield 66, 214, 215

I Zingari 15, *16*, 40, 49, 96, 144, 208, 247, 303; museum 314
Igloolik 65
Illingworth, R. 45, 103
illuminated address 303
Illustrated London News 69, 152
Illustrated Sporting and Dramatic News 22
Imran Khan 48, 175
India 32, 44, 141, 242, 298; tours: England (1932) 300; (1946) 247
Ingram, Isaac 238
inkstands 302; silver 180, 181, 182
Inshaw, David 47

IPM *Catalogue* 255
Ireland, John 100, *101*
'Ireland's Royal Gardens' 63
Iremonger, J. 86
Ironbridge Gorge Museum 165
Isaacs, Vic 314
Islington Albion Club 249

Jackson, A. 207, 232
Jackson, F.S. 84, *85*, 86, 90, 93, 106, 205
Jackson, Randle 173
Jaeger: postcards 256, *257*
Jagger, Mick 48
Jamnagar 161
Jamnagar House 26
Jardine, D.R. 42, 55, 104, 168, 203, 204, 251, 267
Jenkins, David 126
Jenkins, R.O. 248
Jenner-Fust, Sir Herbert 233
Jennings, Grenville 255-6, 259
Jephson, D.L.A. 83
Jessop, G.L. 46, 83, 84, 93, 94, *105*, 186, 201, 227, 231, 236
jewellery 189-90
Jewish Chronicle 196
John Bull 69, 208
John Day Design Studios 177
John Rylands University Library of Manchester 132
John Walker and Sons 217
Johnson, Andrew 310
Johnson, Arthur 195
Johnson, I.W. 217
Johnson, T. 230
Johnston, Andrew Lawson 194-5
Jones, A.O. 233
Jones, Bob 255, 259, 266, 309
Jones, Philip 123
Jonzen, Karen 177
Josset, Lawrence 61
Journal of the Cricket Society, The 21, 165, 197, 201, 207, 233, 262, 307, 308n., 309
jugs 194; silver 179
Jukes, F. 65
Jupp, H. 108, 218
Just Leather, Salisbury 51
J/V Cards 260

K Shoes: posters 214
Karachi: National Stadium 57
Keane, Gary 54
Keats, John 239
Kelly, J.J. 85, *265*
Kelly, Ken 107
Kemp, M.C. 156
Kenfield Hall 34
Kensington District CC (Australia) 174
Kent CCC 51, 101, 106, 145, 146, 167, 181, 182, 207, 234, 235, 237, 256, 266, 271, 276, 302; museum 314
Kent Record Office 209, 238
Kent, William 158
Kent, Wm. *247*
Kepple, S.J., & Sons 165
Keyworth, William Day 173; the Younger 173
Kidson, Hayward 316
Kilner, R. 149, 189, 211
King, G. Lionel 43

King, G.W. 26
King, J.B. 203
King, J.J. 85
Kinnear Ltd.: cigarette cards 265, 266
Kinsella, E.P. 37, 163, 259
Kirby, Thomas 43
Kirkheaton Cricket and Bowling Club 169
Knight, Robert 54
knives, silver 180, 181, 182
Kodak: 'Cricket' film 300
Kortright, C.J. 186, 205-6, 228
Kynaston, R. 73, 78

La Khota Khota 161
Lady Cricketers, Original England 253
Laker, J.C. 118, 144, 177, 224, 241-2, 279, 288, 304
Laleham Green 34
Lalonde and Parham 124, 128
Lambert, W. 26, 131-2, 209
Lambourne Games 285
lamp, silver-plated 302
Lamplough's Model Cricket 285, *286*
Lancashire CCC 118, 180, 187, 215, 291-2, 299; museum 39, 196, 251, 310, 313
Land and Water 107
Langdon, David *100*
Langdon, Rev. G.L. 73, 78
Langford, A.W.T. 100, 109, *286*
Langley, G.R. 290
lantern slides 112
Large, Peter 314
Larwood, H. 178, 267, 273, 290
Laudensark, Frederick 34, *35*
Laughton, Tony 310
Laver, F. 111, 302
Lawrance, Basil Edwin: statue 172
laws 60, 61, 62, 76, 117; handkerchiefs 114-15; *New Articles of the Game of Cricket* 130
Leatham, E.E. 182
Leeds pottery 150
Lees, Frank 161
Lees, W.S. 103
legal documents 23, 218-19
Leicestershire CCC 46, 168, 187, 257, 271, 314
letters 202-6, 211
Leveson Gower, Lady Enid 182
Leveson Gower, Sir H.D. 27, 124
Lewes Priory 34
Lewis, A.R. 144
Lewis, Michael 55
Lewis, Vic 254, 309
Lewis, W.J. 11n.
Leytonstone Academy, Essex 65
"Lib" (Prosperi, Liberio) 80, 83
libraries. public 314-15
Liebig's: cards 219, 266
Lillee, D.K. 91, 98, 177, 252, 294, 316
Lilley, A.F.A. 187
Lillywhite 43; *Guides* 27, 249, 307, 309; publications 73, 135-8
Lillywhite, F. 28, 78, *222*, 236, 242
Lillywhite, F.W. 73, 76, 78, 79, 115, 116, 149, 152, 212, 253
Lillywhite, James 206, 215
Lillywhite, John 77, 183, 208, 215
Lillywhite Frowd 245

limited editions: books 138-44; prints 90
Lindwall, R.R. *202*, 217, 221, 269
Ling, Henry 18, 26, 151, 164
Lipschitz, S. 63
lithographs 34, 51, 70-86
Lloyd, C.H. 45
Loader, P.J. 217, 290
Lock, G.A.R. 217, 290
Lockwood, W. 88, 94, 186, 198, 264
Lockyer, T. 78, 80
Lohmann, G.A. 198
London Cigarette Card Co. 261, 264
London County XI 42
Lord, Thomas 38, 42, 62, 66, 150
Lord's Cricket Ground 32, 34, 39, 42, 44, 51, 54, 61, 62, 70, 75, 76, 88, 89, 90, 92, 96, 115, 188, 208, 213, 301; attendances 210; auctions at 29; benches 301; centenary 65, 188; jubilee 193; Memorial Gallery 42, 253, 311-12; 150th anniversary 162; Tavern 185; Toynbee Rooms 49
Lord's Taverners 110; 'Cricket' (record) 290; *Fifty Greatest* 91, 144, 282
Lorimer, Rev. Malcolm 303, 313
Love (Dance), James 26, 27, 28, 60, 130, 172, 221
Love, Tim 288
Low, David 99
Lowry, T.C. 262
Loxton, Margaret 55
Lucas, Edward George Handel 36
Lucas, E.V. 27, 33, 34, 69, 193, 204, 206, 211, 308
Ludovici, A. 42
Luff, Henry 122
Luke, Clare 178
Lumsdaine, Jack 97
Lurie, cartoonist 101
Lyttelton, A. 81, 82, 84, 200

Macartney, C.G. 100, 104, 266
McCormick, E.L. 56-7
McDermott, C.J. 298
Macdonald, D. & J.: cigarette cards 264, 266
McDonald, E.A. 300, 313
McDonnell, P.S. 260
McEwan, K.S. 267
MacGregor, G. 85, 156, 249
Machado, B. & J.B. 262, 268
McIntyre Bros.: cards 266
McIntyre, M. 218
McKenzie, A.C.K. 210
McKenzie, G.D. 44, 248
McKenzie, J.W. 18, 19, 72, 80, 109, 119, 123, 125, 129, 131, 132ff, 166, 205
MacKinnon, Peter 310
Macklin, Terry 50
MacLagan, T. 96
MacLaren, A.C. 174, 186, 207, 224, 233, 299, 313
McMahon, Keith 54
Maegraith, Kerwin 99
Magdalen CC: scorebook (1827) 225
Magdalen ground, Oxford 69
Maidstone Museum 172
Mail on Sunday 33
Mailey, A.A. 56, 99, 127, 201, 220, 231, 234, *264*

Malaya: tour 104
Manchester Free Trade Hall 171
Mann, Sir Horatio 115, 252
Mann, N.B.F. 44, *202*, 311
Mann, Roger 48, 99, 106, 108, 168, 173, 174, 186, 201, 204, 208, 213, 218, 223, 231-2, 236, 237, 238, 241, 244, 247, 309, 310, 316
Manson, Swan and Morgan 89
Manuel, J.W.T. 41
March, Russell 82-3
Marchant, F. 207, 303
Marlar, R.G. 28, 123
Marlborough, Duke of 209
marquetry: picture 301
Marsh, Madeleine 214
Marsh, R.W. 46
Marsh, Roger 23, 44, 51, *53*, 93
Marshall, George 87
Marshall, Mike 33, 146, 153, 156, 158, 196, 230, 310, *311*, 314
Marsham, C.H.B. 207
Martin-Jenkins, Christopher 316
Martineau, G.D. 112, 289
Martingell, W. 77, 108
MCC 17, 39, 42, 92, 164, 200, 206, 210; Arts and Library Sub-Committee 26, 31; bicentenary auction 25, 26, 29, 31, 36, 84; bicentenary match 44, 234; cap 250; cards 292; Centenary Dinner (1914) 220; collection 27, 33-4, 42-3, 49, 62, 84, 94, 105, 114, 150, 151, 158, 160, 162, 165, 172, 173, 176, 177, 191, 206, 214, 232, 233, 236, 240-1, 243, 266, 279, 299; cricket calendar 282; Diary 283; Jubilee (1837) 116; library 27, 131, 307, 312; life-member badges 280; membership voting boxes 305 ; 150th anniversary 164, 193; red pass 214; shop 296
Mason, J.R. 15, 80, 86, 182, 186, 222, 236, 249, 302
Mason, W.H. 73, 105; Repository of Arts 63; 'Sussex v Kent' print 59, 63-4
"Massie", cartoonist 100
matchbox: labels 269-71; silver 191
matchsticks 23
Mathews, James 37
Matthews, A.D.G. 101
Matthews, Roy T. 81
Maugsch, Julian 177
Mauritius CC *256*
May, P.B.H. 252, 279, 290, 301
May, Simon 292
Mayall & Co. 88
medallions 186-8
medals 186-8
Medici Society 87
Medlock, G.W. 315
Melbourne CC 219, 276; museum 28, 35, 42, 87, 114, 115-16, 150, 162, 172, 193, 213, 218, 236, 302, 315
Melbourne Cricket Ground 76; Centenary Test match 188; postcard 258
Melbourne Exhibition (1881) 238
Melling, John Kennedy 10
Mellini, Peter 81
Melville, W.W.E. 313

Men in White 144
menus: cards 36, 219-20; holder, silver 179
Menzies, Sir Robert 290
Mercer, J. 15
Meredith, Anthony 105
Merigot, J. 65
Merritt and Hatcher 118, 186
Mervitz, Michael 207
metalware 184-5
Mexico 104
mezzotints 66
Michelangelo 47
Middlesex CCC 106, 188, 194, 208, 242
Middleton Cheney 259
Milburn, C. 247
Miles, H.D. 75
Miles, J.O. 229
Millhoff, J. & Co.: cigarette cards 262, 265
Miller, Colin 22, 176
Miller, F.P. 78, 135-6
Miller, K.R. 217, 290
Millington, Terence 283
Milne, F.B. 307
Milton, C.A. 217
Milton, Sir W.H. 278
Minor Counties: Kenya tour 170
Minton 164; tiles 170
'Miss Wicket and Miss Trigger' 66, *67*
Mitcham: cigarette packet 269; public library 314-15
Mitchell, F. 110
Mitchell, R.A.H. 80
Mockford: postcards 256
Möet et Chandon: award 55
Mold, A. 259
Mole, John 187
Moody, Clarence P. 307n.
Moore, Ernest R. 44
Moreland, S.J. & Sons: England's Glory *270*, 271
Morland, George 33, 34
Morphot: postcards 259
Morris, Graham 107
Moses, Harry 182
Moslem Cigarette Co. Ltd. 268
motor cars: mascot 306; MCC 555 plate 305
Mullins, P.J. 206, 309, 315
Mulvaney, John 316
Mulvaney, Richard 316
Murdoch, Mrs W.L. 183, 202, 302
Murdoch, W.L. 17, 118, 203, 227, 228, 230, 233, 234, 251, 302, 307
Murray Cards (International) 262, 265
Murrell, Adrian 107
Museum of Eton Life 225
museums 311-17
Museums Association 29
music, sheet 95-7
Mutch, Duncan 123
Mynn, A. 42, 43, 71, 72, 73, 77, 78, 115, 208, 209, 215, 236, 237

Naïf art 54-7
Napoleon I, willow tree 233
Nash, M.A. 296, 312
National Cricket Association 298, 299
National Film Archive 299

National Portrait Gallery 39, 44, 45, 175
NatWest Trophy: bails 242
Neiman, LeRoy 54
Nettleton C. 105
New Caledonia: postcard 259; stamp 272
New Hall Pottery: plaques 169
New South Wales Cricket Association 182
New Universal Magazine, The 60
New Zealand 144, 194, 262, 274; National Cricket Museum 241, 316
newspaper bills 214, 316
Newton, Charles 191
Nixon, T. 78, 229, 237
Noble Game of Cricket, The 142-3
Noble, M.A. 85, 206, 227, 233
Norman, Philip 26
North Western Reform Synagogue 196
Northamptonshire CCC 194, 257, 264, 266
Northern Cricket Society 36
Nottinghamshire CCC 34, 213, 232-3, 291-2; auction (1984) 228, 248, 254; museum 312-13
Nubern Products: plates 167
Nuremberg Football Club: label 260, 278
Nutting, John 42
Nyren, John 27, 28, 42, 62, 133
Nyren, Richard 200, 235

Ogden's: cigarette cards 260, 262, 265
O'Keeffe, F. 314
Old Judge: cigarette cards 260, 262
Old Trafford 39, 50, 196, 313
Oldfield, W.A. 203
oleographs 86-7
One-Arm v. One-Leg match 213
O'Neill, N.C. 15, 252
O'Reilly, W.J. 203, 286, 298
Orton, T. 221
Osborne, H.A. 110, 313
Oval, The 34, 39, 42, 50, 69, 75, 76, 88, 96, 110, 214, 229, 242, 257, 259, 305, 310, 314
Overend, Leslie 107
Owen, T.J. 287
"Owl" 80
Oxford v Cambridge 63
Oxford University: Almanack 283; Harlequin CC 251
Oxfordshire CC 214

Packer, Kerry: World Series 239
Paddington CC (Australia) 191, 210
pads 21, 237, 253
Padwick, E.W. 128
Padwick, Thomas 17, 34, 132, 135, 307-8
Page, M.L. 252
Painter, Simon 93
paintings 30-57, 311; abstract 49, 54; naïf 54-5, 57; portraits 30-1, 39-47; "Super-Humanist" 51-2; watercolours 37-8
Pakistan: tours: England (1971) 234
Palairet, L.C.H. 313
Pamlin Print: postcards 259
Panini Publishing: stickers 267

Pannett, Juliet 45
paperweights 303
Papua *258*
Pardon, C.F. 138, 205
Paren, G.W. 207
Parian ware 158-60
Park, Chris 107
Park, W. 240
Parker, Purlee 32,
Parkin, C.H. 198
Parkinson, Michael 48
Parr, G. 27, 42, 149, 153-4, 200, 316; tree 235
Parr, Thomas, of Burslem 153
Parry, Bryn 93
Parsons, Canon J.H. 45
Partridge, J.T. 317
passports: Cardus 171; Trumper 23
patch boxes 193
Pattabhiraman, V.: cards 292
Pattreiouex, J.A., Ltd. 264, 265
Payne, J.B. 26, 307n.
Paynter, E. 313
Pears, A. & F. *68*, 69
Pecker, Morley 257
Peebles, I.A.R. 250
Peel, R. 88, 223, 233
Peel, Sir Robert 96
Penang Sports Club 311
pendants 189, 190
Pentelow, J.N. 233, 307
Perachio, Francis 99
periodicals 146-7
Perrier Ltd. 76
Perry, Roy 47, 51, *52*, 93
Pett, William 229, 239
pewter ware 185
Philadelphia 27
philately 271-9; covers 93, 275-6; first-day covers 274; ground cancellations 276-7; medallic covers 188; PHQ cards 274; postal cards 276; postmarks 274
Philipson, H. 83, 260
Phillips (auctioneers): September 1978 sale 25
Phillips, G.H. 63
Phillips, H. 215
photographs 9, 103-11
photogravures 87-90
Picken, L.T. 75
Pickwick Pottery 170
Picture Post Card Monthly 259
pigeon delivery 305
Pilch, F. 17, 59, 71, 73, 76, 78, 91, 96, 115, 133, 149, 152, 154, 237
Pilkington, Chris 165, 180, 239; collection 42, 158, 172; sale (1989) 12, 155
Pilleau, Norman 203
Pilling, R. 196, 260, 314
Pin Cricket: game 285
Pinches, John 188
pins 189, 190
Pinter, Harold 47
pipes 16, 22, 304-5
Pissarro, Camille 30
place mats 302
plaques 169
plates, commemorative 165-9
playbill 212
Player, John, and Sons 216, 260, 262, 265, 267, 268

Playfair Cricket Monthly 147, 311
Playfair: cufflinks 190
playing cards 293
Ploszczynski, N. 72
Plumstead public library 315
Pogson, Rex 123
Pollard, Jack 144
Poilard, James 62
Pollock, R.G. 44, 51, 290, 298
Ponsonby Fane, Sir Spencer 34, 208, 311, 314
Pontefract 182
Pontypool 32
pools coupons 211
Poore, R.M. 231
Porbandar, Maharaja of 278
Port Elizabeth 187, 245, 311
Port Sunlight: Lady Lever collection 30
Portal, Lord 278
Porter, A.D. 96
postcards 255-60
posters 213-14
Potter, Nicholas 31, 58, 317
pottery 170; continental 158, 163; mugs, transfer 163-4
Powell, Robert 48
Pratt Green, Charles 17, 205, 233, 303, 307, 309, 312
Pratt, T. 221
Pratt, W. 34
Premium Bonds 56
Price, A.B. 138
Priestley, Sir Arthur 226
prints 20, 25, 58-94; modern 90-4
Procter, M.J. 51, 91
public houses 293-4; signs 9; tables, W.G. Grace 294-5
Pugh, Michael 177
Pullin, A.W. (Old Ebor) 169
Punch 57, 69, 100, 263, 295
punch bowl, Chinese 150
Pycroft, Rev. J. 26, 59, 69, 134, 249

Qadir, Abdul 102
Quaife, W.G. 99
Quaife and Lilley 243

radio programmes 172
Rafty, Tony 234
Rait Kerr, Diana 247, 248, 250, 312
Ramadhin, S. 93, 289
Ramamurthy, Srikanthan 111, 201, 232, 242, 247, 252, 309
Ramamuthy, S. 177
Randall, D.W. 15
Ranjitsinhji, K.S. *22*, 27, 40, 87, 90, 93, 103, 106, 140, 142, 149, 156, 161-2, 163, 177, 183, 186, 192, 206, 219, 220, 227, 236, 247, 268, 278, 315
Read, W.W. 83, 84, 106, 140
Reader, Alfred 238, 241
'Rebel' tours: ties 254
recordings, gramophone 288-9; tape 290-2; *see also* music
Redfern, Margaret 315
Redman, Joan 102, 234
Reeve, R. 65
Reeve, W. 61
Reflections of a Bygone Age 259
Reid, John Robertson 37
Relf, A.E. 206, 208, 257
Rest of the World XI (1970) 294; signed bat 234

Rhodes, W. 44, 45, 85, 149, *164*, 168, 169, 178, 197, 234, 248, 298
Rice, Tim 48, 123, 141, 309, 311
Richards, B.A. 16
Richards, Colin 46-7
Richards, I.V.A. 20, 45, 46, 48, 90, *91*, 93, 176, 177, 273, 289, 296
Richards, Tim 178
Richardson, T. 102, 149, 186, 219, 239, 260
Richmond Park 62
Ridley, J. 130
Rimmel, Eugene 302
"Rip" (R.P. Hill) 98, 263, 264-5
Ritchie, G.M. 20
Ritchie, John 75
Roberts, A.M.E. 273
Roberts, E.L. 75, 283
Roberts, Henry 61, 62
Roberts, Paul 54
Robertson's jams 281
Robey, George 29
Robinson & Leadbetter, pottery 160
Roller, W.E. 42
Rose, B.C. 188
Rose, Ivan 91
Rosebery, Lord 60
Rosenburg, C., jnr 34
Rosenstiel's, Felix, Widow and Son 91
Rosenwater, Irving 16, 20, 21, 32, 58, 62, 143, 165, 200, 212, 300, 307, 308
Ross, Gordon 188, 218-19
Rossall School 64
Rossi, Henry 171-2
Rothmans: calendar 282
Rowan, Don 290, 309
Rowlandson, Thomas 62, 76, 86
Rowntree's Cachous miniatures 235
Royal Academy 44
Royal Crown Derby 162
Royal Falcon ware mug *164*
Royal family: Duke of Edinburgh 312; King George V 11, 142, 198; Prince Albert 220; Prince Christian Victor 179, 233; Prince Edward 220; Prince of Wales 87, 115, 187; Princess Charlotte, Princess Sophia 70; Queen Mary 56; telegrams 16
Royal Green Jackets 49
Royal Spode: china plate 169
Royal Worcester ware 160-2; plates 167, 168; Bradman vase 161, 316
Royston, H. 78, *79*
Rugby School 65, 253
Rundell, Michael 11n.
Russell, Lord Charles 138-9
Russell, John 42
Russell, R.C. 57, 292
Rutter, I., and Co. 269
Ryman, J. 70

Saatchi and Saatchi 54
Sablet, Jacques 42
St Clair, Henry 43
St Ivel 176
St Kitts: Warner Park, stamp 277-8
St Michael: diary 284; game 285
Salter, Edward 161
Salvadore House Academy, Tooting 64-5
Sampson, Aylwin 93

Sampson, H. 78
Sandby, Paul 34
Sandland plaques 169
Santall, S. 239
Scarborough: Cricket Club 124;
    Grand Hotel 103; handbill (1870)
    213
Scarborough, Joe 55
schools: cricket 210, 250, 253;
    pictures 49, 54, 64-5, 75, 76, 84,
    93
Schweppes: bicentenary plate 169
Scores and Biographies 26, 27, 129,
    135-7
scoreboards 217
scorebooks 9, 208, 225-6, 314
scorecards 63, 92, 192, 207, 221-5
scoresheets 94, 206, 221-3, 225, 305
Scotland 302; cricket bicentenary
    194
Scott, Rosalind 282
Scott-Gatty, Alfred 96
Scotton, W. 227
scrapbooks 206-8, 210
sculptures 171-8
Selangor: cricket ground 311
Sevenoaks Vine 169, 193, 230
Sewell, C.O.H. 204
Seymour, Geoffrey 265-6
Sharp, Nicholas 238
Shaw, A. 177, 206, 233, 312
Sheard, Charles 96
Shearon, Mildred 168
Sheffield, Lord 69, 106, 111, 169,
    196, 201, 219, 232, 241, 243, 307
Sheldon, Tony 310
'Shelley's Ice Cream': cards 267
Shelton, Arthur W. 227, 233, 313
Shepard, Ernest H. 69
Shepheard, George 34
Shepherd Neame: book matches 271
Sheppard, Rt. Rev. D.S. 248, 252,
    290
Sherman, T. 80
shirts 253
Shrewsbury, A. 88, 94, 198, 227,
    231, *232*, 233, 298, 312, 313
Sickelmore, C. & R. 63
silverware 179-83, 189
Simmonds, Hugh 125
Simmons, C.B. 161
Simon, Robin 32, 33, 36, 42
Simpson, R.T. 247
Sims, J.M. 299
Singapore CC 311
Sirra, artist 22
Slatter, Stephen 116
slippers 249
Small, John 130, 198, 208, 230, 238
Smart, Alastair 32, 33, 36, 42
Smart, Larry 55
Smith, G.M. 108
Smith, J. Harcourt 97
Smith, John 204
Smith, Mike 15-16, 44, 112, 169,
    181, 186, 211, 215, 247, 236, 237,
    243, 252, 285, 290, 300, 303, 309
Smith, N. 44
Smith, Sir C.A. 47, 205, 317
Smith, Sydney 19
Smith, W.C. "Razor" 182, 236
smoker's compendium 203, *304*, 305
Smokers v. Non-Smokers:
    photograph (1887) 110; scorecard

223
Snaith, J.C. 313
Sniders & Abrahams: cigarette
    cards 264
Snow, J.A. 45
snuff boxes 305; silver 169, 180,
    181, 182
Sobers, Sir G.S. 44, 170, 233, 273,
    288, 294, *296*, 312, 315
Solarbest Ltd. 97
Somerset CCC 46, 188; museum 314
Sondes children 30
Sotheby's 26, 27, 28, 36, 141, 142,
    156, 202, 259, 304
Soukop, Willie 172-3
South Africa 44, 145, 245, 316-17;
    tours: England (1907) 259; (1929)
    257; (1947) 242; (1955) 194; (1970)
    254
South Australia State Library 161,
    316
South Australian Cricket
    Association 212
Southern Booksellers 18
Southerton, J. 312
Southerton, S.J. 254
souvenir material 19, 296-7
Spalding, A.F. 256
Spear 62
Spear, Ruskin 45, 49
spelter figures 184
Spiers and Pond 117, 218
spill-holders 152
Spofforth, F.R. 42, 51, *53*, 83, 84, 87,
    104, 118, 170, 202, 204, 220, 233,
    245, 300
Spooner, Arthur 31
Sport in Miniature: Century
    Collection 178
Sporting Handbooks 123, 126
Sporting Heritage 91
Sporting Magazine, The 62, 69
"Spy" (Sir Leslie Ward) 80, 84, 100
Sri Lanka 187
Stacey, Gloria 55
Staffordshire ware 149, 150-5
stained glass 195-6
Stamp Publicity (Worthing) 259
stamps 9, 178, 271-4, 277;
    Cinderellas 278-9; cricketing links
    277-8; first postage 271; strike
    issues 279
Stannard and Dixon 77, 78
Staples, R. Ponsonby 87
Star, The: postcards 256
Stark, James 33
Statham, J.B. 217
Stead, Malcolm 93
Steadman, Ralph 97, 98, 259
Steel, A.G. 39, 97
Steel, D.N. 287-8
Steele, D.S. 194
Stephenson, Adrian 100
Stephenson, D.A. 239
Stephenson, H.H. 78, *79*, 105
Stevengraphs 112-13
Stevens, E. "Lumpy" 34
Stevens, Thomas 112
Stockdale, Jean 55-6
Stoddart, A.E. 88, 94, 106, 111, 186,
    203, 219, 226, 233, 298, 303
Stonehenge CC 37
Stratton: jewellery 190
street urchins 108

Streeton, Richard 119
Stroud: stained glass 195
Strudwick, H. 43, 99, 104, 204, *266*,
    300
Studd, C.T. 104
Studd, J.E.K. 260
"Stuff" Gownsman 80, 83
stump-iron 243
stumps 202, 242-3
Stumpz: game 286
Sturgeon, E.R. 51, *52*
Subbuteo 287
sugar bowl 59, 150
Sunday Times, The 204
Sunningdale 49
Surrey 34, 50
Surrey CCC 88, 145, 146, 157, 188,
    222; Centenary Library 314;
    memorabilia 313-14; paintings 34,
    42
'Surrey Cricketers, Sketches of' 78,
    79, 80
Sussex 37, 75, 208, 212, 225
Sussex Archaeological Society 208
Sussex CCC 115, 208, 254, 299, 305;
    auction (1980) 28, 37, 43, 38, 62,
    63, 75, 78, 87, 90, 117, 118, 145,
    208, 215, 224, 228, 302; bazaar
    (1894) 26, 78, 230, 241; museum
    111, 313
Sutch, Henry A. 96
Sutcliffe, H. 15, 149, 164, 203, 228,
    231, *232*, 300, 312
Sutcliffe, W. 164
Swaffham: cricket match (1797) 63
Swanmore Park CC 180
Swanton, E.W. 143, 207, 290, 300
sweaters 248
sweets 305
Swinstead, George Hillyard 57, 219-
    20
Swire, S.H. 313
Swithenbank medallion 187
Sydney Cricket Ground 76, 110,
    111, 310

T-shirts 253-4, 296
tablecloths 302; signatures 202
Taddy, James, & Co. 261, 264
tape measure, cricketer's 244
tape recordings; *see* recordings
tapestry 301
Tarleton, Colonel 115
Tarr, Mike 46, 93, *220*, 234
Tarrant, F.A. 257
Tate Gallery 37
Tate, F.W. 220
Tate, M.W. 99, 100, 204, 300
Tayler, Albert Chevallier 23, 58, 84-
    6, 264, 314
Taylor, Alfred D. 63, 122, 128, 129,
    131, 132, 134, 137f, 302, 307
Taylor, C.G. 73
Taylor, K. 57
Taylor, R.W. 195
Taylor, Rosemary 46
Taylor, Terry 309
tea service, silver 183
Teachers whisky 304
television commercials 298
Tennyson, Hon. L.H. 201, 247, *266*
TCCB 188, 296
Test Match Special: poster 213;
    recordings 289

Test matches: Australia v. England
    (1882-83) 300; (1886-87) 187;
    (1891-92) 110-1; (1897-98) 239;
    (1903-04) 231; (1907-08) 315;
    (1911-12) 111, 239; (1920-21) 111;
    (1974-75) 232; (1977) 188, 220;
    Australia v. South Africa (1910-
    11) 240; Australia v. West Indies
    (1960-61) 242, 298; England v.
    Australia (1880) 243; (1886) 75;
    (1888) 106; (1896) 243; (1899) 251;
    (1902) 236, 277; (1905) 238; (1909)
    239; (1921) 239; (1926) 226, 239;
    (1938) 239; (1948) 110; (1953) 168,
    290; (1956) 241; (1980) 94, 188,
    193; (1981) 118, 240; (1985) 298;
    (1989) 51; England v. New
    Zealand (1983) 194; England v.
    South Africa (1947) 242; England
    v. West Indies (1950) 239; (1984)
    225; scorecards 224; Sri Lanka v
    England (1982) 187
Texaco: posters 214
Thackeray, Lance 258
The Times 45, 81, 101, 112, 161,
    240, 286, 305
theatre programmes 208, 212
Thomas, Percy Francis (H.P.-T.) 206
Thomas, William Meredyth 172
Thompson, G.J. 86
Thompson, Reginald Gorton Barlow
    196
Thoms, R.G. 39, 206, 243
Thomson, J.R. 46, 49
Thorn, Philip 137
Thornbury CC 215
Thornton, C.I. 43, 97, 233
Thorpe, James 38
tickets, admission 62
ties 254, 315; ceramic 169-70
Tinworth, George 155, 156
toast racks 184; silver 180
Tobin, Denis 20, 252, 254, 309
Tonbridge School 49, 75
Top Trumps: playing cards 293
Topolski, Feliks 93
'Tossing for Innings' 34, 87
Towers, Rodger 91
Townsend, C.L. 205, 251
Townshend, Derrick 317
Toye, Kenning & Spencer 188, 193
Toynbee, Lawrence 49
trade cards 264, 266-7, *282*
trays: papier-maché 302; silver 182
Treadwell Art Mill 51-2
Trent Bridge 31, 34, 51, 312-13;
    collection of bats 232-3
Triangular Tournament (1912) 110,
    316
trophies 183
Trott, A.E. *98*, 103, 260, 299
Trowsdale, T. Broadbent 200-1
Trueman, F.S. 45, 49, 100, 216, 287,
    289, 294
Trumble, H. 89, 227
Trumper, V.T. 15, 23-4, 46, 85, 90,
    111, 122, 143, 175, 191, 201, 202,
    210, 218, 227, 228, 232, 233, 293,
    315
Tuck, Raphael 256
Tuke, Henry Scott 22, 40-1, 42
Turnbull, M.J.L. 103-4
Turner, G.M. 316
Turner, Graham 101

Turner, J.M.W. 30
Turner, John 310
Tyas, R. 134
tygs 160, 161
Tyldesley, J.T. 85, 86, 300
Tyler, W. 173
Tyson, F.H. 290

Ullyett, Roy 100, 118
umbrellas 303; stand 303
umpires' clickers 243
Underwood, Derek 50
United States of America 74, 105, 145, 225, 230, 246, 275-6, 317; Peace Corps: film 300

Valadon, Boussod 87
Valentine cards 293
Valentine, A.L. 93, 239, 289
Valentine, B.H. 291
Valentine-Daines, Sherree 47, 50-1
Valentine's: postcards 256
van der Plank, David 271
Van Gogh, Vincent 54
Vanity Fair 9, 59, 80-4, 263; album 82
Vauxhall Gardens 60, 95
Verity, H. 16, 149, 164, 312
vesta cases 192
VICTAD (Victor C. Tipping) 101
Victor, Charles 44
Victoria: v. New South Wales (1882) 302; (1926) 223, 224
video recordings 297-8
Vincent Square 49, 54
Vitale, F. 37
Vizianagram, Rajkumar of 168
Volunteer Rifles: figures 153

Wagner, Anton 22
Wain, Louis 258
Wakefield Art Gallery 31
Wakley, B.J. 303
Wales, Prince of 187
Walford, M.M. *270*
Walker brothers 208
Walker, I.D. 233, 241
Walker, J. 65
Walker, T. 231-2
Walkers Tobacco Co. 268
walking sticks 303
Wallace, C.I.S. 308
Wallis, J. 62
wallpaper, cricketing 301
Walters, F.H. 260
Walters, K.D. 232
Walters, Wesley 94
Walton, W.L. 75
Wanderers Club, Johannesburg 316, 317
Wanostrocht, Nicholas 38
Ward, A. 233, 260
Ward, John 45, 51, 93
Ward, William 61, 73, 238
Wargrave CC: trophy cup 183
Warlock, Peter 288-9
Warner, Sir P.F. 23, 27, 28, 51, 83, 85, 100, 103, 109, 123-4, 141-2, 147, 194, 202, 203, 250, 277, 299
Warren, A. 238
Warton, Major R.G. 138, 141, 187, 210
Warwick, J.B. 304
Warwickshire CCC 182, 258, *264*;

memorabilia 314
Washington, W. 63
Wass, T.G. 294
watches 191-2
Waterlooville 34
Waterman's Ink: postcards 256
Watts, Charlie 48, 247, 248, 305
Watts, George Frederick 59, 71, 77
Waugh, David 101
Weaver, Arthur 93-4
Webb Corbett 194
Webbe, A.J. 303
Webster, Tom 99-100
Weedon, I.F. 75
Weippert & Co. 96
Weir, David 81, 83
Wellham, D.M. 252
Wellings, C. 43
Wells, David 197
Wells Cathedral 30
Wellsteed, Geoff 294
Wenman, E.G. 73, 236, 237
West Africa *108*
West Indies 44, 54, 138, 145, 226, 239, 246, 253, 262; golden jubilee 187; tours: England (1928) 223; (1976) 234
West Kent CC 210
West Sussex Gazette and Courier 115
West, W.A.J. 40
Westminster School 54
Weston, G. Neville 21-2, 135, 169, 173, 204, 235, 307, 308
Wharton-Tigar, Edward 266
Wheeler, John 262
Wheeler, Paul *267*
Whistler, J.M. 42
Whitbread Village championship 295-6
White Conduit Club 115
White Conduit Fields 62, 66
White Conduit House 66
White, T. "Shock" 200
Whitehead, G.W.E. *103*
Whitridge, W.O. 145
Whittam, Billy 222, 223
Whittington, F.H. 22
Whittock, N. 75
Wiggins Teape 293
Wilcox, Leslie 44
Wild, Roland 142
Wildman, Narelle *57*
Williams, Clive 246
Williams, J. 130
Williams, Standring, Sandeman and Heatley 210
Willis, R.G.D. 15, 17, 186, 240, 247, 248, 288
Willis, W.D. & H.O. 260, *261*, 263, 264, 265, 266
Willow Enterprises 285
Willow Stamps 260, 278, 279
Willows Publishing Co. 126
Wills's Woodbine Cricket Game 284
Willsher, E. 78
Wilson, Rev. C.E.M. 135
Wilson, Effingham 62
Wilson, E.R. 16, 17, 32, 60, 114, 135, 149, 151, 173, 185, 191, 214, 221, 301, 302, 308, 312
Wilson, Richard 37, 86, 87
Wilson, Victor 23
Winchelsea, Earl of 28, 38, 62, 150,

152
Winchester College 49, 210, 250, 303; 'Domum Galop' 96
Winder, A.E. 7, 28, 129, 303, 309; sale of collection (1985) 84, 129, 130, 131ff, 144, 226, 259
window bills: *see* handbills
Windsor Castle, china ware 151
Windsor, G. 222
wine: ewer 303-4; labels 304
Wisden, John 42, 73, 77, 78, 119, 178, 202, 242
Wisden, John, and Co. 238, 315
Wisden Cricket Monthly 15, 85, 91, 93, 95, 99, 110, 111, 145, 147, 175, 177, 178, 188, 198, 208, 228, 240, 247, 249, 255, 262, 290, 294, 309, 316; calendar 282
Wisden Cricket Nights: films 299
Wisden Cricketers' Almanack 16, 18, 19, 25, 119-26, 128, 130, 132, 137-8, 141, 144, 227, 308; index 123; rarities 121-2, 125-6; record prices 29, 125
Wister, Jonas 105
Wittersham, Kent 32
Woburn Abbey 171
Wolfe, E.G. 27
Wombwell Cricket Lovers' Society 195
women 10-11, 39, 66, *67*, 69, 70, 223, 241, 253, 259, 282, 300
Women's Cricket Association 176, 253, 300
Wood, A. 16, 149
Wood, Martin 19, 124, 143
Woodcock, John 300
woodcuts 66
Woodfull, W.M. 16, 149, 164, 169
Woodhouse, Tony 266, 309
Woods, J.T. 69
Woods, S.M.J. 83, 98, 156
Woof, W.A. 109, 181
Woolfe, Ken 309
Woolhouse, W.H. 66, 215
Woolley, F.E. 16, 45, 104, 112, 172-3, 181, 216
Wootton, Ronald 91
Worcestershire CCC 188; auction (1980) 28, 224, 228, 248
World, The 80
World Cup (1975) 214, 296; (1983) 94
Worrell, Sir F.M.M. 24, 187, 300-1; Trophy 56
Wortley, Archibald Stuart 22, 39, *40*, 86, 88, 196
Wright, Gerry 48, 94, *310*
Wright, Graeme 267
Wright, L.G. 300
Wyatt, R.E.S. 11, 45, *264*, 290
Wynne, David 177
Wynne-Thomas, Peter 137, 312
Wyvern Software 94, 287
Wyvern Sports Marketing 296-7

Yardley, N.W.D. 103
Yeomans, Ron 22-3, 36, 37, 151, 164, 170, 180, 181, 182, 191, 195, 213, 254, 300ff., 308-9, 314
Yorker, The, public house 27
Yorkshire CCC 36, 90, *107*, 145, 146, 164, 179, 222, 251, 259, 290; Headingley 314; pavilion 170

Young, Alan 170
Young, J.A. 290
'Young England': figure 158, *159*

Zaglo 194
Zimbabwe 317
Zoffany, Johan 30

PICTURE ACKNOWLEDGEMENTS

Where there is more than one illustration on a page, the credits start with the picture furthest to the left and nearest to the top and work down each column.

Colour

William Bowyer ix *a*
Sir Donald Bradman xvi *a*
Bridgeman Art Library x *a,c*
Michael Brownlow xxviii *a*
Burlington Gallery iv *a,b*, xii *a,b*, xiv *c*, xv *b*, xviii *a,b*,
Christie's South Kensington xiii *a*, xiv *a*, xxiii, xxv *b*,
Peter Coombs xxviii *b*,
Mark Ferrow viii
David Frith i *c*, xiii *d*, xv *a,c*, xvii *c*, xx *a,b,d,e*, xxii *a*, xxiv *a,b,c*, xxv *a*, xxix *a,b*, xxx *b,c*, xxxi *a,b*
Jocelyn Galsworthy v *b*
Halcyon Days xix *b*
Ron Harries xvii *c*, xviii *d*
John Hawkins i *a*
Keith Hayhurst xix *a*
History of Advertising Trust xxi *a*
Hilary Humphries xxvi *b, e*
Crane Kalman Gallery xviii *e*
K Shoes xxi *b*
Lennard Books ii *a,b,c*, v *a*, vii *a,b*, xiii *c*, xiv *b*, xvi *b*, xviii *c*, xxi *c*, xxv *c*, xxviii *c*
London Transport xx *c*
Roger Mann xxx *d*, xxxii *a,b*
Roger Marsh xi
Mike Marshall vi *a*, xvi *c,d,e*, xvii *b*
David Messum Gallery iii*a*
Roy Perry iii *b*
Phillips vi *b*, xvii *a*
Gordon Phillips xxvii *b,c*, xxx *a*, xxxi *c*
Bill Prosser ix *b*
Felix Rosenstiel's Widow & Son xii *c*, xiii *b*
Joe Scarborough x *c*
Jackie Shipster ix *c*
Mike Smith i *b*, xxii *b*, xxv *d*, xxxi *d*
Adrian Stephenson xxvii *a*
Jean Stockdale x *b*
Marcus Williams xxvi *a,c,d*

Black & white

Antique Collector 31
Austin Bennett 175 *a*
Enid Bloom 175 *b*
Bonhams 182 *b*
Bruton Knowles Auctioneers, Glos. 103 *a*
Burlington Gallery 21, 42 *a*, 50 *a*, 64, 65, 66, 67, 70, 75, 79 *a*, 80, 88, 89, 96 *a,b*, 98 *a*, 157 *a*, 163, 164,

229 *b*, 286 *a*, 302 *a*
Christie's 41 *a*, 42 *b*, 43, 71, 72, 73 *a,b*, 79 *c,d*, 83 *a,b*, 85 *a,b*, 105, 108 *a*, 111, 112 *a,b*, 115, 139 *b*, 151 *b*, 154, 166, 168, 183 *b*, 184, 185, 189, 190 *b*, 191, 192, 195, 199, 213, 224, 230, 243, 248, 250, 251, 265 *a*, 280 *a,b*, 284, 293 *a*, 301, 302 *b*
Mark Coombs 46
Peter Coombs 306
Geoff Crambie 24
Crane Kalman Gallery 178
Cricket Memorabilia Society 29, 190 *a*
Curry Rivel Gallery 52 *a*
Deighton & Mullen 282
Eton School Library 225
David Frith Collection 22, 26, 40 *a*, 100, 121, 123, 127, 136, 171 *a*, 180 *b*, 203, 204 *a*, 209, 218, 219 *a,b*, 221 *a,b*, 226, 229 *a*, 237, 247, 253, 256 *b*, 288, 291, 299, 304 *c*, 309 *b*
Geering & Colyer 161
John Gill 173
Warwick Gowland 274 *a*
Ron Harries 101 *b*, 309 *a*
John Hawkins 23
Keith Hayhurst 171 *b*, 180 *a*, 310 *b*
Michael Heslop 91
Peter Hicks 176 *a*
Hilary Humphries 268 *a,b*
John Ireland 101 *a*
Raymond Irons Photography 174 *b*
Lennard Books 108 *b*, 116, 147, 200, 207, 212, 215 *b*, 242, 244, 265 *b*, 283
Rev. Malcolm Lorimer 303 *a*
Jocelyn Lukins 156, 216 *a,b*
Roger Mann Collection 40 *b*, 107, 109 *a*, *b*, 174 *a*, 186, 198 *b*, 204 *b*, 214 *a,b*, 220 *b*, 232
Roger Marsh 53 *a*
Mike Marshall 159, 196, 311
Marylebone Cricket Club 40 *c*
MCC 92
J.W. McKenzie 18, 76, 139 *a*
National Dairy Council 103 *b*
National Portrait Gallery 45
Nubern Products 167
Roy Perry 52 *b*
Gordon Phillips 102, 198 *a*, 202, 208, 256 *a,c*, 257 *b,d*, 258 *b,c*, 264 *a*, 269, 270, 296 *b*, 304 *b*, 310 *a*
Phillips 38, 41 *b*, 44, 49, 59, 61, 74, 79 *b*, 86, 106, 130, 131, 133, 134, 135, 140, 142, 151 *a*, 157 *b*, 160 *a,b*,176 *b*, 181 *c*, 183 *a*, 187, 201, 261, 263, 264 *b*, 286 *b*, 295, 304 *a*
Punch 68
Felix Rosenstiel's Widow & Son Ltd. 55
The Royal Crown Derby Porcelain Co. Ltd. 162

Rutland Gallery 35
Bill Smith 303 *b*
Mike Smith 16, 182 *a*, 215 *a*
Sotheby's 33
Ralph Steadman 98 *b*
Adrian Stephenson 266
Jean Stockdale 56
Mike Tarr 220 *a*
Times Newspapers Ltd. 110
Treadwell's Art Mill 53 *b*
Sherree Valentine-Daines 50 *b*
Visnews Ltd. 7
John Walker & Sons Ltd. 217 *a*
Michael Wheeler 181 *a,b*
Ronald White 172
Narelle Wildman 57
Clive Williams 246
Daniel Williams 293 *b*